DEMOCRACY AND CAPITALISM IN TURKEY

DEMOCRACY AND CAPITALISM IN TURKEY

The State, Power, and Big Business

Devrim Adam Yavuz

I.B. TAURIS
LONDON • NEW YORK • OXFORD • NEW DELHI • SYDNEY

I.B. TAURIS
Bloomsbury Publishing Plc
50 Bedford Square, London, WC1B 3DP, UK
1385 Broadway, New York, NY 10018, USA
29 Earlsfort Terrace, Dublin 2, Ireland

BLOOMSBURY, I.B. TAURIS and the I.B. Tauris logo are trademarks of
Bloomsbury Publishing Plc

First published in Great Britain 2023
This paperback edition published 2024

Copyright © Devrim Yavuz, 2023

Devrim Yavuz has asserted his right under the Copyright, Designs and Patents Act, 1988, to be identified as author of this work.

For legal purposes the Acknowledgments on p. xii constitute an extension of this copyright page.

Series design by Adriana Brioso
Cover image: Democracy (1969), by Turhan Selçuk

All rights reserved. No part of this publication may be reproduced or transmitted in any form or by any means, electronic or mechanical, including photocopying, recording, or any information storage or retrieval system, without prior permission in writing from the publishers.

Bloomsbury Publishing Plc does not have any control over, or responsibility for, any third-party websites referred to or in this book. All internet addresses given in this book were correct at the time of going to press. The author and publisher regret any inconvenience caused if addresses have changed or sites have ceased to exist, but can accept no responsibility for any such changes.

A catalogue record for this book is available from the British Library.

A catalog record for this book is available from the Library of Congress.

ISBN: HB: 978-0-7556-4896-2
PB: 978-0-7556-4900-6
ePDF: 978-0-7556-4897-9
eBook: 978-0-7556-4898-6

Typeset by Newgen KnowledgeWorks Pvt. Ltd., Chennai, India

To find out more about our authors and books visit www.bloomsbury.com and sign up for our newsletters.

To my wife, Alison, and my parents, Irène and Erdal

CONTENTS

List of Illustrations	viii
Preface	ix
Acknowledgments	xii
List of Abbreviations	xiv
INTRODUCTION	1
Chapter 1 DEMOCRACY IN TURKEY	21
Chapter 2 CAPITALISM AND DEMOCRACY: THEORIZING THE ROLE OF STATE-BUSINESS RELATIONS	43
Chapter 3 TURKEY'S CAPITALISTS AND THE STATE IN THE WORLD ECONOMY	69
Chapter 4 AWAKENINGS: THE MAKING OF THE BUSINESS ELITE FROM 1960 TO 1980	91
Chapter 5 PROMETHEUS UNBOUND: ECONOMIC POWER FROM 1980 TO 2002	109
Chapter 6 THE CAPITALIST SPIRIT: SOURCES OF POWER AND DEMOCRACY	139
Chapter 7 NEW AUTHORITARIANISM, CONFLICT, AND THE BUSINESS ELITE'S COMMITMENT TO DEMOCRACY	163
CONCLUSION	189
Notes	195
Bibliography	231
Index	245

ILLUSTRATIONS

Figures
5.1	Trade indicators	113
5.2	Share of product type in top eight exports	115
5.3	FDI as a percentage of GDP	124
5.4	R&D as a percentage of GDP	124

Tables
5.1	Turkish Exports' Major Destinations in 2002	120
5.2	Large Holdings Linked to TÜSİAD and Their Sectors of Activity	131
7.1	Share of TÜSİAD Member Businesses in Turkey's Largest 100 Industrial Establishments According to Revenue from Production	170
7.2	TÜSİAD Reports by Topic and Decade	181

PREFACE

I had not planned to write a preface. However, the international news about the capitalist class was rather outlandish during the months I was rushing to complete the current manuscript for publication. As I was typing away about the business elite's potential democratizing role in Turkey and similar newly industrialized countries (NICs), my television set was blaring images of Russian oligarchs' seized assets in response to the invasion of Ukraine. Law enforcement in many paradisaic settings, such as Italian marinas, were showcasing Russian yachts of titanic proportions (pun intended). Posh apartments, shady bank accounts, and football (soccer) clubs further highlighted the extent to which this class had turned global metropolises like London into its own playground. These images were revealing not just because of the huge wealth these individuals were able to amass by being an autocrat's cronies, but also because their lifestyles betrayed a rather peculiar belief: that such outrageous conspicuous consumption would grant them access to a global elite (or maybe they just did not care about appearances and just wanted a luxury yacht).

In parallel, the phone I was trying to ignore was lighting up with waves of tweets about Elon Musk's bid to buy Twitter for USD43 billion. Tweeters were rightfully concerned that Musk's singular take on the freedom of speech would embolden extreme views and drown out what little was left of civility and the clout of objective, expert perspectives on the platform. In a world conjuncture where political polarization put not only democracies but also the health of entire societies at risk, commentators rightfully worried that a whimsical move by one businessperson would negatively impact everyone else's welfare. Many others pointed to the irony that further media concentration in the hands of business tycoons and private interest was being done under the guise of protecting free speech. As is the case for Russian oligarchs, it is the worldview that this grandiose transaction reveals that is rather unusual. A man—who is smart enough to build self-driving cars or send rockets to space—was blatantly doing the exact opposite thing of what media and democracy scholars prescribe to protect the freedom of expression and was boasting about it.

The last few years offer many more similar examples of business behavior, in the United States alone, from campaigns against unionization efforts in Amazon warehouses to fueling an opioid epidemic. As harmful as these acts are, it is the public relations strategies to offset this image that seem stranger, including Bezos's conquest of space and the Sacklers' donations to the Metropolitan Museum in New York to have seven wings named after them. A few decades ago, this type of behavior, like a Russian oligarch's yacht, would have been attributable only to a fictional Bond villain at the movies. It therefore seems rather strange to complete a book on industrial tycoons and their democratizing role. A short autobiographical note as to how the project surfaced, followed by a bit of good and bad news is therefore warranted for the readership.

The impulse to research the business elite came about when I was an undergraduate student in Turkey in the 1990s. I was not very politically engaged, but I had an academic interest in the relationship between economic development and democracy. This was partly fueled by the contrast I saw growing up between the two countries I am originally from, France and Turkey. The summer vacations I spent in France in the late 1970s and early 1980s exposed me to how economic and political welfare seemed to go together, an observation that was undoubtably reinforced by all the Star Wars toys or Playmobiles that my grandparents got me when I was visiting them. By contrast, I remember how during Turkey's debt crisis, at age six or seven, I was tasked by my parents to go from one corner store to another to find for them coffee amid shortages that were crippling the country. I also remember how my mother was the one given the responsibility to call out after me whenever I ran away from my parents on the street; my father figured that in a climate dominated by political assassinations that her risk of being gunned down by fascists was lower compared to his when she yelled my name "Devrim!" (literally revolution) thanks to her French accent and feminine voice.

Thus, when the military stepped in through a coup in 1980 to impose martial law and undertake economic liberalization, it awakened conflicting feelings and experiences. I definitely had an easier time finding coffee. My friends and I also took to constant window-shopping to marvel at the gradual inflow of imported novel items: Converse sneakers one week, Casio calculator watches the next. However, my dad and many of his friends also lost their government jobs (either in protest or because of their left-wing views). They also witnessed a squeeze on their wages and saw their friends being interrogated by the military. It was a period when the grown-ups around me were very worried politically and economically. But … that Casio watch! I therefore grew up with the constant tension and promise of affinity between economic and political freedom. Both seemed to at times develop parallelly and at others conflict with each other. Thinking about these things was probably what propelled me to study economics first and sociology later in life. I wanted to read as much as possible about the relationship between capitalism and democracy (either negative or positive).

Things in Turkey were improving in the 1990s, but slowly. Discussing issues such as the fate of Turkey's Kurds was taboo, so was questioning whether Kemalism was really the best solution to accommodate society's religious impulses or other aspirations. Turkey had industrialized, but perhaps not as fast as it could have. It was in this context that the Turkish business elite started to go beyond what any mainstream, more conservative organization did and started to talk about democratization and many of the politically taboo issues that challenged the state. That calls for reform came from a group I had vilified as a kid during the 1980 coup was surprising to me. I therefore decided to research this shift as a piece of the puzzle I was interested in: at what stage in capitalist development does full democracy emerge? Slowly, I came to be interested in what factors impacted the business elite's political stance and whether they could in fact contribute to democratization. The events that propelled this project were therefore different from what the readers and I have been exposed to in the media lately.

Having said that, I must turn to the bits of bad and good news for the readership. The bad news is that readers interested in understanding how the extreme forms of amoral behavior capitalists demonstrate can change will find little solace or prescriptive value in the book. As a sociologist by way of economics, I always like to think of James Duesenberry's words of caution: "economics is all about how people make choices and sociology is about why they don't have any choices to make."[1] As will be highlighted in this book, one thing that my research revealed was that the business elite in Turkey was acting in a specific context. Their demand for democracy revealed as much about their needs as businesspeople under capitalism as it did about the Turkish state and the legacy of prior state-business relations. They found themselves in a situation where to do well, they also needed for the undemocratic aspects of the Turkish state to change. Embracing a democratizing role also afforded them some ideological legitimacy in a society where capitalist behavior was not always sanctioned. Thus, there are clear limits to the extent their experience is applicable to American capitalism or to the Russian oligarchy.

The good news is that the book and similar work in political sociology, comparative politics, and political economy serve to underscore that the business elite's attitudes under capitalism has not been uniform across country cases and history. As such, work in this tradition reveals that bad capitalist behavior is neither universal nor inevitable. There definitely are other societies or epochs besides post-1990 Turkey where capitalists have contributed to and stayed committed to a democratizing role. The dynamics of these societies are better understood by reading about case studies like the current book (which by no means is the only one as will be shown in Chapter 2). Moreover, given the diversity of capitalist behavior, the case of the Turkish business elite can therefore serve the same role that negative spaces do in visual art. It can provide the reader clues about institutions that are at times present and absent in capitalist societies and that help define the ideological inclinations of the business elite.

ACKNOWLEDGMENTS

Given that the current project took years to complete, many individuals contributed to it either directly or indirectly. As such, I will keep the acknowledgments short and to the point so as to not omit anyone who has supported the project. Having said that, most people I crossed paths with in Montreal, Istanbul, Ankara, Manhattan, and Brooklyn (folks in Ditmas Park in particular) should know that they contributed to the project through support, friendship, and kind distractions.

I would like to thank my informants and staff at TÜSİAD for taking the time to speak with me. Haluk Tükel, when he was general secretary, deployed his staff and resources to make sure that I was given access. Ebru Dicle's contribution to the project as deputy general secretary and general secretary has been monumental. She has taken hours to outline the association's activities and evolution. She has also used some of her connections to help secure a number of interviews. Similarly, Oktay Varlıer used his knowledge of the association and rolodex to point me toward additional members worth interviewing.

While in Istanbul, I benefited greatly from the hospitality of Zerrin and Yasemin Şaka, Melek Ulagay, as well as Mert and Başak Emcan, who have opened their homes (and in the case of Mert, his record collection). The stay in Istanbul was further made easier by Nora Şeni who welcomed me as a visiting scholar with the Institut Français d'Études Anatoliennes. Alp Orçun has provided tremendous help, through guidance, friendship, connections, and knowledge of the topic. This book would not have been completed without him.

The project started at McGill University. I would like to thank everyone in the Department of Sociology, and, in particular, John Hall, Michael Smith, Steven Rytina, and Donald Von Eschen, for always providing valuable feedback. Three people I have stayed in touch with from that period have been pivotal in the project. Raffaele Iacovino made it more bearable through our lovely lunch outings, while Berna Turam and Yeşim Bayar have provided years of friendship, feedback, moral support, and guidance. I thank them for their warmth, resourcefulness, and keen intellect (in the case of Berna also for connecting me with Gayle Sulik who provided great editorial help).

I completed the book at Lehman College and the wider City University of New York (CUNY) system. I am proud of being affiliated with these two institutions for what they have come to be known in the news lately: their ability to provide a quality education to many New Yorkers, outpacing most of the more prestigious institutions in terms of opportunities for social mobility they provide. They are, however, also highly vibrant intellectual communities. The Middle East and Middle Eastern American Center (MEMEAC) at CUNY's Graduate Center has made this project possible by welcoming me, first, as a visiting scholar and, then, as an affiliated faculty member. Anny Bakalian has been pivotal in the completion of the book, thanks to her support and her ability to foster a stimulating environment at MEMEAC. Our union and CUNY have provided financial support for the book through the PSC CUNY grant. Members of the Department of Sociology at Lehman have been tremendous colleagues. They not only have created a very collegiate atmosphere but have also been very encouraging. Several of them have more directly contributed to the project by providing feedback and by sharing ideas. They are, in alphabetical order: Christopher Bonastia, Susan Dumais, Shehzad Nadeem, Susan Markens, Naomi Spence, and Elin Waring. I would also like to thank Madeline Moran and Kofi Benefo who have been very supportive during their tenures as chair of the department. I am, as always, grateful to Miriam Medina for helping us all to keep it together. The School of Natural and Social Sciences, and in particular Dean Pamela Mills, has been pivotal by providing much-needed release time and constant support for faculty endeavor.

As the project was coming to fruition, the editors at I.B. Tauris, Yasmin Garcha and Rory Gormley, have been very helpful. Their ability to secure timely feedback from external readers in our current pandemic environment has been of heroic proportions. Likewise, the production team in charge of the project at Bloomsbury has managed to work at full tilt despite operating in a climate that has impacted the publishing world negatively. Similarly, I am grateful to the two reviewers for taking the time to provide detailed, thoughtful feedback amid all their work. They have vastly contributed to improving the final draft. I am indebted to Aslı Selçuk for supporting the project by allowing us to use her father Turhan Selçuk's editorial cartoon on the cover. As will become apparent in parts of the book, Turhan Selçuk and the generations of illustrators he has inspired have vastly informed the way people from Turkey think about politics despite censorship laws. Thanks to his ability to distill complex social commentary into vivid images, Selçuk's work was probably my first exposure to the sociological lens as a kid, while leafing through newspapers hoping to find something interesting. I am, therefore, thankful for the opportunity to acknowledge the impact his work has had on my career.

This type of academic endeavor is nearly impossible to accomplish without the care of close ones. I am indebted to my parents, Irène Druet and Erdal Yavuz. They have equipped me through encouraging curiosity as well as through their love and support over the years. They always pushed me to question things as I was growing up. My wife Alison Owen has fostered a very loving environment in which I can work. More importantly, the grit and determination she has displayed in her art career has been a source of inspiration. I am forever grateful to her for her affection and for modeling good behavior.

Finally, it is nearly impossible to complete a project on Turkey without somehow being involved with cats. I would like to thank Kedi, Destry, and Marlowe for providing a combined thirty years of needed entertainment and comfort. Above all, their instinct to walk on keyboards and sleep on the warmth of laptops has compelled me to master the art of backing up the files for the current book. I have seen neither Marlowe nor Destry near my keyboard lately. As such, I can confidently aver that all errors, omissions, and shortcomings of the work are my sole responsibility.

ABBREVIATIONS

AKP	Justice and Development Party, Adalet ve Kalkınma Partisi
ANAP	Motherland Party, Anavatan Partisi
AP	Justice Party, Adalet Partisi
CHP	Republican People's Party, Cumhuriyet Halk Partisi
CUP	Committee for Union and Progress, İttihat ve Terakki Cemiyeti
DGM	State Security Courts, Devlet Güvenlik Mahkemeleri
DİSK	Confederation of Revolutionary Workers' Unions, Türkiye Devrimci İşçi Sendikaları Konfederasyonu
DP	Democrat Party, Demokrat Parti
DPT	State Planning Agency, Devlet Planlama Teşkilatı
DSP	Democratic Left Party, Demokratik Sol Parti
DYP	True Path Party, Doğru Yol Partisi
ELG	export-led growth
EU	European Union
FDI	foreign direct investment
FTC	foreign trade company
HDP	Peoples' Democratic Party, Halkların Demokratik Partisi
IEDI	Institute for the Study of Industrial Development, Instituto de Estudos para o Desenvolvimento Industrial
IEMP	ideological, economic, military, and political
IMF	International Monetary Fund
ISI	import substitution industrialization
İSO	Istanbul Chamber of Industry, İstanbul Sanayi Odası
KADIGER	Women Entrepreneurs Association of Turkey, Türkiye Kadın Girişimciler Derneği
MDP	Nationalist Democratic Party, Milliyetçi Demokrasi Partisi
MEDEF	Movement of the Enterprises of France, Mouvement des entreprises de France
MGK	National Security Council, Milli Güvenlik Kurulu
MHP	Nationalist Movement Party, Milliyetçi Hareket Partisi
MSP	National Salvation Party, Milli Selamet Partisi
MÜSİAD	Independent Industrialists and Businessmen Association, Müstakil Sanayici ve İşadamları Derneği
NIC	newly industrialized country
PAN	National Action Party, Partido Acción Nacional
PKK	Kurdistan's Workers' Party, Partiya Karkerên Kurdistan
PRI	Institutional Revolutionary Party, Partido Revolucionario Institucional
R&D	research and development
RP	Welfare Party, Refah Partisi

SEE	state economic enterprise
SHP	Social Democratic Populist Party, Sosyaldemokrat Halkçı Parti
SME	small and medium-sized enterprise
TESEV	Turkish Economic and Social Studies Foundation, Türkiye Ekonomik ve Sosyal Etüdler Vakfı
TİSK	Turkish Confederation of Employer Associations, Türkiye İşveren Sendikaları Konfederasyonu
TOBB	Turkish Union of Chambers and Commodity Exchanges, Türkiye Odalar ve Borsalar Birliği
TÜRKONFED	Turkish Enterprise and Business Confederation, Türk Girişim ve İş Dünyası Konfederasyonu
TÜSİAD	Turkish Industry and Business Association, Türk Sanayicileri ve İş İnsanları Derneği
TUSKON	Turkish Confederation of Businessmen and Industrialists, Türkiye İşadamları ve Sanayiciler Konfederasyonu
UNICE	Union of Industrial and Employers' Confederations of Europe (now BusinessEurope)
YDH	New Democracy Movement, Yeni Demokrasi Hareketi

INTRODUCTION

In 1996, Turkey's largest corporation owners challenged preconceived notions about business conservatism when they took an ideological turn to devote their energies toward the promotion of full democracy. Through their main lobby, the Turkish Industry and Business Association (Türk Sanayicileri ve İş İnsanları Derneği, TÜSİAD), their first significant step was to publish a 176-page report on the need for democratization that tackled a range of timely issues including limits to individual freedoms, lack of minority rights, excessive constitutional powers of the military, and the ongoing imposition of Kemalism (a set of principles named after the founder of the modern Turkish Republic) as a restrictive ideology on civil society organizations and political parties sanctioned by various laws regulating political life. With its emphasis on liberal democratic institutions and values, the content of the report—and TÜSİAD's newfound mission—was highly controversial, given Turkish state tradition and political culture.[1] The current book seeks to understand in comparative light, why and how a privileged group like the Turkish business elite would come to embrace a democratizing role rather than remain conservative and close to the state. By using the ideal-typical case of TÜSİAD (which represents corporation owners who seemingly have little to gain from increased democracy), the broad argument the book develops is that capitalist class's push for democracy in late-developing societies is determined by the interplay of its evolving economic interests with the legacy of established state traditions and state-business relations. This approach is indeed needed because the stance adopted by the Turkish business elite since 1996 represented a major break from the state and its political classes.

Even though Turkey was a parliamentary democracy at the time, the state elite continued to suppress dissent around the above institutions and official ideologies that constituted obstacles to democratic consolidation. The combination of state tradition dating back to the Ottoman era, a top-down nation-building project under single-party rule (from 1923 to 1945), plus three subsequent military coups (1960, 1971, and 1980) that intended to quell social mobilization through ever more restrictive rules were largely responsible for the flawed nature of Turkish democracy.[2] The most internationally publicized example of how these laws impacted citizens concretely was the prosecution, in 2005, of novelist and Nobel laureate Orhan Pamuk. He was charged for "insulting Turkish identity" during a candid interview with the Swiss media when he addressed the military's war against separatist militias and also acknowledged the Armenian genocide. The average person observed or experienced limits on the scope of political movements, evidence of torture in jail, and security courts intended to suppress separatism and freedom of the press. Such actions impacted the strength of civil society to the degree that international organizations such as Amnesty International and Freedom House ranked Turkey as only "partially free" during the period.[3] Thus, the business elite's stance went to the core of the system of government that the state elite had built throughout the twentieth century.

The *Perspectives on Democratization Report* (hereafter *Democratization Report*), however, was significant as much for its tackling of taboo topics as it was for its authorship. TÜSİAD was founded in 1971 by twelve leading industrialists to represent the interests of large corporations from Istanbul, Turkey's economic center. When the report was published in 1997, the association's roughly 500 members and the companies they controlled were responsible for producing one-third of the country's entire value-added (the amount of wealth created through transforming inputs), which is a staggering share for a relatively small number of businesses. As importantly, TÜSİAD had gained notoriety for precipitating the country's military coup of 1980. In the late 1970s when Turkey faced a dire debt crisis, fuel and food shortages due to shrinking oil imports, and armed conflict between extreme right- and left-wing factions, TÜSİAD and its leaders reacted to the situation by publishing full-page advertisements to condemn the civilian government for its inability to adopt market-oriented reforms (including privatization, the liberalization of exports, and an end to price controls). Soon after, tanks rolled through major cities, paving the way for drastic economic measures that seemed at the time to favor employers much more than the middle class.[4]

Given its importance for the economy as well as its conservative past, TÜSİAD's newfound prodemocracy stance is surprising, not only for the case of Turkey but also in light of the comparative literature on the relationship between capitalism and democracy. First, large capitalists generally enjoy a structurally advantageous position that provides privileged access to the state. They are literally a phone call away from government officials, even in the absence of a well-functioning democracy. Second, authoritarian regimes that emerged in capitalist societies typically tended to favor the economic elite by keeping labor and other popular groups, and their demands, in check.[5] Third, and most importantly, both of these factors played an even more salient role in influencing capitalists' regime preferences in late-industrializing societies due to the state's historical role in economic development.[6] As these nations tried to catch up economically to the industrialized North, the state became a much-needed source of resources and protection from competition for a nascent industrial bourgeoisie to develop their enterprise. Given that the business elite in Turkey and in many parts of the developing world owed their success to the state, they have often been dependent on the political elite. Taken together, these factors produce an assumption that the business elite neither needs nor favors democracy and is reluctant to challenge the state.

The counterintuitive prodemocracy position adopted by the Turkish business elite is of further importance, for the comparative literature, because it has endured. TÜSİAD, by and large, has stuck to its position despite a period of political turmoil in Turkey characterized by the rise of the religious Justice and Development Party (Adalet ve Kalkınma Partisi, AKP), constitutional reforms, and a coup attempt.[7] The association had formulated its first push for democracy when the government and state were controlled by secular political actors. The AKP, however, represented a different significant challenge to the Istanbul-based business elite, which was ideologically much closer to the previous political class. The party's success was based partly on the support it received from a budding, more pious, new bourgeoisie which operated in regions distant from Turkey's traditional economic hubs. In addition to the threat the new bourgeoisie posed to the power of the established large corporations, AKP leader Erdoğan attacked big business routinely during his populist speeches. As had been the case in 1980, it would have been plausible for TÜSİAD to adjust its prodemocracy position to protect its members' status.

While the comparative literature recognizes that there are periods when the capitalist class can press for regime change, it is often predicted that this group will revert to conservatism soon as their interests are threatened.[8] Indeed, scholars of democracy have repeatedly cited a historical precedent (across numerous country cases) in which capitalists tend to revert to supporting authoritarian rule or limiting the scope of political liberalization when increased participation of underrepresented groups—in this case, those at the periphery of traditional centers of power in Turkey—appear to be too threatening to their interests.[9] In the case of TÜSİAD, however, the *Democratization Report* has been the organization's ideological anchor since the twenty-five years after its publication. The association and its members appear committed to the democratizing mission, and they have transformed it into more than simply a reactionary stance adopted in a particular policy environment. Hence, TÜSİAD's ongoing adherence to democratic principles for the past twenty to thirty years seems to have eliminated from Turkish politics the reactionary threats historically posed by the business elite.

As significant as the decision to publish the *Democratization Report* in 1997 was, Turkish business leaders were not the only example of pro-authoritarian capitalists who turned prodemocracy. During the "third wave" of democratization in the industrializing world around the same period, countries such as Brazil and Mexico also witnessed the rise of a more reform-minded business class that rebelled against authoritarian governments and called for political change through direct and indirect political actions that ranged from street protests to disinvestment to supporting opposition political parties.[10] Even regimes like Pinochet's dictatorship in Chile, which came to power holding a strong pro-capitalist agenda and mandate to crush distributional conflicts, saw their violent tactics lose legitimacy in the eyes of capitalists who had been "softcore" (more moderate, outsider) supporters.[11] According to Huntington who famously studied the "third wave" of democracy, twenty-seven of the thirty nations that democratized from 1974 to 1990 were considered middle income, further raising the possibility that capitalist support for political change had become pivotal.[12] Thus, TÜSİAD's actions fit a broader global trend where democracy seems to have become more desirable, or at least less threatening, to capitalist interests.

While not a sufficient or solitary factor driving democratization in Turkey, TÜSİAD's changed position can shed light on how one significant obstacle for democratization (the business elite's penchant for more authoritarian forms of rule) can be eliminated. It can also clarify, in a more modern context, how a positive relationship between capitalist interest and democracy can emerge, thus expanding upon classical perspectives that draw primarily from the Western European experience. Recent political developments have unfortunately revealed that the pace of democratization in newly industrializing societies has been rockier than expected, with many autocratic forms of rule or the lack of institutionalization coexisting with electoral politics.[13] Moreover, in advanced capitalist societies, the appeal of what has been broadly termed "populist" political leaders has further put into question the civilizing role of markets. Thus, comprehending the factors that has kept big business committed to democracy has become all the more important. Because understanding the democratic shift undergone by the Turkish business elite entails understanding a process, the book relies on interviews conducted over two decades with TÜSİAD and its members in order to determine which factors have propelled them to press for democracy and stay committed to the mission. The book also fits in the political and historical sociology tradition in which the careful analysis of one case in light of the comparative literature is given primacy. Before further defining the subject and outlining the methodology, a word on where the book fits in the broader theoretical literature is warranted.

Capitalism and Democracy; Economic and Ideological Power

Doing elite interviews for the project had its perks. I was always greeted in cushy offices and was offered an array of hot and cold beverages to choose from. But it also had its pitfalls. One of the first interviews I conducted was in the middle of an Istanbul heat wave when the afternoon sun was at its peak. I was to meet with the late İshak Alaton, a senior and vocal TÜSİAD member. He had cofounded Alarko Holding (a top-ten Turkish corporation) after returning from Sweden in the 1960s, where he had toiled as an immigrant blue-collar worker and had taken advantage of training programs. Alaton successfully applied the know-how he acquired in factories to start his own industrial empire (see Chapter 4). He also became an important public figure as a left-wing capitalist thanks to the social-democratic ideologies he had embraced through his participation in the Swedish labor movement. His office now had dominating views of the Bosphorus Sea in the headquarters he chose to establish in a reconverted historic asylum that towered from one of Istanbul's hills.

I had yet to fully grasp Turkish corporate dress codes and the ways to get taxis past security to drop me off right at buildings' entrances. I ended up climbing the hill to the structure dressed in a dark business suit and tie under the beating sun (instead of the business casual attire that turned out to be acceptable in summer). I finally made my way to Alaton's office, walking past a few security guards and administrative workers who seemed confused to see a disheveled guest about to meet one of the wealthiest individuals in Turkey. As soon as I was buzzed in, Alaton was startled to see his afternoon appointment walk in dripping sweat, shirt drenched. The shock subsided and his familiar working-class demeanor took over as he implored me to take off my tie, offered me "two glasses of water" and a handful of paper napkins. While I gathered my bearings, Alaton, sitting in front of a bookshelf that included works by a few social theorists like Anthony Giddens, got right to the interview by paraphrasing the research I was conducting. He told me that it involved trying to understand why capitalists in whose interest it would be to normally oppose democracy would now turn around and champion it. He then paused, shrugged, and exclaimed: "To answer your question of why we want democracy, you have to go back to Marx [a literature he presumably became familiar with during his youth spent as a union member]. He outlined how the bourgeoisie under capitalism is the champion of democracy."[14]

Indeed Marx (and Engels) did attribute a democratizing role to the bourgeoisie, notably in the *Communist Manifesto*, because the capitalist system that it established needed to break down traditional obligations for the free exchange of one's labor, goods, and capital to occur:

> The bourgeoisie, historically, has played a most revolutionary part. The bourgeoisie, wherever it has got the upper hand, has put an end to all feudal, patriarchal, idyllic relations. It has pitilessly torn asunder the motley feudal ties that bound man to his "natural superiors," and has left remaining no other nexus between man and man than naked self-interest, than callous "cash payment." It has drowned the most heavenly ecstasies of religious fervor, of chivalrous enthusiasm, of philistine sentimentalism, in the icy water of egotistical calculation.[15]

According to Marx and Engels, this occurred in Europe as the bourgeoisie became stronger, first when the manufacture replaced guilds and then, when it was, in turn, transformed by "steam and machinery [which] revolutionized industrial production in order to meet the needs of growing world markets."[16] The bourgeoisies' technological rise was accompanied by its gradual political victory over classes representing the old feudal order, thanks to its help in establishing the modern state, followed by democratic styles of government:

> Each step in the development of the bourgeoisie was accompanied by a corresponding political advance of that class. An oppressed class under the sway of the feudal nobility, and armed and self-governing association in the medieval commune, here independent urban republic (as in Italy and Germany), there taxable "third estate" of the monarchy (as in France), afterwards, in the period of manufacture proper, serving either the semi-feudal or the absolute monarchy as a counterpoise against the nobility, and, in fact, corner-stone of the great

monarchies in general, the bourgeoisie has at last, since the establishment of Modern Industry and of world-market, conquered for itself, in the modern representative State, exclusive political sway. The executive of the modern State is but a committee for managing the common affairs of the whole bourgeoisie.[17]

As will be further examined in Chapter 2, many commentators since (and some before) Marx have used the ideal-typical case of Western Europe to outline the extent to which democracy emerged as a means for capitalists to challenge the *ancien régime* and feudal order in order to push for laws and civil liberties compatible with capitalist activity; only later could organized labor use this political opening to gain more social rights.[18] The initial pivotal role capitalists played in democratization led Barrington Moore to famously declare "No bourgeoisie, no democracy" when describing why early-industrializing societies experienced the rise of liberal democracy whereas societies that lacked a dynamic capitalist class turned to more authoritarian forms of rule.[19]

The real danger in elite interviews (besides figuring out proper attire) is to be swayed by their clout. When one of the biggest capitalists in Turkey (with strong social-democratic credentials and a keen intelligence) avers that the Marxist literature can explain his political stance, it is tempting to believe them and attribute TÜSİAD's push for increased democracy solely to economic change (see Chapter 5 which highlights the ways in which material change in the 1980s made political liberalism more appealing). More specifically, while being close to the Turkish state and its authoritarian practices may have been needed at earlier stages of development, Turkish big business now needed institutions associated with democracy, like the European bourgeoisie had two centuries ago.

However, the classic Marxian approach has been criticized for building an overly functional link between democracy and capitalism. A candid moment shared by another eminent prodemocracy TÜSİAD member can help illustrate this point. I had interviewed Can Paker, not only because he was CEO of a household durables-producing German-Turkish joint venture, but because he was also (according to many TÜSİAD members and staff) one of the more significant driving forces behind the final version of the *Democratization Report*, which placed greater emphasis on liberal democratic values and demonstrated willingness to tackle more sensitive issues (such as minority rights). Can Paker reflected on his early formative years, specifically when he was a university student in the 1960s and most of his peers in similar Turkish elite institutions were taking part in radical left-wing movements:

> You have to understand that at the time my decision to become a businessman was frowned upon. Being a businessman was bad, being a successful businessman was even worse. You were seen as being part of the *comprador bourgeoisie* and as collaborating with the state and with imperialists.[20]

While entrepreneurship is socially and culturally sanctioned in societies like in the United States, the business elite's role under late-industrialization is complicated by the history of state-business relations. The capitalist's position in Turkey and other late-developing nations must be placed into historical and cultural contexts to more fully comprehend the significance of TÜSİAD's ideological transformation toward democratization: not only the material needs of the capitalist class, but its psyche also had to change. Thus, evolving economic needs played a significant role in shaping the business elite's political stance. But this shift was not the sole driving force behind TÜSİAD's demands. This observation underscores the significance of Weber's criticism of or, more precisely, dialogue with the Marxist approach. In writing his *Protestant Ethic*, Weber sought to demonstrate that the type of capitalist behavior discussed by the latter needed a moral justification (or ideological motivation) to be widely adopted by the general population in order to thrive and contribute to the growth of capitalist markets and production. It was precisely because Protestantism and the forms of behavior that it engendered, such as focus on the worldly and the rational use of time, became widely accepted that it facilitated the rise of the bourgeoisie. Only through this parallel ideological shift could markets expand:

> The early progress of such new "ideas" is, however, beset by many more obstacles than the theoreticians of the 'superstructure' assume; they do not blossom like a flower. The capitalist spirit in the sense in which we have hitherto understood it has had to prove itself in a hard struggle against a world of hostile forces ... in ancient or medieval times it would have been denounced as an expression of the most filthy avarice and of an absolutely contemptible attitude. Even today this still regularly happens in all those social groups that are least involved in the distinctively modern capitalist economy or are least adapted to it. This is *not* because the "acquisitive instinct" [*Erwerbstrieb*] was unknown or underdeveloped in "precapitalist eras"—as is often said—nor because there was *less* of the "auri sacra fames" outside of bourgeois capitalism in those days than within the specifically capitalist sphere, as modern romantics fondly imagine.[21]

In many other places, Weber also differed on the causality between the rise of markets and the modern state. Unlike Marx, who saw in Europe's political development the culmination of bourgeois interest, Weber noted that it was actually needed for the expansion of capitalism:

> One element which is certainly important is the rational structure of law and administration. For the modern form of capitalism, based on the rational enterprise, requires not only calculable technical means of production, but also a calculable legal system and administration in accordance with formal rules; without these, adventurous and speculative trading capitalism or any kind of politically determined capitalism may be possible, but not any kind of rational private enterprise economy with fixed capital and sure calculation.[22]

Building on Weber, several historical sociologists have examined how the interplay of state institutions and the expansion of markets led to the rise of the capitalist system. Most notably, while Moore agreed with Marx about the link between democracy and capitalism in places where the bourgeoisie was strong (such as France and England), he also recognized that capitalist development could be promoted through an authoritarian revolution from above in places where a bourgeoisie was lacking (such as Germany and Japan).[23] In the same vein, Tilly highlighted the ways in which military competition between rulers led to the expansion of both the modern state and capitalism.[24] Similarly, given the importance of state tradition and ideology, Chapter 6 of this book moves away from economic explanations to discuss the ways in which the Turkish business elite also underwent an ideological and political transformation during the period, which led it to cut its ties with the political elite. This is warranted because, as discussed further below, state-business relations in Turkey and other late-industrializing nations provided economic benefits to large capitalists at the expense of their ideological legitimacy and political independence.

While the discussion of economic versus ideological-political factors are split into two different chapters for epistemological reasons, the current book combines both traditions. For this reason, I adopt Michael Mann's distinctions of various styles of social power which recognize that the state and social actors rely on a mix of ideological, economic, military, and political power (henceforth referred to as IEMP in parts of the book) to wield influence, which he uses in order to give a fuller description of the emergence of modern states and capitalism in Europe:

> The struggle to control ideological, economic, military, and political power organizations provides the central drama of social development. Societies are structured primarily by entwined ideological, economic, military, and political power. These four are only ideal types; they do not exist in pure form. Actual power organizations mix them, as all four are necessary to social existence and to each other. Any economic organization, for example, require some of its members to share ideological values and norms. It also needs military defense and state regulation. Thus ideological, military, and political organization help structure economic ones, and vice versa.[25]

Even though industrialization and the current international context may impact the economic power of business, capitalists must still build enough political and ideological clout to press for change. Thus, in addition to surveying how the material needs of capital evolved, this book examines how Turkish entrepreneurs accumulated different types of power to formulate a prodemocracy agenda. Such conceptualization enables a deeper understanding of the multifaceted changes impacting TÜSİAD and the private sector, which is a needed comparative exercise to understand the past thirty years of capitalist development and political transformation. It also helps extend the IEMP model to other cases. Although Tim Jacoby has convincingly extended the framework to the study of the Turkish state, I also find it useful to understand the business elite for more contemporary reasons.[26]

Capitalism and Democracy: The Globalization Debate

The capitalist class's more recent ideological shift toward democratization coincided with economic liberalization across the globe and in Turkey, suggesting that this time around, too, as explained by Marx and my interviewee, business leaders adopted a role they were historically meant to play. One of the primary motivations for researching the Turkish business elite and to borrow from Mann was to counteract a recent tendency to see the global diffusion of markets as having a homogenizing political impact across societies and to overstate the role of capital's structural power. "Third wave" democratization was marked by a momentous policy change sweeping late-industrializing societies: the abandonment of state-led models of economic development, such as protectionism, for the benefit of economic liberalization and greater international trade.

The juxtaposition of three momentous shifts affecting late-developing nations seem, therefore, to have influenced the manner in which both academicians and journalists view the relationship between capitalism and democracy in a more globalized world: (1) the (re)democratization of their political systems; (2) the adoption of more market-driven, outward-oriented models of economic development; and (3) the collapse of the Soviet Union, which was the main ideological proponent of state-led models of growth. Taken together, all three transformations created the notion that markets were natural and that the spread of global capitalism and its political institutions were inevitable. This has heavily marred the way in which debates about capitalism and democracy have evolved in recent years.

Optimists in debates about the relationship between capitalism and democracy saw the global diffusion of markets as a way to promote pluralism by limiting resources controlled by corrupt officials and increasing the number of people who have the means to affect policy. As such, economic freedom was seen as going hand in hand with political liberties. Some even proclaimed that the world was witnessing the "end of history" and the demise of cleavages between nations, competing developmentalist ideologies, and even between classes.[27] Skeptics pointed out that income inequality under capitalism functions to erode the ability of specific groups to participate in politics, viewing the global diffusion of liberal institutions as a mere ploy to create environments favorable to investment without much concern for popular participation.[28] Moreover, many see the role of the nation-state as declining in order to promote convergence at the more local-governmental[29] and transnational levels[30] to increase the hold that capitalists have over policy. Though stemming from diametrically opposed standpoints, the positive and negative perspectives converge on the nature and role assigned to the state under capitalism: that its institutions and decisions reflect what is good for the capitalist class by creating an environment favorable to free enterprise. The disagreement has less to do with the political aspirations and power of the economic elite and more to do with the extent to which the rest of society will benefit from a democracy that is oriented to the service of capitalism itself.

Disagreements between optimists and skeptics lie on tacit assumptions about the power of the economic elite and the role of capitalist interests under democracy. The more positive interpretation assumes some level of compatibility between the needs of private enterprise and institutions, such as the rule of law, found under full democracy. Furthermore, they see in capitalists just another group, among many, who can lobby the state under pluralistic principles. The pessimistic view argues that the economic elite hold inordinate power under free-market capitalism through direct and indirect means, including their structurally advantageous position when lobbying the state and the significant role that threats of disinvestment and capital mobility play in governmental decision-making. Yet, reducing the multifaceted trajectory of capitalist societies to a one-size-fits-all guiding principle runs the risk of erasing meaningful variations that occur across country cases and over time.

Economically, there is no doubt that years of capitalist development, growing international integration, and the adoption of more market-oriented policies have shifted the needs of business classes throughout the world since the 1980s. However, it is crucial *not* to overstate capitalists' structural power and material needs during its recent prodemocracy turn in Turkey and other late-industrializing societies. After years of dependence on authoritarianism and the state, any assumption that democracy is inherently in the interest of capital would paint an incomplete picture. The central role played historically by the state and how this has impacted the business elite must be understood, especially in the case of newly industrialized countries (NICs).

Although the business elite (large capitalists) in some countries favored political change over the past thirty years, the democratic transformation has lagged in many parts of the world. In the rest of the Middle East, for example, business leaders continue to support autocratic regimes who promise security and much-needed funds for investment.[31] China's integration into the world economy has also shown that business expansion does not necessarily bring about a parallel political shift. This case demonstrates that it is clearly possible to integrate world markets without achieving significant democratic expansion domestically.[32] In Turkey too, TÜSİAD was the only mainstream business organization to lobby for change; the others did not touch on issues of democratization to the same extent. The more pious and pro-AKP Independent Industrialists and Businessmen Association (Müstakil Sanayici ve İşadamları Derneği, MÜSİAD) published a similar report—Constitutional Reform and the Democratization of the State—but it mainly equated democracy with religious freedom and good governance.[33] Thus, it would be hasty to presume that capital's regime preferences follow a linear path.

The case of the Turkish business elite thus offers a unique opportunity to piece together a broader comparative puzzle at the heart of the relationship between capitalism and democracy. While all full democracies have undergone a period of capitalist development and lower-income countries have tended to be authoritarian, middle-income countries were just as likely to choose between authoritarian and democratic paths. In part, this stems from the capacity of the business elite (within and across various cases) to oppose or favor regime change, at times supporting democratizing movements and otherwise participating in conservative coalitions to protect privilege.

Given these variations, understanding the Turkish business elite and its organization, TÜSİAD, can help explain under which circumstances capitalists in NICs are willing to break their ties from the state and its authoritarian practices to push for increased democratization. In light of differences in business's political attitudes and the importance of various sources of power, the current book adopts an approach that favors in-depth interviews with members of TÜSİAD and the business elite in order to highlight the factors that were at play in Turkey, while shifting away from assertions in the globalization literature that the desirability of democracy will diffuse, almost by default, across borders without concern for the domestic factors that might mitigate them.[34] In other words, the impact of globalization on the economic power and needs of business does not automatically lead to political or ideological transformation. Why the business elite might be particularly resistant to change under late-development warrants further explanation.

The Nature of State-Business Relations under Late-Industrialization

As Ayşe Buğra's seminal work *State and Business in Modern Turkey* demonstrates, the Turkish state became a source of much-needed protection and subsidies for capitalist enterprise for the greater part of the twentieth century, as had been the case in many late-industrializing nations where a weak and budding private sector was catching up to the rest of the world. Most major Turkish corporations owed their first big breaks, and subsequent growth, to resources secured under the auspices of developmentalist policies aimed at industrialization. Buğra and others argue that early state investment shifted businesses away from entrepreneurial activities (such as innovation and management typically found in advanced capitalist societies) and toward maintaining close ties with government officials.[35]

Above all, capitalists' dependence on the state in Turkey, and in many other late-industrializing nations, made them reluctant to oppose some of the more authoritarian tendencies of their governments.[36] Traditionally, they were either co-opted to support the top-down nation-building projects and values of the political elite[37] or they directly contributed to the rise of dictatorships, which they saw as necessary to safeguard the system from potential distributional conflicts.[38] Thus, there are two ways in which capitalists impact the quality of democracy: favors they can obtain from the state through privileged informal channels, and authoritarian reversals to protect their interests.

The former impacts democracy by hurting formalism. Unlike states in advanced industrial capitalist societies that often built formal channels of class representation during early-industrialization, the Turkish state (and many other late-developing nations) relied more heavily on informal channels of incorporation, such as clientelism and populism (see Chapters 1 and 3). In other words, rather than relying solely on more institutionalized forms of class representation (such as political parties, labor unions, and employer's associations that use the existing political system to pursue their interests), state officials and governments tended to reward disparate groups and individuals for regime loyalty. Given that these forms of state-society relations are based more on informal ad hoc linkages used more for co-optation and less on representation of organized societal interests, the establishment of clientelistic networks as such eroded the quality of democracy because it went against the fair treatment of citizens and access to the state through formal channels.

The latter, authoritarian reversals, happens when popular demands or the expansion of political rights become too threatening to the business elite. Thus, they help explain the nonlinear relationship between levels of capitalist development and democracy. The bloodiest Latin American dictatorships emerged during the 1960s and 1970s in the regions' most prosperous economies during higher stages of economic development. Southern Cone nations, where these coups occurred, had already experimented with parliamentary democracy before achieving significant levels of industrialization.[39] Thus, rather than lead to a linear expansion of democratic rights, capitalism at times created tensions that made the business elite more reactionary.

As mentioned above, many Turkish commentators still blame large corporation owners, and TÜSİAD specifically, for precipitating the infamous military coup of 1980. The coup happened at a time when large corporations were starting to feel the limits of developmentalist policies. A strong tension between capitalism and democracy formed in Turkey and the rest of the late-industrializing world as the business elite grew powerful enough to use particularistic channels to gain economic favors and support regime change yet remained weak enough to feel threatened and in need of authoritarianism to protect its interests from international competition and distributional conflicts. Given this tension, the study of Turkish capitalists' prodemocratic transformation, such as the one undertaken in the current book, requires a certain mindfulness to changes in state-business relations.

To this end, I argue that business leaders are more likely to press for regime change when confronted with a political elite that continues to govern through existing arrangements without recognizing the new power or needs of the capitalist enterprise. Cross-country differences are likely to exist due to a combination of divergences in material interests of the capitalist class and variations in the adequacy of existing business-state relations to accommodate them.

As for capitalists' long-term commitment to democracy, I further argue that the democratizing role capitalists adopted is not, in some cases, merely a narrow, instrumentalist position that can easily change. My interviews with TÜSİAD members revealed many instances when they seemed to relish the opportunity to speak to a sociologist about their role in democratization. In a politico-ideological climate where business leaders historically felt inadequate to protect their interests, discussing their prodemocracy stance seemed to provide legitimacy—a socially sanctioned goal perhaps, much like the Protestant ethic gave a sense of purpose to Weber's capitalists during the reformation period when customary economic relations prevailed. Given the centrality of this democratizing role as a new source of ideological power for capitalists, TÜSİAD will be less likely to rely upon authoritarianism in the face of challenges to their interests. Since ideology does not develop in a vacuum but needs institutions, like business associations, to formulate and diffuse them, the capitalist class is more likely to uphold its official prodemocracy stance for longer stretches of time once established.

This book thus relies upon, and helps to confirm, the usefulness of Mann's framework as well as the state-centric literature, which avoids the excesses of more recent writing on global capitalism. The book "brings the state back [again]" to refrain from overstating the structural power of business and the transformative power of markets by recognizing that states can, at times, be autonomous from class interests and the economic elite to pursue their own goals (such as consolidating rule over a given territory). Previous scholarship extensively demonstrated that varying degrees of state autonomy can lead to differences in (1) forms of rule,[40] (2) successful development outcomes,[41] and (3) types of welfare regimes.[42] State autonomy also means that economic policy can be used not only to cater to the whims of capitalists, but also to co-opt them in order to garner support for nation-building projects envisioned by the political elite. When this is the case, state autonomy can lead to situations, like in Turkey, where business feels at once weak and powerful politically.

The state's economic favors to business come at a price. The founder of Koç Holding, the largest corporation in Turkey, famously lamented that he was coerced into abandoning his life-long membership to the Kemalist Republican People's Party (Cumhuriyet Halk Partisi, CHP) in order to continue receiving subsidies from the Democrat Party (Demokrat Parti, DP) when they won the elections in 1950.[43] Similarly in Mexico, up until the 2000s, industrialists from the Mexico City region dared to make only anonymous donations to the opposition National Action Party (Partido Acción Nacional, PAN) for fear of attracting the ire of officials of the Institutional Revolutionary Party (Partido Revolucionario Institucional, PRI) who successfully remained a single-party regime for decades.[44] Recognizing that states are sometimes autonomous and that they use both formal and informal channels to incorporate society is a useful tool to understand potential frictions between political and economic elites, and to gauge the relative weakness of the capitalist class. Thus, seeing societies as networks of power, like Mann, where nation-states have caged and greatly shaped the capitalist economy and forms of interest representation is more useful than the globalist perspective in understanding the propensity of the business elite for change. A careful examination of this group through a single-case study that represents an ideal-typical case of business's push for democracy can help in this endeavor. A word on what is meant by the business elite is therefore warranted.

The Business Elite in NICs

Scholars of capitalism treat business interests differently depending on the research question and level of analysis. Analyses of investment flows, specific sectors of the economy, and entrepreneurial behavior or the lack thereof, for instance, have provided great leads on how to think about the relationship between democracy and capitalism in terms of capitalists' structural power (investment flows), state-business relations (sectors), and the values of the business class under late-industrial development (entrepreneurship).[45] This book, however, focuses on the business elite and, more specifically large industrial capital, as a class and assumes to some extent that their structural position in society shapes their common economic interests, political preferences, and worldviews. TÜSİAD is an ideal-typical case study for treating capital as such.

TÜSİAD was founded by and represents mainly the interests of the business elite who are the owners of large conglomerates, or holdings as they are called in Turkey. As Chapter 4 will highlight, these are large family-owned, rather than publicly owned, firms that are considerably bigger than other indigenous private-sector establishments. Because of regional inequalities in levels of industrialization, they also tend to be based in Istanbul, which has traditionally been Turkey's main industrial and commercial hub. Moreover, they are active in the production of a much wider array of goods than is customary for businesses in advanced capitalist economies like the United States, which typically focus on their core competencies (such as GM or Boeing). The Koç family, for instance, who for decades has been in leadership positions within TÜSİAD and owns the largest Turkish holding, is engaged in the military industry, agribusiness, consumer durables, as well as automotive sectors, in addition to running a national chain of supermarkets, among other activities.[46]

At least two factors help explain family control and diversification among the business elite under late-industrialization (see Chapter 4).[47] First, development policies in Turkey, and elsewhere (most notably South Korea), gave an edge to established capitalists families when vying for state subsidies aimed at stimulating new sectors of activity, thereby allowing them to grow by diversifying production.[48] Whenever government credits or subsidies became available, established firms with more experience and connections were more likely to benefit than were newer companies. Second, lower levels of wealth across society inhibited expansion through the stock market and ensured that ownership would primarily remain in the hands of one family. Remaining under family control was all the more important because it also allowed holdings to maintain their interpersonal connections with the political elite, something professional managers often lack. Because large industrial families in Turkey and in other NICs are active across a plethora of sectors, along with their regional proximity to one another in a commercial hub, there is greater overlap between the interests of these individual entrepreneurs and the capitalist class to which they belong. Being owners, as opposed to managers, and producing an array of goods and services gives them a vantage point about what is good for capitalist interest as a whole (rather than narrowly focusing on the interests of a single firm or specific sector of the economy).

Interestingly, scholarship also reveals that business associations play a pivotal role in allowing the capitalist class to act politically. To avoid intra-class conflict among various businesses, the capitalist class (like the working class) needs ideological and political institutions to formulate a common identity and goal.[49] Thus, business organizations such as TÜSİAD play a more significant role than scholars of pluralism typically attribute to them. Pluralists tend to see business associations as a civil society organization (like any other) that represents its members (in this case capitalists within the state) by serving as the sum total of their individual interests. Yet conceptually and empirically, business associations carry much more weight than that in shaping the goals of the capitalist class through their "logic of influence" and their ability to affect member opinion and gain loyalty for longer-term goals.[50]

For instance, business associations in Latin America facilitated entrepreneurs' acceptance of broader goals, such as democratization.[51] In the Middle East and North Africa, where business tended to be more reticent, associations have served as channels between capital and the state to allow for greater private-sector dynamism and commitment to development goals.[52] In sum, the establishment of business associations and think tanks reinforces belonging to a network and exerts some degree of influence over members of the group itself to make them act as a unified class.[53] Similarly, TÜSİAD has played a role for the Turkish business elite that cannot be overlooked. As will be seen in Chapters 3 and 4, Turkish holding owners historically did not find existing business associations, created top-down by various governments, to be adequate vehicles for their interests. They believed that these organizations overrepresented small and medium-sized enterprises (SMEs), which did not give them enough authority over policy given their size and importance for the economy. Ergo, they founded TÜSİAD in 1972 (as a voluntary, invitation-only membership association) to better represent the interests of large industrial capitalists. Even after the association's membership grew from around 100–200 members in the 1970s to more than 600 today to include a more diverse base, the association has retained its focus on the interests of large capital. In addition to some of the founding members' heirs, TÜSİAD leadership tended to invite like-minded individuals (including professional managers from members' holdings, a few handpicked representatives from smaller firms, and consultants who could bring technical expertise to issues they faced). In fact, private-sector consultants became highly active around the topics TÜSİAD tackled. Thus, TÜSİAD's broader membership base further served to formulate a coherent goal and create a class identity for the business elite.

This logic of influence was key to increasing the ideological power of capitalists and ensuring commitment to the broader direction of TÜSİAD by, among other things, allowing for charismatic and prodemocracy leaders to set association goals and shape capital's ideology. Many of the members I interviewed emphasized the pivotal role that a handful of more politically liberal TÜSİAD members played when drafting and publishing the *Democratization Report* and the work that went into making the report palatable to other members. Some Turkish academics I spoke to about the project viewed the association as the business elite's "political party" in a country where class interest had not been incorporated into the state more formally. Thus, private-sector associations have, at times, been essential in allowing capitalists to act as a class. For this reason, this book focuses as much, if not more, on TÜSİAD as it does on the individual perspectives of its members. TÜSİAD's ideological turn toward democratization, and its commitment to serving as a prodemocracy force, greatly reflects what the Turkish business elite as a whole believed would be good for Turkish capitalism.

Single-Country Case Studies and Elite Interviews

In any society, there are macrolevel actors (the elite) who wield more power than most other individuals. The above discussion has shown that TÜSİAD members are such a group. Many recent studies on democracy, due to assumptions about the uniformity of globalization, have either focused on microlevel actors, such as popular movements, or have ignored the mitigating role that the political and economic elite can play in domestic matters (perhaps due to assumptions that economic and political institutions diffuse naturally). Both of these choices tend to overlook that some events really do take place at a macrolevel; a meeting between, say, an industrial tycoon and a government official about trade policy may have more of an impact on society than do the ordinary interactions of everyday life.[54]

Hence, studying elite actors (like TÜSİAD and the business elite in Turkey) sheds light on underlying mechanisms of influence on broader social change. I was in a fortunate position to consider *how the business elite can become more prodemocratic* by studying the evolution and stability of TÜSİAD's stance through a series of in-depth interviews during various phases in Turkey's recent history. With a theoretical focus on mechanisms and processes, I purposively sought out individuals who would offer a unique vantage point (such as TÜSİAD's administrative staff or former chairpersons, owners of large corporations, people with an advisory capacity for the association including consultants, and TÜSİAD members directly involved in preparing the 1997 *Democratization Report*).

The first wave of interviews (2001 to 2002) with sixty respondents aimed to determine why Turkish capital initially pushed for increased democratization (with the *Democratization Report* and by other means).[55] The second wave (2008 to 2012) with twenty more interviews (including ten follow-up conversations) sought to determine how the association had evolved and why capitalists remained committed to democracy despite potential threats to their interests from the rising Muslim bourgeoisie and the AKP. Moreover, the addition of new respondents allowed for the inclusion of perspectives from Turkish Confederation of Businessmen and Industrialists (Türkiye İşadamları ve Sanayicileri Konfederasyonu, TUSKON) and MÜSİAD[56] as well as more TÜSİAD members and staff, such as the head of its DC office. Given the current political environment and threats to civil society organizations, the final interviews (2021 to 2022) favored confidential interviews with three key informants who could speak openly about their ideas as insider-outsider observers of the association's activities. A final conversation with TÜSİAD's current general secretary, Ebru Dicle, confirmed some of the information they provided. This final exercise allowed for deciphering TÜSİAD's actions and official statements through a careful examination of its archives from the last decade. Thus, I was able to build on my earlier analyses to gauge the association's future directions and ability to continue pressing for democracy under Erdoğan's increasingly autocratic presidency. Taken together, these interviews painted a fuller picture about how the needs of the private sector had evolved, how capitalists' relationship to the state had changed, the inner workings of TÜSİAD, and the degree to which its members were willing to embrace their new prodemocracy role.

The study of how the business elite can become more prodemocratic is essentially the investigation of a process. By focusing on one country case (Turkey) and grounding the analysis in historical narratives and informant-based perspectives (TÜSİAD and the business elite), this research provides detail on mechanisms for change. It examines three key questions: (1) What, if anything, in contemporary capitalism makes democracy appealing? (2) How essential is a prodemocracy stance for the business elite? (3) What are the roots of cross-country variation in capitalist's loyalties to the state after years, if not decades, of dependence upon it?

Outline of Chapters

Chapter 1 outlines more clearly the nature and extent of the ideological turn TÜSİAD took by placing it in the context of Turkish politics. In addition to giving a fuller picture of the association's activities during the period, it highlights the ways in which Turkish democracy was lacking. In so doing, it provides readers who may not be familiar with the case of Turkey and the broader democratization literature with some factual information and conceptual tools to understand the more substantive parts of the research and the book.

Chapter 2 takes a comparative historical perspective to give an overview of existing theories on capitalism and democracy as well as business's political loyalties. It provides a chronological account of how authoritarian and democratic regimes emerged under capitalism, and it highlights explanations as to why capitalists in certain countries supported change during the latest wave of democratization. Much of what we know about capitalism and democracy comes from scholars' concerns during varying epochs of global economic development. While studies on the rise of capitalism in Western Europe explored its affinity with democracy, scholars who witnessed the rise of authoritarian developmentalist states focused on its antagonisms. Understanding the link between capitalism and democracy, why the interests of capitalists change, and the political transformation of the capitalist class requires a *comparative historical perspective*. That is, being mindful of differences within and between countries that span historical periods and diverse empirical foci on business politics offers scholars explanations that go beyond a particular context. To that end, the chapter describes further notions of state autonomy and Michael Mann's IEMP model as a theoretical frame, and builds on them.

Chapter 3 offers a background to readers who may be unfamiliar with the case of late-industrializing nations (particularly Turkey) to establish how state tradition impacted capitalists' political weakness and the nature of state-business relations. It outlines how state-business relations and the Turkish state evolved over key periods significant to all late-industrializing non-Western nations, such as: (1) the Ottoman Empire during Western industrialization, when most other nations (especially when compared to Britain, France, and Germany) fell behind in terms of levels of industrialization; (2) the nation-building phase during the interwar period, when the political elite around the world developed strategies to incorporate society and rule over a given territory; and (3) the state-led industrialization phase spanning World War II through the 1980s, when states actively participated in the economic development projects of their countries largely due to favorable global economic and geopolitical conditions. This accounting sheds light on why Turkish capitalists felt dependent upon the state and politically weak up until the 1990s. Against this background, I argue that the political elite used informal channels of incorporation to build the state's ideological power and, in the process, created a national bourgeoisie concerned with preserving particularistic ties to the state.

Chapter 4 centers on the 1970s, when the Turkish business elite saw their economic power grow and their interests diverge from the rest of the private sector. Because of existing state-business relations, TÜSİAD and large corporation owners did not feel represented within the state and did not witness a parallel increase in political power. Interviews with TÜSİAD members with insider information about the period the organization was founded illustrate the travails of the association's early days. Thus, the chapter highlights how various challenges triggered the group's aspirations to increase the political power of large capitalists, laying the foundation for the association's more recent activities.

Chapter 5 surveys how the material needs of large Turkish industry changed after the military coup of 1980 up to the early 2000s and AKP's reign. Drawing heavily on interviews with members of TÜSİAD, it analyzes how the business elite increasingly integrated into world markets and became gradually more capital intensive after years of endogenous growth. While the interviews revealed a greater desire among them to compete with the rest of the world economically, they also exposed problems such as the lack of skilled labor and the uncertainty of long-term investment. These problems suggested that the nature of state-business relations had not changed much over time; the political elite were still unwilling to cater to the needs of capitalists.

Chapter 6 helps give a more complete picture of TÜSİAD's and the business elite's turn to democracy by bridging two traditions in the social sciences—one that emphasizes the importance of material conditions and another that stresses the primacy of state-society relations. Relying on interview and archival data, the chapter argues that economic changes alone are not sufficient to explain the democratizing mission of Turkish capitalists. In fact, these were significant only in light of the national bourgeoisie's relation to the state and the latter's unwillingness to incorporate class interests. Members of the industrial elite embraced capitalist's historical, democratizing role (as outlined by Alaton and Marx above) because they perceived it as a way to increase their ideological and political power in the face of an unresponsive state. Thus, the chapter argues for looking at capitalist interest in a more multifaceted way.

Chapter 7 examines the period of AKP's reign from 2002 to 2021 to determine the extent to which factors that had shaped the business elite's and TÜSİAD's earlier prodemocracy stance (a combination of their economic power with their growing political and ideological powers) also impacted their stance in the face of mounting threats to their privileged position. While the literature would predict that AKP's rise would have made TÜSİAD more conservative, the chapter reveals that its stance has become long term. In that sense, the chapter provides some further suggestions about the position the business elite can take for the long-term prospect of democratic consolidation in the face of increasingly authoritarian leaders around the world. The concluding chapter offers comparativists analytical tools to think about the relationship between democracy and capitalism by discussing further the implications of looking at different sources of power when studying the business elite and taking the state as being autonomous at times. More specifically, it discusses the business elite's stance in the face of the current rise in authoritarianism to assess the extent to which an elite endorsed process of democratization is still possible.

Chapter 1

DEMOCRACY IN TURKEY

As one of the first Middle Eastern countries to hold multiparty elections, Turkey fared comparatively well (three military coups in twenty years notwithstanding) in providing universal suffrage since the end of its single-party regime in 1946.[1] Still, Turkish democracy has suffered several major flaws throughout its history. Before the book turns to an analysis of why the business elite pushed for democratization, it is worth highlighting how Turkey's political class hurt democracy between 1980 and 2022.

The expression "deep state" and how it became popular best typifies what was wrong with the Turkish political system during the period. The term is now commonplace in English. It increased nearly fivefold from 2000 to 2020 in the English-speaking world and almost tenfold in US English publications (based on mentions in Google Books).[2] According to a 2017 ABC News/Washington Post poll, 48 percent of Americans believed that the "deep state"—a network of "military, intelligence and government officials who try to secretly manipulate government policy"—was real and, according to 58 percent of those, constituted a "major problem."[3] Before the term made it into the English language and ultimately encapsulated what some Americans believe to be a threat to pluralism in their country, the "deep state" (*derin devlet*) originated in Turkey, was widely used throughout the 1990s, and gained further traction in 1996 following a high-profile road crash. The accident involved an ultra-rightwing militant (wanted for murder and drug trafficking), his "beauty queen" girlfriend, a police chief, and a parliamentarian who were all travelling together (like the protagonists of a bad joke) in the same vehicle. The punchline, it turns out, was that some members of the Turkish state, government, and security forces were colluding with a network of mobsters and militants to sow instability and carry out extrajudicial murders. These secret activities were mainly intended to derail the peace process with Turkey's minority Kurdish population (internally) and to quiet what the state perceived to be anti-Turkish foreign agents (externally), all funded with drug trafficking money.[4]

The story grabbed public attention by echoing what many citizens already believed to be wrong with their democracy. First, it underscored the dual nature of the Turkish state in that despite its seemingly bureaucratic Weberian features (including an impressive size and competitive entry–examinations for civil service positions), significant decisions about policy were still being made and implemented through informal (aka "deep state") networks.[5] This not only violated notions of accountability but also underscored the particularistic nature of some actions by the state elite (such as selectively seeking out allies while excluding others). Moreover, it brought to light the extent to which some groups (such as high-ranking members of security forces and organized crime) had greater influence over the state than did civil society actors. Second, it showcased the lengths to which the political elite would go to insulate key policy areas from public pressure, especially those that cut to the core of Turkish national identity (particularly ethnic identity and geopolitics). Taken together, these two points embody a degree of continuity with Turkish state tradition, which has tended to be top-down and patrimonial throughout most of the country's history.[6]

Given that the main thread of this book is etiological, more fundamental structural obstacles to Turkish democracy like state tradition are favored throughout its pages over legal formal impediments. Focusing on structural factors that limit pluralism have the double advantage of making comparisons to other countries more amenable, as discussed in the next section, at the same time as simultaneously explaining how business's political power has been affected. As will be seen in Chapter 3, state-business relations have been persistently impacted by the political elite's propensity to rule top-down by using the central bureaucracy and a set of informal state-society relations, rather than trying to build formal linkages with civil society actors.[7] Because many of TÜSİAD's demands cover formal aspects of democracy, however, the goal of this chapter is to present a brief review of how laws and institutions that limit pluralism reflect these broader underlying factors. Hence it provides context for the business elite's political stance during the post-1990 era by outlining the extent to which Turkish democracy, despite frequent elections, is lacking when measured against notions found in the comparative literature as to what the minimal requirements for democracy should be. The following pages provide a rudimentary guide aimed at a readership familiar with business politics and issues of democracy within the context of advanced capitalist liberal democracies in North American and Western European societies. It also offers a refresher on what was going on in Turkey from 1980 to 2022. The reason why this is needed is twofold.

First, even though citizens in most societies at the turn of the twenty-first century were able to vote in elections, scholars of democracy note persistent roadblocks (and at times outright authoritarian governmental maneuvering) that diminish the quality of (re)emerging democracies. Since such obstacles vary from country to country, Turkey's democratization process provides an illuminating backdrop for the period as a whole. In the case of Turkey, both those in power and their opposition tended to adopt a "modernization" or "Westernization" discourse as a source of legitimacy.[8] To an outside observer, the cloak of modernization may imply a genuine desire on both sides to protect democratic institutions and religious freedoms, but this was not the case as both camps have resorted to autocratic measures to advance their goals. Second, given that our understanding of business interest has been shaped by scholarship that assumes some level of capitalist structural power (by building on Marxist notions of bourgeois democracy or theories of elite pluralism), this chapter highlights further how TÜSİAD and its members' political actions were novel in an environment where state and government agents tended to insulate policy and rule from on high. Thus, the scope of this chapter is to provide context about the state of Turkish democracy during the post-1980 period and highlight that the manner in which the business elite tackled issues of democracy during this time was something new and unexpected.

Notions of Democracy

That the "deep state" was alive and well during a period when Turkey was on its path to becoming more democratic helps underscore the complexities involved when discussing the nature of regimes. Since these kinds of illiberal practices have coexisted with democratic institutions, defining democracy during the past thirty years of the "third wave" has presented comparative sociologists and political scientists with a conceptual challenge.[9]

In the scholarly community, there has been disagreement as to what is meant by "full democracy" and what nations should be striving for to begin with. Debates about the extent to which socioeconomic rights should be part of democracy was (and still is) particularly salient due to the juxtaposition of economic and political liberalization in many newly industrialized democratizing nations. As countries were transitioning from authoritarianism, the role of the state in the economy was redefined through economic reform and deregulation, raising concerns over how declining resources and safety nets at the disposal of citizens would impact their political voice.[10] Thus, some championed the establishment of participatory democracy to provide citizens the means to substantially engage and shape polity whereas others advocated for enhancing the social dimensions of democracy, and still others emphasized (given the size of societies in the modern era) the challenges of establishing anything beyond the more limited and formal definition of a democracy, conceptualized by Dahl as "polyarchy."[11]

Regardless of its definition, obstacles to full and consolidated democracy remain in place in many societies around the globe; the transition to more inclusive rule is not always immediate, clear, or enduring. Challenges to democracy take many forms including, but not limited to, pre-transition authoritarian rulers entrenching some of their powers in constitutions, elected leaders centralizing government in the hands of the executive, and the persistence of corruption that violates notions of equality and creates an impression that something is lacking in the way new democracies are being governed.[12] To complicate matters, many enduring autocratic rulers, perhaps swayed by a global discourse favorable to democracy, started to create a semblance of participation through tightly controlled elections or tolerance for heavily regulated civil society organizations. Such endeavors aim to increase their legitimacy through limited governing coalitions and consultation with potential challengers while keeping them at arm's length.[13] Therefore, not only is there a lack of consensus about what democracy should encompass, but most nations have also implemented elements of both authoritarianism and pluralism simultaneously. These factors compelled scholars of government to use a myriad of qualifiers to characterize post-1990 regimes ranging from "competitive authoritarian" to "illiberal democracies" to "hybrid regimes," making comparisons between country cases difficult.[14]

Rueschemeyer, Huber, and Stephens eloquently resolved the first problem of definition by underscoring why the establishment of even limited notions of democracy is a worthwhile goal in itself:

> We care about formal democracy because it tends to be more than merely formal. It tends to be real to some extent. Giving the many a real voice in the formal collective decision-making of a country is the most promising basis for further progress in the distribution of power and other forms of substantive equality.[15]

Hence, even procedural democracy can constitute a pathway toward greater pluralism through the promise of increased participation and the expansion of social rights. This is particularly meaningful for country cases where too radical or sudden a shift in the distribution of power may appear threatening to an elite that is less willing to relinquish privileges.[16]

The problem of multiple regime trajectories rightfully led some to ponder whether transitory regimes were indeed moving toward democratic consolidation or in the direction of something else entirely.[17] The variety of regime outcomes that lie somewhere in between authoritarianism and democracy along with their seeming durability compelled several scholars to depart from a strictly taxonomic study of semi-democracies, shifting attention to structural factors that impede change. Rather than classifying these regimes based on the multiple strategies they use to limit participation, scholars identified factors common across all of them that were conducive to illiberal practices. This analytic shift helped make cross-country comparisons more manageable and meaningful. In sum, a legalistic study of regimes (which results in too many variants to develop a consolidated theory) has been abandoned to make space for the consideration of shared factors such as socioeconomic context, state traditions, and structural conditions that impede participation and good governance from the get-go.[18]

A structural comparative approach is also useful for explaining the shape that state-business relations have taken in Turkey throughout its history. In other words, some of the factors that traditionally hurt democracy also determined the relative weakness and power of the business elite and shaped the articulation of capitalist interest. For reasons of parsimony, these will be discussed as appropriate in the rest the book. The next section focuses more narrowly on some of the more formal restrictions to democracy from 1980 to 2020 (starting with the military junta and extending to AKP's rule under President Erdoğan).

Turkish Democracy from 1980 to 2022

In this section, I discuss the structural limits to democracy in Turkey only to the degree that they affect legal-institutional elements important to the period under study in order to avoid overlaps with subsequent chapters. The main focus, however, is on the narrower procedural notions of pluralism that were lacking during the post-1980 period. To do so, I turn to a basic, easy to operationalize definition of formal democracy offered by Huber, Rueschemeyer, and Stephens, who define the concept as

> a political system that combines four features: regular free and fair elections, universal suffrage, accountability of the state's administrative organs to the elected representatives, and effective guarantees for freedom of expression and association as well as protection against arbitrary state action.[19]

Even according to the definition above, Turkish democracy during these last four decades has exhibited significant shortcomings. Specific challenges varied in accord with the nature and goals of those who governed, including: the military junta (1980 to 1983), followed by a center-right-wing party that undertook economic liberalization under the watchful eyes of the generals (1983 to 1991), followed by various coalitions between right- and left-wing parties that sought to democratize some institutions while suffering governability crises (1991 to 2002), ultimately paving the way for the religious AKP whose rule culminated in the establishment of Erdoğan's more centralized presidency from 2014 onward.[20]

Despite each administration and period's unique characteristics, two overarching issues (and the way they were dealt with) greatly hurt the quality of democracy during the forty years following the coup. This period was marked by armed conflict against Kurdish rebels and tensions between secular and Islamist citizens, compelling state and government agents to tap into Turkish state tradition and its repertoire of illiberal tactics to deal with these crises. As will be seen below and in Chapter 3, non-elected state officials trying to protect what they saw as national values and institutions has been a running theme throughout Turkey's modern political history. Thus, despite the chapter's focus on procedural notions of democracy, the significance of these two structural obstacles lodged in ethnic and religious tensions are worth outlining at the onset, in order to understand how they impacted Turkish democracy, even according to narrower definitions.

The Kurdish Minority

The state's dealing with the Kurdish issue hindered democracy in several ways. As a sizeable stateless group spanning Iraq, Syria, Iran, and Turkey, the Kurds represent roughly 15 percent of Turkey's population. Even though many nations around the world since the 1980s have felt growing pressure to adopt various forms of multiculturalism to accommodate their minority populations, this process proved thornier in the case of Turkey for two reasons.[21] First, since 1924 the Turkish state and its various constitutions combined civic and ethnic notions of citizenship, defining anyone from Turkey as "Turks."[22] The political elite chose to emphasize the latter because of the perceived threat posed by nationalist movements in former colonies during the last days of the Ottoman Empire,[23] a large Kurdish uprising in 1925,[24] and the state's general inability to incorporate (through formal channels) the various groups on the territories it controlled.[25] Ultimately, by choosing to blend notions of Turkishness based on ethnicity with a sense of belonging to the nation, the state opened avenues of assimilation for minorities willing to embrace Turkish national identity while at the same time limiting multiculturalism through policies such as banning the use of minority languages in public spaces, like the education system and government offices.[26] Second, while a large portion of Kurds migrated to cities in the western parts of the country, as did other populations from Turkey's more rural communities, many still live in southeastern regions, which have been underfunded and less developed throughout the twentieth and twenty-first centuries.

The combination of assimilationist policies and disparities in the socioeconomic experience of individual Kurds created variability in the degree to which social mobility made integration possible, leading some to assimilate and others to be segregated.[27] The latter compelled organizations such as the Kurdistan's Workers' Party (Partiya Karkerên Kurdistan, PKK) to demand outright secession from Turkey through violent political action, intensifying during and after the 1980s.[28] The Turkish state classified these kinds of groups as terrorist organizations and implemented highly repressive measures including, among other things, the imposition of martial law throughout heavily Kurdish regions, the prosecution and outright banning of political parties and leaders organized around ethnic identity, and state-sponsored violence against Kurds. The state, throughout the period under study, thus eroded the quality of democracy as these strategies raise issues of accountability, freedom of expression and association, and lack of protection against arbitrary government action.

Secular-Muslim Conflict: The Center-Periphery Dichotomy

Tension between more secular and Islamist segments of society and its impact on democracy are also rooted in deep structural factors that explain the state's inability to incorporate the interests of various groups found mostly in the rural parts of Turkey. An overly simplified, birds-eye view of the struggle between the two groups over the period pits a more urban, secular bureaucratic elite that seeks to protect the gains it made under the republic's modernization project against a more rural and pious rising middle class that seeks greater representation through increased religious rights. As is often the case, such characterization misses the point that neither group is a monolith.

The term secular includes not only staunch supporters of the Kemalist state, such as the military and state prosecutors, but also left-wing or liberal intellectuals critical of the former and the authoritarian institutions they seek to protect.

Islamists have included members of the current AKP who sought to solidify their hold on the state and revive their version of neo-Ottomanism as well as sects that tried to incorporate religious freedoms into the public sphere.[29] Moreover, as further demonstrated by Berna Turam, this tension is not a zero-sum game but rather can be characterized as what she calls the "politics of engagement."[30] Conflict between the various groups that represent secular and Muslim sectors of society often lead them to develop new strategies that ever so slightly shift the nature of the Turkish state. Thus, there have been instances when elements from both camps contributed to the development of rights we associate with democracy and, conversely, when they supported autocratic measures to solidify their reign (ranging from the secularist elite's attempt to stop political Islam's rise through threats of military coups to the AKP's use of the state's coercive capacities to quell opposition).

Two factors central to Turkish politics have further complicated the conflict's relationship to democracy and authoritarianism. First, rather than crush religion outright, the secular state elite at various times during the twentieth century promoted Sunni Islam (through, for instance, instituting mandatory religion courses in public education to make it an important part of national identity) while opposing the display of religion in public life, the same way it opposed the expression of minority cultures.[31] Second, notions of modernization and secularism embraced by the state elite is unique to Turkey, and to some extent France.[32] More specifically, secularism or laicism has been interpreted not as sheltering religious life from state involvement (as proffered in the United States), but as protecting the state from pious influences. Likewise, as will be seen in Chapter 3, the state elite took modernization throughout the twentieth century to mean the Westernization of bureaucracy and imposition of sociocultural change from the top down, rather than democratization or widespread economic development.[33]

To understand why these two factors came about and how they caused the secular (or laic)-Muslim conflict to negatively impact democratization, it is helpful to use a conceptual lens developed by Şerif Mardin, a preeminent scholar of Turkish society. Mardin notes the existence of a tension between the center, made up of the urban ruling elite seeking to protect the state, and the periphery, which included atomized rural populations not formally incorporated into the state.[34] Within this framework, the significance for Turkish politics of this center-periphery tension can be traced back to the Ottoman state structure and the manner in which it was later adopted by republican reformists in the twentieth century. The state throughout most of Ottoman reign ruled by focusing on its more despotic functions and ideological power for various structural reasons explored in Chapter 3, such as: patterns of land control, the existence of a centralized bureaucracy, the segmented nature of Ottoman society, and the deliberate travails of the empire to insulate itself from potential challengers (for instance, by recruiting non-Muslims with little or no ties to society into civil service). In sum, so long as the sultans were able to finance their military expansions through taxes, they did not feel the need to engage with various groups in society.[35]

According to Mardin, the tendency to insulate the state as such created a tension between the center (seeking to protect the state) and the periphery (made up of atomized groups). He further notes that the limits of this structure, specifically the lack of economic dynamism that it created, were felt geopolitically when the Ottoman Empire's main Western European rivals entered a more rapid pace of industrialization after successfully modernizing their nation-states. This imbalance culminated in the Ottomans' defeat in World War I by Allied forces and resulted in the loss of its colonies and occupation of Anatolia (modern-day Turkey's borders). The Turkish Republic was founded soon after in 1923 by Mustafa Kemal (Atatürk) and other influential military leaders recruited from among the Young Turks who waged a war of independence against occupying Allied nations. When defining the contours of the new regime, three particular actions had a long-lasting impact on the direction of the republic and on future tensions between secular and religious segments of society.

First, Mustafa Kemal and his allies abolished the caliphate (the supreme leader of Muslim lands, a title controlled by the Ottoman Emperor) to sever any potential source of political or ideological claim the sultan had over the nation. In so doing, they formulated the Turkish model of laicism. Because the new political elite wanted to consolidate power and because cultural factors (i.e., Islam), not state structure, were seen as the root cause of the Ottoman Empire's weakness, the first step was to shield the government from religion. Thus, reforms to the nature of state-society relations that were more immediately needed to modernize the state were ignored.[36] Second, while the first National Assembly that helped define the new regime included a diverse range of local emissaries, Mustafa Kemal effectively eliminated potential sources of opposition by creating a single-party regime gathered under the CHP's roof. Third, as was seen in the discussion about Turkey's Kurdish minority, the state opted for an ethno-civic definition of citizenship. National identity conceived as such, however, created a contradiction. Because the territory inherited by the republic was composed of several different ethnic groups (including the Kurds) and because peoples from Christian and Jewish backgrounds were viewed with suspicion, Islam and Sunni Islam in particular were used as a rallying point for most of society.[37] Thus, the state was shielded from religion, while religion defined Turkish society.

As momentous as these shifts might seem, according to Mardin, the CHP did not make significant attempts to reform the centralized state structure it inherited from the Ottoman Empire. It tried to insulate the bureaucracy and continued to rule top-down rule. As such, even if Mustafa Kemal and the CHP claimed to be populist and modernizing on the surface, they did not try to build formal channels of inclusion (see Chapters 3 and 4). When combined with their definition of secularism and ethnic national identity, this meant that any local power broker wishing to gain influence needed to embrace the Kemalist vision of Turkishness and Westernization to advance within the ranks of civil service or to get involved in electoral politics. Hence, the tradition in Turkey has been for the military, the state, and its bureaucracy to try to protect themselves from societal, religious pressures through this common ideology.

Contemporary Secular-Religious Conflicts

Society at large continued to embrace Sunni Islam as the common glue holding the nation together. However, conservatism based on piousness was not granted formal representation and remained in the periphery. It found expression around religious civil society organizations and ethno-religious notions of nationalism as a unifying identity.[38] The state at times used these religious sentiments and blended them with its ethnic notions of nationalism when, for instance, non-Muslim minorities were the target of an arbitrary local wealth tax imposed during World War II[39] or when they suffered violent state-condoned attacks and intimidation in the 1950s.[40] Although Islam was in the periphery, it always remained a resource in the background that the central state could use to pursue its own authoritarian ends.[41]

According to Mardin, the juxtaposition between laicism and religiosity as such crystalized to form what he called "Turkish exceptionalism." He explained that because of the primacy the central bureaucracy played for Ottoman rulers and the modern Turkish Republic, "the state continues to come before religion by 'one millimeter.'"[42] In other words, ruling classes have been inclined to "protect" the state from social and religious influences, but it used Sunni Islam to achieve specific political goals as illustrated above. Thus, while in Europe conflicts between Church and state were resolved through compromise and defining more clearly the former's role in civil society (such as in the field of education), the pattern in Turkey was to allow religion to play a significant role for national unity, while insulating the bureaucrat and state from it.

Two institutions played a particularly significant role in this dynamic. The Directorate of Religious Affairs (Diyanet İşleri Başkanlığı), established in 1924, has regulated Sunni mosques by appointing Imams whose sermons were shaped by the secular state.[43] Moreover, the state enacted the laws that regulated the assets of religious foundations, which often restricted what non-Muslim congregations were allowed to do with their property. Given the central place that Istanbul and Turkey hold for the Orthodox and Armenian churches, such restrictions limited the resources these communities had to practice their religions. Thus, despite its secularist bent, the state greatly shaped the religious arena across the country.[44]

In terms of democratization, secularism allowed for some non-negligible gains, such as enabling women to enter the public sphere early on without a veil and to participate in active politics or civil service.[45] Yet this kind of change broadly speaking was really a form of limited modernization that fit the state-imposed "westernization of the bureaucrat."[46] In the specific case of women, it was only a form of "emancipation" and was not a "liberation" from the patriarchal structure of society[47] Just as local elites had to adhere to Kemalist ideals, women's social ascent was still defined within the parameters of a state-controlled structure rather than within a truly inclusive system that allowed for diversity.[48]

"Turkish exceptionalism" and the juxtaposition of a secular bureaucracy and Muslim society continued to hinder democracy further in the post-1980 period. This apposition has become even more significant from the 1990s onwards with the success of the religious AKP, which managed to mobilize the periphery to challenge the secular establishment and vie for control of the state. Both secularist and more Muslim camps tried to use state institutions to effectively quiet the opposing camp, and both have quelled Kurdish dissent. During this time, various governments succeeded in curbing freedom of expression around these topics, heightening the arbitrary nature of the state through reliance on unelected state prosecutors to prosecute opponents for such alleged crimes as wanting to overthrow the state, and damaging the competitiveness of elections (and weakening civil society) by banning political movements organized around debates over Islam and the Kurdish issue. With this in mind, I turn attention to the specific limits imposed on pluralism during each period.

The Coup of 1980 and Its Impact

Nicos Mouzelis identified a pattern in late-industrializing nations; when states do not have the capacity to accommodate demands ignited by modernization, dictators tend to step in to crush competing interests.[49] In Turkey, the center-periphery dialectic and tendency to rule top-down meant that civil society organizations such as employers' and workers' unions and their activities were either tightly controlled by the state or used by the local elite to gain political capital (see Chapter 4). In the absence of efficient vehicles for the formal inclusion of societal interests, significant changes to the country's social structure often engendered protest and civilian strife. Whenever this happened, the army took control of the polity, resulting in three military coups from 1961 to 1980 to replace government structures that seemed incapable of accommodating new and competing demands.[50]

The third military government and its leader Kenan Evren shaped the post-1980 period with the imposition of so-called solutions to political polarization, which in the 1970s culminated in violence between extreme right- and left-wing organizations and fierce competition for influence over the bureaucracy and its resources. The military was further motivated by the desire to implement structural adjustment programs imposed on Turkey by the International Monetary Fund (IMF) because of the country's debt crisis. Thus, Evren and the generals implemented measures with two primary goals: to eradicate (top-down) the fragmentation of the political system and to eliminate opposition to economic reforms. The coup itself had already interrupted democracy. The constitution drafted in 1982 and the first civilian election of 1983, both of which occurred under the watchful eyes of the military, had even longer-term pervasive effects on procedural democracy and the structural obstacles it faced for several reasons.

First, the military defined who could compete in elections and the kinds of platforms they could embrace. The leaders of pre-1980 parties, who the generals blamed for instability, were barred from active politics, so too were civil servants, students, and union leaders unless they resigned their positions. Moreover, the ideological spectrum of political parties narrowed. The explicit identification of Kemalism as a set of values to uphold, or at least align with, restricted the political platforms of ethnic, religious, and class-based movements. In addition to operating under the constant threat of closure, an electoral mandate requiring parties to receive at least 10 percent of the national vote to gain seats in the National Assembly further marginalized these kinds of movements. Such measures weakened procedural democracy by curbing the competitive and representative nature of elections themselves in addition to perpetuating the weakness of Turkish politics, by continuing to exclude the periphery's interests from formal representation within the state. Laws barred parties from having formal ties with civil society organizations. And the generals undermined left-wing movements further by severing the influence of unions over electoral politics. Ultimately, the desire to combat polarization and fragmentation resulted in the further weakening of civil society.

Second, the constitution of 1982 violated notions of formal democracy by giving inordinate powers to unelected officials. Not only did Evren, the head of the junta, serve as president until 1989, six years into the civilian government's term, the military's top brass continued to have influence over civilian governments according to the constitution. More specifically, generals remained overrepresented in the National Security Council (Milli Güvenlik Kurulu, MGK)—a cabinet which dictated policy measures elected parliamentarians were forced to adopt when it came to matters concerning the integrity of the Turkish state and territory. The hold that the military had over legislation came to an end only after the constitutional reforms of 2010 gave control of military decisions and the MGK to the president and prime minister. A similar feature inherited from the 1961 coup gave state prosecutors and the State Security Courts (Devlet Güvenlik Mahkemeleri, DGM) the authority to pursue individuals and groups they believed to "threaten the integrity of the Turkish nation." However, concepts such as the latter further weakened civil society (see Chapter 4) because they are vague and expose individuals, organizations, and political parties to arbitrary state action.

Finally, the military government instituted mandatory religion classes in schools in an attempt to combat the perceived threat of left-wing extremism. The hope, according to Arat and Pamuk, was to reinforce religious affiliation, not class consciousness, as a unifying societal identity.[51] Given the historical tensions between the center and periphery in conjunction with an absence of significant reforms to state-society relations, the measure served to only incite future conflict between secularist and religious Turks.

ANAP's Majority Rule and Democracy

While the military constitution significantly limited the scope of procedural democracy, subsequent elected governments (either due to lack of will or influence) were unable to significantly liberalize policy. The first democratically elected post-coup Motherland Party (Anavatan Partisi, ANAP) government actually heightened some of the formal and structural limits to pluralism. ANAP was not the generals' preferred party. In fact, the junta endorsed a pseudo-party, the Nationalist Democratic Party (Milliyetçi Demokrasi Partisi, MDP), which was led by a former general. The MDP dissolved in just a few years for lack of popularity and a significant social base. Nevertheless, leaders of the coup tolerated ANAP because it had a center-right-wing bent and commitment to economic liberalization. Moreover, its leader Turgut Özal was a career technocrat, who had helped draft the stabilization package in 1979 while he oversaw the State Planning Agency (Devlet Planlama Teşkilatı, DPT) as undersecretary to the prime minister before the coup. He had also proven his conservative and pro-Western credentials through unsuccessful electoral bids in the country's various right-wing parties and a stint working for the World Bank.[52] Özal and ANAP were also a safe, less authoritarian choice for voters due to its lack of connection to previous political parties and to the military. ANAP's aim was to be a governing majority and establish itself as a "big tent" party, able to draw from the urban middle classes from the center and conservative voters from the periphery. This had both positive and negative impacts on Turkey's path to democracy.[53]

Like Özal himself, ANAP's cadres were mainly technocrats drawn to the private sector from previously excluded social groups such the upwardly mobile children of families in peripheral towns and cities; a practice later replicated by the AKP.[54] Given Turkish state tradition and the nature of the bureaucrat, this was a novel development that expanded the range of voices in politics. Özal and ANAP leadership's greater affinity to Islam in their personal and public lives, especially when compared to the previous political elite, further expanded the party's ideological representation. ANAP brought religion and the periphery to the fore while, as noted by Arat and Pamuk,[55] contributing to greater pluralism in several ways including: beginning European Union (EU) membership talks in 1987, liberalizing mass media when there were previously only state-operated TV channels, and emphasizing values such as greater individualism and personal responsibility. Before his death in 1993, Özal even seemed personally inclined toward a more peaceful resolution of the Kurdish issue.

Despite these benefits to democracy, ANAP also damaged it in two crucial ways. First, in the attempt to build a strong majority party, the civilian government did little to try and change aspects of the military constitution that were undemocratic. Because laws adopted by the military limited the social base and ideological scope of opposition parties and because they hurt the appeal of more marginal parties (as a result of the 10 percent electoral barrage), they suited ANAP's political ambitions. Second, the manner in which ANAP implemented economic reforms (addressed in Chapter 5) initially weakened the middle classes, did not combat problems of state clientelism, and altogether eroded the power of civil society.[56] Thus, the more structural and social limits to democracy persisted.

Weak Coalition Governments (1989 to 2002)

During the parliamentary elections of 1989, the first to allow pre-coup leaders back into active politics, ANAP's lackluster performance in the area of democratization created enthusiasm for two other parties as a possible path for reform. The first was former prime minister Süleyman Demirel's center-right-wing True Path

Party (Doğru Yol Partisi, DYP) that he led to victory after being allowed back into politics. Demirel and his movement traced their roots back to the 1950s' DP, which had successfully put an end to the Kemalist single-party era. The fact that the DP had done so thanks to its appeal to the periphery further reinvigorated some hope for change this time around too. The second was Erdal İnönü's Social-Democratic Populist Party (Sosyaldemokrat Halkçı Parti, SHP), which included some left-leaning members of the CHP from before its ban during the coup. The electorate gave them enough votes to form a coalition government with a mandate to liberalize the political system.

The DYP-SHP government made certain democratic inroads by getting rid of laws that restricted parties' connections to civil society organizations or that barred various members of specific professions from entering active politics unless they resigned their posts. However, intensifying conflict against the Kurdish PKK during the same period increased the hold that the military had over politics. As such, weak coalition governments were powerless in the face of undemocratic measures such as martial law and the closure of parties with ties to Kurdish nationalists. Moreover, they were unable to weed out members of the "deep state," who pursued a nationalist agenda and engaged in efforts to insulate the state. Coalition members ultimately ended up using the clientelist networks established by the state elite to enhance their own political ambitions. When combined with economic instability and high inflation rates, the rest of the period was characterized by a succession of unsustainable coalition governments, which were punished during elections by voters who saw their purchasing power decrease due to economic mismanagement.

Two coalitions are worth mentioning in terms of their impact on the subsequent AKP period. The first coalition was forged between the DYP and Welfare Party (Refah Partisi, RP). The RP was the main openly Islamist party and was led by pre-coup politician Necmettin Erbakan, who historically had been the chief figure of Islamists in electoral politics. Under his leadership, the RP obtained its first significant national victory in the 1996 parliamentary elections, in part because centrists were not as successful as Özal's ANAP in attracting the religious vote. Unsurprisingly, the Kemalist state elite saw the DYP-RP coalition as too big of a threat. Thus, in 1997 the military intervened to ban Erbakan and his party for allegedly plotting to overthrow the secular order. While the coalition was short-lived, the RP had two significant impacts on the future of Turkish politics. First, the more technocratic and centrist cadres of the party would later form the AKP as a less threatening alternative, almost akin to ANAP during Özal's reign, blending notions of Islam with economic liberalism. Second, as will be seen below, the RP's chief success was in its capacity to win key mayoral races locally thanks to the draw of future AKP leaders, including Erdoğan whose first significant political role was as the mayor of Istanbul under the RP umbrella. Their success in running local governments would herald the AKP's subsequent appeal, during a period when other parties' influential members dismissed local office to focus on national elections, which they myopically saw as the sole pathway to greater national notoriety and potential cabinet positions.[57]

The second coalition was another unlikely marriage between the social-democratic Democratic Left Party (Demokratik Sol Parti, DSP), the ultra-nationalist Nationalist Movement Party (Milliyetçi Hareket Partisi, MHP) and post-Özal ANAP. Nevertheless, the DSP was led by Bülent Ecevit, a charismatic leader, who in the 1960s and 1970s had used his political appeal to steer the CHP toward a more left-wing bent. Thus, his becoming prime minister generated some enthusiasm and gave the coalition a mandate to push through EU candidacy, which many voters associated with increased democracy. However, disfunctions within the coalition and its inability to govern were largely perceived as causing the major financial crisis of 2001. In 2002, voters punished the coalition (as well as most of the parties that had been perceived as ineffective during the 1990s) by rewarding the AKP (formed from RP's ashes) with nearly 35 percent of the votes, which translated into two-thirds of the seats in the assembly thanks to a fragmented electorate and the electoral threshold. Amid economic mismanagement, some of AKP's cadres' former success in managing cities as mayors made them an appealing if not sensible choice. The rest of the electorate defected to three other parties, which along with the AKP would dominate the Turkish political landscape for the greater part of the following decades: the CHP, which regained some of its pre-1980 clout and managed to unite Kemalists and some social-democrats as a secular opposition to Erdoğan, the ultra-nationalist MHP, which always enjoyed the support of a solid ethno-Turkish (and not religious) core, and the various iterations of parties representing Kurdish and minority interests (when they were not dissolved by the state elite).

The AKP Government (2002 to 2021)

The RP, led by Erbakan, was fundamentalist and seemed, for many secular commentators, set on creating an Islamist state. The new AKP, however, was seen as safer and was often likened (at least in its early days) to Christian democrats in Europe or the Republican Party in the United States, combining elements of economic liberalism and religiosity.[58] Despite the divergence between the two parties, Erdoğan and other AKP leaders were able to capitalize on their past mayoral success with the RP.[59] More specifically, the AKP cadres' effective management of large metropolises greatly increased their appeal for marginalized groups who migrated from rural regions and allowed them to mobilize members of the periphery. The newly formed AKP thus continued to use grassroots organizing and basic service delivery at the level of local government.[60] Moreover, it also followed in Özal's footsteps by creating a dynamic sector of SMEs in the periphery and bolstering consumption through targeted aid and construction projects.[61]

In sum, the party became the voice of a rising new middle class and could boast about very tangible accomplishments through visible improvements in cities. At a time when coalition parties experienced governability crises that impacted the economy negatively, this type of efficacy proved to be valuable political capital, and the AKP has remained in power since 2002. As importantly, the movement's seeming ability to marry religiosity with liberal political and economic values in order to incorporate previously marginalized groups gave it legitimacy in the international arena, with many hailing the "Turkish model" as an answer to Islamic fundamentalism in the rest of the Middle East.[62] According to scholars who studied the movement throughout its two-decade rule, however, three distinct phases characterize the AKP government.[63] The first was from 2002 to about 2007 when the party seemed not only willing but also eager to advance Turkey's candidacy to the EU. The second, from 2007 to 2014, represents a time when secularist fears about the government's growing ability to solidify its reign created tensions in society, particularly about constitutional reform. And the third, from 2014 to today, has been characterized by Erdoğan's presidency and the growing influence of the office he holds.[64]

During AKP's first phase, Turkish citizens from various ideological backgrounds were hopeful that Erdoğan's government would deepen democratization, despite its religious bent. Turkey's EU candidacy had, according to many commentators[65] invigorated previously excluded civil society organizations such as those representing Kurds, women, and religious groups. The AKP was favorable to membership chiefly because one of its strongest supporters MÜSİAD, the largest autonomous business association to represent SMEs and more religious entrepreneurs from the regions, had outward-oriented members interested in deepening ties with Europe.[66] The AKP undoubtedly considered reforms needed for EU membership as promising greater political and religious freedoms in an environment where the state elite used undemocratic means to protect secularism. Moreover, as seen above, the AKP enjoyed the blessing of Western powers for its advancement of the "Turkish model" as a possible path toward democracy in the Middle East.[67] Overall, the constitutional debates centered around EU membership, thus, created a "politics of engagement" through which various Muslim and secular groups could forge the type of democracy they longed for.[68] Notably, the business elite and TÜSİAD seized this opportunity to continue pushing for the democratic reforms it had advocated for since 1996. In the early days of AKP, this engendered some level of cooperation between the association and the party elite in Turkey's push for EU membership, despite their ideological differences (see Chapter 7).

Secularist Turks were split in their beliefs about AKP's true intent in carrying out such reforms. Some feared that talks about declawing the military or expanding individual freedoms were intended to remove obstacles to the party's majority rule and extend religion into the public sphere, while others simply welcomed constitutional reform. The fearful camp dominated much of the country's political arena in 2007 when it became apparent that the AKP was poised to nominate one of its own leaders for the country's presidency.[69] Given that Turkey was a parliamentary system, the prime minister and the cabinet determined the legislative agenda, and the National Assembly (indirectly) chose the president. The position, therefore, did not hold much political clout except for one crucial aspect: the ability to nominate members of the executive branch (thus the state apparatus), ranging from regional governors to chiefs of police to university rectors.

From 2000 to 2007, the position was held by Necdet Sezer, whose term was ending and who had been chosen by the DSP-ANAP-MHP coalition thanks to his inclination to balance the safeguard of state institutions with the democratization process. Thus, the prospect of an AKP president, especially an Erdoğan presidency, worried the supporters of the old secularist guard because of the newfound possibility to staff the state bureaucracy with more religious technocrats. This propelled secularist Turks and the CHP (now positioned to become the main secular opposition) to organize "democracy protests" throughout the country.[70]

In the face of passionate and vigorous opposition, the party chose the then minister of foreign affairs, Abdullah Gül (and not Erdoğan), whose political experience and gentler demeanor were thought to make him a palatable candidate. But in a country where Kemalism had been imposed top-down throughout the twentieth century and news about the existence of a "deep state" was still fresh, the possibility of a state bureaucracy governed by religious groups rather than secularist civil servants made even the compromise choice unacceptable to the traditional elite. Soon after, the military (emboldened by public support) intervened for the third time in less than thirty years by publishing a memorandum that threatened the removal of AKP from power. Given the deadlock, the presidential election went to popular vote and Gül was elected to a seven-year term, thus allowing the AKP to continue to solidify its rule, but only after heightened political conflict with the secularist camp.

The years from 2007 to 2014, until Erdoğan's presidency, were in all a vibrant period for Turkey. During this time, it seemed like the AKP would continue to liberalize the polity, despite earlier opposition to its rule. Indeed, it made several symbolic, if not significant, overtures to Turkey's various communities by, for instance, going on official visits to Armenia or by starting the peace process with Kurds through the liberalization of the Kurdish language in the media and public spaces.[71] Moreover, they passed amendments to the constitution in 2010 thereby removing some key obstacles in front of democracy by, among other things, decreasing the military's influence over legislation and expanding individual freedoms.

However, at the onset of the third phase, around the time Erdoğan, the AKP's natural leader, was elected president in 2014, a combination of events threatened his party's rule. The manner in which Erdoğan decided to deal with them signaled a move away from the democratization efforts and the "end of the Turkish model."[72] In 2013, an "Occupy"-like grassroots movement, "Occupy Gezi," took over an Istanbul park of the same name to protest a significant plan for its development by the AKP. The protests grew into a coalition of various movements that advocated for democratization.[73] When the AKP decided to crack down on the protests, serious confrontations with police ensued. Still, the movement gained in popularity. Even hooligan groups from Istanbul's three major football clubs (particularly "Çarşı," Beşiktaş's anarchist supporters) used their game-day fighting prowess to protect protesters from law enforcement violence.[74] In a country where there is even a saying about how the sport is more important than politics, their support spoke volumes about the traction that the movement was gaining. [75]

Another sign of the AKP's waning popularity was the success of the Kurdish Peoples' Democratic Party (Halkların Demokratik Partisi, HDP) during the 2015 parliamentary elections. The movement sought to organize Kurds as well as marginalized groups like the LGBTQ community and won 13 percent of the national vote. Thanks to the strategy of forming a broader democratizing coalition, the HDP surpassed the 10 percent threshold needed to participate in the assembly. By securing its place in the parliament as such, the HDP usurped a number of seats the AKP would have held as the runner-up in the southeast through its appeal to more religious Kurds. Just as it did to thwart the opposition of the Gezi protests, the AKP resorted to repression and military violence in Kurdish towns that voted for the HDP, only doing so under the pretense that the towns were threatening to secede.[76]

Lastly, in 2016, an attempted coup (allegedly organized by the Muslim Gülenist community) further threatened to remove the AKP from power. The putsch was foiled, but it propelled the party to rid the state of anyone they perceived as sympathetic to the military's actions and the Gülenist movement. The purge, however, was wider-reaching and targeted countless individuals for being even softcore supporters of various political movements.

Hence, although the government and state were governed by more pious members from the periphery, rather than Kemalist bureaucrats from the center, it retained several continuities with Turkish state tradition. First, the AKP followed in the footsteps of Özal's ANAP in its desire to forge a majority party led by career technocrats who used their office to build clientelistic networks.[77] Second, although it moved away from Kemalism, it remained focused on ideological power and the top-down imposition of national identity. This was most evident in the shift in tone against the Kurds and other ethnic minorities: rather than accepting their unique identities as legitimate, the AKP (similar to previous periods) sought to unify them under Sunni Islam as a source of integration.[78] Third, like the republican state before it, the AKP embarked upon highly visible and prodigious projects as illustrated by Erdoğan's affinity for building new national monuments (in the form of mega-mosques) and developing major infrastructural projects (such as a massive airport and excessively long canal in Istanbul).[79]

AKPs continuities with Turkish state tradition are revealing. With its reluctance to accept and incorporate various identities through channels besides Sunni Islam, the AKP did not change the dual nature of the Turkish state. The AKP does appear to be highly capable of transforming society by focusing on more symbolic functions of government, but it has been unable or unwilling to build formal state-society relations. Taken together, these trends have compelled prosecutors and bureaucrats under the AKP to prosecute voices of dissent (as attested by the jailing and closure of Kurdish political leaders and parties), as did state officials before them during the republican era.

Turkey's political trajectory during the period can therefore be characterized as a period of slow democratization after a military coup, followed by more rapid political change under the AKP government, followed by a period of de-democratization during the third phase of its rule. During the period, the

Turkish business elite, as stressed in the introduction, managed to stay on point. To highlight the significance of this position, the next section will conclude the chapter by briefly putting into context the past, historical social role of capitalists in Turkey and by emphasizing further the extent to which TÜSİAD's demands were novel for this group.

Turkish Democracy and Business

While the concept of "deep state" nicely encapsulates problems of Turkish democracy, two popular cultural representations defined how the business elite entered the collective imagination of Turkish society. The first was as one of the most notorious antagonists in Turkish melodramas of the 1950s–1970s— an industrial tycoon, a "fat cat" who schemed to keep his child from marrying a working-class hero. Turkey's Hollywood, Yeşilçam (Green Pine Street) in the heart of Istanbul, produced upwards of 200 to 300 movies annually during its heyday, heavily reinforcing how society perceived the business elite. The industrial capitalist, cast as an aristocratic, shadowy figure nestled in an isolated seaside villa while deliberately obstructing the social ascent of a deserving protagonist was etched into the collective consciousness of generations of cinemagoers. The second emerged during the military coup of 1980 when two humor magazines, *Gırgır* and *Fırt*, reinforced a similar trope in their weekly publications. Using satire to circumvent media censorship and critique the junta's draconian economic measures, the two publications often ran panels of famished workers ogling a table full of calligulesque capitalists feasting with military generals on lavish meals that they washed down with imported whiskey. For individuals coming of age during a period when the military government froze wages, downsized public employment, and crushed any dissent, this imagery transformed the capitalist from an antagonist simply protecting his social status to a powerful political actor willing to plot with an authoritarian government.

The center-periphery dynamic described previously to explain social tensions and the nature of the state can be used to understand these two images as well. Business elites in Turkey were successful in that they were members of the center who benefited from helping protect the state from societal pressures. However, this position shifted dramatically in the 1990s when, compared to the slow pace with which various governments engaged in democratization efforts, the business community appeared to change faster. Recall that TÜSİAD published its *Democratization Report* in 1997 when coalition governments seemed reluctant to take on the military and the state elite to push for change.

Turkish capitalists did not see themselves as caricatural figures feasting with officials or operating in the shadows to maintain their privilege anymore. They felt increasingly capable of transforming society and the political arena. Some even took over areas previously controlled by the state such as education and culture, by founding museums and private universities. Most importantly, TÜSİAD's specific political demands and positions during the 1990s and 2000s drew attention for tackling sensitive issues because they went to the core of the Kemalist state. Though controversial in the context of Turkey where the state imposed a dominant ideology, TÜSİAD's *Democratization Report* (as a document) gave mostly a linear and academic account of the deficiencies of formal democracy. Because it was prepared by a left-leaning law scholar (Bülent Tanör), with input and contribution from more progressive TÜSİAD members, the *Democratization Report* served as a liberal dissection of Turkish law in the tradition of the enlightenment. By proposing to replace legal restrictions with laws that would align more clearly with universal citizenship rights and liberties, the report primarily dealt with the formal definition of democracy. Even in this limited form, however, the publication tackled issues entrenched in Turkish political tradition and presented a break from the state and the political elite.

The Business Elite's Break from the State and the Kurdish Issue

The way the business elite, either individually or through TÜSİAD, addressed Turkey's conflict with its Kurdish minority is a good indicator of the growing schism with the political class. The Kurdish issue was by no means the sole or prime topic they dealt with. As noted above, the fact that TÜSİAD's *Democratization Report* partly blamed the imposition on political movements of Kemalist values for the deficiencies of Turkish democracy was equally, or more, controversial. Chapter 7 will also highlight how the official pro-reform stance taken by TÜSİAD during the secularist-Muslim conflict (through its emphasis on the need to draft a constitution that respected individual and religious freedoms) made it a more moderating voice during the country's political debates. The business elite's focus on a peaceful resolution to the Kurdish conflict, however, encapsulates its shift away from the state well. To this end, some collective and individual actions on the topic are worth noting.

Sakıp Sabancı, the head of the second largest family-owned corporation, one of the major founding members of TÜSİAD, and an industrial tycoon who used a rural inflection to great effect in his public statements did not shy away from the issue. In 1996, he authored (or at least signed) a report that he published on socioeconomic solutions to the armed struggle between the Turkish state and Kurdish rebels.[80] His ideas, at the time, were contentious because they moved away from the military strategies endorsed by the state and drew attention to regional inequalities. To this day, some Turkish commentators, including a handful of individuals close to the business community I spoke to, connect the assassination of Sabancı's brother to members of the "deep state" who wanted to send the influential family a message.[81] Whether founded or not, the existence of such rumors is, at the very least, an indication that the family was moving ideologically away from the state according to public opinion.

Cem Boyner, a younger industrial tycoon and former chairperson of TÜSİAD, entered politics in the 1990s as one of the founders and the spokesperson of the New Democracy Movement (Yeni Demokrasi Hareketi, YDH). YDH sought to appeal to former members of the 1960s' radical youth movements by bringing liberal democratic solutions to the Kurdish problem and other restrictions on freedoms of speech and conscience, when other parties seemed unwilling to tackle them. In 1994, Boyner moved away from the ethnic "Turkish" definition of the nation when he described Turkey as a "cultural mosaic made up of Kurds, Lazs, Circassians and Albanians" during public debate.[82] Though not active in electoral politics anymore, Boyner was spotted—years later—in Istanbul joining prodemocracy protestors at Gezi Park, further challenging presumptions of capitalist conservatism and their commitment to holding the center intact. In light of the negative depictions of industrial capitalists heaving in the collective consciousness, such actions were deemed controversial and counterintuitive.

These individual efforts have continued until recently. In 2019, the Turkish Economic and Social Studies Foundation (Türkiye Ekonomik ve Sosyal Etüdler Vakfı, TESEV), a think tank founded and financed by the Eczacıbaşıs—another TÜSİAD founding family—commissioned and published several reports on the southeast penned by renowned Turkish scholars on the socioeconomic conditions of the region.[83] Like the act of founding museums and educational institutions, individual efforts to move the debate forward on the Kurdish issue and eastern parts of Turkey is probably driven by a newfound desire to find solutions to what are the country's major shortfalls. As will be seen in Chapter 6, however, some informants from within and outside TÜSİAD also provided a material explanation to the desire to find a peaceful solution to the conflict. Large corporation owners felt that they were financing a war that was costly (through taxes that they paid), which they also thought was hurting Turkey's economic potential by keeping one significant region underdeveloped. Though only part of the explanation, it is therefore not surprising that it would also compel TÜSİAD to adopt a less ethnonationalist position in its official statements advocating for peace.

TÜSİAD has traditionally organized yearly official visits to the leaders of various mainstream political parties to express the views of the business community. Throughout the 2010s, it also made a point to include the HDP among its stops rather than shun the movement for its platform to gain greater autonomy for Kurds. Even though the HDP has suffered from Erdoğan and the state's backlash for chipping away at AKP's reign through its electoral successes, TÜSİAD's tone toward the movement has been milder and much more critical of Turkish conservative parties. For instance, during an official visit to HDP headquarters after its first major electoral success in 2014, the association's president lent support to a peaceful solution to Kurdish demands for greater autonomy and defined a role for the business elite:

> [The peace] process is only a process that can be solved through dialogue. We find the current environment highly positive. For the resolution to be sensible, there needs to be economic development in the region. To this end, we organized numerous meetings with TÜSİAD members in order to increase awareness among the business community. We are going to Mardin this month, to discuss alternative tourism. Next month we are going to Van. TÜSİAD is embracing responsibility for the economic side of the peace process.[84]

During the general elections of 2015, when the movement was met with significant hostility from nationalist circles (including physical violence), TÜSİAD put out a statement that condemned the political climate and promoted pluralism:

> During this election campaign, we observed heightened societal tension, polarization and widespread intolerance that has had a damaging effect on confidence, at a level beyond typical election cycles. Confidence in the economy and the country as a whole can only improve with freedom of thought, democratic participation, rule of law and public reason. As TÜSİAD, we believe that confidence can be strengthened with transparency and accountability, and with the effective participation of civil society.[85]

In parallel to these official positions, the association worked with local business organizations to promote regional development through panels, reports, and, as indicated in the above presidential statement, organizing visits to southeastern regions (see Chapter 7). Though hardly revolutionary, these kinds of positions toward an ethnic conflict were considered contentious in a country where the state elite had tried historically to impose a top-down definition of ethnic identity. Thus, how TÜSİAD's foray into issues of democracy was received by individual members of the business elite (my interviewees) warrants some consideration given their historical dependence on the state.

Individual Attitudes toward Democracy

When TÜSİAD leadership first introduced the *Democratization Report*, it created internal strife within the association between those who took the state's official position and criticized the document and those who lauded its liberal democratic bent. Nonetheless, as will be discussed in Chapter 5, most of the members I spoke within a few years after its publication aligned with its new mission due to the logic of influence that business organizations hold over their membership combined with TÜSİAD's internal governance structure, which primarily favored the voice of large corporation owners (see Chapters 4 and 6). This is not to suggest that the association is a monolith. My interviews revealed a broad spectrum of what individual capitalists understood to be their democratizing mission. Some focused on elements that dealt only with good governance and the rule of law, while others incorporated increased civil rights and protection from arbitrary state action. Still others emphasized social dimensions of democracy such as the education system, gender equality, minority rights, and income inequality. Since the more influential TÜSİAD members owned multisector corporations, differences in perspective likely reflected the individual ideological bent of respondents, rather than specific sectoral interests.

Two common themes in interviews I conducted with TÜSİAD members touched upon historical factors driving the group's call for increased democracy. The first was that the state and political class were not swayed by the organized societal interests of the capitalist class. The second was the feeling that the Turkish capitalist lacked ideological legitimacy and, therefore, historically avoided pressing for broader demands. Taken together, these themes point to structural constraints that impinge upon democracy. Throughout its history, the Turkish state tradition relied on ruling top-down, developing despotic functions (the "stick"), and enhancing its ideological power rather than building formal ties with civil society actors. Thus, it presented obstacles to democratization beyond its formal definition, but also weakened the formal power of the business elite.

What is striking about TÜSİAD's demands for democracy is that it survived political turmoil. Neither the military's war on the Kurds nor the ascent of the AKP or its suppression of civil society seems to have deterred the association. While most secular Turks felt threatened by AKP's constitutional push, TÜSİAD was a secular ally for reform. And when the AKP became more threatening, TÜSİAD emphasized the need for a resolution to Turkey's social tensions that respected democratic norms, instead of calling for an intervention by the military or unelected officials, like state prosecutors. The next chapter offers a theoretical background to explain how under capitalism the business elite, at times, adopts a prodemocracy stance and why it is willing to break away from the state, even one that has been able to forge such a strong center as the Turkish state.

Chapter 2

CAPITALISM AND DEMOCRACY: THEORIZING THE ROLE OF STATE-BUSINESS RELATIONS

A discussion of capitalists' attitudes toward political change is intrinsically linked to the relationship between capitalism and democracy (or the lack thereof). Neither is straightforward. The introduction to this book reported two separate conversations I had with two prominent members of the Turkish business elite who had a deeper understanding of the topic thanks to their different trajectories. They both also happened to be the most active figures behind the more progressive tone of the *Democratization Report* TÜSİAD eventually embraced. One, İshak Alaton (born in 1927), had been part of the Swedish labor movement before coming back to Turkey to build his own industrial empire. He was well-versed in the Marxist literature of his youth as a factory worker, which attributed to the capitalists a democratizing role through the destruction of the aristocratic order and establishment of a modern state to "manage the common affairs of the whole bourgeoisie."[1] The other, Can Paker (born in 1942), was exposed to the same literature as a university student, but through the prism of his Turkish radical peers, who were anti-imperialist and more alert to the role of indigenous bourgeois classes at the service of Western imperial powers and local authoritarian states. Turkey's military had already carried out two coups with the pretense of quelling social unrest before the time Paker turned thirty. He therefore fretted being perceived as a *comprador* bourgeois by members of his generation when he embarked on a business career. Even the Marxist tradition (and its Maoist, Leninist, or dependency theory variants) cited by Alaton and Paker attributed different roles to the bourgeoisie and varying regime outcomes under capitalism. Theories about the business elite's political loyalties are, thus, largely shaped by the period and context they examine.

Alaton was right to bring up the *Communist Manifesto* to the extent that nineteenth-century and early-twentieth-century commentators, such as Marx and Weber, constituted one of the most significant cornerstones of the social sciences owing to their efforts to grapple with the juxtaposition of two colossal shifts affecting their societies: the rise of the modern state and more representative forms of government alongside economic development and the expansion of capitalism and industrialism. The first line of investigation this tradition engendered was naturally concerned primarily with the first nations to industrialize. The ideal-typical case of Western Europe suggested that democracy went hand in hand with capitalism because it offered new commercial classes increased representation, which they lacked under the feudal order, and provided individual freedoms necessary to engage in commercial activity.[2] Hence, Moore famously evoked "No bourgeoisie, no democracy" to emphasize that a large commercial class was necessary to push for increased political liberalization.[3] However, the persistence of poverty and political conflicts between various classes, despite remarkable improvements in productive capacities, also pointed to a fundamental tension that survives to this day even in most mature democracies: economic resources are allocated unevenly under capitalism, while democracy promises to afford each individual or group some clout over policy.[4] Marx and Engels used this contradiction to view the capitalist class's transformative capacity and bourgeois democracy as necessary to set the stage for an impending socialist revolution. Schumpeter offered a different interpretation when he envisioned modern capitalists as individuals who could be moved enough by the ideas and political fervor engendered by inequalities under capitalism to extend democracy and social rights top-down as rational solutions to society's ills.[5] More recent scholarship, however, revisited the same tensions between capitalism and democracy to observe that the capitalist class in Western Europe supported democratization so long as it did not threaten its interest by expanding the power of popular groups.[6] This newer strand, therefore, often attributes the rise of democracy to strong popular classes who championed equal rights, and not to the capitalist class. Hence, Alaton was partially wrong in the sense that, even where the association between full democracy and capitalist development has been strongest, there has been no clear consensus on what entrepreneurs' regime loyalties were during Europe's transition to pluralism. This is even clearer in the case of late-industrializing nations, as pointed to by my other interviewee Paker.

Soon after nations' independence from colonial powers in the twentieth century, the above questions have been extended to the case of late-developing societies in Latin America, Asia, Africa, and the Middle East to determine whether they would follow a path similar to Western Europe's as they grew richer. Half a century of research on the Global South has only added layers of complexity to our understanding of capitalists' regime loyalties by highlighting even further that the relationship between capitalism and democracy is as varied as the types of country cases studied. First came modernization theorists who asserted that it was the more aristocratic values of the domestic economic elite in late-developing societies that crippled both democratization and growth by inhibiting the emergence of a more entrepreneurial, meritocratic, and egalitarian culture.[7] This approach assumed that with the right amount of economic stimuli, in the form of government or foreign investment, and with the right kind of social engineering, in the form of education, prodemocracy classes would emerge as a result of growth, social change, and industrialization.

However, throughout the period, not only did many military dictatorships topple nascent parliamentary democracies after they had reached substantial levels of economic development, but some, like South Korea from the 1960s to the 1990s, seemed to manage their economies better when compared to societies with more open political systems. This perceived advantage has even compelled scholars of development to weigh the tradeoff between extending democracy or achieving rapid economic growth under the hospices of an authoritarian state (referred to by Kohli as the "cruel choice" thesis).[8] In a nutshell, this line of investigation wondered whether the redistributive impact of rapid capitalist growth would overwhelm fragile democracies through popular demands placed on the state. Despite the large sample of nations studied, however, no overarching pattern was found in the relationship between regime type and successful capitalist development, leading some to even conclude that authoritarian rulers tended to face the same policy demands and pressures as their democratic counterparts.[9] Hence, to clarify why some democracies had fallen at higher stages of development came the more class-based and structural explanations to reveal that when moving to more advanced capital-intensive manufacturing, budding industrialists were likely to support authoritarian regimes, which they saw as more capable of channeling resources toward subsidizing the private sector and more willing to quell distributional conflicts, which modernization had engendered.[10] Within this approach, capitalists were perceived—as will be explored further in the next chapter on the historical conditions that shaped the Turkish business elite's position—as at once powerful and weak: they could precipitate regime change but did so because of their dependence on developmentalist states and their mission to promote and protect a national bourgeoisie.

Given such variations, it is therefore not surprising that research focused on the (re)democratization and economic liberalization processes of many late-industrializing countries during the past thirty years would also reveal differences in business's political stance from one case or from one scholarly tradition to another. As noted in the introduction, business in many Latin American countries contributed to the collapse of authoritarian regimes and adopted a prodemocracy stance during the region's political transition in the 1980s. While some legitimately raised concerns about the quality and scope of democracy achieved under the control of ruling classes,[11] others underlined the role played by the business elite and posited that it would need to stay committed to pluralism for democracy to become further institutionalized.[12] Yet, studies of enduring authoritarian regimes, such as in China or the Middle East, highlight that capitalists there are a far cry away from becoming a democratizing force given their continued dependence on patronage and stability afforded by the state.[13] More recently, the rise around the world of autocrats with a tendency to centralize power[14] and the slow institutionalization of formal state-society relations[15] are also reminders that the relationship between capitalism and democracy is not linear and that the position adopted by classes is still important to predict regime outcomes. These variations thus bring capitalist interest to the fore of predicting democratization, democratic consolidation, or authoritarian reversals. After all, if some of the most structurally powerful allies of authoritarian regimes can oppose or promote more open political societies, their specific interests should be examined more closely. Numerous scholars have offered potential areas of investigation.

However, previous theories we have about the capitalist class and its relation to the state have been the product of a wide range of research with similar objects of study but different dependent variables. Some have focused on regime outcomes,[16] others have tried to underline the conditions for successful development policy,[17] while another tradition has tried to theorize about the nature of the capitalist state.[18] In light of the impressive span of previous research and theorizing, the chapter undertakes a broad chronological overview, starting with the rise of Western European capitalism and democracy and ending with the more contemporary cases of late-industrializing societies, in order to tease out building blocks to understand why the business elite in Turkey would abandon its pro-authoritarian ways to push for democratization.

As emphasized in the introduction, the central argument of the book is that cross-country differences in business's political attitudes exist because of variations in established state-business relations, the level of responsiveness of political classes to capitalist interest, and changes in the power and needs of the business elite. Central to this argument is my use of Michael Mann's IEMP framework which sees states and social groups as using varying combinations of four sources of power in order to exercise control over others. More specifically, I trace differences in state-business relations, and in turn regime outcomes, to variations in the manner both state and private-sector actors have accumulated and used different forms of power. This framework has, for instance, already been used successfully to explain differences in development outcomes,[19] the failure of US foreign involvement,[20] and the impact of globalization on economic policy.[21] Before I can proceed with a review of how this approach can be more amenable to understanding the political attitude of business across several different cases and epochs, however, state autonomy must be defined to make one significant piece of the framework more accessible to a wider readership. Once this is done, the chapter will trace how the capitalist class's regime loyalties throughout various periods has shaped scholarship on capitalism and democracy (from early-industrialized nations in Western Europe to the case of late-development) to then highlight how some have made sense of the role capitalists have played during the "third wave" of democracy.

State Autonomy and Social Power

State Autonomy and Capitalist Interest

In a study of Latin American businesses' active role in the democratization process of the 1980s and 1990s, Bartell and Payne note a certain contradiction in the manner with which we imagine and overestimate capital's political power when it comes to its impact on regime change.

> Despite an apparent departure by the business elite from past authoritarian attitudes, scholars studying transition from authoritarian rule have viewed this

change with great skepticism. They distrust business leaders' commitment to democracy. They assume that if they prove unable to control the democratization process—which, given their limited political power, is a plausible assumption—and if liberalization goes "too far," business leaders will again unite with other social sectors and reverse the process. In other words, according to skeptics, the only variant of democracy business leaders will accept is a highly restricted one. Once again, then, business leaders are too weak to assert their demands in a democratic context, although powerful enough to replace democracy with authoritarian rule, and generally preferring authoritarianism or highly restricted democracy to democratic rule.[22]

The authors raise a series of interesting and interrelated questions about state-business relations. If capital is strong enough to precipitate regime change in the first place, why was it not able to suppress the mounting popular sector demands through existing institutions during the pre-1980 era without calling on the barracks to intervene? Similarly, when business leaders grew wary in the 1980s of military dictatorships' violent excesses, why were they not capable of reining them in without resorting to a full-on regime change? These questions have strong ramifications for the case of Turkey and TÜSİAD through a puzzle they set. If the business elite has enough influence, it should be able to promote the creation of a business-friendly environment without pressing for further democratization. Capitalists have undeniably some structural power and clout over policy that ordinary citizens lack, but the answer to the above questions and the key to the puzzle partly lie in the observation that states have at times the power to act autonomously or independently from social groups. Moreover, the type of access that the business elite has to the state has tended to vary. Thus, it is useful to depart from pluralist as well as classic Marxist accounts of the state that solely see it as representing the interests of various groups in society.

The concept of state autonomy was first born out of a methodological critique of classic Marxist thought. As noted by Schumpeter, it is always possible to attribute, ex post, a pro-capitalist agenda to most policies that states enact. While he did recognize the importance of class interest in understanding political change, he also advocated that it should be used more carefully to understand the state:

> All that is worth while troubling about is the Why and How of that vast majority of cases in which the theory either fails to conform to fact or, even if conforming, fails to describe correctly the actual behavior of those "committees for managing the common affairs of the bourgeoisie." Again, in practically all cases the theory can be made tautologically true. For there is no policy short of exterminating the bourgeoisie that could not be held to serve some economic or extra-economic, short-run or long-run, bourgeois interest, at least in the sense that it wards off still worse things. This, however, does not make that theory any more valuable.[23]

State autonomy has, since, been used by neo-Marxist authors to fine-tune our understanding of state-business relations under capitalism in order to make sense of a range of outcomes that seem counterintuitive given the structural power of capitalists. For instance, state autonomy was introduced in Marxian debates about the emergence of pro-labor policies and social spending in advanced capitalist societies that would seemingly go against capitalist interest. One camp spearheaded by the sociologist Poulantzas who echoes the same idea as Schumpeter's to understand such phenomena as the resolution of the May 1968 crisis in France maintained that states care more about the long-term survival of the capitalist system than the short-term interest of capitalists:

> According to Marx, Engels and Lenin, the members of the State apparatus, which it is convenient to call the "bureaucracy" in the general sense, constitute a specific social category—not a class. This means that, although the members of the State apparatus belong, by their class origin, to different classes, they function according to a specific internal unity. Their class origin—class situation—recedes into the background in relation to that which unifies them—their class position: that is to say, the fact that they belong precisely to the State apparatus and that they have as their objective function the actualization of the role of the State. This in its turn means that the bureaucracy, as a specific and relatively "unified" social category, is the "servant" of the ruling class, not by reason of its class origins, which are divergent, or by reason of its personal relations with the ruling class, but by reason of the fact that its internal unity derives from its actualization of the objective role of the State. The totality of this role itself coincides with the interests of the ruling class.[24]

In other words, given intra-class conflicts among capitalists, whose specific short-term goals might clash, the state and its bureaucracy need, at times, to maintain an equal distance from individual members of the private sector to ensure the longer-term survival of capitalism. For instance, if giving benefits and concessions to workers, like the French government did in 1968, is needed to maintain labor peace and help at the same time boost demand, states can decide to extend these despite opposition from individual members of propertied classes.

This approach was later picked up by more Weberian, state-centric sociologists as a critique of both Marxism and pluralism. The perspective was fully synthesized and articulated by Skocpol, Rueschemeyer, and Evans who advocated for "bringing back the state" to make sense of cross-country divergences in policy outcomes. Their approach underscored that the goals of the state, its structure, and its institutional elite were, depending on the context, as likely to impact the direction of polity as pressure from society and powerful interest groups.[25] As will be mentioned throughout this chapter, this approach also led to focusing on the quality of state-society relations rather than the quantity of state intervention. Most notably, Evans compared state efforts to expand IT sectors in late-industrializing nations and demonstrated that divergences in outcomes were caused by differences in the nature of state-business relations and not the size of government.[26] In one extreme, he observed that when states are too insular, like in Mobutu and his cronies' Zaire, their powers go unchecked and the political elite use their office and state resources for personal gain. When states lack autonomy, like his examples of Brazil or India, their bureaucracies grow to distribute rent without coherent developmentalist goals, despite the existence of some well-performing agencies (or "pockets of efficiency") staffed by goal-oriented civil servants. Positive development outcomes are most frequent in places like Korea where the state has a cohesive bureaucracy that is at once autonomous from private interest and embedded enough in society to get frequent policy feedback. Similarly, Weiss has illustrated that the historical presence of networks can help predict the extent to which policymakers can successfully mobilize the private sector to formulate efficient industrialization policy through state-business interactions (or "governed interdependencies"), even under the existence of global pressures to limit the size of state intervention.[27] Although this approach's dependent variable is positive developmentalist outcomes, it also is useful for understanding the political position of the business elite in Turkey and elsewhere because it underscores variations in the nature of state-business relations across capitalist societies. More importantly, by focusing on relations this tradition cautions that even under periods of economic liberalization and changes in the size of the state, existing channels of incorporation can have varying success in accommodating the needs of the business elite. Like any other useful conceptual tool, however, state autonomy and different notions of state-business relations can benefit from some fine-tuning for two different reasons.

First, as Domhoff has illustrated in his critique of the state-centric literature, the question of the level of independence the state has from the influence of powerful groups should be an empirical one, where the influence of the capitalist class, or lack thereof, is studied through the presence of business representation in policy networks.[28] The latter is accomplished, for instance, by assessing the extent to which the economic elite's think tanks shape policy debates or change the fields of university research through funding and agenda-setting. Second, although the existence of a Weberian rational bureaucratic state has been widely noted as a necessary precondition for the formulation and promotion of economic development, many states since the end of colonialism have exhibited features of such government organization without witnessing the success of ideal-typical bureaucratic states such as Japan or Korea. For instance, modern Middle Eastern states had through large militaries and education systems considerably expanded the size of their bureaucracies as one way to integrate their societies.[29] This, however, did not translate into coherent economic policy or the creation of a competitive private sector. The fact that the expansion of civil service was impressive without compelling leaders in the region to translate this capacity toward successful industrialization should require us to hone our conceptualization of the state so that it can be used for comparative research.[30] To this end, an approach that recognizes the structural power of capitalists, but leaves room for variations in its exact level and interplay with the state should be developed. I borrow from and combine several conceptual tools (including Mann's IEMP model) in order to arrive at a typology of states and state-business relations that can be more amenable to empirical research on type of access capitalists have to policy makers, which is particularly important for cases of late-industrializing nations such as Turkey.

Typologies of Power, State Traditions, and the Business Elite

The first typology of states has to do with the types of power that they have and distinguishes between their levels of *infrastructural power* and *despotic power*, which can help explain part of the tension described about the growth of Middle Eastern bureaucracies that did not engender considerable economic development. As noted by Mann:

> [*despotic power*] derives from the range of actions that state elites can undertake without routine negotiation with civil society groups ... A state with despotic power becomes either an autonomous actor, as emphasized by true elitism, or multiple but perhaps confused autonomous actors, according to its internal homogeneity ... *Infrastructural Power* is the institutional capacity of a central state, despotic or not, to penetrate its territories and logistically implement decisions ... Infrastructural power is a two-way street: It also enables civil society parties to control the state, as Marxists and pluralists emphasize.[31]

These are ideal types of course, and many states have had elements of both, especially in our modern context where many seemingly despotic states have had to develop infrastructural power in order to increase their reach. However, it is still possible to point to general tendencies that states have chosen or been forced to adopt to govern over a given territory. Historically, for instance, European feudal states during the late Middle Ages were so decentralized that in order to secure the allegiance of local power holders and tax society they had to provide services such as roads and bridges, which increased their infrastructural power. Society thus became economically more dynamic thanks to the trade networks this helped build, while the state increased its extractive capacity by expanding its reach and tax base. Some states, however, have been able to rule through despotic power without choosing the route of power sharing, such as the more centralized Ottoman or Chinese Empires that have allocated more resources on repression and the symbolic powers of the state (see Chapter 3 for the Ottoman Empire and Turkey).[32] These tended to be more fearful of any potential local power holders who would have been able to challenge their rule. As such, the Chinese and Ottoman Empires chose to build their extractive capacities by establishing large bureaucracies manned by tax farmers rather than develop their infrastructural powers. The ideal-typical despotic state thus inhibits economic growth and can see groups in society with economic power, such as commercial classes, as a potential threat.[33] Similarly, modern era Middle Eastern states have tended to use their impressive bureaucracies for top-down sociocultural policies designed to breed nationalism, while using economic incentives only to secure the allegiance of various groups through patron-client relations.[34] In this situation, the capitalist class can at times benefit from the resources distributed by despotic states, without benefiting from the more diffuse expansion of infrastructure across society. Hence, we can have the growth of bureaucracy without the formulation of coherent developmental goals and without a dynamic private sector. One can therefore distinguish, within infrastructural power networks, power that is more extensive (or diffuse, such as markets) and authoritative (or direct, such as military command).³⁵

The second useful analytical tool to discern the real influence of the business elite over varying types of states is Mann's distinction between ideological, economic, military, and political sources of power (IEMP). States and groups in society, including capitalists, wield varying levels and types of power derived from a range of institutions:

> *Ideological Power* derives from the human need to find ultimate meaning in life, to share norms and values, and to participate in aesthetic and ritual practices. Control of an ideology that combines ultimate meanings, values, norms, aesthetics, and rituals brings general social power.
>
> ... *Economic Power* derives from the need to extract, transform, distribute, and consume the resources of nature. It is peculiarly powerful because it combines intensive, everyday labor cooperation with extensive circuits of the distribution, exchange, and consumption of goods ... All complex societies have unequally distributed control over economic resources.
>
> ... *Military Power* is the social organization of physical force. It derives from the necessity of organized defense and the utility of aggression. Military power has both intensive and extensive aspects, for it concerns intense organization to preserve life and inflict death and can also organize many people over large sociospatial areas. Those who mobilize it, as military elites and castes, can wield a degree of general social power.
>
> ... *Political power* derives from the usefulness of territorial and centralized regulation. Political power means *state* power. It is essentially authoritative, commanded and willed from a center.³⁶

Within this framework, the differing combinations of power the state and social actors hold within specific societies lead to singular "crystallizations," or the emergence of unique state traditions and modes of incorporation within state institutions. Thus, Western European feudal states relied much more on economic and political power to incorporate society than did states that relied more on military power. This engendered the birth of the ideal-typical liberal democratic state, which rules through consensus and incorporates class interests within formal institutions. The Ottoman Empire and Turkish Republic have relied more heavily on ideological and military power to rule over former Ottoman colonies and what is now modern-day Turkey, first through the symbolic power of the sultanate which held the caliphate and then through the pillars of Kemalism that the Turkish Republic used to forge a national identity (see Chapter 3). Once the state has established control over several spheres of life in this manner, it would become highly suspicious of competing sources of power and rule in a more top-down fashion than is customary in liberal democracies. Thus, the infrastructure developed within this framework was more authoritative and less extensive.

The competition for power is not necessarily a zero-sum game, as noted by Parsons.[37] It can be "distributive" (power over someone) but can also be collective to the extent that it can be used to improve the situation of all actors. For instance, a national bourgeoisie that does well can also increase the power of the state through a larger tax base. Thus, the manner in which states have chosen to rule is impacted by and in turn also affects the power of social actors. In terms of the topic at hand, capitalists as a class also wield economic and ideological power. The fact that they are a source of employment and impact the lives of their workers is an undeniable source of economic power, which they can use to influence the policy decisions of governments. And, as proposed by Marx, "the ideas of the ruling class are in every epoch the ruling ideas, i.e., the class which is the ruling material force of society, is at the same time its ruling intellectual force"[38] mainly because they also control the cultural means of production. However, my claim is that the power of business and the relationship between economic power and ideological power is neither uniform nor direct across different cases. While, for instance in the United States the business elite has been able to build a sphere of influence in policy networks[39] and in Germany it has found a place in corporatist structures,[40] it has been heavily dependent on the government for patronage in many late-industrializing societies. Whenever this has been the case, business has been economically weak and has tended to adopt the dominant ideology of the state or aristocratic classes. As noted by Schumpeter, it is in societies where the capitalists can use rational decision-making to advance their social ranks that they have been more inclined to embrace the democratizing ideas of popular groups.[41] One important narrative thread in this book therefore traces how and why Turkish capitalists' power has changed to the point that it is able to challenge the state.

As importantly, power is derived through institutions which are controlled by the state and social actors. While the business elite's economic power can derive from the growth of the private enterprise, ideological power is not created and accumulated in a vacuum: it needs churches, associations, and organizations to coalesce. Hence, the business elite needs to build institutions, such as effective associations and think tanks, to increase and translate their economic power into ideological power. Moreover, ideologies can be borrowed and need not necessarily be created by classes to fulfill a materialist function. As illustrated by Poggi in his Weberian study of Calvinism and capitalist development, Protestantism became appealing to the new commercial classes because it meshed well with their economic activity. In other words, ideologies are not created to attain materialist goals, but can be adopted and embraced by classes if they help make sense of their day-to-day activities and social roles.[42] The claim I develop throughout the book is similar. Championing liberal democracy was appealing to business in Turkey and elsewhere in the late-developing world because it is, first, a mission that was actively cultivated by TÜSİAD and other business associations they established and then, it was a way to increase their ideological legitimacy and political voice in a manner that was proportional to their increased economic power.

Within this framework, globalization and free trade are important because they have the potential to shift power toward the capitalist class by putting the bulk of the responsibility for economic progress on the private sector and by offering alternative sources of ideology, such as liberal democratic values. However, I depart from basic diffusion models because external pressure can become salient only if the capitalist class has the necessary institutions to embrace and diffuse new ideas, and if these fit together well with their endogenous economic power and needs. As importantly, societies have varied in the way that they have implemented economic liberalization. Thus, the types of relationship the business elite historically have had with the state determine the extent to which these ideas become salient.

The final important characteristic of states is the distinction between informal and formal channels of incorporation. Mann admits that for the period covering the emergence of the modern state, he limited his IEMP model to the study of the United States and Western Europe, where industrialism emerged first.[43] Thus, his framework does not explicitly tackle informal state-society linkages, which are crucial to understanding cases like Turkey. In attempting to integrate society and rule over a territory, states can build formal mechanisms of representation through elections, the integration of civil society organizations, and universalistic laws that apply to most or all citizens equally. At times, however, as will be further discussed below, states have had to rely on informal channels of incorporation to garner the support of various individuals and groups in society. This has included populism that uses a mixture of charismatic rule with rewards distributed directly to various groups in society by bypassing formal channels. Populists have often attempted to replace existing civil society groups with organizations established and controlled by the state, such as the various workers' and women's branches of the Peronist Party in Argentina[44] or the PRI in Mexico.[45] Another strategy adopted by rulers has been the use of clientelist networks to gain the support of key allies that have some influence over large constituencies, by providing them with benefits or key roles within the state. This has been used to secure the support of the landed aristocracy in Latin America, who control a large labor force,[46] or the elite in the Middle East, who have tribal or sectarian affiliations which help guarantee the allegiance of specific segments in society.[47] As was hinted at in the previous chapter and will be covered more extensively in Chapter 3, the Turkish state has often used a combination of both at the detriment of civil society actors.

From the perspective of the business elite, the distinction between formal and informal channels of incorporation is significant since the ability to obtain resources is based on personal ties rather than on objective meritocratic factors, when entrepreneurs have to compete for state subsidies. This gives an advantage to structurally powerful actors and perpetuates unequal access to the state, as already established enterprises have an advantage when competing for government aid. However, these types of relationships can become highly unpredictable because they can change at the whim of state officials and can be impacted by changes in government. Informal access therefore presents a contradiction in terms of business's power: it has privileged access to state resources, but this access often depends on the allegiance of individual entrepreneurs to the regime and not on the broader powers of capital as a class. As such, business is at once weak and strong politically in settings where the state has relied extensively on informal channels of representation. The contradiction in business's power noted by the Latin Americanists Bartell and Payne stems exactly from the fact that capitalists have connections to the political elite but that their interests as a class are not always incorporated into the state through formal channels.[48] Thus, the nature of power the state relies on to rule and the types of access the private sector enjoys all work in tandem with the needs of the capitalist class to affect its regime loyalties and the level of influence it enjoys. Accordingly, the following historical review will survey how various theories about business's political position have evolved from case to case, while incorporating into the discussion, state autonomy, the four types of social power, and the role of (in)formal channels of interest representation.

Regimes and Capitalism in Western Europe

Early Liberal Democracy

The ideal-typical case of Western Europe development was the first one to compel commentators to note an affinity between capitalism and democracy (including my interviewee İshak Alaton). The appeal of self-regulating markets and trade as a way to achieve not only prosperity but also political freedom has constituted one of the cornerstones of Western philosophical tradition. As noted by Smith in 1776:

> commerce and manufactures gradually introduced order and good government, and with them, the liberty and security of individuals, among the inhabitants of the country, who had before lived almost in a continual state of war with their neighbours and of servile dependency upon their superiors. This, though it has been the least observed, is by far the most important of all their effects. Mr. Hume is the only writer who, so far as I know, has hitherto taken notice of it.[49]

This idea seemed to be embraced by many of Smith's contemporaries and authors of the Enlightenment. Through an extensive examination of writing predating the emergence of full on capitalism, Hirschman reveals that the "invisible hand of the market" gave ammunition to many opponents of absolutist monarchies, who found in the concept of a self-regulating economy a legitimate argument for curbing the powers of rulers.[50] Throughout the period, the burgeoning capitalist class pushed for "bourgeois democracy" in order to advance its interests and gain political representation, which had previously been reserved for the European aristocracy.[51] The relationship between democracy and capitalism appeared to be linear and a strong bourgeoisie was believed to be its champion. As bureaucratic states replaced traditional customs and forms of rule, so too did the economic enterprise become more rational and concerned with efficiency according to Weber.[52]

> At present under our individualistic political, legal, and economic institutions, with the forms of organization and general structure which are peculiar to

our economic order, this spirit of capitalism might be understandable, as has been said, purely as a result of adaptation. The capitalistic system so needs this devotion to the calling of making money, it is an attitude toward material goods which is so well suited to that system, so intimately bound up with the conditions of survival in the economic struggle for existence, that there can today no longer be any question of a necessary connection of that acquisitive manner of life with any single *Weltanschauung*.[53]

Much of the political transformation undergone during and after the rise of capitalism in Western Europe, and some of the interpretations put forth to explain this change, indicate that the rise of capitalism and emergence of democratic institutions were intrinsically intertwined. The first mechanism linking the two was political. The rise of commercial activity increased the role and wealth of capitalist classes and led to the feudal aristocracy's gradual absorption into the new economic system. In England, capitalist demand for raw materials and foodstuffs led the gentry to transform feudal lands and do away with customs in order to profit from agriculture, rather than stay shackled by their obligations to provide for their populations. As stated by Marx:

> The spoliation of the church's property, the fraudulent alienation of state domains, the robbery of common lands, the usurpation of feudal property and clan property and its transformation into modern private property under circumstances of reckless terrorism, were just so many idyllic methods of primary accumulation. They conquered the fields of capitalistic agriculture, made the soil part and parcel of capitalism, and created for the town industries the necessary supply of a "free" and outlawed proletariat.[54]

Once this process was set in motion, commercial classes gained political representation in line with their growing economic power to push for their specific needs. From the perspective of a more class-based analysis, the extension of representation to a wider segment of society than the aristocracy was needed to help tame the struggle emerging between business interests and the members of the *ancién regime* by incorporating it within the state.[55] This struggle was at times mitigated, as noted by Schumpeter, in instances where the aristocracy joined capitalist enterprise.[56] In France, where the aristocracy was reluctant to do away with its feudal privileges and was resisting the rising power of the bourgeoisie, it was overthrown forcefully through the revolution of 1789.[57]

The second mechanism, linking the rise of capitalism and democracy, stems from the previous and deals with the compatibility of capitalist interest and the institutions associated with liberal democracy that are conducive to commercial activity. The disintegration of the traditional feudal order and dissolution of ties to the land benefited the rising bourgeoisie which could now gain access to politically free labor, expand markets and seek profits without customary and cultural restrictions on investment decisions and the manner in which private property could be used.[58] Feudal ties and obligations were local, while capitalism required more extensive or diffuse institutions to grow for the promotion of trade and economic transactions. Cultural restrictions on the use of time and resources were binding under the old order, while the management of private enterprise needed constant calculation and tinkering in order to improve production and achieve future profits.[59] Thus, transition to liberal democracy was more likely to happen in societies where commercial activity had led to the rise of strong capitalist interest and had eroded feudal obligations and cultural mores. Once capitalism was set in motion, the possibility for upward social mobility became alluring, and the rational thinking that this entailed transformed society.[60]

The More Arduous Path to Democracy in Europe

The historical affinity described above should not imply a clear linear or causal relationship between capitalism and democracy where capitalists (or the bourgeoisie) always champion political change. First and foremost, the rise of democracy was fraught with obstacles. The seeming compatibility between capitalist interest and institutions associated with democracy, as well as the new capitalist class's desire for increased representation, did not translate to full democracy immediately.

Less linear accounts further emphasize that landed and capitalist classes at times even supported authoritarian reversals when the mobilization of popular groups became too threatening. For instance, in France, the restoration of the monarchy followed by the Second Empire would suggest that propertied classes were afraid of the revolutionary zeal of working classes. In their extensive comparative study of various societies, Rueschemeyer, Huber, and Stephens reveal that the European capitalist class was interested only in the rights that facilitated economic activity and increased its representation within the state.[61] It had no immediate interest, however, in extending increased representation to labor. A positive relationship between democracy and capitalism emerged only when economic development led to the expansion of working and middle classes in whose interest it was to actually champion universal suffrage and increased social rights. Capitalism engendered the rise of democracy only in cases where these groups were able to build interclass coalitions. Hence, even linear accounts such as Marshall's or Schumpeter's suggest that it is through the passage of time and through demands for greater equality that full democracy eventually emerged.[62]

Second, on a more meso level, Marxist studies of the factory shopfloor have revealed that the manufacture underwent a transformation during the rise of industrialism, where employers sought to take away knowledge of production from skilled craftworkers through increased control and automation. The outcome of this conflict was projected to the more macronational arena through the emergence of a class of laborers resigned to accept that its role would, at best, be limited. Working-class movements had to accept reformism over revolutionism in a system where capitalists had made themselves essential in the production process.[63] On a more structural level, this meant accepting the rules of the game established by the capitalist class, and on a more political level, it meant supporting political parties that were able to build interclass coalitions through less threatening ideas.[64]

Finally, theories about the linear affinity between capitalism and democracy have been criticized as centered mainly on the British experience.[65] In fact, Mann classifies the latter as an "anomaly" because the rise of industrial capitalism did not radically disrupt class relations but was characterized by gradual reform.[66] The expansion, early on, of a more representative political system was able to accommodate the demands of landlords who were already integrated in capitalist trade networks, the petit bourgeoisie, and, later on, larger industrial capital, all of whom did not see a need to challenge or vehemently oppose each other's interests. The transition to capitalism in the two other significant cases of the continent was far more disruptive, and as noted by Moore,[67] was brought about either through revolution (France) or through top-down authoritarian reform (Germany).

This observation has led comparative sociologists to focus on explaining the divergence of these two societies from the more ideal-typical Anglo-centric case. In his classic study noted above, Moore concluded that it was the relative balance of power of classes that led nations to adopt three different routes to modernization. While it was the presence of a strong bourgeoisie in England and its incorporation into existing channels of representation previously reserved for landed classes that led to the emergence liberal democracy, it was the resistance from the aristocracy that led a similar class in France to push for a violent overthrow of the *ancien régime*. As for the case of Germany, it was the relative weakness of the capitalist class and strength of the old, landed warrior classes that propelled the state to spearhead capitalist development. The initial impetus behind state-sponsored modernization was the need to catch up geopolitically to early-industrializers like England who could invest newfound resources and technology toward military might. However, in the absence of a strong industrial sector, Germany had to channel resources to the few capitalists who could achieve capitalist growth, especially in sectors benefiting the military. As for the aristocracy, it was the highly nationalist tones of the developmentalist project combined with the fact that this group was absorbed into high positions in the bureaucracy that made the transformation far more acceptable. However, this class alliance, according to Moore, led to the achievement of capitalist development under the hospices of a pro-capitalist authoritarian state and not under liberal democracy. Thus, in the case of Western Europe alone, we see the capitalist class at times champion some form of increased participation, either through gradual reform or revolution, and at others gain from the nationalist and authoritarian character of the state.

These variations have led some scholars to delve deeper into the importance of ideological-political institutions and, in particular, borrowing from the work of Weber, the impact that preexisting state traditions can have on both capitalist development and political change. Weber had already broken away from economy-centric perspectives partly because he felt that they did not explain why and how the motivation of individuals to act like capitalists emerged in the first place. In doing so, Weber engendered scholarship that saw the relationship of democracy and capitalism less of a causal mechanism, but as more of a fortuitous juxtaposition of different conditions. Newer perspectives[68] have pieced Weber's writings on capitalism together more comprehensively in order to show that political institutions and values we associate with liberal democratic were not products of capitalism or the capitalist class but that they emerged, like the new economic order, because of preconditions present in European societies that meshed together. For instance, a universal definition of citizenship was pivotal for capitalism because it helped promote long-distance trade by replacing the distinction between the in-group and out-group. It also shielded individuals and their property from arbitrary state intervention. Notions of citizenship, however, were the legacy of merchant cities, universalistic religious values, and bureaucratic states able to enforce the rule of law. In sum, all these taken together helped shape the institutions of Western European capitalism, spark the emergence of liberal democracy, and orient the behavior of individuals toward more profit-seeking behavior.[69]. Thus, within this perspective, capitalism has a historical affinity with institutions we tend to associate with democracy and not with democracy itself, so long as a predictable environment where agents can make rational choices based on calculable profits emerges.[70]

Hence, Mann asserts that the rise of citizenship and political rights should not always be linked to capitalist development, like more linear accounts do, but should instead be traced back to British constitutionalism, which emerged under feudalism before the rise of enterprise.[71] In this specific case, economic power was diffuse across society and the British landed aristocracy had, before even the industrial revolution, already entered capitalist markets. The rising petit bourgeoisie had no political power, but parliamentary representation of landed classes ensured the adoption of pro-capitalist laws. Ultimately, class compromise between the aristocracy and bourgeoisie was achieved through the widespread adoption of the Enlightenment's political ideology, which meshed well with the two groups' economic interests.[72] As for the case of authoritarian Germany, Mann argues that more labor-intensive repressive forms of agriculture combined with an absolutist state structure predating the emergence of capitalism was highly conducive to the top-down model of capitalist development discussed by Moore.[73] Thus, even in the "ideal-typical case" of Western Europe, we see large variations in state traditions that can impact the position of the capitalist class. In sum, the existence of different sources of power—IEMP—allowed states to use different strategies in order to cage capitalist relations within its territory by forging different class alliances.[74]

Regardless of the path they adopted, a final characteristic of Western European societies was that they benefited from the gradual pace of industrialization and the rise of capitalism. This meant that states had more time than the rest of the world to establish the institutions needed to incorporate the interests of new classes. Whether autocratic or democratic, they faced a decentralized political system, but could use the resources generated by economic expansion toward building their infrastructural powers gradually. This would lead to the more formal representation of capitalist or working-class interest within the state throughout Europe, which afforded entrepreneurial classes some political power. In a nutshell, classes were incorporated into the state gradually through formal representation. In cases where the shift to democracy was slow, the bourgeoisie was further moved by political currents that capitalist inequality engendered to find solutions to societal problems through top-down democratization.[75] However, as the next section will show, for other cases the nature of late-development inhibited the development of similar channels of representation and, because class interest was often incorporated through informal means, prevented business from being politically powerful.

Late-Development and Dependent Business

The Role of the State

In an essay trying to grapple with the violent nature of Latin American dictatorships, "The Turn to Authoritarianism in Latin America and the Search for its Economic Determinants," Hirschman[76] admits that his *The Passions and the Interests*, cited earlier on these pages, was an escapist project where he found solace in the thoughts of the Enlightenment, which saw arguments for democracy and against absolutist governments in the idea of a self-regulating market. To remember, the Enlightenment perceived the market equilibrium as too natural and delicate a balance to be meddled with by mercantilist absolutist rulers. Alas, Hirschman felt that twentieth-century dictators in late-developing societies used the same exact pro-market arguments to legitimize the use of violence against various organized economic groups and their economic demands:

> "If it is true *that the economy must be deferred to*, then there is a case not only for constraining the imprudent actions of the prince but for repressing those of the people and for limiting watch" ... As Tocqueville was to express epigrammatically: "A close tie and necessary relation exist between these two things: freedom and industry." Yesterday's hopeful doctrine and today's dismal reality could not be farther apart and Tocqueville's sentence would seem to be more applicable to the Latin American experience if it read instead: "A close tie and necessary relation exist between these two things: torture and industry."[77]

The above can in part be explained by the peculiar aspect of late-development: once other nations have industrialized, for instance Great Britain, competing nations by default become "late-developers" and the immediate task at hand becomes to catch-up.[78] A combination of geopolitical strategic aspirations and the desire to develop for the sake of progress can for certain states add a sense of urgency to the project. As mentioned in the previous section, early-industrializers have indeed more resources and technological knowledge to channel toward military power. And, as noted by world system and dependency theorists, they can use this might to dictate unfavorable terms of trade onto the rest of the world through direct or indirect intervention in other societies' affairs.[79] Hence, while an endogenous drive toward industrialization pushes first developers forward, exogenous factors do form an additional impetus in the case of other nations.

Late-developers, assuming they are sovereign nations, have an advantage, however: states can intervene in the economy to leapfrog through stages of development with the help of planning, subsidies, and direct participation in the economy (as attested to by the success of Germany in the late nineteenth century and East Asian nations in the twentieth century). The nature of late-development, from a state-centric perspective, often engenders the creation of a bureaucracy and military able to act as arbiters to mitigate the demands of different elite classes in society, including landlords and capitalists, to bring about a revolution from above[80] However, because development projects have often been directly tied to the state's geopolitical goals, the levels of capital's ideological and economic powers have tended to be negatively impacted, as they have had less autonomy from the political elite. As in the case of Germany discussed above, because resources obtained by capitalists were usually part of a broader nationalist projects, it made this group more dependent on states and more likely to support "modernizing" autocrats rather than democratic governments. As will be seen in Chapter 4, this was also the case for Turkey and hurt substantially the power of the business elite.[81]

In addition, the nature of underdevelopment itself, according to scholars from both a materialist- and political-centric perspectives, imposes certain constraints on the national bourgeoisie. In terms of economic power, the size of entrepreneurial classes has been heavily impacted by factors like narrow domestic markets and the lack of capital for investment inherent to late-development. Industrialization had to be, therefore, typically promoted by the state through direct and indirect means that took the shape of state ventures, subsidies to industries, and in more general terms a set of policies that have been characterized as import substitution industrialization (ISI) aimed at shielding infant industries from foreign competition. This led to the centralization of economic power in the hands of the state that played a greater distributive role. Within this system, only a handful of capitalists enjoyed enough connections to the state to benefit from some of the development policies, yet they were too weak to act autonomously or press for changes to state-society relations. These general trends help explain why underdevelopment tends to be associated with authoritarianism or, in the least, states that have some tendency to centralize power. However, they also beg the following questions: why have more nations not experienced a more linear path to more open forms of government once some level of development had been achieved? And, why have capitalists typically continued to favor authoritarianism even after periods of expansion, till at least the 1980s?

Bureaucratic Authoritarianism

This question can best be answered by examining the case of bureaucratic authoritarian regimes, a concept developed by the Latin Americanist O'Donnell to understand the emergence of highly technocratic and very bloody dictatorships in the Southern Cone when these societies were relatively industrialized and had already had experience with one form or another of parliamentarism.[82] The problem stemmed from the fact that higher stages of economic and political development created strains and cleavages that did not exist in the past. Rising tensions, thus, created an environment ripe for the military to step in. Commentators, however, vary on the exact root cause of the problem. Some believe that higher stages of development bring about authoritarianism because of economic factors and the nature of capitalism, while others adopt a more political-centric view to highlight the inability of states under late-development to accommodate various tensions..

More materialist Marxian world-system and dependency theorists have adopted a class-centric approach to underscore that "dependent development" had to be achieved in environments that were particularly prone to creating inter- and intra-class conflicts at higher stages modernization, thus creating a vicious cycle where more economic development was likely to engender higher levels of authoritarianism.[83] More specifically, many countries in the Global South still had a landed elite, which favored traditional forms of labor control rather than institutions favoring capitalism; they were already connected to capitalist markets through foreign trade that often bypassed the local urban bourgeoisie. This meant that states and capitalists were often faced with opposition from an aristocratic caste to development projects. On another front, they were confronted by increasingly militant working classes, which had been mobilized through modernization and the compression of time and distance through urbanization and the development of modern transportation and communication networks.

Therefore, the rise of bureaucratic authoritarian regimes typically occurred to crush distributional conflicts when the state's desire to channel resources toward industrialists was met by resistance from the landed elite who could use the poor urban working classes to build an alliance against the capitalist class. Thus, the state and military focused on its technocratic function to promote development and used greater repression to control a disenchanted peasantry and working class mobilized through modernization. As to why these cases were different than Germany in their ability to achieve successful development through a compromise between the aristocracy and merchant classes, the world-system and dependency schools would suggest that the late-industrializing societies of the twentieth century had to operate on a world map already dominated by international capitalism, which engendered two peculiar conditions. First, propertied classes were already heavily tied to foreign interests and markets, thus eliminating the need for domestic class compromise because they could sell abroad. Second, unlike the gradual rise of European states which slowly incorporated emerging class interests, the industrialization of the South had to be achieved fast and, often, under the watchful eye of world powers that had a stake in ensuring that the regimes would be faithful allies regardless of their human rights records. Thus, the capitalist class found itself in a tripartite alliance with transnational capital and with authoritarian development-minded local technocrats where they were politically weaker.

However, more Weberian interpretations see the rise of authoritarianism as emanating less from the economic structure of nations, but more so from the informal, as opposed to formal, nature of state-society relations they have inherited from previous despotic states. This perspective agrees with the Marxian interpretation that the timing of the nation-building and industrialization processes of these societies created distortions that were absent during Europe's development. However, authors in this tradition focus also on the nature of the state to explain the mechanisms at play: states under late-development have had to rely on informal channels of incorporation as opposed to incorporating class interests more formally. For instance, Mouzelis has argued that, during the postcolonial era, newly independent nations in the Balkans and South America, unlike Western European states, had to incorporate society fast in order to rule over newly delineated territories.[84] But, because they lacked the tax base that industrialization would have provided, they did so less by building up their infrastructural power and formal channels of representation and more so by relying on existing forms of traditional informal control such as clientelism, charismatic rule, and populism. These means of incorporation were initially adequate during the lighter phase of industrialization as the lack of strong vested interests meant that there were not many demands placed on the state. At higher stages of industrialization, or just before the emergence of bureaucratic authoritarian regimes, however, these channels became insufficient to cater to social groups that became hypermobilized as a result of such socioeconomic changes as urbanization and the emergence of new classes. Whenever this happened, the military usually stepped in to crush popular protest and to carry out distributive policies, whether it was in America's Southern Cone, Greece, or Turkey. Thus, because of state tradition, business has, at best, been a weaker partner in an authoritarian developmentalist alliance led by the political elite. This observation ties in to the question asked in the initial pages of this book: what kinds of changes need to occur for the former to break away from existing state-society relations?

Capitalists' Ideological and Political Power under Late-Development

Business's dependence to the state has been all the more accentuated by ideological elements. Many, regardless of scholarly perspective, agree that the capitalist class has been weak ideologically and has had a tendency to lack a certain entrepreneurial spirit due the conditions of late-development and the active role played by the state. In many cases, business has been timid and has sought the protection of a paternalist state rather than be open to social, political, and economic change. In Latin America, modernization theorists had traced the root cause of this reticence to the dominance of aristocratic values in late-developing societies and the organic family ties usually found between the landed elite and capitalist class, since the former were the first and primary source of wealth in society.[85] Dependency theorists, on the other hand, focused on structural factors impacting the economy and capitalist behavior.[86] While modernization theory fails to recognize the role of the state, authors who focused on the structure of late-development also pointed out to the fact that revolutions from above carried out by the military and technocrats has had a tendency to breed nationalism and traditional values among the capitalist class.[87] Regardless, of perspective, there is some agreement the conditions of late-development have impacted the ideology of the business elite.

It should be underscored, however, that I also prefer more politico-economic rather than cultural explanations behind the lack of entrepreneurship. The active role states played in development policy and reliance on informal ties in distributing resources had a significant impact on capitalists' behavior and their ideological orientation for several interrelated reasons (see Introduction and Chapters 3 and 4). First, the organization of firms has been impacted by the fact that capitalists allocated much more time and resources to maintaining close ties to the state rather than concentrating on their prime entrepreneurial functions. As was the case in Turkey, capitalists preferred to maintain family control, which hindered the rise of the managerial function in society. Owners and not professionals were more likely to have ties to the state and, thus, private-sector establishments remained under the control of families.[88] Second, and as importantly, the collective political power of business (not just the character of firms and level of entrepreneurship) has suffered as a result of late-development. More specifically, the importance of individual action in obtaining benefits from the bureaucracy hurt capitalist collective action by diminishing the value capitalists attached to political associations representing them. Many entrepreneurs were better served investing time and energy to obtaining individual benefits by using personal relationships they had to members of the state, rather than try to act through business associations.[39] Because of this collective action problem, private-sector associations were historically either created top-down by the state or easily co-opted with the broader goal of managing societal pressures.[90]

In sum, the ideological and political power of entrepreneurs have been hurt because the development of private-sector institutions, such as complex economic enterprises and business's political associations, has been hindered through dependence on the state. The above has occurred in environments where business's success has often been tied to top-down developmentalist and, often, nationalist policies that have propelled the capitalist class to embrace the ideology of the state. However, as will be seen below, democratization around the world during the post-1980 period signaled a change in the ideological, political and economic position of the business elite.

Business during the Transition to Democracy

The transition to democracy in the 1980s and 1990s, or so-called "third wave" democratization, was according to Huntington fueled by a combination of transnational organizations' push for pluralism, the expansion of the middle classes, and rapid economic growth which created hard to accommodate interests for authoritarian governments.[91] Also, the transition occurred under a particular global economic conjuncture: most late-industrializing societies were undergoing a debt crisis fueled by years of foreign borrowing. In order to tackle the crisis, many nations undertook structural adjustment programs that led them to abandon state-led development in favor of export- and market-oriented reforms, often pushed by international institutions such as the IMF. Because they represented cuts in spending and the loss of government jobs through downsizing or privatization, these reforms generally were unpopular among domestic classes. As such, they either precipitated the fall of authoritarian governments or posed a challenge to newly emerging democratic governments that were reticent to impose unpopular cuts.

The juxtaposition of vast economic change and political opening is seen as significant in terms of the power and regime loyalties of capital for two interrelated reasons. First, the coincidence of democratization and economic reform had revived among some economically more liberal commentators the hope that private-sector activity was a panacea for the abuses of the state and that free trade would bring about political change, in the same manner that the rise of capitalism had led to the expansion of civil society in the past. Second, and undeniably, the changing role of states in the economy has redefined the role of the private sector as a more significant engine of growth in many late-industrializing societies, potentially increasing the power and ideological legitimacy of entrepreneurs. However, my position is that when one investigates individual cases the real impact on business of these changes has been mitigated by a series of factors, including the legacy of previously established state-business relations, potentially leading to cross-country variations in the current period. To this end, four major factors that can impact business's political stance are worth emphasizing: (1) the business elite's greater openness to change, (2) its greater propensity to act through associations representing capitalist interest, (3) the greater responsibility for growth shouldered by the private sector under new development paradigms associated with economic liberalization, and (4) the legacy of previous state-business relations, which can mitigate the impact of all of these factors.

Capitalists' Commitment to Democratization after the "Third Wave"

Given the historical weakness of the business elite under state-led models of development, the first interesting change during the 1980s has been the support that the business elite, in some cases, has provided to the push for democracy. The debt crisis and failure to generate significant economic growth during the late 1970s and early 1980s was a major setback for dictatorships, as most autocrats had based their legitimacy and justified the use of violence on the promise that they were better than civilian governments at promoting development. This usually created splits within the elite and proponents of the regime, between hard-liners, who favored an escalation of coercion, and soft-liners, who wanted some degree of political liberalization.[92] In some instances, the economic elite felt that these regimes and their teams of technocrats had become too insulated, even from capitalist interest that they were seeking to promote. For instance, established Chilean industrial capitalists were critical of Pinochet and his, so-called, Chicago Boys who became too close to newer investors who had made their fortune through speculation and insider information.[93] Wherever this was the case, capitalists pressed for democratization and even took to the streets to protest authoritarianism, as they had done in Brazil.[94]

However, there have been fears that democracy achieved through the economic elite would have some limits. Some worried that transition would be carefully managed and characterized by pacts among the elite in order to curb popular groups' ability to participate in newly emerging democracies.[95] For instance, even in Chile, where business was partly responsible for the liberalization of the political system, its prevalence within the decision-making process greatly constrained the policy options available to labor-backed political parties when it came to social spending and labor right.[96] In El Salvador, while more capital-intensive industrialists promoted political liberalization, they continued to align with landed classes around issues dealing with the social rights of workers.[97] In cases, like Turkey, where the military helped weather the debt crisis and was the institution that brought about economic stability and social peace, there was the added concern that democratization would be slower.[98] These instances and the historical record have naturally raised concerns over the degree to which the business elite will stay committed to the democratization project if they felt as though they were losing power or popular groups became too threatening. When we jump two decades ahead to today, however, we notice that the rise of more populist governments around the world did not cause much change in business's position. There is no guarantee that this stance will be permanent, but it brings about the importance of the three other conditions present during the period: that business is more organized, enjoys greater legitimacy as an engine of development, and is impacted by the legacy of state-business relations.

Thus, the second big change compared to the pre-1980s period that has positively impacted the power of capitalists is the fact that, as is the case with TÜSİAD for Turkey, capitalists had increasingly started to act through business associations. This was true of large industrialists around São Paulo in Brazil, who founded the Institute for the Study of Industrial Development (Instituto de Estudos para o Desenvolvimento Industrial, IEDI)—a think tank seeking to contribute to political debates. It was also the case—for capitalists in Argentina and Chile who used their business associations to press for democratization.[99] What is new about these organizations when compared to previous forms of interest representation is that they claim, like TÜSİAD, to advocate for capitalist interest in general as opposed to narrow sectoral or firm-based demands. Moreover, through their support for democracy, they have shown signs of becoming more autonomous from states that had used them to co-opt business interest. As such, they have increasingly become institutions capable of formulating and diffusing through the "logic of influence" the broader ideology of capitalists as a class. Furthermore, these associations have benefited from charismatic leadership that has been able to make individual members accept the longer-term goals of the associations and the ideologies they try to embrace.

Within the context of late-development, embracing "democratization" as a goal has served several purposes to increase the ideological and political power of business according to Cardoso.[100] On a more instrumentalist level, the democratization discourse has been a way to for capitalists to address the problems of economic and political uncertainty, which had plagued late-developing nations historically. By pushing forward notions of democracy, the business elite has participated in national debates about the future of developmentalist projects during a period of structural adjustment. Moreover, embracing democracy, according to Cardoso, has allowed for building alliances with other groups in society and transnationally. My interviews, for instance, have revealed that one of the most left-leaning Turkish labor unions, namely, the Confederation of Revolutionary Workers' Unions (Türkiye Devrimci İşçi Sendikaları Konfederasyonu, DİSK), agrees with TÜSİAD on more procedural issues impacting democracy, while the United States Chamber of Commerce has been in talks with the association to propose it as a model of business representation for late-developing nations. An additional point based on a Weberian framework is worth adding to Cardoso's observations. In places where the business elite has lacked ideological legitimacy and has been a minor partner to the political elite, adopting a democratization mission can provide an ideological justification for private-sector activity.

The third big change impacting business has been more structural. Economic liberalization following years of industrialization policy has shifted economic power away from the state and toward the capitalist class. In tandem to democratization, the period was characterized by the internationalization of most economies, the shift from ISI to export-led growth (ELG), and structural adjustment programs that occurred during the period and had transformed the power of the capitalist class. I do not agree with the Washington Consensus'[101] optimistic view that these reforms were a magic wand that curbed the arbitrary power of states and made economies perform better. Limiting the state's involvement in the economy did not lead countries to uniformly have more efficient development policies. Practices such as clientelism still prevailed after the reforms primarily because, even under ELG, states have the ability to affect policy and distribute resources to varying effect.[102] Moreover, through a decline in social spending and the size of the bureaucracy, and by extension urban middle classes who lost employment and benefits, these reforms have been shown to actually hurt the quality of (re)emerging democracies at least in the short term by taking away resources from groups who could potentially check the state.[103]

The significant impact of the reforms for the topic at hand has been the fact that increased trade and less government involvement have taken the responsibility for industrialization and growth away from the state and placed it on the private sector. Capitalists' performance in this new economic environment has varied greatly from case to case, and business has not always heeded the call.[104] In places where they have performed better, however, it has had an impact on the perceptions of capitalists about their own strength and role in society and vis-à-vis the state, as they lacked legitimacy in previous periods.[105] Wherever this has been the case, we can expect an increase in the ideological power of business in parallel to its economic power, making it easier for it to mobilize around broad policy demands.

The final, and perhaps most important, factor that has served to mitigate these changes and determined capital's stance has been the shape of previous state-business relations and the extent to which they have changed. One of the reasons the economic performance of nations under ELG and structural adjustment programs has varied greatly is linked to the fact that decreasing the size of state alone does not change the nature of state-society or state-business relations. Though the shift away from ISI policies has limited the amount of protection national industries enjoy, outward-looking models of growth have created their own sources of rent. Export-oriented sectors and establishments have continued to receive subsidies under the new strategy and newer sources of rent created by speculation have emerged due to the lack of regulation in various financial markets. This has certainly been the case for Turkey's experience with economic reform in the 1980s.[106]

Furthermore, limiting the size of the state and cutting social policies can potentially eliminate the only existing channels of formal incorporation (as opposed to informal) by eroding state institutions.[107] As mentioned earlier, state-centric accounts of authoritarianism demonstrated that the problem under late-development was not necessarily excess state intervention in the economy but more so the over reliance on informal channels of incorporation.[108] Thus, eliminating civil servants and decreasing the resources that popular sectors get has eliminated potential checks on the state and channels of incorporation. The period has also witnessed a centralization of power within the executive. Politically, the urgency of these reforms has given the government increased legitimacy when bypassing democratic and formal channels for their implementation.[109] The concentration of decision-making in the hands of the executive and not bureaucracy can be advantageous to groups close to the state in the acquisition of these resources.[110]

As such, when dealing with the state, the extent to which capitalists still have to rely on informal channels of interest representation, as opposed to formal ones, has greatly varied from case to case. Consequently, one can observe a tension arise in the juxtaposition of the growing powers of capital alongside previous state traditions and channels of incorporation. The argument I develop throughout the book is that this conflict has led to Turkish capitalists' political mobilization because they felt that the state and members of government could not adequately incorporate their new interests. To understand why the political elite in Turkey was not in tune with the business elite's demands, the next chapter will highlight how the state tradition in Turkey impacted their relationship and the latter's political role.

Chapter 3

TURKEY'S CAPITALISTS AND THE STATE IN THE WORLD ECONOMY

Turkey embodies several tensions, which have made its road to democratization a rough path (see Chapter 1) and which has impacted the nature of its state-business relations. The first one, among others, is between the authoritarian tendencies of its state and the semi-competitive nature of its political system. Even though Turkey has held multiparty elections since 1946, it has undergone three significant military coups between 1960 and 1980, each eroding some of its democratic institutions even further by restricting the freedoms of its citizens and political organizations.[1] Today, the current AKP government's tendency to centralize power in the hands of the executive, despite having made inroads in other areas like declawing the Turkish military in its first decade in power, has naturally given commentators additional concern about the attainability of full democracy. This raises the question of whether a fundamentally undemocratic state tradition is well entrenched in Turkey.[2]

A second tension, which just serves to accentuate the above problem, is between the state's seemingly strong bureaucracy juxtaposed with its reliance on informal channels to incorporate society.[3] An outside observer might be impressed by the grandeur of government buildings in Ankara and the entry examinations one must pass to work in them, but also equally surprised to notice that bribery, the use of patron-client relations to gain leverage, and corruption have also been widespread.

Within this environment, a third tension is between the significant levels of capitalist development the country has achieved without the expected impact on regime liberalization and changes to state-business relations. While GDP per capita more than tripled to jump from around USD3,000 in the 1990s to over USD10,000 in the second decade of the new millennium, commentators still pointed to the deficiencies of Turkish democracy (see Chapter 1), and my interviewees from the private sector still lamented at the lack of good governance. The goal of this chapter is to outline how the above tensions find their roots in historical factors and long-standing state traditions which, in turn, have had pervasive effects on state-business relations and the power of the capitalist class. The exercise will, thus, put TÜSİAD and the business elite's shift in its proper context by stressing the conditions that had led to their historical weakness before their recent transformation. Before moving to a broad historical overview, it is

The Dual Nature of the Turkish State

As mentioned in the previous chapter, very few states fit neatly in the ideal-typical category of developmentalist states, able to formulate coherent long-term goals through the help of a meritocratic bureaucracy. Rather, they might experience the growth of their administration for certain functions but rely on more traditional forms of incorporation and rule in other areas.[4] Thus, the aspects of life they are able to wield power and direct society in might seem impressive when compared to other domains where their range is limited. This juxtaposition impacts levels of democracy concretely because the development of some functions can increase the coercive capacity of the state at the same time as the selective use of rewards through informal channels can raise issues of fairness through unequal access to the state. These same factors also have impacted state-business relations because members of the capitalist class must use similar particularistic channels to gain the favors of the state. For this reason, the current chapter will focus on the nature of state-society relations throughout Turkey's history (in line with the work of scholars such as Collier and Levitsky) rather than focus on the legal, formal deficiencies of democracy.[5]

To use some of the tools developed in the previous chapter: the Turkish state has high levels of despotic power and is able to control ideology and the political process, while its weakness and pragmatism in economic policy prevents it from staying the course on long-term rational policies in the area of economic development. In a nutshell, the state's ability to impose a dominant ideology has been notable, but its record on economic development and on incorporating society through formal channels has been mixed, especially in light of its impressive size.[6]

More specifically, commentators generally agree that the Turkish state has been powerful to the extent that it has historically been quite capable of suppressing a diversity of opinions and identities to impose its own definition of the Turkish nation by drawing on its ideological power and coercive capacity. Examples of this include the cultural policies of the Kemalist government that undertook broad sweeping reforms throughout the first half of the twentieth century, such as latinizing the alphabet and imposing Turkishness as an ethnic definition of nationality in an otherwise culturally diverse territory.[7] However, as noted by Mardin, such policies were really meant to protect the state (or center of power) from the periphery—or margins of society (see Chapter 1).[8] Hence, the state has wielded some ideological power, but this has tended to be through top-down policy, insulated from popular debate and civil society actors.[9]

Economic policy, however, has been used for the shorter-term concern of harnessing support and opposition for these policies.[10] Even though development may, at times, have been a genuine goal for the state elite, economic and political actors willing to be co-opted and accept the dominant ideology have been rewarded with access to the center and state resources.[11] These observations remind us that the existence of rent and patronage generated by the state as such indicates that it is at once insular and quite permeable depending on the policy area. As I will outline in the following pages, this dual nature can be traced back to the top-down state structure of the Ottoman period and has further been reinforced during the post-1923 republican period when attempts to incorporate society rapidly and centralize power were undertaken during the single-party rule of the Kemalist CHP.

The chapter will further highlight that this trajectory, combined with geopolitical factors, considerably impacted the capitalist class's position in society by weakening its political and ideological powers. This has been the case even if this class greatly benefited from state resources and regimes willing to crush labor mobilization. Several broad periods are thus worth examining to understand this dynamic, with a particular emphasis on the capitalist class: (1) the early period of the Ottoman Empire when the state structure was established, (2) the late period of the Ottoman Empire and the transition to the Turkish Republic, when attempts to reform the state led to the demise of an autonomous bourgeoisie, (3) CHP's single-party rule and the period of early ISI, during which the state was able to create a politically dependent capitalist class, and (4) the multiparty period and the more capital-intensive phase of ISI during which many of the more influential members of TÜSİAD emerged. At each stage, how the manner in which the state incorporated society impacted the relative strength of the bourgeoisie or capitalist class will be highlighted. Because developments in the rest of Europe and the world affected the Turkish state and the capitalist class, each section will incorporate a comparative note.

The State and Classes during the Early Ottoman Period

Two Models of Political Organization

Two ideal-typical state models dominated the Old World during the Middle Ages after the decline of the Roman Empire and the constriction of European trade. The first was the centralized administration of the Ottoman Empire, the second, the more diffuse European feudal state which replaced the vacuum created by the fall of Rome's western lands.[12] In many ways, the Ottoman Empire was more successful at centralizing and reproducing power to establish its longevity (it survived from around 1300 to 1918, longer than current nation-states have been in existence). More recent Ottoman histography has, therefore, proposed moving away from interpretations of the empire from the prism of its inevitable demise during World War I to focus on its endurance.[13]

In addition to its span (in time and space), historians point to the empire's considerably larger population when compared to European societies, and its vital role in Mediterranean trade through the control of port cities and East-West trade routes.[14] Politically, Ottoman sultans are increasingly thought of as shrewd innovators, borrowing from already existing state traditions that suited their needs (from the Roman and Byzantine Empires that they supplanted) and choosing from various strategies to accommodate, assimilate, or crush local resistance to stay in power.[15] They were also adept at innovating their fiscal institutions in the face of changing world economic conditions.[16] With these features in mind, the fact that the imperial system did not trigger the transition to capitalism and the rise of a strong capitalist class should be discussed to understand the backdrop of more current state-business relations.

The Western European Feudal Dynamic

While the Ottoman Empire was successful in establishing a permanent administrative structure able to suppress challenges to its rule, commentators generally agree that Europe's more decentralized nature and its rulers' inability to eliminate local power holders set in motion a series of dynamics that were conducive to the emergence of capitalism, a strong entrepreneurial class, and a modern state that incorporated class interests (see Chapter 2). As such, a few notes on the nature of feudalism are warranted to understand why the Ottoman Empire did not witness similar changes.[17] Throughout most of Western Europe, the collapse of the Roman Empire led warrior tribes to establish rule over sparsely populated agricultural land and its peasantry by relying on a Germanic system of reciprocal fraternal bond linking several warlords together, thus leading to the foundation of the feudal state.[18] As an economic system, feudalism gave control of land to the aristocracy so that it could harbor a population of dependent serfs and finance armies to support the monarch. Economic power was thus spread across landed classes who were able to trade their surpluses with cities; centuries later and in many cases, this class eventually joined the bourgeoisie and modern state bureaucracy or was removed forcefully through revolution, during the region's industrial revolution.[19] Through this dynamic, as stressed by Marx and Engels, feudalism also created opportunities for trade that the bourgeoisie took advantage of in order to build its economic power.[20]

As a political system, feudalism through vassalage similarly created competing powerholders and diffused military and political might. Rulers who wanted to centralize their coercive capacity to establish control over wider territories had no choice but try and gain the loyalty of local lords. In order to create a strong administration and increase military power, states thus had to grant some form of representation in government and had to provide infrastructure in exchange for loyalty and much-needed taxes.[21] This system was conducive to the economic dynamism discussed above to the extent that it gave control of the land to local aristocrats or the peasantry who had great incentives to improve production, as they were the ones reaping the benefits of improvements and investments to the land. Moreover, the services that monarchies had to provide led to the creation of a trade network through the help of infrastructure.[22] An additional feature of feudalism was the emergence of self-governing autonomous merchant cities.[23] The power vacuum created by the competitive feudal geopolitical system allowed for the emergence of independent cities that catered to the needs of its merchants and citizenry, which created a blueprint for future forms of government that sought to incorporate class-based interests. Combined with the gradual growth of generalized trade, the above allowed for an environment that was fruitful for the emergence of a capitalist state in which the bourgeoisie had a say. Because trade led to the emergence of an autonomous capitalist class in a gradual manner, entrepreneurs were able to press for increased representation within existing channels during the continent's transition toward the more modern model of the nation-state.[24]

The state tradition developed as such can be characterized as exercising low levels of despotic power and high levels of infrastructural power, mainly because European monarchies had to enter into mutually beneficial relationships with the continent's aristocracy and cities, thus unleashing the diffuse, extensive power of markets and causing the rise of powerful commercial interests.[25] While the initial shift to capitalism was accidental, the success of the European nation-state lied in its ability to "cage" the power relations the transition had engendered during the industrial revolution.[26]

Despotic Power and the Empire's Longevity

The Ottoman Empire was much more stable. Even if recent histography, as mentioned above, paints a much more adaptable form of rule, it also helps understand more concretely how, despite the periodic rise of strong local power holders and the existence of trade, the empire continued to exercise despotic (rather than infrastructural) power and authoritative (rather than extensive) power, unlike feudal Europe. Thus, it allows for also a deeper appreciation of why the capitalist class has continued to remain weak throughout the twentieth-century republican period.

When the Ottomans conquered Constantinople in 1453, after successfully chipping away for 153 years at Byzantium's local allies and its Anatolian lands (modern-day Turkey), they established a center with a more permanent administration. They also put themselves in a position to gain further ideological legitimacy by establishing a strong base from which they could represent Sunni Islam and by claiming both the title of Roman emperor and the caliphate (in 1517). The conquest was made easier because Byzantium had been considerably weakened by the emergence of local lords, who had accumulated land and had amassed military power that could challenge the state.[27] However, the new invaders still found it advantageous to revive the previous Byzantine landholding system and state-society relations to establish their rule.[28] The fact that they borrowed from traditions and practices, which their predecessors had in turn inherited from the successful Roman Empire, made it easier to reintroduce previous laws and landholding arrangements without resistance.

More specifically, the sultans established what was called the *timar* system, by bringing Anatolian lands back under the state's domain. Within this pattern, sultans granted usage rights of small parcels in exchange for taxes and military service, primarily cavalry units living off the land.²⁹ The *tımar* system established as such intended to maintain the military power of the state without creating strong local power holders which could challenge the center. Several factors contributed to the stability of the system and prevented it from sliding into the same power grab that existed under feudalism or that had caused the demise of Byzantium. Structurally, the relatively small size of land holdings created opportunities for peasant families to move without being beholden to individual landlords. Hence, attempts to intensify production or expand land to amass individual fortunes were, for the most part, futile.

Administratively, the state managed to centralize the coordination of land use and tax collection by developing the *devşirme* system, where civil servants were recruited and trained from among young subjects of the empire's Eastern European and Balkan colonies, and not indigenous feudal lords. The *devşirme* also constituted the sultan's own private cavalry, further tilting the balance of power in favor of the empire's center.³⁰ The former's lack of local ties within society ensured that their allegiance was to the sultan. These arrangements were reminiscent of the Romans, who had built their success on their ability to establish a cosmopolitan elite, gaining the loyalty of their provinces. The stability of the system was further reinforced through the ownership of land by the sultan and through limits on inheritances. Both the *devşirme* and the local lords were barred from passing on their fortune, position, and privileges to descendants, thus guaranteeing that there would not be an accumulation of power in the provinces.³¹ Moreover, sultans had the discretionary power to revoke these privileges as a further mechanism to curb the rise of local dynastic power.

These practices overall underscored the first key difference with European feudal dynamics. The arrangements under the *tımar* and *devşirme* systems prohibited the rise of large landholdings and decreased the incentive for intensive production, which meant that landed classes who in most other comparative cases gradually moved to commercial activities were lacking. Indeed, an examination of the twentieth-century Turkish business class, for instance, demonstrated that the majority commercial and industrial families did not come from the landed elite.³² Also lacking (or easily crushed) across the empire were potential reformers or revolutionaries with ties to society's class structure.³³ Instead of a mutually beneficial relationship that Western European monarchs had to develop with powerful local interests conducive to infrastructural and economic change, one witnesses the emergence of a state with great despotic power.

As emphasized earlier, characterizing the Ottoman imperial structure as stagnant is a broad generalization and a form of description that makes use of ideal types. There periodically were the rise of powerful landed interest and state administrators. During the second half of the empire's existence, the sultans also supplemented the *tımar* mode of land control with the *ayan* system where, much like France's *noblesse de robe* (nobility of the robe), the authority to collect taxes was sold to local notables, or *ayans*. This had the double goal of increasing revenue while curbing the power of established landed elite. The more enterprising *ayans* could have potentially created pressures for reform and greater representation.

The reason that they and landed interests before them did not pose a challenge to imperial rule helps bring additional insight into the structure of the Ottoman state. Sultans and their administration (much like a network with hubs and spokes) entered into a vertical relationship with local power holders, with little horizontal connections between classes.³⁴ This reinforced the patrimonial nature of society by affording the state the ability to selectively reward and punish members of the landed and political classes. Thus, rather than focus on economic and political power to try and absorb or cage social power relations through the state, the Ottoman Empire could focus on its ideological and military powers as sources of legitimacy. The sultan, as the caliphate and Roman emperor, was able to reproduce his rule by adopting the role of ultimate deliverer of "justice" without feeling the pressure to grant universal rights to or consult with groups who lacked the capacity to organize horizontally. Moreover, so long as the empire collected enough taxes for military conquests, it did not feel the need to modernize the system.³⁵

The Bourgeoisie during the Early Period

The impact of the Ottoman politico-economic system on the emergence of an autonomous capitalist class has been more mixed and is harder to fit neatly into a clear ideal-type, where it can be deemed completely absent.³⁶ While strong landed interests were lacking, there have been times during the Ottoman period when the nucleus of an independent bourgeoisie was becoming apparent. The same way that the Ottoman state tried to control land use, it also oversaw urban guilds through price and supply controls. However, given the central role of the empire in Mediterranean and East-West trade, their revenues were more directly tied to world prices and the main control was exercised through taxes. More importantly, while the *timar* land control system was mainly binding for Muslims, non-Muslim communities were granted self-rule, as part of the Ottoman strategy to *selectively* accommodate diversity to gain loyalty. Because these groups represented a steady source of taxes, the empire did not see a great benefit in regulating them heavily.³⁷ This provided local Christian Greeks, Armenians, and Jews as well as Levantines of European descent greater economic autonomy and allowed them to undertake many of the crafts and commercial activities in urban centers across the Ottoman land.³⁸

Even though Muslims could and did also participate in commercial activity, external factors created a particularly favorable environment for non-Muslim capitalistic enterprise.³⁹ For one thing, the bulk of commercial activity within the empire passed through the western part of modern-day Turkey, which demographically harbored vast religious and cultural diversity. International trade conducted with Europe also gave Christian and Jewish entrepreneurs a competitive edge thanks to cultural affinities they shared with partners. This was reinforced by bilateral treaties known as capitulations to encourage trade with European powers (particularly France) which shielded foreign commercial emissaries from Ottoman state action. Thus, in Weberian terms, not only did capitalists from non-Muslim communities work with more calculable laws but were also part of a broader transnational in-group. This bourgeois class was therefore well positioned to accumulate high levels of economic power. Despite its commercial success, however, this group was not part of the Ottoman political system. Sultans did not feel the pressure to provide them with the same types of rights or representation that their Western counterparts had acquired under European states, as they were able to levy taxes from commerce to finance the empire's administration and expansion. As will be discussed in the next section, the period during which the empire tried to reform the state did not allow for this group to have greater power either, as geopolitical factors combined with ethnic cleansing policies weakened it considerably.

Overall, commercial and agrarian interests did not translate into pressures on the state. There was a relative absence of horizontally organized classes in whose interest it would have been to gain increased representation or public services. The sultans were able to use vertical channels of integration to selectively deal with potential threats or reward allies. Furthermore, cohesion was achieved in part thanks to the ideological power Ottoman state tradition afforded them. In sum, the state exhibited high levels of despotic power and did not feel any significant pressures, from below, to develop infrastructural power. If the Ottoman conquests are any indication, however, this state model was able to compete with or even outperform European states during the late Middle Ages. It was when capitalist activity and industrialism really took over Europe and rising nation-states were able to increasingly invest in their military conquests that the Ottoman Empire started to lag behind. Given the relative absence of reformers in society, to use Barrington Moore's famous framework, any meaningful change, therefore, had to come through "reforms from above" initiated by the state for Turkey to remain geopolitically competitive.[40] As will be shown below, this influenced the nature of reforms undertaken both during the modernization period of the Ottoman Empire, under the Young Turks, and during the transition to the republic under Mustafa Kemal because they reflected the ideologies and preferences of the political elite rather than interests of social classes.

The Later Phase of the Empire

Reforms from Above

The relative backwardness of the Ottoman Empire's political and economic structures was particularly felt during Europe's second Industrial Revolution, as economic development in Britain, France, and Germany had helped fuel stronger armies and made more direct colonial rule through military expansion possible. The problem was exacerbated at around the same time because growing nationalist movements across its colonies started to pose a challenge to Ottoman rule.[41] As a result, the state emptied its coffers and saw its debt rise to finance military competition. European powers' rising dominance and the empire's inability to keep up fiscally propelled several reform movements to save the Ottoman state between the nineteenth and twentieth centuries, including a short-lived constitutional and parliamentary system (1876 to 1878), the centralization of the military, and modernization of the bureaucracy.[42]

The road to reform was rocky and interrupted by what can be considered authoritarian reversals in the hands of Sultan Abdul Hamid II (who suspended both the new constitution and parliament). But Ottoman reformists had a newfound zeal in the desire to modernize the empire. The most significant of these movements were the Young Turks, a group of middle-class army officers, professionals, and intellectuals who organized under a revolutionary movement and political party—the Committee for Union and Progress (İttihat ve Terakki Cemiyeti, CUP). These reformers were united around the desire to modernize the empire through the adoption of both European-style political institutions and Turkish, not Ottoman, ethnic nationalism. To this end, the CUP organized through revolutionary cells and forced the revival of the parliament in 1908 to pass a series of measures that have had long-term pervasive effects on Turkish state-society and state-business relations, ranging from the impact of its genocidal nationalist policies to its intellectual influence over the later republican period. More specifically:

1. The reforms were top-down, given the lack of Young Turks' connection to social classes.
2. They focused particularly on cultural change, which they felt had held the Ottoman Empire back, at the expense of socioeconomic development.
3. They were, for the most part, nationalist in character.
4. Their economic policy favored the creation of Muslim capitalist enterprise, undermining the burgeoning non-Muslim bourgeoisie.
5. Their ethnic cleansing policies radically deepened the above problems.

The Young Turks were the direct product of the imperial system and its attempts at renewing itself. Many of them were army officers trained in military schools, which was the only Western-style education available to upwardly mobile middle-class Muslims. Thus, as a status group they were disconnected from landed classes and the non-Muslim bourgeoisie.[43] As such, their desire for change was less rooted in material interests or conditions but more so on what they ideologically perceived to be reasons for the relative weakness of the empire through the prism of the education they received. More specifically, they were exposed to the ideas of the French Revolution and the Napoleonic project. Not only did the movement borrow its name from the French revolutionary slogan *union et progrés*, but the Young Turks also believed that social and cultural modernization could be imposed top-down (much the same way the Jacobins had done in France).

The movement was nationalist in character. The Young Turks had observed that the spread of French revolutionary ideas and new nationalist feelings had compelled Ottoman provinces, such as Serbia and Greece, to successfully mobilize for their independence. They also (astutely) observed that the empire lacked formal channels of incorporation and needed to create a sense of belonging to the nation, instead of the patrimonial model of vertical integration. To recall, the Ottoman Empire had ruled over Anatolia by excluding the small peasantry from the center, by curbing the power of local notables, and by allowing self-rule for non-Muslim populations. Hence, hopes for a multicultural Ottoman model, formulated in the early days of reformist movements and where subjects of different faiths would be treated equally, gave way to growingly ethno-religious conceptions of what the Turkish nation should be.[44] For the most part, the Young Turks believed that Turkey should be independent of foreign influences and as such wanted to build the country around an indigenous identity. Afterall, the rise of European capitalism and modern states had been accompanied by the emergence of nationalism. These observations led the CUP to lend more weight to cultural policies to integrate society around Turkishness. However, in the absence of a strong Turkish identity under the Ottoman Empire, the notion of citizenship, and Turkishness, the CUP—and later Kemalists—developed was closely linked to Muslim identity (despite claiming to be secularist, see Chapter 1).

The above also had significant impact on the future shape of state-business relations. Indeed, the Young Turks' nationalism, military background, and their penchant for top-down reform had long-term pervasive repercussions on the character of the Turkish capitalist class through the shape their economic and ethnic policies took. The reformists were not completely hostile to capitalism. On the contrary, they wanted to create a Muslim capitalist class as part of a broader nationalist modernization project. This was partly fueled by the fiscal woes of the empire, but also the Young Turks' negative perception of non-Muslim capitalist classes. They viewed the latter as being largely in the service of Western European creditors (because of Ottoman capitulation treaties discussed above) and as active supporters of Greek and Armenian independence movements. They thus longed to supplant them with a new Turkish domestic bourgeoisie. However, the economic structure of the Ottoman Empire and relative absence of large landholdings or Muslims in commercial activities left very few individuals that could be recruited into this new class.

Thus, one of the primary policy tools that the CUP developed was to build *partenariats*, or joint ventures, between the state and private entrepreneurs in the establishment of manufacturing firms.[45] The state went far beyond providing the capital needed to finance such enterprises. It also guaranteed that if individuals entered certain desired sectors, the state would take over the firm in case of economic difficulties.[46] Given such an attractive prospect, most individuals who benefited from the CUP's policies were actually recruited from the bureaucracy, political classes, or individuals close to them, thanks to their personal connections. The new capitalist class thus lacked autonomy from the state. Because this group was ideologically close to the Young Turks, the period set a precedent where economic policy was largely used to co-opt groups and gain support for political reforms. Unsurprisingly, the politicized nature of these establishments and the fact that they were helmed by individuals who lacked business acumen ultimately meant that they would be short-lived. Thus, rather than form the nucleus of a potentially strong capitalist class, the group would end up ceding this role to a new cohort of entrepreneurs who would be the beneficiaries of state policy during the twentieth century.⁴⁷ Indeed, Buğra's seminal work on Turkish capitalists has highlighted that very few current large conglomerates have deep roots. Nevertheless, these policies ultimately weakened the non-Muslim bourgeoisie who had been well positioned to play a role similar to the democratizing capitalist class found in Western Europe by giving the bulk of state subsidies to new entrepreneurs. While the Young Turks' economic policy had a significant impact, its ethnic policies, as explored in the next section, had an even more dramatic impact on the country and its capitalist class.

Minority Capitalists under the Young Turks

In his *Dark Side of Democracy*, Mann notes the existence of an unfortunate tension in the rise of pluralism: it often engenders ethnic cleansing policies as a result of competing claims over the nation and its resources.⁴⁸ The Young Turk movement, according to Mann, best typifies this unfortunate pattern. As seen above, the new political class was wary of Ottoman minorities. Not only was the movement nationalist, but it was also bent on scapegoating non-Muslims as being at the service of Western powers during the empire's decline and as supporting Armenian and Greek independence during its demise.⁴⁹ Ultimately, the CUP's stance toward Turkey's minorities and its participation in World War I led to the gradual displacement of the country's Greek Orthodox population and the Armenian genocide.⁵⁰

Multiple scholars have noted that the exodus of Turkey's Greek population, which took place from 1912 well into the republican period, helped garner support for CUP's desire to create a Muslim Turkish propertied class. This was evidenced by the fact that local landowners lent their support to the movement after acquiring abandoned Greek property in the western parts of Turkey at extremely moderate cost.⁵¹ The fate of the Armenian population further crystalized the CUP's policies toward its minorities. Recent Turkish historiography on the Armenian genocide has been particularly illuminating thanks to scholars' privileged access to Ottoman archives.⁵² They have been able to highlight the fact that the CUP employed the same modern communication techniques (such as the telegraph) that it had used during its earlier power-grab in order to launch coordinated attacks and forced migration policies against Turkey's Armenian populations. The enterprise led to the deportation of 800,000 to 1,500,000 Armenians from Anatolia, with little concern for their physical safety or their protection from violence perpetrated at the local level.⁵³

As importantly, for the current discussion, this scholarship also reveals that the violence became linked to the desire to create a national bourgeoisie.⁵⁴ In his exhaustive review of the evidence, Akçam notes that decrees drafted by Ottoman officials initially emphasized (on paper) that they intended to compensate displaced Armenians by sending them their assets or (in the case of fixed property) the revenue obtained from their sale.⁵⁵ In practice, however, he found no official directives as to how this plan should be carried out or how the sale receipts should be disposed of. Moreover, there is evidence to suggest that the handling of Armenian property intrinsically became part of the desire to create a Muslim bourgeoisie, such as the following cable sent by the Ministry of the Interior to local governments:[56]

> It was previously communicated that, in order that those [commercial] establishments left by the Armenians, such as factories, shops and mills, not be left empty and unused, they [the establishments] were to be turned over, under the appropriate conditions, to Muslim companies, and all manner of facilitation and assistance be afforded for this purpose. It is suggested that they be rented or sold to Muslim applicants at low prices and that they be shown the necessary assistance [for this to happen].[57]

Two characteristics of Turkish capitalism were thus established under the later period of the Ottoman Empire. First, given that it was created within the framework of building Turkish identity and also benefited from the Turkish state's policies toward minorities, the Muslim capitalist class is going to embrace the dominant nationalist discourse and is going to lack ideological autonomy. Indeed, while some scholars have highlighted the fact the growth in the number of Turkish Muslim enterprises is heavily correlated to the erosion of minority populations,[58] Göçek further argues that modern Turkey's reluctance to officially acknowledge the Armenian genocide is intrinsically linked to the role it played in nation-building, including the emergence of its elites.[59] And as such, the economic transformation of the empire is not going to be conducive to the emergence of an autonomous bourgeoisie able to press for liberal democratic reforms or for representation based on class interest. If anything, it led to the demise of the earlier bourgeoisie.

Second, the economic dependence of the Turkish capitalist class meant that its economic success was heavily dependent on the state and therefore, as will be further discussed throughout the book, its composition heavily correlated with shifts in government and political allegiances. It has been observed that the latter factor greatly impacted the makeup of modern-day enterprises too: many of the big corporations still in existence today are the ones that have been fortunate enough to have access to state resources during various political eras and very few date back to the early 1900s.[60] The fact that the Young Turks saw in their nation-building projects a way to cage capitalist activity around a strong national identity meant that the business elite entered the twentieth century with little economic and ideological power. They were dependent on a state that relied on revolution from above to transform society. But, as will be seen below, this is as much the product of the CUP rule as it is of the political system established under the Turkish Republic throughout the period.

The Republican Era

A National Bourgeoisie? The New Republic and Statism (1923 to 1946)

After the defeat of the Ottoman Empire at the end of World War I, Western powers had gained control of its former colonies as well as territories in parts of modern-day Turkey. In response, the Turkish independence movement moved the national assembly from Istanbul to Ankara, abolished the sultanate, and waged a war of independence, effectively ending the rule of the Ottoman Empire. Following the recapture of Turkey's current borders, Mustafa Kemal and other officers originating from the Young Turk movement are going to dominate political life through the establishment of the single-party regime of the CHP up until 1946, when open elections were first held.[61]

Given its clear roots, many of the new republic's impulses during the consolidation of political power were borrowed from the CUP[62] and Ottoman state tradition.[63] Comparatively, however, the two and a half decades of Kemalist rule can be likened to the postcolonial states' mission of establishing the nation-state and of adopting a national development strategy that had compelled Latin American states in the 1930s and then African and Asian states in the 1950s to intervene more actively in economic and social life. When thought of in terms of the degree of state intervention in developmentalist projects, the CHP's reign can be broken down into two distinct periods. The first, from 1923 to about 1930, is characterized by competition from within the party for control of government. Thus, during its first few years, the CHP did not move too much away from the Ottoman reforms already started by the CUP and which exhibited a rather casual pragmatic adherence to free-market principles.[64] The second period, which lasted until the multiparty period of 1946, however, is characterized by a more deliberate attempt to centralize power within the CHP and establish a more interventionist style of government, thus crystalizing the traditional tendency of the state to adhere to top-down policies.[65]

Regardless of the difference between the two, it should be stressed that both stages of nation-building were characterized by the CHP's reliance on more traditional, informal channels of incorporation. The pervasive nature of state-society relations from earlier periods impacted interest representation and the position of business fundamentally due to three interrelated reasons. First, the two periods were affected by the historical weakness of civil society and the patrimonial legacies of the state. This initially made it easy to impose reforms from above without much resistance from society. Second, the absence of strong industrial classes (dating from the end of the empire) prohibited the emergence of class-based politics and the incorporation of economic interests in policy, impacting both capitalists and the working class.[66] The CHP, as a result, had a freer hand to focus on more cultural channels of incorporation and ethnic definitions of citizenship rights and obligations. Finally, the lack of economic development combined with the need to gain control of the Turkish territory fast compelled the state during both periods to rely on informal channels of incorporation to gain support for its policies; a problem that was, according to Mouzelis and as seen in the previous chapter on capitalism and democracy, characteristic of many states in the semi-periphery.[67] In the absence of a strong tax base, states have tended to turn to clientelism and populism, and not formal channels of representation, to curb the demands engendered by modernization.

If one looks at the two periods separately and in greater detail, however, the CHP's first years in power exhibited clear continuities with the CUP's rule under the late Ottoman period. Kemalism in its early stages, like the ideology of its Ottoman predecessors, showed a clear preference for social and cultural policy as a path to modernization.[68] Members of the CHP instituted a set of reforms reaching most areas of life, ranging from the Latinization of the alphabet to imposing dress codes to the creation of a secular state and regulation of religious life.[69] Thus, as was the case for the Young Turks, the CHP's penchant for ideological change turned economic policy as a means to an end rather than an objective onto itself during the early republican era (until the 1930s). As significantly, the lack of strong class interests meant that it did not have to undertake significant redistribution policies. Within this framework, the state continued a market-friendly attempt to establish joint partnerships with a weak bourgeoisie.[70] The creation of a domestic bourgeoisie was still favored as a path to independence from foreign influences; however, several factors pushed active development policies to the background. First, there were some members among the CHP who valued liberal economic principles and who saw in them a way to emulate Western developed nations; thus, during its first congress, the party affirmed its commitment to economic liberalism. Second, the Lausanne treaty, which marked the end of the war, pretty much constrained Turkey's policy options by forbidding the state to adopt quotas or tariffs in foreign trade after its loss in the world war. Consequently, *laissez-fairism* was the generally preferred economic philosophy toward private enterprise.[71]

However, the desire to create a domestic industrial sector led to the adoption of a few policies that dated back to the CUP's rule. State credits to promote private-sector enterprise as well as the involvement of civil servants in business organizations were two sets of national development strategies deployed to this end. Furthermore, because the CUP's approach to Turkish nationalism did not change dramatically under the CHP, Turkey's religious and ethnic minorities will continue to suffer from a shift of activities and resources to the nascent Muslim capitalist class. Postwar treaties led to the further displacement of Greeks and transfer of their property to local notables.[72] During the period, entrepreneurs still associated their existence with the nationalist project of the CHP and, as such, lacked ideological autonomy despite a more liberal economic period.

The second era, from 1930 onward, however, ushered in a radical shift that made business even more dependent. More specifically, the Great Depression of 1929 constituted a turning point in Turkey's nation-building project by offering a ripe environment for the CHP to formulate a much more interventionist developmentalist program. As was the case for several Latin American nations, who were at about the same stage of political and economic development, the world slump afforded Turkey the opportunity to implement active industrialization policies thanks to relative global prices that had shifted in favor of primary export goods at the expense of capital goods.[73] Turkey could now sell raw products in order to obtain capital for industrialization at cheaper prices than before. In the specific case of Turkey, the end of restrictions imposed by the Lausanne treaty also allowed the CHP to regain access to a broader set of policy instruments it had previously lacked control of, such as tariffs and exchange rates.

Ideologically, leaders from within the CHP and other nations saw the crisis as a failure of free-market policies and were inspired by more state-centric alternatives, such as those envisioned by the political economist List during Germany's push to industrialize. Due to Russia's geographic proximity and some of CHP members' affinity with the Soviet model, bolshevism also offered a strong pull and was a source of inspiration when designing the developmentalist strategy. Thus, the policy tools adopted combined a blend of measures, including protectionist trade policy through tariffs, quotas and strict controls on foreign currency exchanges, the creation of a central bank and state economic enterprises (SEEs), and the adoption of a five-year plan drafted with the help of Soviet advisors.[74]

Even though the CHP turned to the Soviet Union as a potential industrialization model, it should be emphasized that it remained committed to capital accumulation through private enterprise.[75] What was, nevertheless, significant in the case of Turkey for the private sector was the interplay between economic policy and the CHP's sociopolitical project to consolidate power and nation-build. The opportunity to control economic life more tightly allowed the Kemalist wing to further its influence over the CHP, formulate a "statist" ideology, and extend its control over society.[76] As such what Kemal Atatürk and the CHP officials referred to as *Étatism* (statism) accentuated the Turkish state's seeming strength in some areas and weakness in others.

Economically, the model or ideology was intended to be a middle-path between capitalism and socialism, where Turkey's dependence on foreign economies would considerably be decreased through ISI under the guidance of the state. Politically, however, the state's more active role in the economy was used to justify its widespread intervention in other areas of life, further weakening civil society.[77] The CHP had, from its beginnings, defined itself as a populist party. However, in the 1930s it changed its definition of populism from "the state for the people" to its newer more statist version "the people for the state." To this end, the CHP even built new channels of incorporation for various segments of society around Turkish identity, inspired partly by Mussolini's corporativismo (corporatism) under fascist Italy.[78]

Given the strong political motivation behind this shift, its impact on the capitalist class was also ambiguous. The CHP was able to garner the business's support, partly, by stressing its commitment to private capital accumulation and, in part, thanks to entrepreneurs who were ideologically open to state-sponsored industrialization. However, the approach to economic policy under *Étatism* was most often pragmatic and haphazard, used mainly for political goals. As such, capitalists could never gauge the state's commitment to specific policies and could not make long-term plans for fear that the economic environment could change easily.[79] As importantly, CHP officials often betrayed a mistrust toward members of the business community.

Two measures can be cited as significant examples. The first revolved around the implementation of policies to restrict black market activity during World War II. Instead of persecuting a few guilty entrepreneurs, the state adopted stricter widespread measures, like price controls, that hurt the entire capitalist class and bred public mistrust against it.[80] Another, even more traumatic, event for the capitalist's place in society and position vis-à-vis the state was the institution of a one-time wealth tax. Local governments during the war were granted the discretionary power to impose a flat levy and given leeway in determining the individuals it would be collected from. Within this framework, officials mainly targeted Jewish entrepreneurs arbitrarily and, to a lesser extent, some Muslims who had been denounced by other businesspeople as allegedly engaging in illicit activities.[81] The event was significant in shaping the capitalist class. It further strengthened the position of Muslim entrepreneurs in society, in line with the Young Turks' and CHP's previous ethnic policies. As importantly, it created a long-term atmosphere of mistrust among the business community toward both the state and other members of the capitalist class.[82] If one considers that some members of the bourgeoisie witnessed their business partners go through hardship, their social position became tenuous and depended on the mercy of others.

Overall, the single-party period was characterized by the formulation of a state-driven industrialization policy and the establishment of a national bourgeoisie. However, the role assigned to economic policy and the mistrust that officials bore against capitalists did not lead to significant improvement in the incorporation of economic interests within the state. Rather the approach to the private sector was arbitrary and pragmatic, mainly seen as fulfilling a role within the wider nation-building project centered on the ideological power of the state. During the period one can, therefore, more clearly see the dichotomous nature of state polity in Turkey: it tends to enhance its authoritative power over politico-cultural aspects of life by using economic policy as a tool.

The "Paradox of Turkish Liberalism": Multiparty Democracy (1946 to 1960)

The Turkish Republic witnessed its first transition to democracy in the post-World War II period, which also coincided with greater economic prosperity around the world fueled by the end of the war, the Marshall plan, and increased global demand. Western powers were willing to allow protectionist industrial policies in the semi-periphery as the general boom enabled manufacturing in industrialized powers to remain sufficiently profitable by catering solely to their local markets.[83] Moreover, a burgeoning industrial sector in less-developed nations meant that richer countries could now import consumption goods from overseas and mainly focus on greater value-added production. For Turkish economic policy, aid provided under the Marshall plan offered a path for transitioning from a mainly agrarian economy to devote its energy to the development of even more capital-intensive private-sector establishments (see Chapter 4). It also led Turkey to gravitate away from the lingering appeal of the Soviet statist model to more openly embrace the West and its economic plan for late-industrializing societies: a period of industrialization through subsidies following a first phase energized by agricultural development.[84] Hence, there were strong conjunctural factors for the liberalization of polity.

As for the first push for democracy, it came from within the CHP itself when two key members, Celal Bayar and Adnan Menderes, broke rank and were joined by several other deputies to form the DP. The movement was sparked by its members' desire to adopt the rights covered in the United Nations Charter and found its support base among agricultural and commercial classes that had felt neglected because of Turkey's center-periphery dynamic and CHP's inability, or unwillingness, to integrate economic interests. The DP thus participated in the first free general elections of 1946. It built further momentum in the 1950 election to gain 55 percent of the votes and an imposing majority with more than four-fifth of the seats in the National Assembly. This victory guaranteed Bayar the position of president and Menderes that of prime minister until their overthrow in 1960 by the first military coup in the republic's history.[85]

The party's success was a clear signal that agrarian and business communities favored more liberal economic policies and that its democratizing mission more widely resonated across society. Decades later, it would also become apparent that many of the country's influential post-1980 politicians (such as Özal), who combined an appeal for conservative voters with Western-style institutions, traced their ideological roots to the enthusiasm generated by the DP during the 1950s.[86] As importantly, the success of economic liberalism highlighted several reasons why CHP policies did not connect with Turkish society.

First, the CHP's arbitrary approach to economic policy never let it gain the trust of the business sector. To solve this problem before the 1950 elections, the CHP had created through legislation an umbrella business organization, the Turkish Union of Chambers and Commodity Exchanges (Türkiye Odalar ve Borsalar Birliği, TOBB), to incorporate formally representatives of all industrial and commercial chambers into the decision-making process. However, as will be discussed in Chapter 4, the role of this semiformal institution was very limited and was perceived as political maneuvering rather than real commitment to capitalist enterprise.[87] As such, the DP's ideological commitment to private enterprise and liberalism seemed more sincere to commercial classes that had been left out of the state.[88]

The second problem with the CHP was its approach to rural sectors of society. Not only did the movement exclude members of the periphery from formal channels of representation,[89] but its economic policy actually hurt agriculturists during Turkey's attempt to compete in world markets.[90] More specifically, the cost of agricultural inputs ballooned because of protection granted to unproductive manufacturers, increases to the price of goods produced by SEEs, and heavy taxation on imported industrial goods, all of which were used by rural sectors. However, it also artificially kept the price of agricultural products low in order to gain foreign exchange through their exportation. As such, the countryside, which still employed 75 percent of society, witnessed its relative income deteriorate during the period.[91]

The DP's campaign promise, however, was to create "one millionaire in every neighborhood" through economic liberalism. From 1950 until its overthrow by the military coup of 1960, the DP indeed followed policies that appealed to the commercial and agrarian sectors of society. Moreover, given the Marshall plan and the fact that the international climate was generally favorable to Turkish exports and the industrialization of the semi-periphery, the early years of DP's rule were overall successful owing to the rise in prosperity that citizens witnessed.[92] In terms of more specific policies, the DP loosened controls over agricultural prices, liberalized the import of some capital goods to help Turkish manufacturing move into the production of domestic goods, and heavily invested in infrastructure, such as transportation networks, to further promote growth through trade. Within three years, the prices of primary export products such as wheat and minerals increased, generating further investment in these sectors and a 50 percent increase of land brought under cultivation. The general rise in income thus led society to buy into the DP's campaign promise of individual prosperity.

However, the favorable global economic climate that helped the DP in its first years was short-lived and the party's economic woes helped underscore some of its own difficulties to connect with society and the private sector. Prosperity ended when world agricultural prices decreased during the second half of the 1950s. In response, the DP focused on increasing income and not investment. For example, it tried to sustain the newfound wealth enjoyed in rural areas by buying agricultural products directly at above market prices despite the global slump. But subsidizing agricultural income became unsustainable. Combined with the DP's investments in infrastructure, this policy increased debt and inflation, thus crowding out industrial investment.[93] It is, therefore, during this period that Turkish industrialists were going to be faced with what Buğra has termed the "paradox of Turkish liberalism" to describe the juxtaposition of the DP's (and subsequent center-right-wing parties') generally more favorable attitude toward private enterprise, alongside the inability to fully adopt economic liberalism.[94] During its handling of the downturn, the DP was neither able to reduce the size of the government in the economy nor able to increase industrial investment despite its generally pro-business discourse. Buğra underscores that, after all, the DP's slogan was not "an entrepreneur in every neighborhood," but a "millionaire."[95]

Most importantly, the "paradox of Turkish liberalism" encapsulates why the DP and subsequent center-right-wing governments never had the expected impact on the creation an autonomous capitalist class. Government overcrowding meant that the latter still continued to rely on state resources for much-needed investment and suffered from unpredictable economic policy.[96] Furthermore, the DP inherited the CHP's and the Young Turks' state tradition of using economic incentives to co-opt members of the private sector to support the party. To illustrate this point, Buğra points to an infamous episode in Turkish business and political history, which was also touched on the introduction to the current project: the founder of the largest Turkish corporation Vehbi Koç was forced to refute his CHP membership after receiving threats from the DP. He had no choice but to bend to DP's demands, as he was well aware of the need to maintain close relations to government in order to remain successful in business.

Ethnic policy during the period did not help the entrepreneur's tenuous social position. In 1955, diplomatic tensions between Greece and Turkey triggered mob attacks on Greek-owned businesses in major cities. These pogroms were perceived to be state-sponsored and, as had been the case in earlier periods, led to exodus and the sale of minority-owned property at cheaper than usual prices.[97] Hence, the bourgeoisie witnessed once again the extent to which its security and prosperity depended on the state, even when those at the helm of government were not from the Young Turk movement.

State-Led Development and State-Society Relations (1960 to 1980)

The end of DP's rule came in 1960 after it was brought down by a military coup and its key officials were sentenced to either life in prison or death, accused of violating the constitution and attempting to form a dictatorship.[98] This occurred after the DP tried to put limits on the freedoms of speech and assembly in response to widespread protests and opposition to its policies, some of which came from key intellectuals and students. When these restrictions further emboldened protesters, the military stepped in to curb civil unrest. In January of 1961, the military junta created what it called the "Committee for National Union" (Milli Birlik Komitesi), and along with civilian constitutional law professors, it drafted a new constitution, giving rise to what sometimes is referred to as the "Second Republic." For reasons of parsimony, I will skip a lengthy discussion of the economic and industrial policies adopted by post-1960 governments as these are discussed in greater detail in the next chapter on the political mobilization of capitalists in the 1970s. However, a few notes on how the coup and attempts at reform impacted the broader aspects of state-society relations are warranted.

The constitution of 1961 initially hoped to tackle one key problem that had plagued Turkey, specifically the inability of the state and governments to incorporate various segments of society through more formal channels. In doing so, it recognized many of the problems that characterized Turkish state tradition and that have been outlined here in the book. Within this framework, there was an attempt to build a more Western European style corporatism to give representation to business and labor. One of the first things members of the coup did was to, therefore, reaffirm their commitment to capitalist industrial development as a means to solve distributional conflicts.[99] Within this framework, the constitution of 1961 foresaw the creation of the State Planning Agency (Devlet Planlama Teşkilatı, DPT) and the adoption of five-year development plans combined with the deeper, more capital-intensive phase ISI policies. These measures also had the advantage of meshing well with what the Marshall plan had envisioned for Turkey and similar nations: the transition to state-led industrialization,

However, several persisting problems made it difficult to achieve the goal of crafting Western European style corporatism. First, labor and business unions, such as TOBB, were not granted formal political power.[100] As will be shown in the next chapter, the military often made apparent the distrust it had for civil society organizations by limiting the scope and power of what could have been class-based corporatist institutions. Second, the measures adopted under ISI and the heavy role of SEEs led to industrial concentration both regionally and in terms of patterns of ownership and control. As such, the industrialization project did not affect all segments of society equally and economic incorporation was limited.[101] Third, the measures did not achieve much in ameliorating the business environment in Turkey. While ISI policies greatly benefited large capitalists, as will be seen in the next chapter, they continued to engender wariness about the exact boundaries of state intervention and control.[102] More specifically, the period was characterized by the considerable growth of the state through SEEs' involvement in production, the control of the planning agency by the more Nationalist Kemalist wing of the state, and the fact that it was never legally made clear whether the economic plans were only indicative or mandatory.[103]

Consequently, the attempt to incorporate economic interests was by and large a failure. This can be seen as being in line with the general framework built to understand the Turkish state, that its emphasis on ideological and despotic power makes it pragmatic or weak in the area of economic policy. If anything, the military government of 1961 accentuated these tendencies as the impetus behind the coup was the military's conviction that the DP had moved away from Kemalist ideology. As such, the 1961 constitution reinforced its commitment to Kemalism and Turkish nationalism, which were the more symbolic ideological aspects of state power. Moreover, the military already enjoyed great legitimacy because of the role played by Mustafa Kemal and other Young Turk officers in the foundation of the republic. The military's intervention to remedy what it presented as a politically unstable situation further increased its legitimacy among some segments of society. Another problem in terms of state-society relations was the fact that subsequent elected officials during the post-1960 period could increasingly rely on clientelistic networks of support because uneven economic development created disparate segments in society. More specifically, increased economic diversity alongside the persistence of small commerce and crafts, as well as small farmers, created a pool that parties could selectively tap into through political patronage and populist policies without incorporating the rest of society.[104] Thus, economic policy and state resources were increasingly used by civilian governments to distribute short-term rewards through direct populist rule and clientelistic networks. This hindered the coherence of long-term industrial policies and the formal incorporation of interests within the state. By keeping the formal ties that civil society has to the state weak, these measures also insulated the more ideological dimensions of power from popular contestation.

Concluding Remarks: A Weak Business Elite

The first military intervention of 1960 combined with Turkish state tradition set the stage for political developments during the next few decades, both in terms of the quality of Turkish democracy and in terms of state-business relations. During the next decades, Turkey witnessed two other military coups, in 1972 and in 1980, and an arduous road to democratization during the post-1980 period for structural reasons already discussed in this chapter. More specifically, as will be shown in the next chapter and as hinted to above, military officers, the political elite, and the state never established formal representation of class interests mainly due to a distrust of civil society activities. While there were attempts to write into the constitution a more concrete role for business, labor, and civil society organizations, the extent of their political power was often ill-defined and these were often very vulnerable in the face of the coercive power of the state. More concretely, there was always an attempt to impose a top-down ideology on associations, the rules governing their freedoms were often blurry, and it was thus always very easy for the state to curb their activities. As a result, what could have been more formal vehicles of interest formulation for large capital were never clearly established, as will be shown in the next chapter.

In addition, the state continued to focus a great deal on enforcing a dominant ideology and used economic policy only pragmatically to gain support in the absence of a strong civil society. As was seen above, during periods of military rule, economic ministries were mainly controlled by individuals close to the Kemalist ideology, and the military sought to increase its legitimacy by playing the role of night watchman. Moreover, during periods of multiparty elections, governments used economic rewards mainly as a way to gain support through populist and clientelistic channels of incorporation. Thus, while the Turkish state has demonstrated a commitment to private-sector capital accumulation, it never was able to create a stable environment for capitalist enterprise. As will be seen in the next chapter, the deeper phase of industrialization policies of the 1960s and 1970s will lead to capital accumulation within a handful of private-sector establishments close to the already industrialized region of Istanbul, without increasing their political power because of a lack of formal channels of interest representation. And as will be seen in Chapter 5, the period of economic liberalization, like it had during the DP's rule, would be accompanied by a period of economic uncertainty and overspending because of governments' desire to create rent. Thus, in neither period will large capital enjoy political power.

More concretely in terms of business power, this meant two things according to Buğra's seminal work. First, the need to maintain close ties to the state and wade through an economically uncertain climate meant that the Turkish industry would favor large family-controlled corporations, as they were seen as better able to build personal ties with governments and diversify activities in the face of potential change. Second, even though individual capitalists were able to secure rewards from the state, capitalists as a class never gained formal representation within the state that still preferred to insulate certain policy areas from societal debate and influence. As the next chapter demonstrates, this partly contributed to the establishment of TÜSİAD by large corporations and, as covered in Chapter 5, it led the association to press for increased democratization and state reform as a way to affirm some of its power.

Chapter 4

AWAKENINGS: THE MAKING OF THE BUSINESS ELITE FROM 1960 TO 1980

TÜSİAD's current headquarters is a neoclassical-style building erected in the 1800s by Joseph Baudouy, a French entrepreneur who quite fittingly made his fortune when the Ottoman Empire gave him monopoly over the construction of lighthouses in ports it controlled. When one enters the renovated building in the historic neighborhood of Tepebaşı, a modern waiting room adorned with art, presumably donated from members' personal collection, is immediately noticeable. On the upper floors, one is gleefully greeted by a team of young professionals with degrees from top Turkish universities, busy doing research for the various commissions (or roundtables) they work for on issues ranging from democratization to competitiveness to gender equality. There are various offices and meeting rooms surrounding the common work areas on every floor, all with original art, large flat screens for presentations, and imposing solid-wood conference tables. During most of my interviews there, an attendant, who could have been employed in any number of upscale restaurants, courteously offered me coffee in fine china and premium bottled-water. All the while, the general secretary, his two deputies, and several staff members took turns to meet with me and painstakingly described TÜSİAD's positions on a range of issues and its organizational structure, with its board of directors and commissions.

The fact that an institution representing some of the wealthiest individuals in Turkey, if not the world, would have such an impressive setup is hardly surprising. What is striking is how far it has come since its humble beginnings in the 1970s. Feyyaz Berker, the founder of Tekfen Holding and president of TÜSİAD's board of directors throughout the 1970s, described to me a period when he carried most of the association's business out of a small office with no permanent administrative staff to speak of. The editor of a business weekly I interviewed also spoke of brainstorming sessions the founders of TÜSİAD used to hold over tea in members' homes or offices, more likely to be located on the mezzanine of a factory shopfloor. This was a far cry away from the high rises overlooking the Bosphorus Sea where I conducted many of my interviews and was offered an array of coffee and premium water. Unlike the broad political and economic problems they tackle today, some of the ideas to increase business's political voice they came up with during these early meetings were as simple as 'giving factory tours to members of the government and state so that they understood the private sector's contribution to society." The next three chapters explain the significant transformation TÜSİAD has undergone in the span of thirty years and the prodemocracy stance it has adopted by focusing on the shifts in its members' economic, political, and ideological power and on the changing nature of state-business relations in Turkey.

When I set out to do research on Turkish capital, I had two conflicting images of TÜSİAD in my head, as did many other commentators and the press. The first was the TÜSİAD of the 1970s that many, to this day, hold accountable for precipitating the coup of 1980. Turkish newspapers and satirical magazines published caricature drawings of burly corporation owners leading lavish lifestyles, running around with military generals so regularly that the image became part of the consciousness of many who grew up during the period (see Chapter 1). The second was of post-1990 TÜSİAD that heavily criticized the state and pushed for democracy through a collection of young, dynamic, as well as older, more established leaders. The initial questions I approached my interviewees with carried the imprint of this dichotomy and would always be centered on trying to explain a "break" from the past or a "radical shift." Many members I interviewed, however, felt uncomfortable characterizing it as such. While they did note major changes in the nature of Turkish industry, the role of the entrepreneur in society, the global economic climate, and TÜSİAD's activities, they still saw a logical continuity between its new democratizing role and with the association's raison d'être during its early years.

The initial decision to create TÜSİAD would suggest that there is some truth to this perspective. The twelve founding members, who were the owners of the largest private Turkish corporations, were already part of other semiofficial mandatory business associations and were connected enough to gain favors from the state through informal channels. Hence, the act of founding the association alone should be perceived as a new orientation, first, as a way to supplant existing organizations and, second, as a move away from individual to collective action in order to tackle broader policy objectives as opposed to gaining personal favors.[1] TÜSİAD's initial mission statement reflected a desire to address the broader role of capital in society, defined as "promoting development through private enterprise within the principles of a mixed economy and Atatürkism, [...] free enterprise is the foundation of economic life and the guarantor of democracy."[2] Speaking to me about the disposition of founding members in relations to the newer democratization initiatives, one of their heirs further added:

> If there had not been the support of the earlier generation none of this [TÜSİAD dealing with political and social issues] would have happened ... There have been very respectable members since the founding moment that have opposed this, but the core founding group has always been very open to new ideas.[3]

Many commentators, from within and outside, I spoke to drove home this point by emphasizing that the original core members have always had a tight grip on any broad project undertaken by TÜSİAD, including the push for increased democratization. Hence, the association's concern with sociopolitical issues

4. Awakenings

over material demands should be read as the product of a steady evolution since its founding moments in the 1970s rather than as a break. But as noted by my interviewee above, this should not imply a unity of vision within TÜSİAD members. My research revealed a division between members, or entire families, who were viewed as politically "more liberal" and those who were considered "more conservative" or closer to the official ideology of the Kemalist state. As will be discussed at length in the following chapters, the association offered these two camps a way to formulate a coherent business-class ideology and political stance, despite their conflict.

One cannot deny the fact that several of the reasons for founding TÜSİAD were also pragmatic and lodged in economic interests. It was, as will be seen below, to some extent a defensive organization that reacted to the politico-economic climate of the time and organized to be a better vehicle of the interests of large industry, when it was diverging from the rest of the private sector. But the next few pages will also show that while TÜSİAD members' changing economic position was a strong impetus behind forming the association, the travail that went into it was also geared toward increasing the ideological and political power of large capital. The presentation is neither a pluralist one, which views organizations as natural vehicles of business representation, nor is it a Marxist one, which assumes that capital, in particular large business, has some de facto hold on the state. Rather, the chapter shows how the nature of state-business relations in Turkey propelled Turkish industrial capital to forge a political organization which would in later years press for radical change after somewhat of a timid start. To do so, the chapter will first highlight the nature of holding companies (the business elite's preferred form of private-sector establishment) and their relation to the state. The discussion will then show how the business elite's interests started to diverge from the rest of the capitalist class in the 1960s and how this compelled them to organize politically in the 1970s.

Holding Companies and State-Business Relations

As described in the previous chapter, Turkish state-business relations have historically been characterized by a weak capitalist class and a political elite that approached economic policy as an instrument to rally support behind its nation-building project. This—as illustrated very well by Buğra in her study of Turkish capitalists, which my interviewees often cited—has led to a particular type of private-sector establishment: large family-owned multisector holding companies that were better able to operate in Turkey's politico-economic climate.[4] Because these families play a significant role in the economy and because they are TÜSİAD's founders, a brief examination of their history by looking at several interlinked factors is thus warranted to understand the post-1970 period and the emergence of the association, a point emphasized by many individuals I spoke to from within the Turkish private sector and by the literature on Turkish industry. These establishments, as described by Buğra, evolved in response to the nature of late-development and characteristics of state-business relations in Turkey, as had been the case in other late-industrializing societies in which the state played a prominent role.[5] Like Korean chaebols, the two largest corporations, namely Sabancı and Koç Holdings, produce goods as varied as bottled water and automobiles, in addition to owning retail chain stores. Besides the diversity of activities that they are engaged in, one important feature of holdings, as stressed above, is the fact that control has remained mainly under families as opposed to public ownership and professional management. Several interlinked causes, as highlighted by Buğra and my interviewees, help explain their particular nature.

First and foremost, broadly speaking, the rise of large manufacturing firms around the late-industrializing world is due to the nature of underdevelopment and the active role the state plays in trying to catchup to the rest of the world through protection, subsidies, and cheap credits. Within development projects, larger establishments have tended to receive the bulk of state aid partly because of an ideological preference that governments have had toward supporting big ventures, which they genuinely perceived as epitomizing economic progress. However, there are also strong structural factors in the case of Turkey that explain the competitive advantage the owners of such establishments have enjoyed when accessing government aid. Turkey, like many late-industrializing societies, lacked a historically strong capitalist class and suffered from a scarcity of wealth across society. In Turkey, the problem was further amplified by the destruction or exodus of ethno-religious minorities, who had formed the nucleus of an autonomous bourgeoisie during the Ottoman period (see Chapter 3). This prohibited the use of tools such as joint ventures or stock markets to fuel capital formation, leaving a handful of entrepreneurs to compete for state subsidies. The national bourgeoisie was relatively new during the republican era and most of contemporary manufacturing firms really got their first big breaks thanks to state subsidies by venturing from small beginnings to larger projects toward the end of the 1950s.[6]

Once established, the rise and concentration of holdings were inevitable, as the owners of established businesses had an easier time using personal connections compared to new entrants and they also undoubtedly developed more technological know-how, which made them legitimate contenders for subsidies. In turn, aid compounded over several decades and directed toward the same entrepreneurs led to their remarkable growth compared to the rest of the private sector. The diverse activities these holdings are involved in are also products of the experience their owners had developed. The personal connections, capital, and experience they accumulated as first entrants in manufacturing without a doubt gave these entrepreneurs an additional edge even when they were competing for state subsidies and contracts to enter newer and different sectors of activity.[7]

While the importance of subsidies and nature of late-development help explain the concentration of manufacturing, the intrinsic nature of the state also contributed to family ownership and diversification. A running theme throughout this book is that economic policy has been often used by governments in a patrimonial fashion in order to co-opt various groups in society. Since there were no clear established guidelines or certainty about competing for subsidies and since the bureaucracy was complex to navigate, personal ties with officials and some experience in obtaining resources were essential. Thus, the control of private-sector organizations by families, who were able to tap into existing connections, and not professional managers became the favored mode of management. As for diversification, it was preferred because it helped absorb the potential negative impact of unforeseen changes in economic policy that was not always based on predictable rational goals but could vacillate at times based on the self-interest of the political elite.[8]

Most of today's large holding companies have followed a trajectory similar to the one described above. Alarko Holding, which is active in climate control and is among the largest in Turkey, is a good example of how initial experience in one sector combined with being early entrants afforded great opportunities for growth, even if it was just from very small beginnings. It was founded in 1953 by İshak Alaton, and Üzeyir Garih who had opened a small shop inside an office building in order to install AC and heating units. Alaton had migrated to Sweden in his early twenties following World War II because his family was too impoverished to provide for his higher education, presumably because of the wealth tax levied from minority groups. As briefly mentioned in the introduction to the current book, he had first gained experience in manufacturing by working as a welder in a locomotive factory. There, he not only earned enough money to pay for courses in industrial design, which provided him with experience, but he also developed a strong social-democratic political identity, which later in life has guided a lot of his political action within TÜSİAD and in the Turkish public sphere.[9] His partner, Üzeyir Garih, had a master's degree in mechanical engineering from Istanbul Technical University but only two years of work experience in the field of climate control, which he had acquired working at the American Carrier Corporation's Istanbul dealership. In 1963, however, they managed to use their experience in the field to obtain a Development Bank loan and establish a factory to produce their own units. Today, thanks to similar breaks, the holding is active in construction, power generation and supply, seafood, tourism, and real estate, in addition to its core activities. This case is not unique by any means: the founders of the two largest holdings, Sabancı and Koç, were merchants from Anatolia who managed to enter manufacturing through state subsidies. Enka Holding, one of the major construction companies, owes its growth to two government contracts awarded to build seaports in the 1960s and 1970s, respectively.

The above discussion, however, should not create an inflated image of the Turkish industrialist as someone necessarily behaving in entrepreneurial fashion, nor as someone who holds an inordinate amount of political power. As illustrated very well by Buğra, because the energy spent and patterns of business organization were geared toward staying close to the state, the type of amoral market-oriented maximizing behavior characteristic of the ideal-typical Western businessperson was inhibited.[10] The nature of holdings, like the concentration of capital characteristic of late-development, further created several tensions in the power of business that are not necessarily present in the cases of industrialized nations and that help explain business's historically pro-authoritarian tendencies (see Chapter 2).

Since their proximity to the state and size provide holdings a privileged access to subsidies and protection, they inhibit the need for further democracy or the establishment of formal channels, privileging particularism over universalism. Attitudinally, entrepreneurs felt as though they were at the mercy of the political elite and often acted defensively to protect, or justify even, their socioeconomic position. This was further reinforced by the fact that, oftentimes, the fortune of the capitalist class had been dependent on Turkey's ethnic policies during its nation-building project (see Chapter 2). However, we can also note a countertendency. Given that holdings are diversified, they do not represent the narrow sectoral interest of one establishment but are able to have an all-encompassing view of the needs of capitalism as a system. Moreover, as noted by one of my informants with vast managerial experience in holdings, being active in multiple sectors had started in the 1970s to instill in the founders a sense that they could find solutions to society's problems through private enterprise. For instance, one holding owner (in almost ingenuous fashion) felt that starting the production of garbage trucks would help resolve Turkish cities' sanitation problems. These Schumpeterian impulses to trust top-down capitalist change, thus, occurred in a context where there were multiple conflicting tendencies. To remember, large owners might act alone to secure privileges, but may also see ad hoc patrimonial state policy as a problem for the broader economic system. They might have enough power to secure access to resources but might fear reprisals if they publicly call for changes that go against the position of the political elite.[11] As multiple interviewees reminded me:

> [In Turkey] the tradition is for the entrepreneur to be dependent on the state. Firms have developed and businessmen have become stronger under a closed economy. In this environment incentives and contracts from the state play major roles.[12]

The establishment of TÜSİAD and its subsequent activities can therefore not be isolated from these conditions. The association was created by individuals who enjoyed a certain vantage point and, because of family affiliation, identified as being part of the capitalist class. Members of this group felt that they had enough power to obtain individual favors through informal channels to the state but did not have a collective political voice. Put differently, holdings and their owners individually enjoyed some economic power, but this made them politically weaker as they had to appease the political elite. With this in mind, the next sections will further investigate the rationale behind creating TÜSİAD and its evolution by disentangling the various sources of power, namely economic, ideological, and political.

Capital-Intensive Production and Representation

The period from the 1950s to the 1970s brought about a more concrete political desire to achieve industrialization through private-sector accumulation under the Marshall plan. Several significant interrelated changes to economic policy and the Turkish economy, thus, led to the expansion and further concentration of production within Istanbul and holdings. Even though the political class (including the military) was still committed to the active role of the state, it also feared growing distributional conflicts and saw in the growth of private manufacturing a way to generate additional sources of employment and income.[13] To remember, the period was marked by two military coups. The first military coup of 1960 sought to incorporate society more formally (even if unsuccessful because of legal limits imposed on associational life) through a desire to create a more corporatist structure on paper (see Chapter 3). The second in 1971, even if attempts to establish long-term military government was thwarted through successful political maneuvering by civilian political leaders, sought to crush distributional conflicts engendered by the more capital-intensive phase of industrialization and sought to keep political radicalism in check (especially left-wing movements) by banning them.

Economically, the political elite started to move development policy away from state-owned enterprises and more clearly toward the expansion of the private sector's role as an engine of change. Policies pursued till then were driven by import substitution and included an overvalued exchange rate, quantitative restrictions on imports, as well as bilateral trade agreements and high tariffs, which were accompanied by measures such as tax and credit incentives directed toward industry.[14] These were complemented by the state's involvement in the economy through SEEs as providers of raw materials and employers of last resort, in line with the more populist policies of the time.[15] The set of measures used in development policy were fine-tuned over the period to favor the manufacturing sector even further. As a result, the importance of the capitalist class and its economic power increased. More importantly, the material needs of large industrialists changed over the period and diverged from the rest of the private sector, contributing to the establishment of TÜSİAD as a way to supplant already existing organizations as their main channel of representation.[16]

Key aspects of the deeper phase of ISI help explain this transition. The five-year development plans, under this new state-sponsored mixed economy period, placed greater emphasis on rapid industrialization propelled by the development of capital-intensive sectors. Previous policies were deepened by targeting more specifically the needs of manufacturing in order to help the sector transition to the production of capital-intensive and intermediate goods. To this end, the state reevaluated the role of SEEs and focused them more directly in the production of inputs rather than crowding out private entrepreneurs in consumer goods' sectors. Moreover, import licenses were implemented so that manufacturers could have more flexibility to acquire the capital goods they needed from abroad. As a result, the manufacturing sector's share in GDP rose from 14.1 percent in 1963 to 19.1 in 1979, placing Turkey fifth only behind Brazil, China, Mexico, India, and South Korea during the same period in terms of manufacturing value-added in the developing world.[17]

The aggregate growth of manufacturing, however, misses the specific transformation large Istanbul-based establishments were undergoing. Given that they were involved in sectors favored by the state, they became the intended and unintended beneficiaries of the economic transition Turkey was undergoing. Some policies benefited them directly. For instance, between the 1950s and 1960s, 63 percent of all 402 projects funded by the Industrial Development Bank (responsible for channeling US aid toward industry) were in Istanbul and its heavily industrialized neighboring region of Marmara.[18] Other policy goals, like attempts to develop banking and savings in the countryside, unintentionally also boosted the power of Istanbul capitalists. While the government had really envisioned the expansion of commercial banking to fuel the development of the periphery, in practice the policy only served to channel savings toward the metropolis where holdings were looking for loans to finance capital investment. By the 1970s, the manufacturing sectors in Istanbul and the Marmara region, thus, became markedly more capital intensive than the rest of the country, with some estimates highlighting that the average Istanbul worker was capable of producing two and half times as much as someone from the rest of the workforce.[19]

As a result, once established, TÜSİAD would voice quite distinct interests from the rest of the private sector and from other existing business associations. Its members had started to move away from light industry to the heavier phase of industrialization and increasingly needed to import technology and machinery from abroad. To this end, a growing need for foreign exchange and credits for investment led the future founders of TÜSİAD to be more favorable to lifting trade restrictions when compared to smaller establishments and commercial capital. They also disagreed with the employers' union, Turkish Confederation of Employer Associations (Türkiye İşveren Sendikaları Konfederasyonu, TİSK), over labor relations, in particular wage levels. For one thing, future TÜSİAD members were already willing to pay their workers more than smaller industrial and commercial establishments, and for another, they wanted to expand the domestic market through a general rise in income.[20] In broader political terms, TÜSİAD leaders increasingly tied the need for increased labor rights and wages to the need to maintain social peace. Holding owners therefore started to see their interests not only as being tied to narrow material needs, but also as being linked to broader societal issues affecting them as a class.

The growth of Istanbul manufacturing, rising class consciousness, and the new economic strength of holdings did not, however, automatically translate into increased leverage over state policy, unlike what the Marxist scholarship would predict. It also did not, as pluralists foresee, lead to a parallel increase in the voice of Istanbul manufacturing within existing channels of representation. As will be discussed in the next two sections, the impact has been more nuanced. For one thing, the business elite (and later TÜSİAD) were increasingly at odds with the rest of the private sector. For another, the state and political elite used these intra-class cleavages in patrimonial fashion to secure the support of only part of the capitalist class, thus decreasing TÜSİAD members' political clout and ability to obtain the full benefits of economic policy. And finally, the political role and ideological legitimacy of the private sector were not any more secure than had been in previous periods. Although the new five-year plans increasingly highlighted the greater role of the private sector, the growing size of the state in many strategic sectors and the political class's more markedly populist discourse of the 1960s and 1970s posed a perceived threat to large capital. These factors combined with the bourgeoisie's historical weakness put the ideological legitimacy of this class in jeopardy. The next section will, therefore, show that large business representation was crafted in an ad hoc manner by its members to increase the political and ideological power of business.

The Birth of the Business Elite's Political Power

The current book maintains that nature of state-society relations can undermine the political power of business despite its rising economic power and that the establishment of associations can be an attempt to increase it. Studies on business organizations have usually had as a main focus, or dependent variable, the ability of governments to achieve good economic policy. One of the questions about associations these have asked has been whether they were able to restrain self-interest rent-seeking behavior on the part of their members to actually get them to accept (or lobby for) government policies that overall would be good for the economy.[21] Within this framework, some have been cautious about TÜSİAD's effectiveness as an association, as its powerful members have had traditionally more to gain from acting individually rather than collectively in order to affect specific industrial policy.[22]

Adopting this approach to understand TÜSİAD misses the point that it is not an instrumentalist organization, but a political one. During the period under study, the association has voiced the broader concerns of the capitalist class in the 1970s and 1980s and then tackled even wider sociopolitical issues after the 1990s. The claim I am making is not that TÜSİAD's demands are completely a-material, but that its establishment epitomizes the perceived need for formulating the broader demands of capital. Put differently, given that most of its members already have the power to act alone on issues related to the minutia of specific policy implementation, the very act of creating an association was, thus, done to enhance the political voice of large capital. This section examines the dynamics behind the formation of TÜSİAD as a political organization.

Even though the policy transformation discussed above was increasing the economic power of would-be TÜSİAD members, the weakness of civil society and the manner in which policy was carried out still continued to undermine the power of capital as a class. To emphasize, legally holding companies and their owners, like any other private-sector establishment, were mandatory members of business associations created in top-down fashion by the state. These included TOBB, TİSK, and a more regional association, the Istanbul Chamber of Industry (İstanbul Sanayi Odası, İSO). But, by law, these afforded each firm only one vote and did not take into account their size or economic power. As such, TÜSİAD founders were seeking a parallel and more salient route to voice their needs because existing organizations had been ineffective from their inception.

In response to the rift that was forming between the business elite and the rest of the private sector, twelve of the leading industrialists from the main Turkish industrial corporations joined together in 1971 to sign TÜSİAD's Founders' Memorandum drafted by Vehbi Koç, the patriarch of the largest holding in Turkey. Shortly after, they were joined by eighty-six other large industrialists also from around Istanbul.[23] The establishment of TÜSİAD was a political action geared toward finding alternative ways to institutionalize the representation of large business, in the hopes that it would be more effective than the several organizations already in existence.[24] The fact that the business elite saw existing institutions as ineffective had deeper political roots than just the lack of representation. Why this was the case, therefore, warrants greater scrutiny.

The state had first founded semiformal mandatory associations in 1950 to try and incorporate civil society actors, more specifically small entrepreneurs from the periphery that the Kemalist CHP had historically ignored (see Chapter 2). The military junta of 1960 further sought to increase their functions to try and institutionalize class representation within the state through a corporatist structure, meant to curb distributional conflicts. The generals also founded TİSK in 1962 to encourage centralized bargaining with labor. However, in addition to the fact that the business elite did not see eye to eye with other establishments represented in these organizations, broader political factors also impacted their appeal. The main problem was that, despite the seeming importance state actors placed on formalizing state-society relations, the manner through which they legislated associational life always betrayed a historical mistrust of civil society actors and sought to control top-down rather than empower various socioeconomic groups. In the specific case of business, a truly corporatist structure or effective societal organizations never materialized for several interrelated reasons.[25]

For one thing, the exact legal framework through which these organizations would function within the state was never clearly defined. Most laws passed in the twentieth century regulating associational life always used vague language that made it possible for the state to control the leadership of organizations and prosecute or even shut down groups that "threatened" national interest.[26] For another, business associations lacked a clear mandate. As such, any genuine attempt the state made to give them actual powers to increase their members' stake in participation ended up undermining their intended effects by leading to distortions and misuse. For instance, the state granted TOBB the authority to distribute import licenses that were direly needed by manufacturing establishments during the ISI period in order to import capital goods. TOBB was specifically chosen because, by law, it was the umbrella organization representing several chambers. The hope was that licenses dispensed as such would provide a broader pool of entrepreneurs the chance to acquire the much-needed resources. In practice, however, TOBB did not have clearly articulated goals or policies as to how they should be handled. Moreover, the organization tended to overrepresent smaller enterprises throughout the country, some of which were not even involved in manufacturing but in commerce. As a result, TOBB's control over such desirable material rewards as licenses combined with its ability to reach smaller entrepreneurs from the periphery turned it into an appealing target for politicians seeking their support at the detriment of larger capitalists. Politicians from the periphery (or outside of the urban political establishment) thus sought to capture TOBB as a tool to co-opt the leadership of chambers and build patron-client relations with entrepreneurs from outside major metropolitan areas. Indeed, Bianchi's detailed study of Turkish associational life illustrates many instances when noteworthy politicians such as Demirel of the center-right Justice Party (Adalet Partisi, AP), an offshoot of the DP, or Erbakan from the religious National Salvation Party (Milli Selamet Partisi, MSP) secured the support of the rural periphery by influencing or, in the case of Erbakan, outright capturing the TOBB presidency.[27]

Thus, in a context where civil society was weakened through state action and formal state-society relations were not as formalized, attempts to build business representation further created political rent. The result has been detrimental for the representation of large capital because it further undermined the effectiveness of TOBB as an autonomous political organization. The episode also had real material consequences for the business elite. By giving import rights as a source of political rent to smaller nonmanufacturing merchants who used them to acquire commercial goods for short-term gains, the measures siphoned the licenses away from Istanbul entrepreneurs who would presumably have used them to acquire capital goods needed to move to the heavier phase of industrialization, .[28] Hence, large capital was effectively pushed out of leadership position of these organizations and, despite being in a structurally powerful economic position, did not gain any material benefits from being members in them. To this day, some of my interviewees still emphasized that the leadership of these organizations were really mouthpieces of the government. They have further underscored that an institution that affords every member a single vote (such is the case in semiformal organizations such as TOBB) was not reflective of the structural importance of holdings, echoing some of the similar misgivings that entrepreneurs in comparative cases, like Brazil, have voiced about umbrella organizations.[29]

Thus, the establishment of TÜSİAD was a clear and deliberate attempt to move away from existing organizations that had undermined large capital's potential influence. TÜSİAD sought to represent a much smaller, select, and cohesive portion of the Turkish private sector, as opposed to try and work as an all-encompassing association. To this end, the founders established early on that membership to TÜSİAD would be through invitation only. Furthermore, it would be granted on an individual basis to ensure the inclusion of only like-minded businesspeople, as opposed to all private-sector establishments active in some sector or region.

> TÜSİAD is an association. It has a 7,000 dollars membership fee ... TOBB or İSO are places where everyone is officially a member, even small commerce. This is why TÜSİAD can look at the needs of medium and large enterprises and the issues more rationally. It has more flexibility because it is an NGO.[30]

As will be discussed in greater detail in the next chapters, the founders, all of whom owned the top Turkish corporations, structured the association so that they would maintain some control over it. The selective TÜSİAD membership process meant that the founders could invite individuals who shared their core values to join, such as their heirs, top managers, and consultants. In so doing, large holdings not only maintained their grip over the association, but they also ensured some level of ideological affinity. It therefore became an organization that was at once the product of a similar structural position and of shared class consciousness.

These observations, when combined with the fact that holdings were already capable of obtaining individual favors from the state and that the political class was seeking to capture other associations, suggest that TÜSİAD was first and foremost an attempt to increase large capital's political voice rather than act solely as an instrumentalist lobby. TOBB's and TİSK's stance against this new association highlights that it was somewhat successful in achieving this goal. Various accounts show that the two formal associations expressed discontent with government officials' growing willingness to include TÜSİAD as the third representative of business interest in policy debates. As for labor organizations, they remained heavily suspicious of the timing of TÜSİAD's creation, which coincided with the military intervention of 1971, and saw in it a blatant capitalist attempt to control the state.[31] Regardless of TÜSİAD's motivations, the fact that small entrepreneurs and labor perceived the new association as being all-too-powerful is a strong indication that it was becoming politically more effective than the previous individual lobbying efforts of its members. The next section will outline how concerns over the ideological power and legitimacy of the capitalist class further affected the association's activities.

Organizing the Business Elite's Ideological Power

As outlined in the previous chapter, commercial and manufacturing classes under the Ottoman Empire were composed of ethno-religious minorities. These were replaced in the twentieth century by a Muslim capitalist class created by the Young Turks and the CHP with the aim of establishing a national bourgeoisie through protection and direct transfers of wealth. Hence, this group saw its raison d'être as intrinsically linked to the nationalist agenda of the state. As revealed through some informal conversations I have had, as well as scholarship on the issue, the capitalist class continued to carry the weight of owing its existence to the destruction of ethnic communities.[32] This feeling was sustained throughout the twentieth century through the implementation of policies directly targeting ethnic minorities, such as the wealth tax during World War II levied arbitrarily mostly on Jewish families or state-condoned violence against Greeks in the 1950s. Measures such as these affected the psyche of the entire entrepreneurial class and its members as everyone witnessed firsthand the impoverishment of their main business partners and saw more concretely the extent to which the state was willing and able to arbitrarily punish specific groups. The problem was compounded during the second half of the century, as seen above, by the fact that the Turkish industrialist was someone who owed their first break to the state in a politico-ideological climate where development policy was used in tandem with nationalist-populist discourse to co-opt society. Many interviews repeatedly echoed the need to stay close to the state during the period:

> Up to the 1980s, under the import substitution industrialization period, under high custom walls and protection, TÜSİAD could not afford to oppose the state.[33]

> TÜSİAD is not a monolithic group, and it never was. It has always been a platform where different views were put forth. But before the last decade, in an environment where most enterprises were doing business with the state, not to step on the state's toes, not to be in opposition to the state, to do what the state wanted ... was a practice generally preferred by firms.[34]

This type of allegiance to the state and its policies inhibited capitalist activity. Weber's classic insights into the 'capitalist spirit" can help understand why the Turkish business elite needed to find a new ideological bent. To remember, Weber outlined the peculiar orientation that entrepreneurship under capitalism entails: instead of being bound by stable traditional ties, the capitalist must perpetually make rational use of resources based on a calculation of future profits.[35] This type of behavior is amoral and goes against the demands that more traditional forms of allegiance require. For widespread capitalism to be successful, profit motivation takes precedence over customs, relationships with workers go against feelings of loyalty or obligation, and the rational use of resources requires a new orientation toward time. Hence, the entrepreneur must find some new form of meaning to their actions to replace traditional obligations.

During the period Weber was writing about, the establishment of manufacturing and generalized trade in Europe was gradual, and individuals already involved in capitalist enterprise could slowly embrace religious beliefs or ideologies giving capitalist behavior some justification until they attained a critical mass that ensured the establishment of generalized trade. As discussed in previous sections, in Turkey and other late-developing societies, spending energy to enjoy close ties with state officials and accepting the dominant ideology enabled entrepreneurs to gain access to traditional patron-client networks. However, while this type of orientation is appropriate to obtain subsidies and protection when entering ventures for the first time, the growth of capitalist enterprise in Turkey most likely created the need to develop a more rational orientation in the 1970s. The expansion of private-sector establishments, the increasing complexity of production, and greater integration with world markets would all require the type of long-term planning discussed by Weber. But this does not happen instantaneously as Poggi sought to emphasize by revisiting Weber's work. According to his analysis, it was the slow, gradual co-development, rather than a causal relationship, that led the rise of ideologies associated with Protestantism and entrepreneurship to mesh well together. European capitalists wanted to make sense of their inclinations and found it in religion.[36] Hence, during the 1970s, the Turkish entrepreneur was someone seeking meaning to the new types of action needed to govern a modern capitalist enterprise. TÜSİAD inherently became a vehicle to collectively, as a class, seek this new orientation.

As important as the ideological function of the association was, however, its establishment cannot completely be disentangled from the political climate of the 1970s either. The period, as was the case in other parts of the world, was characterized by growing conflicts between the traditional left and right. In Turkey, there was specifically fear of distributional conflicts as well as the polarization of political movements, which competed against each other to capture various sociopolitical institutions, such as unions, the civil service, and education. The conflict which turned violent, in the form of political assassinations and terrorist attacks, also impacted mainstream political parties, who tried to pander to radical groups that controlled political capital.

This affected economic policy and the role of capital in society. The Ecevit controlled CHP government moved further toward the left. Even though there was a role intended for the private sector, especially for large manufacturing as seen earlier in the chapter, the CHP started to strongly emphasize its commitment to state-led models of growth. In so doing, it further blurred the boundaries of the private and public sectors. As such, although most state measures since the 1950s had ended up favoring large business, the period only served to add to the uncertainty tied to the social role and ideological power of the bourgeoisie at a time when it was actually becoming stronger economically.[37] The ideological-political weakness of large capital during the period was a theme that was constantly echoed during the interviews I carried out with members of TÜSİAD.

> A study was conducted in the 1950s, 1952 or 1953, by the Chamber of Industry. [The study] listed the most respectable institutions in Turkey; ... a question like "what comes to your mind when you think of respectable?" [was asked]. The first one was the Turkish army, the second parliament, third universities, fourth something like the bureaucracy ... the eleventh was business at the lowest rank. During the 1950s the entrepreneur was seen as a robber who only thought of his profits, because industry was not that developed.[38]

> During the [1970s] I also was a bureaucrat at DİE [State Statistics Institute, Devlet İstatistik Enstitüsü]. The image of businessmen was negative then. This is why they felt the need to establish TÜSİAD then. It is the opposite now. There are people who want a smaller state. Things that were not talked about before are discussed now. The word "Kurd" is being pronounced now. Turkey is living the growing pains of these changes.[39]

Thus, TÜSİAD's actions also demonstrated an attempt to solidify and expand the ideological and political power of capital as a class. From the onset, TÜSİAD tried to act as a think tank and started to publish various reports on a number of issues affecting the private sector. During its earlier days, from its establishment to the mid-1970s, hints about the type of discourse TÜSİAD was trying to build can be found in the yearly activity reports and in its mission statement. While its first mission statement acknowledged the virtues of a mixed economy, where the state still played a prominent role, the association's founders also tried to carve a role for themselves by asserting that the private sector was the main vehicle of development and progress.[40] As importantly, TÜSİAD included macroeconomic comparisons in its annual activity reports that demonstrated the greater efficiency of the private sector when compared to the state in such areas as job creation and productivity.

Within this context, the fact that most of TÜSİAD's publications at the time were more economic in nature when compared to the subsequent period of the 1990s is not surprising. Indeed, of the fifty research papers and books published by TÜSİAD (from 1974 to 1979), thirty-five were dedicated to economic issues, compared to only twelve on social-political issues, while three contained elements of both (see Chapter 7 for a full comparison). However, it would be inadequate to say that they were only concerned with instrumentalist demands. The publications reveal a concern to legitimize the private sector and touch on broader debates about state-business relations. Some of TÜSİAD publications of the time, even if more economic in nature, thus also touched on liberalization and on the greater role of the private sector, such as *Business State Relations, The Business Community and Education, Industrialization and Regional Balance, Views and Suggestions on Measures to Prevent Waist, EEC-Turkey Relations*. Even its more narrow instrumentalist publications dealt with the issue of red tape involved with state intervention such as *The Actualization and Difficulties of Investments Obtaining Support Certificates*.

Many members I interviewed saw an attitudinal shift, both in terms of developing a culture of moving public debate through reports and in the desire to press for economic liberalism. Feyyaz Berker, TÜSİAD's president in the 1970s who presided over this transformation, confirmed that the association had already started to tackle the topics of economic liberalization and, to some extent, democratization. The feeling was echoed by others:

> TÜSİAD has from the beginning been at the vanguard of such [sociopolitical] issues. It is not something specific to 1996. From its beginning TÜSİAD published reports, gathered leading experts in their fields and financed them to prepare these reports and presented them to the public. Some attract less attention, others more.[41]

The emergence of TÜSİAD and its activities in the 1970s are, therefore, testament to the existence of a tension between large business's desire to carve a role for itself and an environment where particularistic ties granted privileges to business while making it politically weaker. The main goal behind its activities, as Buğra maintains, was to participate in the long-term development debate.[42] Hence, three sources of power—ideological, economic and political—were intertwined and characterized the steady evolution the association underwent. The reports also demonstrate how TÜSİAD not only sought to impact political debate, but also to influence its own members' ideological orientation and increase their legitimacy in society as capitalists. As noted by several of my interviewees, one way the founders sought to form a coherent front and forge the capitalist class's ideology and goals was by sticking behind the content of the reports.

A Prelude to the 1980s: Capital's Political Power and the Military Coup

The tentative and gradual attempts to build the business elite's ideological power culminated in the association's greater involvement in politics from 1978 to 1980. TÜSİAD started to tackle the debt crisis and, in more general terms, economic mismanagement more actively.[43] TÜSİAD's publications from the late 1970s indeed reveal that the business elite drew an even sharper contrast between the performance of its members and the public sector in areas such as productivity, employment creation, and value-added.[44] In so doing, it went beyond legitimizing private enterprise to offering an alternative, and what it perceived to be a more efficient, model of growth than state-led industrialization.

This is partly why members who I interviewed and who were active in the 1970s refused to see the 1990's *Democratization Report* as a radical break, since they felt that TÜSİAD's push for economic liberalization was the first meaningful step they had taken politically against the state and government. Indeed, the association accelerated its efforts to press for change when it actively and heavily supported the economic liberalization and stabilization measures advocated by the IMF to tackle Turkey's debt problem. The position crystalized in 1979 when TÜSİAD took an unprecedented turn for a private-sector organization to publish four full-page newspaper advertisements to criticize the then prime minister Ecevit and his left-wing government's reluctance to fully embrace reform. The advertisements which linked arbitrary state intervention, bad governance, and corruption to the lack of democratic rights and increased poverty were seen by some of my informants as the association's first big political action.[45]

Ecevit and his CHP's reluctance to implement the reforms combined with the atmosphere of political unrest in the country eventually led to his resignation in October 1979. While the center-right Demirel and his AP took over the helm of government, they also were soon faced by the January 24, 1980, resolutions, a set of draconian measures borrowed from the IMF and developed by the State Planning Agency (DPT). Given the atmosphere of political polarization that reigned in Turkey, the reforms would have likely been a political suicide for any elected government. Thus, Demirel's lukewarm attitude toward the new economic measures eventually led to the military junta taking over the country's government.[46]

This succession of events, which paved the way for the military coup, is to this day seen as being triggered by TÜSİAD's advertisements and by the strong pro-reform stance adopted by the business elite. More critical writing in Turkey blames the association for the turn to authoritarianism and sees it as a sign of capitalists' strength in classical Marxian terms.[47] Scholars of state-business relations like Arat and Buğra, however, further add that it was also the product of tensions between the state and industrialists created by the latter's dependence and lack of legitimacy during the period leading up to the coup.[48] From a more comparative perspective, this period does confirm some of the findings of the existing literature on the role of the business elite in regime transition. Economic mismanagement, in the form of the debt crisis, combined with unclear boundaries of state intervention, had led TÜSİAD to take stronger action for change. TÜSİAD's rise in the 1970s also confirms that the more recent emphasis on business organizations to explain the process is a highly legitimate area of research to get a full understanding of instances when business becomes a political force. Most of TÜSİAD's activities during the period and its willingness to press for change reveal that this was part of an effort to change the relative political weakness of business. While the demands of TÜSİAD at the time were not as radical or political as in the 1990s, it can therefore be said that the nascent organization was trying to change the characteristic of state-business relations by giving large industry a political voice, and as such the period was a strong precursor to the 1990s.

The period foretold the shape that 1980s' politics and economic liberalization would take in another significant way, by introducing a major actor to Turkish politics: Turgut Özal who served as prime minister from 1983 to 1989 and greatly shaped the process of economic liberalization and the tone of Turkish politics through his ideological impulses.[49] Özal epitomized the upwardly mobile middle-class technocrat that has dominated most of Turkish politics during the post-1980 period. He grew up in what Mardin would sociologically consider the peripheral regions of Turkey (Malatya and Silifke). His worldview was greatly shaped as an undergraduate student in the late 1940s during the DP's rising popularity, when he was moved by the same conservative, anti-communist, and pro-American ideologies. Later, his admiration for the United States would further deepen in graduate school and a stint working in the World Bank from 1971 to 1973. He spent most of his life working for the DPT, which he helped establish and led as its undersecretary, during which time he also was an advisor to Prime Minister Demirel (in 1966). Özal's first entrance to the scene of electoral politics in 1977 was not successful. An engineer and technocrat by training, he still lacked the popularity to be successful in electoral politics, as attested by an unsuccessful bid to win a seat to the National Assembly under the umbrella of Erbakan's religious MSP. However, he was adept at networking and felt comfortable navigating and making connections between conservative political parties, the business elite (members of TÜSİAD specifically), and transnational organizations. In this capacity, he sat on the board of several holdings, including Sabancı, and was tapped to not only continue working for the DPT, but would also author the draconian stabilization package, which ushered in the military. Although, as will be seen in the next chapter, he did not always see eye to eye with the putschist generals, his career and ideological inclinations, according to Karataşlı, made him the ideal candidate to push through a much more pro-Western, neoliberal agenda with the additional goal of integrating the periphery into Turkey's center.[50] The next two chapters will trace how the economic and political changes ushered in this way impacted the business elite's prodemocracy agenda.

Chapter 5

PROMETHEUS UNBOUND: ECONOMIC POWER FROM 1980 TO 2002

> Everyone should realize that democratization is an issue that Turkey cannot overlook in building its future in a healthy way. Strong economies will catch the wave of globalization only to the extent that they are built in an environment shaped by democracy and the law's universal measures, with a modern state, and a transparent and enlightened social base.[1]

Like in Feyyaz Berker's (the head of a major holding and TÜSİAD's first ever chairperson in the 1970s) 1997 speech above, many of my interviewees also built broad sweeping linkages between democracy's institutions and a well-functioning economy. Given the global ideological-economic climate that dominated the post-1980 period, this line of reasoning was to be expected to a certain degree. Turkey and most nations around the world underwent a period of vast economic change during the 1980s and 1990s. Globally, the expansion of world trade, the liberalization of capital flows, and increased competition from nations such as China compelled countries to adjust in order to perform well economically. In Turkey, as in many late-industrializing nations, state-led models of development (mainly through ISI) were being replaced by more market- and export-driven policies such as ELG.[2]

Thus, the business elite lost some of the privileges it enjoyed (in the form of import restrictions, subsidized government credits, and cheap inputs) as private-sector performance was increasingly promoted through export incentives, privatization, and greater openness to trade.[3] During our personal interview, Berker (quoted above) used his years of experience in manufacturing to recall a period three decades earlier when Turkish industrialists had been able to "sell anything they wanted" thanks to state subsidies and lack of meaningful competition. The post-1980 period put an end to this, according to Berker, because they now had to adjust by constantly improving the quality and cost of their products to stay competitive.[4]

As momentous as these shifts in economic paradigm were, the collapse of the Soviet Union and the disintegration of the socialist bloc were also significant politically. Their downfall eliminated one of the most substantial arguments for state-led development and gave ideological ammunition to proponents of liberal economic policy. The 1990s thus seemed to usher in a global victory for what has been widely termed neoliberalism, where economic dynamism was linked to trade, less government intervention, and stronger civil society. For Turkey and other nations in the EU's gravitational economic pull, the Union's emphasis on democracy made the connection between political and economic liberalism even more salient.[5] The fact that TÜSİAD took its major turn toward a more democratizing role in 1996 with the publication of its *Perspectives on Democratization Report* undoubtably speaks to the significant impact that these changes have had on local capital.

Although the business elite has historically done well under authoritarianism, a range of theories, presented in Chapter 2, made a case about why they might also be likely to favor political liberalization to advance their own interests. There are strong arguments for why institutions associated with democracy go hand in hand with a well-functioning capitalist economy and, in turn, why an enlightened bourgeoisie would favor change. The current chapter, thus, will focus on this instrumentalist relationship by outlining the ways in which the economic power and needs of Turkish corporations changed during the period to make democracy more appealing.

However, changes to the global economic environment alone provide only a partial explanation of why the Turkish business elite changed its political position. During the expansion of world trade and liberal economic policy, many political sociologists have demonstrated that liberalization was not an immediate panacea for all the ills of previous forms of state intervention, such as the prevalence of corruption.[6] Moreover, despite globalization and the need to stay competitive, many states have preserved their key characteristics lodged in the state-society relations they had built.[7] Although liberalization in Turkey brought about significant changes, such as privatization and the dynamism of SMEs, the manner in which the state carried out deregulation did not eliminate corruption, as the Özal government and the state were able to create new sources of rent and state intervention.[8] This can be partially explained by the fact that economic liberalism in Turkey not only was carried out to remedy the distortions of the previous ISI period (see Chapter 4), but also had political motivations. In their attempts to align with the West, the military and Özal had strong incentives to implement economic policy with the chief goal of ending societal conflict by integrating the periphery into new middle classes and by combating the appeal of leftist ideologies.[9] As seen in the previous chapter, in his position as a government technocrat in the 1970s, Özal was already a powerbroker between various domestic agencies and transnational organizations, and he had already demonstrated a penchant for conservative ideas combined with an admiration for the West. Thus, not only the economic dimensions, but also the political dimensions of globalization must be taken into account when examining the reforms' impact on the Turkish economy and state-business relations.[10] Adopting such an approach is needed for several other significant interrelated reasons linked to the nature of the business elite.

First, as mentioned throughout this book, the push for democracy was not uniform across and within country cases. Capitalists around the world have not all embraced a democratizing role to the same extent despite operating in a similar global environment. Within Turkey too, TÜSİAD was the only business association that promoted democracy in the 1990s and even then, some of its own more conservative members were lukewarm about pushing through rapid political change.[11] Second, my interviews revealed that, while they agreed with the general policy direction of the country, there still was a lot that could be done to make the Turkish private sector more competitive by focusing on the broader institutional setting. This view confirmed the broader comparative literature's observation that the period did not bring about the parallel institutionalization of state-society relations,[12] but also the Turkey-focused literature's assessment that the set of liberal economic policies produced mixed results.[13] Third, and linked to this point, the same way that economic liberalization did not translate into good governance right away, state-business relations also remained informal in nature. Thus, as covered in previous chapters, the kind of changes endorsed by TÜSİAD still represented a rift between the state and the business elite, despite the transformation Turkey had undergone. As such, given the importance of the state as a source of rent for capitalists, its willingness to break away from it as early as the 1990s must be examined more closely. To go back to one of the questions raised in the introduction: if capitalists have historically benefitted from the state, why resort to demands for radical political change rather than influence the government through existing channels? Finally, centering the discussion around instrumentalist goals overlooks the deliberate travails, from changing TÜSİAD's structure to the leadership role some played, that went into making it an organization better equipped to tackle broad objectives and press for democracy.

The last two caveats deserve special attention and will form the basis of Chapter 6, which will examine how the ideological and political power of Turkish capital evolved under the period covered, with a particular focus on state-business relations. The current chapter, however, will deal with the first by disentangling the evolution of the private sector and its material needs during the first two decades of the post-1980 period to show why political change was particularly salient for large Turkish corporation owners. In so doing, the chapter will outline changes in material interests, a necessary but not sufficient condition, that make democracy desirable to the business elite. The focus of the chapter will be on the direct links that the TÜSİAD members I spoke to had built between their own needs and democracy. As will be revealed, these were lodged in a combination of exogenous conditions, such as trade, and endogenous factors, such as the growth of private establishment that created new opportunities and constraints. Before delving into the relationship between capitalist interest and democracy, however, it would be appropriate to start by surveying the extent to which the business elite's economic power grew despite significant changes to the policy regime.

Liberalism, Manufacturing, and Economic Power

The General Environment

The reforms ushered in by the military dictatorship and deepened by the subsequent civilian government of Turgut Özal (1983 to 1989) brought about greater economic openness and deregulation. Thus, they included the structural adjustment program proposed by the IMF, the liberalization of capital markets and foreign trade, as well as the redefinition of the role of the state through privatization and export-led development.[14] They had been drafted in 1979 by technocrats, including Özal himself, with a deep admiration for the United States and conservative political roots, closer to the periphery of the country. Thus, examining the 1980s and the reforms, several scholars have pointed to aspects of economic policies that were potentially harmful to the interests of the business elite, including the loss of state subsidies as well as the rising importance of financial capital and of smaller entrepreneurs from regions away from Istanbul.[15] Regardless, the Turkish business elite fared relatively well during the new liberal economic regime. Large capitalist families from within TÜSİAD kept growing and diversifying the same way that they had done in the preceding periods, leading to an increase in their economic power. While industry (including manufacturing sectors, construction, and energy) was already developing in the 1960s and 1970s, the sector really flourished in subsequent decades when it started generating nearly 30 percent of all Turkish value-added at the turn of the century (up from 20 percent in the 1970s).[16]

To recall, Chapter 4 had already revealed that the business elite started to witness the limits of the Turkish state-led model of growth because they were entering new sectors of activity after years of development. In the 1970s, this led them to experience the adverse effects of distortions in input prices caused by government intervention. More specifically, the state's control of foreign exchange, tariffs, and import licenses made it hard for capital-intensive producers to innovate through the transfer of foreign technology. These problems had already been one of the primary impetuses behind forming TÜSİAD to represent the business. They also help explain why the association was initially highly supportive of economic liberalization from 1980 onward.

The loss of protective barriers did not seem to be damaging to the Turkish industry. Even though foreign competition grew (with the imports of goods and services rising from less than 10 percent of GDP throughout the 1970s to around 30 percent in 2000), the domestic private sector also managed to keep up with increased trade. Turkey's exports rose from just above 20 percent of GDP in the 1970s to consistently stay at just under 30 percent throughout the post-1980 period, suggesting that the economy was not vulnerable in the face of competition. As significantly for the case of TÜSİAD and the business elite, the manufacturing sector became the main engine behind the rise in exports. While Turkish manufacturers were responsible for only 14 percent of all exports in 1970, they started to outperform all other sectors of the economy in the 1980s and 1990s to accomplish more than two-thirds of all international sales (see Figure 5.1).

As mentioned above, however, there were aspects of the new policy environment that were potentially harmful to the business elite. These aggregate figures, therefore, cannot reveal the extent to which large capital was impacted by the economic paradigm shift. These types of radical turns often create policy winners and losers, and establishments that had benefited from developmentalist policies are typically more likely to suffer from declining state protection. In the specific case of

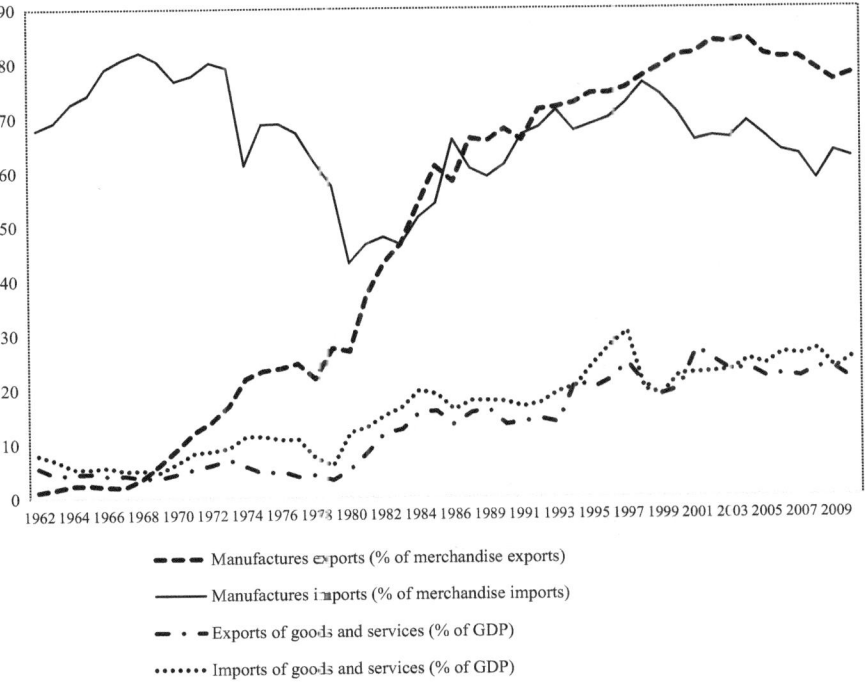

Figure 5.1 Trade indicators.
Source: World Bank, "Turkey Trade Statistics," https://wits.worldbank.org/countryprofile/en/tur. Accessed August 5, 2022; World Development Indicators," https://databank.worldbank.org/source/world-development-indicators. Accessed August 5, 2022.

Turkey, there was some attempt to favor previously neglected smaller entrepreneurs and develop the financial sector as a way to encourage the ascent of individuals from the periphery into the center of the country.[17] As a result, SMEs in regions far away from the traditional business centers have undergone a great surge in activity after economic liberalization. Dubbed "Anatolian tigers" for their dynamism, these new entrepreneurs contributed greatly to Turkey's surge in manufacturing exports.[18] It should therefore be underscored that TÜSİAD members managed to carve out a share of private-sector expansion and export performance. In 1997, businesses owned by the association's members had created about 40 percent of Turkish value-added and were responsible for about 35 percent of all Turkish exports.[19] Moreover, the interviews conducted with them highlighted the extent to which they had changed and were willing to become more dynamic under the new policy regime.

Paradigm Shift and the Business Elite

Despite losing the state protections they had previously enjoyed and rising competition from newer capitalists, the business elite benefited from a set of fortuitous circumstances which allowed them to build on the capital they had accumulated during the 1970s. First, as had been the case in many societies implementing liberalization, the shifts in policy did not bring about a deeper, more structural change in state-business relations. Not only has the latter been proven to be resilient in many comparative cases,[20] but in the specific case of Turkey, informal linkages remained in place.[21] As will be seen below and in the next chapter, this ultimately created contradictions for the business elite, and it would eventually compel the group to press for state reform. In the more immediate term, however, large capitalists continued to leverage their privileged access to government officials to make new economic policies more palatable. More specifically, they were able to lobby the Özal government behind closed doors to influence the pace of liberalization. Import restrictions were being lifted in phases, and, thus, individual members of the business elite were able to selectively negotiate the kinds of products that would remain shielded from foreign competition by using their own particularistic access to legislators in order to do so. Moreover, the fact that Özal centralized economic policy in the hands of the executive and that he had already worked as a well-connected technocrat during the 1970s' ISI period made these types of negotiations easier. In this manner, large corporations were able to use existing state-business relations to mitigate the potential negative impact of trade for their companies while competing in sectors they were more productive in.[22]

Second, the legacy of state-business relations also provided the business elite the opportunity to build foreign partnerships rather than compete directly with multinational corporations. The red tape involved with investing in Turkey compelled foreign businesses to seek out local partners with established connections to officials and more experience navigating the bureaucracy. Companies such as Ford, Mannesman and Philip Morris have all started production in Turkey with the help and lobbying power of the major traditional holdings. Capital-intensive goods (such as Toyota and Fiat vehicles) destined for the European market were increasingly produced by joint ventures involving TÜSİAD members (such as Koç and Sabancı Holdings). In return, Turkish entrepreneurs have been able to acquire know-how, import foreign technology, and produce higher quality products locally.[23] The Turkish business elite was, therefore, not only shielded from direct rivalry, but it was also able to enter new sectors of activity by working with multinational corporations as local distributors or as subcontractors.

In the process, automotive and consumer durables industries linked to TÜSİAD have become national champions of exportation toward the EU. For instance, according to a study of its own members, more than 120 firms linked to the association were exporting toward Germany, while around 100 were selling to the UK and Italy.[24] As importantly, the types of goods that were exported were increasingly capital intensive. Export data show that four such sectors (capital goods, machinery, electrical goods, and transportation) have become more important drivers behind Turkey's trade performance. These four sectors taken together had made up less than 10 percent of Turkey's top eight exports in the late 1980s. However, their share doubled and then quadrupled to reach about

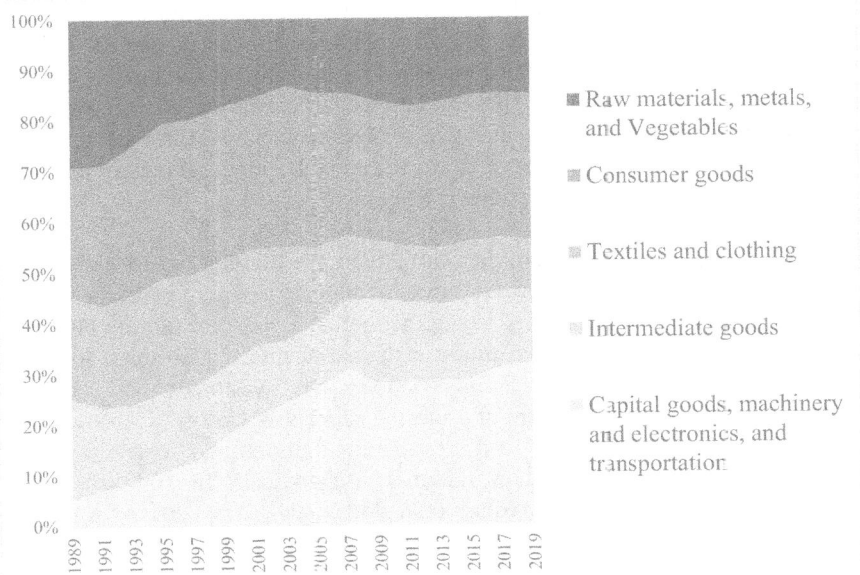

Figure 5.2 Share of product type in top eight exports.
Source: World Bank, "Turkey Trade Statistics," https://wits.worldbank.org/countryprofile/en/tur. Accessed August 5, 2022.

20 percent in the mid-1990s and 40 percent in 2006 (when TÜSİAD was actively pushing for reform). Notably, while still among the top eight Turkish exports, the share of less technology-driven sectors such as raw materials, vegetables, food products, and stone and glass fell from about 40 percent at the beginning of the period to less than 20 percent at the turn of the century (see Figure 5.2).

Finally, specific legislation to promote international trade (adopted as early as the summer of 1980 by the military government) ended up favoring large capitalists and the corporations they controlled. More specifically, when determining who could actually trade and who could benefit from subsidies intended to stimulate Turkish exports, the state chose to favor larger private-sector establishments. To this end they introduced a legal framework and incentive system for the creation of "foreign trade companies" (FTCs) that were large import-export companies. In terms of size, the first step had been to set minimum standards by defining which FTCs could gain access to favorable treatment:

- Minimum export earnings of $15 million during the year preceding the application, with the additional condition that at least 50 percent of all exports would consist of mineral and manufactured products.
- An initial capital of at least TL 50 million (equivalent to $640 000) paid up over a twelve-month period [and] export growth at a rate of 10 percent per annum.[25]

These requirements may have been partly motivated by an ideological, almost romanticized, desire to create large national champions of trade (the same way South Korea had done with Chaebols). But it was also done with the more rational expectation that large establishments would be better positioned to benefit from economies of scale (or lower average costs from producing in large volumes), increasing the likelihood that they would become competitive. Under the new ELG model of development, the privileges and benefits these companies enjoyed were defined as:

1. The ability to use credits from the central bank's rediscount facilities with one-year maturity at favourable interest rates of 50 to 60 percent of commercial rates. 2. Allocation of foreign exchange from the "Export Promotion Fund" for importing raw materials required in the manufacture of products to be subsequently exported. 3. Permission to import investment goods and spare parts of up to 60 percent of projected exports. 4. Export tax rebates corresponding to 6 percent of export value in addition to tax rebates for which all exporters qualified on an item-by-item basis. 5. The right to maintain foreign currency holdings on a global basis, to be used in importing raw materials for the manufacture of exportable commodities embodied in the FTC's program. 6. The ability to contract (with government approval) medium term foreign credits up to two years. 7. Monopoly rights (jointly with SEEs) to import commodities from countries associated with COMECON.[26]

Thanks to these benefits and the volumes that needed to be achieved to obtain them, Öniş estimates that only a handful of sizeable FTCs were able to really expand their share of total exports throughout the 1980s. More importantly, he reports that this led the top FTCs to achieve roughly half of all Turkish exports by the end of the decade. This put the business elite and TÜSİAD members at an advantage. The trade companies with formal or organic ties to already established major corporations (which had the necessary capital to produce and trade in large volumes) were the ones that were positioned to take advantage of this new incentive system. For instance, the two major players from TÜSİAD, Koç and Sabancı Holdings, controlled RAM and EXSA, two of the top five Turkish FTCs. Öniş estimates that these two holdings were integrating world markets at a higher speed than the rest of the Turkish economy, given that the largest four FTCs (of which they were a part of) were responsible for 30 percent of the trade accomplished by all twenty-four Turkish trade companies. Hence, it can be said that TÜSİAD members were able to capitalize on their experience and connections to continue expanding into new sectors and to do relatively well in terms of trade.

However, despite these favorable changes, the momentous shift from ISI to ELG and navigating a new global economic order also engendered challenges that shaped the demands of the business elite. The growth in the size of capitalist enterprise under the business elite combined with increased trade created in the case of TÜSİAD members two sets of needs that made democracy more appealing and that can be characterized as: those that are exogenous (and more immediate or reactionary) and those that are more endogenous (and based on the long-term structure of the private sector). Exogenous and immediate factors refer to competitive edges Turkish business needed to acquire fast in order to stay above water in a more global economy (such as developing opportunities for trade or attracting foreign investment). These became salient not only because of the pressures trade created, but also because of a newer mechanism my interviews revealed: the business elite's increasing cosmopolitanism and the more mobile nature of capital. The rivalry between different countries to attract foreign investment meant that TÜSİAD members were approached with incentives by foreign governments, which made them size up their own political class and its shortcomings.

The endogenous evolution of the private sector, however, included deeper shifts firms underwent over decades (such as the growth in the size of private-sector enterprise) and the broader policy environment they needed in order to operate more efficiently. Taken together, both sets of changes made democracy and its institutions appealing to the business elite. While the chapter will reveal the link the business elite built between political change and economic needs by focusing on all of the above, the next two sections will turn attention to how the international environment and Turkey's place affected the needs of TÜSİAD members, by mostly relying on perspectives gathered during interviews. Needless to say, when the bulk of the interviews were conducted in 2001 and 2002, Turkish capitalists, like entrepreneurs in many other late-industrializing societies, saw themselves as being affected greatly by increased international competition.

Exogenous Factors

EU Integration and Democratization

Bülent Eczacıbaşı (the owner of one of the largest holdings and TÜSİAD chairman in the early 1990s) summarized the predicament of capitalists in late-industrializing nations well:

> You cannot achieve anything by imitating what everyone else is doing, even if you have cheap labor it does not work. If you decide to do something with cheap labor, there is always something that is produced in a place with cheaper labor. It comes out of Latin America, Asia or Africa, as such it is not a reliable competitive advantage. You have to do something.[27]

Eczacıbaşı's statement also highlights one of the main tensions NICs face as a result of international competition. Countries like Turkey who cannot compete on labor cost by entering a "race to the bottom" in global markets have to now innovate and increase productivity through more capital-intensive production. In the specific case of Turkey, the promise of a large market with the proximity of the EU played an important part of the business elite's perceptions. The maturity of capital (that production does not rely on labor control anymore) has propelled scholarship on TÜSİAD's democratizing role to overemphasize the role of EU membership by linking the timing of the association's demands to the ascension process[28]. As much as EU membership was important for the association's members (as will be outlined in the next few pages), the rest of the chapter also demonstrates that a deeper examination of business interest uncovers more fundamental and, at times, endogenous factors at play behind the appeal of democracy.

One telling sign that EU integration had become important for TÜSİAD by the 1990s and 2000s (and also the extent to which the association was increasingly willing to draw from the knowledge of experts) was the fact that several members and staff I spoke to suggested that I interview Cem Duna. Though a TÜSİAD member, he was not a businessperson by training. Duna had graduated from Ankara University's prestigious Faculty of Political Science in 1968, which at the time not only produced some of the country's highest-ranking bureaucrats but also some of the members of its left-wing intelligentsia (given the importance of student activism on its campus). After graduation, Duna entered the foreign service where he spent many years as ambassador in several European countries before becoming Turkey's representative within the EU and one of the chief negotiators in the country's membership process before retiring. I interviewed him in the offices of the consultancy firm that he had established in an Istanbul villa (rather than a high-rise dominating the Istanbul hills), from which he offered advice to Turkish businesses on entering foreign markets. These roles also allowed him to become a TÜSİAD member, where he was highly active in formulating the association's stance on the reforms needed to join the EU.

Unlike the fluid image of globalization in popular imagination, where capital moves freely and international trade is borderless, Cem Duna gave a different assessment of the post-1980 economic environment. He saw the world as being made up of three major trading bloc, or poles, within which most of economic activity took place. TÜSİAD's official position and other members I spoke to offered the same assessment. More specifically, the business elite was aware that the bulk of world trade and direct foreign investment took place within Europe, East Asia and North America. As a result, a majority of TÜSİAD members I interviewed underscored repeatedly that they dreaded the prospect of Turkey's isolation and felt that it should stay connected to the EU so that the private sector could continue to do well. Eczacıbaşı summarized the risk that they saw well:

> Turkey lives, even if not fully, in an economy that is integrated with the rest of the world with liberalization, the custom union, and an open economy ... As I mentioned earlier, we worry that we will be isolated from the rest of the world. There is the worry that the current situation will gradually push us into the status of a Third World country that loses its chance to integrate with the rest of the world. We worry that we are losing our chance to enter the European Union. Because unfortunately this is a real eventuality. As long as we continue adopting archaic measures the risk is very real. Europe can close its doors. Businesspeople see this. Faced with the risk of seeing doors closing and opportunities fleeing, [businesspeople] with the financial and organizational means, who are open to the world, who are forced to be open, who have very intensive relations with the

rest of the world realize that they must do something. [TÜSİAD's demands] are a product of this thought process.[29]

Although only in passing, Eczacıbaşı also touches on a fundamental theme that was raised often in my interviews: what he (and other entrepreneurs) sees as capitalists' unique vantage point embedded in their cosmopolitanism, or the observation that, unlike others, "businesspeople see" the problem because of their greater openness to the world. This point will be discussed further below as a factor that crystalized TÜSİAD's position. But as to why democracy was important to stay connected to the European bloc, Eczacıbaşı added:

> Why democratization? Why work to improve democratization? When we ask these, "the improvement of the economy must go through this" is not a complete explanation. We see that if we do not improve on these shortcomings that we will be left out from the rest of the world. We want to join the European Union. There are certain values that are valid around the world now, there are human rights, there are indicators of democracy, as long as we stay behind on these issues we will be pushed outside the world. We have seen to what stage we have come with the European Union, countries that have entered the European Union before us have passed us. There is the realization that we are missing the train.[30]

For TÜSİAD, the more immediate task was to therefore make sure that Turkey remained committed to European integration, its more natural and closest trade partner.[31] Within this framework, the desire for democratization was imposed through external forces. This point was further reinforced by Kayhan, a TÜSİAD member who had a broad vantage point about Turkish capitalism thanks to his role as a consultant:

> This is also what the international community wants of Turkey. We [Turkey] have always seen those who have said that Turkey needed democratic reforms as our enemies. If we continue to hold this opinion, Turkey will not have that many friends anymore. The democracy and human rights agenda always came about in relationship to the EU. However, we have seen that this is also of highest importance in the USA's agenda with Turkey. We should not be surprised or show any reaction. Because these are also universal values we seek to attend, they will always come about … Closed politics' inevitable result in the long term is a closed economy. A closed economy loses its competitiveness. It cannot find any sustainable markets. It will start to face problems of employment. As long as Turkey delays its democratic reforms, the international community's pressures increase. We close ourselves the more we react instead of dealing with this pressure by surpassing ourselves and changing.[32]

A cursory glance at Turkey's trade partners (Table 5.1) during the period confirms the central role that Europe, and EU member countries in particular, played in increasing the urgency of the reforms the business elite was pressing for.

Table 5.1 Turkish Exports' Major Destinations in 2002

Country	Value in millions of USD	Percent share of total exports
Germany	5,869	16.3
United States	3,356	9.3
England	3,025	8.4
Italy	2,376	6.6
France	2,135	5.9
Spain	1,125	3.1
Holland	1,056	2.9
Russia	1,172	3.3
Israel	861	2.4
Romania	566	1.6
Total	21,541	59.7

Source: World Bank, "Turkey Trade Statistics," https://wits.worldbank.org/countryprofile/en/tur. Accessed August 5, 2022.

It should be emphasized that, at the time, other business organizations representing the more pious and smaller-sized sectors of the Turkish bourgeoisie were building networks to try and trade with the Middle East (and in more general terms the Global South), which they saw as culturally closer to Turkey and as being ripe for change.[33] This was also confirmed through my interview with the president of TUSKON, which was closer to SMEs from the religious Gülenist movement. He took great care to illustrate how his association had built ties with African as well as Balkan nations, which the traditional business elite tended to ignore. For the latter, as underscored by a TÜSİAD member, Northern partners seemed to remain preferable, making the EU all the more central:

> What does Turkey have as an alternative? There is no viable pact beyond the European Union. I do not believe in the Black Sea Economic Cooperation, I do not believe in the Middle East, Turkey's natural ally is Europe. But for trade its natural allies are both going to be Europe and Russia. We have to expand our relationship with Russia. We angered Russia a bit much when we got close to places like [unintelligible], Azerbaijan, Turkmenistan. I think it is a mistake. As a businessman I support the development of trade, political, and economic relations with Russia.[34]

Thus, economically staying close to the EU was important. The central place that my informants gave to the need to stay connected to an economic pole (or bloc) raises the legitimate question of whether TÜSİAD pressed for democratization with the only end goal of joining the EU (as political reform in the country was one condition put forth during Turkey's membership negotiations). In fact, a consultant and TÜSİAD member I spoke to built this link quite clearly:

> Why is TÜSİAD speaking of the equality between men and women? Because it is a criteria of the European Union. In 2002 the EU is the most important thing. We, as TÜSİAD, concentrate on every subject to be able to enter the EU ... There

is a win-win situation between the EU and Turkey. The EU wins from Turkey joining. Turkey also wins. This is why like TÜSİAD I support that [Turkey] joins the EU even if it is done haphazardly.[35]

This, in of itself, would be an interesting finding about the exogenous democratizing impact that the EU, unlike other trade blocs, has on countries in its periphery. The central place of the EU has also been used by Bayer and Öniş in their analysis of TÜSİAD's demands in order to assert that the business elite's interest in democracy was limited to the ascension process[36] As such, in order to understand the relationship between capitalist interest and democracy, any meaningful discussion linking the economic interests of TÜSİAD members to their political action must assess the degree to which they were only passively responding to pressures for change from outside or whether they had some level of agency and were driven equally by endogenous factors when pushing for democracy. This question is, first and foremost, worth addressing to make the findings in subsequent sections and chapters amenable to comparison with other country cases and other writing that deal with democracy and capitalist interest. On this point, there is some evidence to suggest that integration to the EU was not only seen an end in itself for, but more so a means to an end in order to push for democracy. Determining whether democracy was appealing intrinsically entails a broader birds-eye view of the period that goes beyond focusing on TÜSİAD's role in the ascension process. There are several factors that suggest this was the case.

First, TÜSİAD was the only Turkish association at the time that pressed for the types of democratic reform needed for EU ascension. Thus, the unique factors that shaped TÜSİAD' tripolar vision of the world and made its members see greater material benefits associated with being part of Europe (or conversely great perils should Turkey be left out) should be considered. Second, and related to this point, choosing to be part of Europe was a strategic deliberate move, as attested by several individuals I spoke to. Here, someone in upper management at Koç Holding emphasized why it was important for Turkey to join to capitalize on its potential for great political power:

> What would happen if European integration does not work? When Turkey considers its trade balance with Europe it becomes apparent that we are already integrated in terms of industry. There are no other alternatives, that is the situation. If we stay out of this community, we will have wasted everything we have accomplished so far. This has to go forward now. I just told you the economic and industrial element of the story. I will also touch on the other dimension. Turkey is now Europe's seventh largest economy. In 2010 it will be the fifth largest economy. This is in terms of size, in terms of volume these figures are still very low, but in terms of size it is the seventh largest among the twenty-eight countries. If you look at its population and contribution, it is the fifth largest ... This entails the following, Turkey would be the fifth largest country after France, Germany, England, and Italy in the European parliament. It will be the largest represented country in the parliament. Soon there will

be 900 parliamentarians, ninety could be Turkish. This means that not only economically, but also politically, Turkey could take part as an important nation in the European decision-making process ... If this does not happen [Turkey] will face the problems of Third World countries. The integration with Europe will continue the way it is, but it will fall to the status of a Third World country. When we could be part of a team as a leading force, we will become a Third World country like Pakistan, Bangladesh, and India. [Integration] is to Turkey's advantage industrially, commercially and socially. This is why we as industrialists support European integration.[37]

Thus, TÜSİAD members not only saw some risk in remaining a peripheral economy, but they also emphasized the political opportunity that being a full-fledged EU partner entailed. Third, as will be covered at the end of the current chapter, TÜSİAD member firms had undergone significant structural changes that made democracy appealing for more reasons than just belonging to a bloc. Many interviewees touched on the social dimensions of democracy (such as education) as needed to have a dynamic capitalist economy domestically.

Finally, the political reforms TÜSİAD proposed were not solely guided and constrained by the necessary reforms to enter the EU. My interview with its deputy general secretary at the time reconfirmed the fact that TÜSİAD's more political activities were burgeoning in the late 1980s and early 1990s, before talks of official membership to the EU. But the issues the association tackled prior to 1997 were approached in ad hoc fashion. As a result, membership talks helped anchor and focus some of the activities that TÜSİAD was already undertaking by offering a roadmap for change. If anything, the EU tended to be relatively vague when proposing a list of needed reforms for Turkey's membership. TÜSİAD's demands provided more depth, breadth and clarity to what was needed to be done in order to democratize Turkey.[38] Thus, it can be said that EU ascension bestowed the business elite's demands with greater legitimacy and provided a concrete direction. But it was not the sole goal. Thus, factors that both created the need to integrate and made democratization more desirable for intrinsic reasons will be explored next. These were not only guided by the appeal of the EU, but were also driven by the fact that capital was operating in a different, more competitive environment.

Foreign Investment and State Reform

In terms of short-term solutions for the business elite's ability to stay competitive, international pressures made reform appealing for two reasons: the need to increase foreign investment in order to increase productivity, and the shortcomings of the Turkish state when it came to providing the private sector with competitive edges. As seen in previous pages, many interviewees had stated that competitiveness based on product and process innovations, rather than cheap labor, had become crucial during the post-1980 period. The central role that foreign partnerships play for Turkish holdings to produce a range of goods and import technology combined with the lack of domestic investment in research and development

(R&D) made foreign direct investment (FDI) particularly desirable. The central role played by foreign partnerships was summarized well when asked whether TÜSİAD members pushed for reforms to remain competitive or whether they did so because they already felt they had the strength to compete, a top-ranking professional at Koç Holding gave the following answer outlining the importance of FDI and competition:

> There has been the emergence of an industrial structure capable of merging with Europe … We have to consider the role of joint ventures here. There are 3,600 joint ventures in Turkey and foreign organizations. These are mostly industrial organizations, I want to give a few examples: Mercedes, Daimler-Benz has been in Turkey for thirty years, Siemens for forty years, Bosch has been in Turkey for twenty-five years. These firms had already chosen Turkey as a production base, before our integration into Europe had even started. These started for the domestic market, before, it started with import substitution, when we decided to produce instead of importing, for example the automotive sector started this way. After going through a period of infancy and reaching adolescence, at that moment industry became capable of exporting. Today [Turkey] exports Dunlop to the rest of the world, FIAT, Renault builds the Megan for the entire European region here, Daimler-Benz builds buses for Europe and the rest of the world here in Turkey, all the parallel [automotive] industries started this way. There are now international brands in textiles, from Lafayette to Burberry's.[39]

In sum, foreign partnerships had long roots and had started as a way for their foreign partners to sell in the country during the protectionist era in the 1970s. It had allowed the business elite to move into many new sectors, such as automotive. In the 1980s, it became a strategy to export from Turkey toward Europe. In the process, holdings had acquired much-needed investment and the necessary know-how to develop new industries. However, this approach hit a roadblock in the late 1990s and early 2000s when financial deregulation and uncertainty made Turkey particularly attractive for "hot money" seeking short-term rents as opposed to longer-term investments.[40] During the period, when TÜSİAD members were first interviewed for the project, Turkey's FDI as a percentage of GDP hovered only at around 0.4 percent. OECD (Organisation for Economic Co-operation and Development) members and middle-income countries, however, were on average able to attract 1.5 to 2 percent of their GDP as foreign investments. More importantly, FDI flows were, everywhere, on the cusp of increasing during the period, while they seemed to remain stagnant in Turkey (Figure 5.3).

Turkey's lackluster performance in terms of FDI became a central concern for my respondents because they felt that combined with Turkey's lack of R&D they would not be able to compete based on innovation (Figure 5.4). Duna for instance, during our interview, emphasized that the innovation time gap has decreased considerably and believed that TÜSİAD members needed to attract foreign investment and transfer technology lest they become even more isolated in the tripolar world they all described.[41] This feeling was also shared by my other interviewees, who saw the Turkish private sector's ability to compete as being heavily dependent on its ability to adopt foreign technology through partnerships, in the face of a lack of R&D in Turkey:

> [To maintain competitiveness] you must do something. You must renew the process or the product. And this requires R and D activity, it requires spending. Institutions do not have the means. There are very big problems.[42]

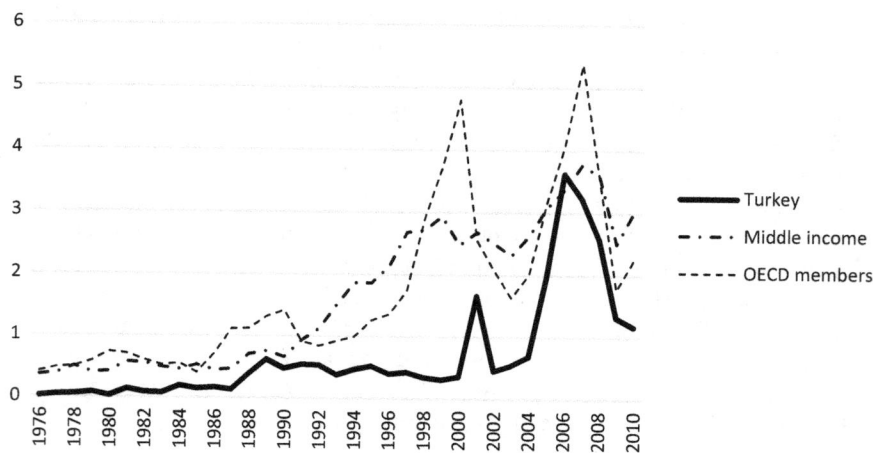

Figure 5.3 FDI as a percentage of GDP.
Source: "World Development Indicators," https://databank.worldbank.org/source/world-development-indicators. Accessed August 5, 2022.

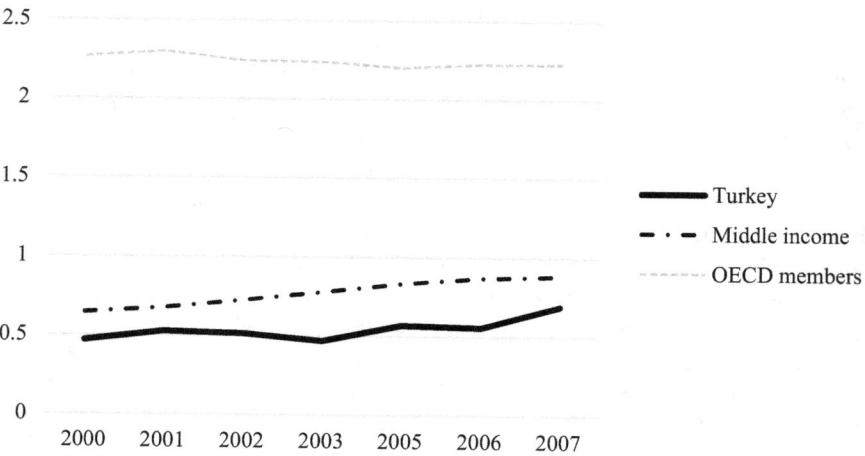

Figure 5.4 R&D as a percentage of GDP.
Source: "World Development Indicators," https://databank.worldbank.org/source/world-development-indicators. Accessed August 5, 2022.

Given low levels of research, political elements such as international respectability, stability, and overall state reform were often associated with the need to attract investment to Turkey.

Kaslowski put it bluntly "[When speaking of the importance of the rule of law and certainty] "I would not want to invest in Burundi; I cannot expect someone to invest in Turkey."[43] Many other interviewees and the organizations' leadership built more detailed linkages between the need to attract investment and Turkey's political situation at the time, as echoed by a higher TÜSİAD advisory council speech delivered by its president:

> Foreign capital entries to Turkey have decreased to their lowest level of the past ten years. We can interpret this as the most obvious indicator of negative expectations about our country's economic and political stability. Although Turkey needs foreign capital to accelerate its development, and has the potential to realize this, it gradually gets a smaller share of foreign capital flows.[44]

TÜSİAD's official stance and my interviewees, thus, underscored the importance of such themes as political and economic reform and the rule of law and certainty, which they began to perceive as needed to attract investment and develop production. However, these issues became particularly salient because by operating in a more international environment the business elite not only felt pressures, but also gained new perspective about the kind of state intervention it needed thanks to what can be broadly called business cosmopolitanism.

Business Cosmopolitanism

In-depth interviews with members of the capitalist class offer the opportunity to witness how globalization has made them personally more cosmopolitan and how this, in turn, has impacted their worldviews. Rather than treat "capital flows" as impersonal and abstract, it allows for understanding how entrepreneurs navigate the global economy. A nonnegligible number of TÜSİAD members (often during the more conversational portions of our meetings) lamented that their foreign business partners frequently asked them questions about the political situation in Turkey. Some felt embarrassed about being repeatedly put on the spot rather than be allowed to focus on their business trips. In that sense, as will be seen in the next chapter, embracing a democratizing role was a way to shed the weight of having to constantly justify their country's actions. There was, among interviewees, the shared feeling that the state could do more to increase the international respectability of Turkey by enhancing democratic norms. For the immediate focus of the current chapter, however, this growing internationalism was pivotal to the extent that it gave them an additional vantage point from which they could judge the Turkish state in terms of economic policy and efficiency. First, they have been able to contrast the services and business environment offered by the Turkish state to other business opportunities. Second, partnerships with foreign companies and trade further reinforced skepticism about the Turkish government by offering possibilities for growth that were previously not present under state-led models of development.

On the first point, two interviewees outlined specific examples of instances when foreign governments offered them very advantageous conditions for investment in their countries. Meltem Kurtsan, whose family holding has specialized in natural pharmaceuticals, listed several Eastern European governments which approached her with tax-free incentives to establish factories within their borders. Similarly, Erkut Yücaoğlu, who runs an industrial logistics company from a modest office space in the heart of Istanbul, described how he had been wooed by a Balkan nation to invest in a power plant construction project. These types of interactions led them to witness firsthand the kinds of incentives that were available to them elsewhere and highlighted the shortcomings of the Turkish state. This, they both pointed out, stood in sharp contrast to the lengthy bureaucratic process involved with investing in Turkey.[45]

Second, these kinds of comparisons and the need to stay competitive more broadly impacted TÜSİAD's perception of the Turkish state by making problems with the general business environment visible. For instance, a striking majority of my interviewees complained about the higher energy costs and increased input prices they had to operate with compared to foreign competitors. Many also stressed the lack of adequate infrastructure (mainly transportation and communication) which hindered private-sector efficiency by increasing production costs. Hence, operating in an international environment, while trying to stay competitive, further crystalized in the business elite's minds that political reform, a new development paradigm, and a new role for the state all went hand in hand to improve private-sector performance. Investment opportunities abroad were really linked to the question of good governance and good development policy and not directly linked to issues of increased democracy. However, it was often intertwined with the interviewees' desire for political reform broadly speaking as it had brought a fundamental change to their relationship to the state. TÜSİAD and its members have increasingly talked of good governance as a way to make the private sector more efficient. Furthermore, they have underscored liberalization of some sectors of the economy, like energy, as a way to make more efficient use of resources to increase the Turkish private sector's ability to compete. Hence, the juxtaposition of a private sector willing to compete and an inefficient state in light of globalization transpired as a recurrent theme in many of the interviews.

Third, the above transformation was made even more salient because of the metamorphosis undergone by the private sector as a result of integrating the global economy. More specifically, being in joint ventures with foreign partners and turning outward through exports enhanced the business elite's and members' sense of legitimacy. One interviewee (Mehmet Şuhubi), who owned a smaller manufacturing company by TÜSİAD's standards, outlined in detail how he had formed a partnership with an American firm and how this eventually has changed his entire operation and perception of the Turkish state:

The partnership in 1998 started with thirty workers. How large is it now? 380 workers. And what is the difference between my revenue today and my revenue in 1998? It is ten times more. How is this possible when everyone is going bankrupt in Turkey? It has to do with exportation. People who have decided that they have no other option than exporting are in [TÜSİAD] now. What has this brought us? A high value-added automotive sector and the exportation of textiles ... The businessman's mentality has changed ... Why does Turkey not go bankrupt with this political system? Because exports are still at 34 to 35 billion dollars.[46]

Finally, foreign partnerships, like the one described by Şuhubi, put a more structural or fundamental strain on the informal nature of state-business relations in Turkey. Trade and being accountable to foreign partners compelled more outward-oriented businesses to adopt international norms and more formal reporting tools. In more general terms, one of my interviewees close to TÜSİAD, who knows the needs of the private sector well, emphasized the fact that doing business internationally has forced the members of TÜSİAD to adopt "codes" that did not exist in Turkey before. This theme was also echoed in one of my interviews by a TÜSİAD member:

> Large businessmen, bosses do not usually want the type of reforms pushed by TÜSİAD. But the world has become global. In a global environment, international capital prefers more transparent, more ethical and straightforward places. For this reason, Turkey has two worries in the long term. One is to increase exportation and the second is to attract foreign capital. Issues such as transparency, ethics, and corporate governance are very important for both. In an environment where the legal system is not working properly this takes time. So, I think that the number one priority for firms should be to internalize these practices.[47]

As such, the more pervasive impact on the Turkish capitalist class of expanding global trade and partnerships is not only the need to stay competitive, but to be compelled to adopt international norms of corporate governance. Greater formalism, as will be discussed in more detail in the next section and chapter, created tensions between the patrimonial nature of the Turkish state and the greater bureaucratization of the private sector, which started experiencing limits to the advantages they could obtain from informal relations to the government that existed and the new norms that private enterprise has had to adopt.

Taken all together, the new global environment in which TÜSİAD members operated represented a mix of opportunities and constraints. While the manufacturing sector grew over the period and was able to take advantage of expanding trade, as evidenced by the data, they also became increasingly aware of the Turkish private sector's vulnerabilities and of the shortcomings of their own state. In other words, TÜSİAD members are confident enough in their strength to accept a new politico-economic arrangement yet they feel vulnerable enough to seek reforms that would help the private sector. The existence of this tension raises the following question. Why did the business elite choose to press for significant political reform and further integration instead of working as a reactionary force to maintain protective barriers and its access to rent provided by the patrimonial Turkish state? For an answer, one must turn to the structural changes that the business elite and TÜSİAD member firms had been undergoing for many years prior to the period. When combined with international pressures and the desire to be competitive, the endogenous evolution of Turkish capital made political reform even more necessary.

Endogenous Factors

Capital-Intensive Production and Expansion

As illustrated by a high-ranking executive from a major holding company (Alarko), there was a tendency among some TÜSİAD members to link democracy's multiple facets to a range of economic opportunities and challenges the private sector was facing:

> [The only factor] is not the EU. [TÜSİAD] realized what the absolutely necessary conditions after the transition to a liberal economy [were]: labor rights, civil servant rights, and political stability. [TÜSİAD] became conscious of the fact that these could promote foreign investment and expand markets..[48]

The range of connections built in this manner cannot be fully understood without seeing the pressures faced by the business elite in the context of deeper changes they were undergoing domestically, namely: the growing capital intensity of production and expanding size of private-sector establishments. Thus, democracy did not only become more desirable as a result of globalization, but also because international integration was specifically happening during a period in Turkish history when large capital was undergoing significant changes itself. Moreover, the business elite's transformation was juxtaposed to and brought to light domestic problems that made it harder for the business elite to operate. These included, more specifically, factors such as uncertainty, low domestic consumption, and the lack of skilled labor, to name just a few. In a nutshell, as industrialists moved toward more capital-intensive production and greater levels of bureaucratization, they increasingly needed the broader environment to adjust in order to make long-term planning possible. Hence, the maturity of capital made change attractive.

The politico-economic environment of the post-1980 period left the business elite in a quagmire. Outward models of growth through FDI and exports became more appealing to make up for the shortcomings of the Turkish economy and state, but at the same time staying competitive internationally required some of the domestic conditions business was facing to change in order to build the necessary capacity to remain competitive. Most TÜSİAD members I spoke to underscored that firms linked to the association had become more capital intensive and required greater levels of investment to achieve productivity. They needed greater certainty in order to achieve this. Thus, tensions between a changing private sector and an inadequate business environment not only made turning abroad more appealing to TÜSİAD, but also served to highlight the problems to be solved domestically to sustain growth and become competitive internationally. Taken together, these factors put demands for democracy front and center as a way to not only address short-term problems created by internationalization, but also tackle some of the deeper transformations the business elite was experiencing.

The Heavier Phase of Industrialization

One of the most revealing aspects of TÜSİAD's desire to bring about change to the broader environments is the fact that the Turkish business elite and its holdings had previously developed strategies to cope with economic uncertainty. Historically, building particularistic ties with state officials, diversifying their portfolios, and investing in wide-ranging sectors provided holdings, as revealed by Buğra's study, an effective strategy to adapt to precariousness.[49] In addition, holdings had been able to absorb some of the cost of uncertainty by acting, for all intents and purposes, like financial institutions that benefited from the high interest rates that uncertainty created and yields on government bonds that state spending engendered. More specifically, the negative impact that high government spending had on the real sector was buffered by two strategies that holdings used in tandem: they received cheap subsidies from government for their industrial investments at the same time as they were issuing high interest bonds through their financial subsidiaries.[50] How the Turkish private sector operated is well summarized by Mehmet Şuhubi in his interview:

> Governments constantly had recourse to easy external debt; they then used this in wrong places and eliminated the opportunity to service the debt. Banks turned a blind eye on this businessmen were also ignoring it; they were investing in government bonds without risking losses; banks were borrowing from outside and investing it in [bonds]. Businessmen were using the advantage of rapid growth and expanding fast with the "I will grow as much as I can get from Ankara [the State]" mentality, creating employment. Turkey's population was constantly growing, investments were directed to wrong places, easier investments were chosen, and chances of servicing the debt were lost due to low value-added investments. In an environment like this, it was apparent that the end was in sight; the 1994 crisis was an alarm bell.[51]

However, according to my interviewees, this strategy of hedging their investments had become unsustainable because the business elite needed greater certainty in order develop capital-intensive production and increase productivity. While the previous discussion about the business elite's export performance in newer sectors (such as machinery and transportation) suggested that the move to capital-intensive production was indeed happening, a closer look at industry in general and large establishments in particular further highlights this fundamental shift.

A clear indication that the Turkish industry has become more intensive can be found in labor productivity measures. Even though the percentage of workers employed in the sector decreased to about 22 percent in 1996 (down from 32.6 percent in 1984), the share of industry in value-added increased from an around 20 percent in the 1970s to about 30 percent during the period from 1985 to 1996. Thus, industry could produce a greater share with a smaller proportion of the workforce. As importantly, the increase of productivity was accompanied by a shift in the sectoral makeup of manufacturing sectors. The share of value-added of what could be considered heavier sectors, such as transportation and machinery, was only 8.5 percent in the 1960s and reached 16–18 percent in the 1990s. This change was already underway in the 1970s when these more capital-heavy sectors were producing around 15 percent of value-added.[52]

The particular position of the Turkish business elite makes these aggregate observations even more salient. Chapter 4 had highlighted that decades of developmentalist policies (starting in the 1950s) had really been focused on large establishments around Istanbul. The chapter had further demonstrated that this had been one of the main impetus behind forming TÜSİAD to represent the interests of larger capital during a period when its interests were diverging from the rest of the private sector. Because TÜSİAD members were already involved in heavy industry and capital-intensive production, the development of the Turkish economy discussed above likely affected the business elite more than the rest of the capitalist class. As such, the fact that industry kept a similar pace toward more capital-heavy production in the 1980s and 1990s placed the business elite in a distinct position, especially when combined with its growingly outward-oriented nature:

> Turkey was a country that was exporting raw materials and agricultural products. During the fifties and sixties Turkey was selling wheat and salt. In the 1980s, Turkey has tried to catch up to world technology and in doing so turned from its characteristic specialty agriculture to industry. Today 85 percent of its export are in industry, so it is the exact opposite of what it was fifty years ago. We are not entirely an industrial nation, but despite this the intermediate products we produce, not high-tech products, we are not Japan or South Korea, has created an industry capable of merging with Europe. In doing so, Turkey has reached world standards in consumer durables, in automotive and textiles.[53]

The manufacturing sector reaped the benefits of this change (as was seen in earlier sections) through a surge in its exports. Manufacturing made up a measly 2 percent of exports throughout the 1960s and witnessed a hike in the 1970s to reach about 27 percent in 1977, before Turkey's debt crisis. It is in the late 1980s, however, that manufacturing exports soared to make up around two-thirds of all exports and continued to climb to reach 75 percent in the mid-1990s.[54] There is strong evidence to suggest that the business elite was specifically impacted by these broad general trends in the rise of productivity and exports. In 1997, around 200 members' firms

Table 5.2 Large Holdings Linked to TÜSİAD and Their Sectors of Activity

Name	Date	Sectors started	Sectors active in 2000
Alarko Holding AS	1954	Heating/air conditioning	Contracting, land development, heating/air conditioning, tourism, seafood, energy
Borusan	1944	Steel pipes	Steel (pipes and sheets), automobile and machine dealership, IT, and communication (2002)
Eczacıbaşı Holding AS	1942	Pharmaceuticals	Pharmaceuticals, construction material, consumer products, IT, finance, and welding technology
Enka Holding	1957	Construction, industrial contracting, steel hand tools and plastics	Construction, engineering (highways, power plants, airports, industrial complexes)
Koç Holding	1926	Small store and construction material sale, move to industry with GE light bulbs	Automotive, consumer durables, food processing, banking, tourism and services, construction
Sabancı Holding	1925	Cotton trade	Automotive, finance, food, IT, tires and transmissions, chemicals, cement, paper products, tourism, and international trade
Tekfen Holding AS	1957	Construction, light bulbs (35% of Turkish market share until the end of 2002)	Construction and engineering (pipelines, refineries, industrial complexes, telecommunication, power stations, airports and seaports), agricultural products (fertilizers), finance, real estate, foreign trade (revenue of 3.4 billion USD in 2002)

Sources: Alarko Holding, "Alarko Holding Groups," https://www.alarko.com.tr/en/groups/overview. Accessed August 5, 2022.
Borusan Holding, "Borusan Group Companies," https://www.borusan.com/en/group-companies/group-companies-borusan-holding. Accessed August 5, 2022.
Eczacıbaşı Holding, "Eczacıbaşı Markalar," https://www.eczacibasi.com.tr/en/brands. Accessed August 5, 2022.
Enka Holding, "What We Do," https://www.enka.com/what-we-do/. Accessed August 5, 2022.
Koç Holding, "Sectors," https://www.koc.com.tr/activity-fields/sectors. Accessed August 5, 2022.
Sabancı Holding, "Sabancı Ventures," https://ventures.sabanci.com/en/. Accessed August 5, 2022.
Buğra (1994).

surveyed by TÜSİAD during an internal study produced over 40 percent of the value-added in the manufacturing, construction, and banking sectors of Turkey.[55] Moreover, establishments in Turkey with over 1,000 employees, which are where the TÜSİAD members are originally drawn from, represented just over 1 percent of businesses from 1993 to 1999. However, these also produced roughly 34 percent of all the value-added in 1998.[56]

This would suggest that years of capital accumulation (starting as early as the 1950s and 1960s) eventually made the business elite and their establishments more capital intensive than the rest of the economy (Table 5.2). The move to the heavier, more complex phase of production has inevitably increased TÜSİAD members' stake in the stability of the politico-economic environment. The type of sectors they operated in, such as automotive, and higher levels of productivity they were trying to achieve required longer-term investment in capital-heavy machinery. The latter often comes with a steep price tag (or sunk costs) and requires a longer-term outlook to become profitable, which led members of the business elite to value some level of certainty. Yet, around the time TÜSİAD published its *Democratization Report* the Turkish economy was far from being predictable. The country was plagued by financial crises, high inflation, and extremely variable growth rates since the end of the 1980s.[57] From the start of market reforms in the early 1980s up until 1989, the annual growth in GDP fluctuated between 3.5 and 7.01 percent to reach a high of 9.48 in 1987. However, after a low of 0.25 percent in 1989, GDP growth went on to fluctuate extensively between periods of expansion above 9 percent in 1991 and 1992, and recession of -5.45 percent in 1994. TÜSİAD's leadership have, accordingly, often addressed in speeches how state reform and more democratic institutions were necessary to decrease economic uncertainty:

> Speculations about early elections are always on the agenda. The next election becomes the determinant of every political and economic decision; there is no one able to look beyond the next election left ... As long as political instability remains, it becomes impossible to take the necessary measures to ensure economic stability. The economy is forgotten and loses its place in the country's agenda, while everyone is busy dealing with political struggles. That the economy does not enter a crisis becomes the only measure of economic governance. We then realize that we have become the world champions in inflation, but we are not even aware of it.[58]

> ... That Turkey's democracy and all of its institutions function well concerns also the Turkish economy closely. I want to substantiate this claim by drawing your attention to a recent issue ... All the constitutions to this day have given governments the responsibility to draft the yearly state budget. The budget has to be approved by the National Assembly. But in practice there is no role given to the National Assembly to check whether spending has been done according to the approval.[59]

The issue was of particular importance because most of the burden of capital investment fell directly on firms' own capital given several factors. First, as seen before, the share of FDI in capital formation is low. Second, state subsidies to industry have declined since the 1980s and the period of economic liberalization. And third, the stock market represents a very small share of each firm in Turkey where firms are mostly family owned. During the first decade of the twenty-first century, the average market capitalization (or the value of a company's outstanding shares) never went below 35 percent of GDP in middle-income countries taken as a whole, and domestic credit to the private sector always hovered at above 60 percent of GDP. In Turkey, however, most of investment comes from businesses' own accumulated capital as credits to the private sector were only 33 percent of

GDP in 2008 (and reached 60 percent only in 2014) and market capitalization oscillated between 14 and 44 percent between 1994 and 2010.⁶⁰

Thus, it was not surprising that the members I spoke to and TÜSİAD in its official stance increasingly saw democratization as a means to tackle levels of uncertainty that were plaguing Turkish politics and the economy. More importantly, this shift also suggests that the strategies that holdings had developed to deal with uncertainty had reached their limits. Demands for democracy thus signaled that TÜSİAD increasingly represents the interests of its members as real sector producers, and that adapting to uncertainty through diversification and financial gains had lost their viability. With more capital-intensive investments financed by the business community itself, the stakes have therefore gotten bigger for capital that needs a longer-term prospect and protection for its operations. As noted by the General Secretary of TÜSİAD Haluk Tükel, "[TÜSİAD members] want to use capital well, but crises take away most of the investment."⁶¹ The vulnerability of even large Turkish corporations to the crises was echoed by two other interviewees, Kaslowski and Şuhubi, who have emphasized the fact that even most large corporations have lost a sizeable portion of their assets due to the crises.⁶² The solutions typically presented by TÜSİAD speeches were political stability, mainly through electoral reforms, good governance, and the rule of law in order to implement medium- to long-term growth strategies. For instance, the TÜSİAD chair (who presided after the *Democratization Report* was published) linked frequent changes in government to incoherent policy:

> We have changed governments five times just in the last two years. Within this environment governments have always shunned from taking political risks. Long term decisions have always been postponed and economic policies have only been directed to controlling short term fluctuations.⁶³

While the proposed medium-term economic plan usually included the following themes, as summarized by Chairman Komili, who had really been pivotal in pushing for democratization, in a 1995 speech:

> The Turkish economy strongly needs [a medium-term stability program]. This program must include certain reforms, which are: (1) Increasing the productivity and competitiveness of Turkish industry through privatization, attracting foreign capital into the country and incentives to renew technology. (2) Developing institutional restraints on state spending. (3) The development of all necessary laws and institutions that permit the collection of taxes on a fair, widespread and in a manner that promotes recorded economic activity, so that it becomes an efficient fiscal policy tool. (4) The reform of the bankrupt social security system.⁶⁴

This situation is therefore a shift in the preferences of TÜSİAD from the period when large capital could hedge uncertainty in the ways it organized and built its relations to the state. Capital-intensive production therefore dictated new sets of relations to the state and the need for a new politico-economic environment.

Capital-Intensive Production and the Social Dimension of Democracy

One of the areas that was made salient by the expansion in productive capacities was the need for a larger domestic market and a more qualified labor force. For this reason, social dimensions of democracy, as opposed to its narrow procedural notion, also came to the fore in TÜSİAD's activities and the individual forays of its members in civil society. Education as a topic was extensively dealt with by TÜSİAD in a series of reports and in the publication of two "model textbooks" in high school history and geography. The latter emphasized greater critical-thinking skills and more global knowledge, instead of linear accounts that textbooks typically offered. At the same time, two foundations linked to TÜSİAD's largest holdings established Koç and Sabancı Universities to compete directly with the country's top prestigious public universities. In addition, the Sabancı Foundation, with the goal of providing free quality education, has been operating thirty-eight primary and secondary schools across eleven municipalities. In terms of income distribution, in addition to a TÜSİAD report on the topic, Sakıp Sabancı (the founding owner of the second largest corporation) authored and published a study that investigated economic inequality in the southeastern Kurdish part of Turkey.[65] The interviews I conducted with TÜSİAD members revealed why the issue was of particular importance. Many specifically pointed to the fact that poverty and conflict in the region between military forces and Kurdish militia further limited the size of the Turkish market. However, they also emphasized that the war had drained taxes, which they felt was mostly financed through large corporations.

But education and income distribution were also seen as being paramount for the general economic environment by the members I spoke to (particularly those from larger holdings making long-term investments). The high capital-high productivity production complex they were moving to made change on these two dimensions especially important. Income distribution was needed to achieve economies of scale (or decrease the cost of production by churning out goods in larger numbers) through expanding the domestic Turkish market. In other words, the sunk investment costs required by the deeper, more capital intensive phase of production necessitated a bigger domestic market to make it viable. Within this context, given the progress that industry had made in Turkey, purchasing power had not undergone as considerable an increase during the two decades preceding TÜSİAD's *Democratization Report*. GDP per capita in 1996 had gone up only to around USD2,900 compared to about USD2,100 on average over the 1970s.[66] Hence, the size of the domestic market was presented as one major area of concern that explained TÜSİAD's desire for more meaningful political reform, and this for several reasons.

First, my interviewees felt that income redistribution was key in stimulating growth and giving business access to a larger market.[67]

> We have to achieve growth. Increasing the purchasing power must go through growth but also by correcting income distribution. What is important again is to have economic equilibrium. We are happy because we are growing fast for two

years in a country where there is macroeconomic disequilibrium; we then realize that this growth has been offset by large drops, the national income has not grown in a country where the population growth is 2 percent. In this environment the market does not grow, and the private sector cannot find markets. Worsening income inequality is also a function of inflation. As such, when we speak of creating markets, we have to speak of fast and balanced growth.[68]

Second, the limited domestic market was seen as an element forcing Turkish business to look for an outward-oriented growth model in order to have access to larger markets. These two factors taken together created a tension for the Turkish industry: it could operate with a small domestic market thanks to exports, but at the same time expanding demand in Turkey would also allow Turkish capitalists to be more competitive abroad. During our interview, Oktay Varlıer,[69] also linked to one of the larger holdings, felt that Turkey could take even greater advantage from trading with the EU only if it developed its own market and looked to trade with countries in Central Asia in order to benefit from economies of scale; he added that this was pretty much what Spain had done to increase its competitiveness in the EU by achieving economies of scales owing to its cultural and historical proximity to South America.

As for education, the common underlying factor was that productivity had gained primacy in being competitive over cheap labor. Most of my interviewees highlighted the lack of a skilled workforce as a problem faced by the Turkish economy and realized that Turkey could not compete in world markets based on a wage advantage. This is why the lack of a properly functioning training and education system, which is able to create a skilled workforce, was one area of complaint coming from both my interviewees, TÜSİAD speeches, and publications.

> There is a need for skilled labor now. For these reasons issues such as education, democracy, Cyprus, and human rights have come to the forefront of the agenda ... There is a private sector that is ready to compete, instead of selling to the state.[70]

It can therefore be said that the 1990s became a period when the need to sustain a high productivity-skilled labor complex was felt strongly, compelling capitalists to focus on the more social dimensions of democracy. Outward-looking models of growth through exports could have been a possible way to overcome the shortcomings of the domestic economic environment. But, in addition to creating its own intrinsic pressures for democracy (such as being part of the European bloc), the need to stay competitive internationally also made domestic limitations more noticeable. TÜSİAD members needed a larger national market to achieve economies of scale and also needed a more skilled workforce. Hence, the juxtaposition of increased competition and endogenous changes has worked to make democracy appealing both for external and internal reasons.

Microorganizational Changes and Democracy

A final factor worth noting are the microorganizational changes that firms linked to TÜSİAD underwent, as they are fundamentally linked to a tension in state-business relations. Even if the trend has been slow in comparative terms, holdings have grown in size and have increasingly relied on professional managers throughout the post-1980 period. This is significant for the discussion on democracy and state reform because, as illustrated by Buğra (and emphasized throughout the book), informal state-business relations and the benefits that entrepreneurs got from maintaining close ties to the state had propelled holdings to remain under family control. Moreover, this was a significant strategy the business elite had employed in order to adjust to uncertainty and also the patrimonial nature of the Turkish state. As such, some scholars, like Biddle and Milor, are skeptical about the degree to which an association such as TÜSİAD, whose members have benefited from informal channels to the state, can be committed to increased professionalization within their organizations and (by extension) to state reform.[71] Not surprisingly, two consultants with outsider-insider perspectives to the business elite I spoke to, Başaran-Symes and Kaynar, also stressed that professionalization had been slow to achieve within large corporations. Başaran-Symes noted that firms were still very family centered and patriarchal, which made it difficult for qualified professionals to excel in, while Kaynar emphasized the fact that professionalization of enterprises impacted only a segment of the private sector and was only a recent trend.[72]

> How are managers going to be recruited with inheritance and the increase in the number of family members? This is why firms like ours [head hunting] have started to play a very important role in the past three years in terms of: choosing the board of directors, CEOs, and the transition to fully professional firms. If out of hundred we gave a grade of seventy to England [in terms of professionalization], I would give Turkey a thirty. We are very far behind. But we are very advanced compared to Iran or Syria ... But we are at a turning point, last year's [2001] crisis was a turning point. Up to now everyone was growing and earning or losing money. They have noticed this now. In 2001, banks that were well managed did not go bankrupt ... Firms that are managed well do not go bankrupt. The real [production] sector is likely to follow the same trend as in banking.[73]

Nevertheless, they both noted that professionalization was an inevitable outcome and was slowly happening in Turkey. This is largely due to the increased reliance on high capital-high technology complex discussed above, which requires more elaborate industrial organizations. It is, however, also simply driven by the expansion of enterprise, which make family control hard to maintain. On this point, the sheer number of subsidiaries holdings own and the size of the workforce they employ make professionalization necessary. In 2002 (just a few years after TÜSİAD's enhanced political activities), the two biggest and most diversified holdings, Sabancı and Koç, owned sixty-six and ninety-six subsidiaries, respectively. Among the other founding members of TÜSİAD, Eczacıbaşı owned thirty-six, Borusan owned twenty-one, while Enka controlled fourteen. The biggest in the group Koç employed 54,000 individuals and the more moderately sized Eczacıbaşı employed 7,300 people.

As a result, compared to the 1970s, when holdings had only a handful of subsidiaries and could manage their production, the post-1980 period required an expansion of the managerial function. This change was attested to by some of my interviewees. Feyyaz Berker, of Tekfen Holding, as well as Varlıer, a professional manager at Alarko Holding, reflected on the fact that more and more bosses were trusting professionals to run important aspects of companies.[74] Others, like Eroğlu, noted the contribution of professionals to Turkish holdings:

> There are more professionals. This is the way I see it. The boss is one of the players who plays soccer on the field, but there is a need for professionals who can look at the game as a spectator from time to time. Because the [boss] is personally invested, they cannot see in a very clear way; they can make mistakes. Professionals have an advantage; they can look from outside. The businessman constantly thinks of his work, of his money and investment. His twenty-four hours are spent like this. Professionals spend eight hours like this and rest for eight other hours. Because they can rest, they do have more perspective. They can see things that bosses do not. As such, there contribution to the business community is clear. Within places like TÜSİAD, this presents different perspectives. I don't know if there are many professionals [in TÜSİAD], what the exact ratio is but there are probably 10 to 20 percent.[75]

The same way that doing business with foreign partners (as seen in earlier sections of this chapter) had compelled private enterprises to adopt more formal reporting practices, so too did adopting a more bureaucratic structure create a need for increased corporate governance. As importantly, the growing formal nature of companies and their greater reliance on professionals also served to highlight a tension between the private sector and the state: these changes require day-to-day interactions with officials at all levels of government through people who lack informal access to the state. Thus, as noted by one TÜSİAD member:

> Firms tied to TÜSİAD are fed up with the following: they make considerable efforts to manage their firms, but because there is bad governance at some level of government ... not the people in power but in practice it is very bad. In Turkey, for example, the cost of energy or telephone. It is very easy to meet the minister at the top, they would even grant me a meeting, but in practice at the level of low-ranking officials there is no good governance ... TÜSİAD member firms are on an everyday interaction with the state and feel that there should be a public-sector reform.[76]

It can therefore be said that, in addition to the broader macrolevel changes that have impacted the business elite, the evolution of their firms also requires a greater level of formalism, which brings about increased interest in corporate and good governance to the fore. Two high-ranking bureaucrats I spoke to informally also confirmed this by noting that TÜSİAD (unlike other business associations) made it a point to send representatives to any informational session they organized. The association wanted to keep its members up to date about any changes in regulation; something that had become important with growing complexity and formalism.

Conclusion

The period spanning from the 1980s to the 2000s was undeniably one of momentous change for the Turkish private sector in general and for the industrial business elite in particular. Economic liberalization created new opportunities, but also new pressures to stay competitive and integrate new markets. Despite these challenges, the chapter revealed that the business elite was open to change because it had to managed to perform relatively well under the new economic regime. However, democratization became more salient among the business elite in order to address more immediate needs such as attracting foreign investment and staying connected to the EU. Moreover, these factors and their relationship to issues such as good governance had become more noticeable to TÜSİAD members because they were personally navigating in a more cosmopolitan world. They concretely witnessed the types of incentives that existed in nations that competed with Turkey or had been in partnership with foreign firms that demonstrated concern over Turkish politics or required greater formalism in economic transactions.

The chapter also demonstrated, however, that the need to stay competitive and how this relates for business's demands for democracy cannot be understood in a vacuum. Endogenous growth and decades of development policies that were, as seen in Chapter 5, mainly targeted to large establishments from Istanbul had created a more capital-intensive industrial sector that needed to compete based on productivity. Thus, the move away from cheap labor and investing in process innovation in more capital-heavy sectors, such as automobile, had created a desire to have greater long-term stability and larger markets to make investing in big projects profitable. Moreover, with more complex production also came more formal, bureaucratic private enterprise structures that made informal ties to the state less viable. The chapter also revealed that interviewees from TÜSİAD were able to draw clear links between these changing material conditions and multiple aspects of democracy. These ranged from those that are typically found less threatening to capitalists in the comparative literature, such as aspects to good governance and stability, to more significant changes, such as issues relating to education, income distribution, and minority rights.

Given, however, that these demands taken together put the business elite in direct opposition to the Turkish state it had benefited from for years, the next chapter will outline the more political labor that went into making TÜSİAD an organization for change.

Chapter 6

THE CAPITALIST SPIRIT: SOURCES OF POWER AND DEMOCRACY

When Komili, TÜSİAD's chairman in 1996, unveiled the association's *Democratization Report* and called for significant changes to the Turkish constitution, a schism that had existed within the organization became apparent to the press. A more "liberal" wing lauded publicly TÜSİAD's new democratizing mission, while more "conservative" members lamented that they were moving away from its core mission and from Kemalist tenets, formulated by the founder of the modern Turkish Republic. My interviews revealed that although the decision to commission the report had gone through all the formal channels, the end product, with the incorporation of more democratic liberal values critical of the dominant ideology, was the pet project of the chairman and several other more "liberal" members. Moreover, the report included a preface by the former who penned a strong pro-reform position in which he called on TÜSİAD to embrace a democratizing mission. Previously, many members felt that TÜSİAD publications were "objective studies" written by the subject's experts and not political documents. Thus, some of my informants felt that the more "conservative" wing was most likely as irked by the chairman's personal plea as its actual content.

Eventually, most of the members ended up standing behind the report and, when I interviewed individuals from different ends of the ideological spectrum, a few years after its initial publication, they all were keen on explaining why it was crucial for capitalists to adopt a democratizing role. While some of them conceptualized democracy as being close to full democracy, or embodying some of its social elements, others had a more limited view that incorporated chiefly elements related to issues of good governance. Despite these differences, however, they all seemed equally willing to embrace TÜSİAD's new mission. As pointed to by former TÜSİAD chairman Erkut Yücaoğlu during our conversation, other members were capable of observing a basic empirical link between countries' levels of democracy and economic development or performance.[1] He stressed this point by drawing for me a plot diagram during our interview, marking various nations on a piece of paper along two axes that he labeled "democracy" and "development," emphasizing that this was a presentation he had made in many different forums. Other members also seemed to believe that economic change went hand in hand with political change. To use Marxian terms, the formation of consciousness seemed to be a process rather than immediate, and, as will be seen in this chapter, it was the product of a deliberate attempt to architect the organization in a way that was conducive to using what Schmitter and Streeck called the "logic of influence"[2]—something that was crucial in managing differences and convincing all members that liberal democratic values were in the interest of the capitalist class as a whole.

Thus, given the initial division and eventual cohesion, an examination of large entrepreneurs' changing stance cannot be confined to the study of their material interests and involves an examination of how and why their political and ideological power grew during the period. The process operated on two separate levels. One, as it has been hinted at throughout the book, has to do with TÜSİAD's deliberate attempts to formulate a coherent ideology and build an effective political organization to represent the interests of large capital. Yücaoğlu emphasized that the scatterplot he had just shown me was something he liked to share with other members of the association as well as with state officials, hinting at regularly scheduled meetings and discussions.

The other has to do with tensions between the evolving nature of capital and the lack of formal representation it had within the state. Many of my interviewees lamented the fact that the political elite was not responsive to their demands, but some further outlined the ways in which they did not depend on the state in the same way as they used to. By touching on both factors, the chapter outlines why the period culminated with a greater desire to confront the political elite's unwillingness to bring about significant change to state-business relations. The exercise will be useful for the comparative literature on the state and the capitalist class because it reveals that the economic elite's hold on the state cannot be taken as a given and that variations in the form and level of access can lead to divergent political outcomes. Before presenting how the organization's structure evolved and how members' perception of the state changed, however, the chapter will trace TÜSİAD activities surrounding the publication of the report and, in more general terms, its prodemocracy stance.

The Evolution of TÜSİAD's Political Activities

Despite the internal strife that the "Democratization Report" engendered and despite the seemingly radical nature of its contents, my research showed that there had been an actual build up to its more prodemocracy mission since the 1980s. The evolution was not immediate; it spanned several years, and it was something that was deliberately brought forth by what we can call TÜSİAD's inner circle. Indeed, the most important, yet less publicly advertised, step in the direction of heightened political activity was the passing of the torch from leaders of the older generation, who had founded the association, to second-generation businesspeople. As will be discussed in greater detail later in the chapter, this was a momentous decision for the organization because it was taken informally by its small core group of leaders during closed-door meetings and was driven by the feeling that the younger generation would be more capable to oppose the state and to press for reform.³

This decision's impact was not visible until the early 1990s, however, and the early 1980s (post-coup years) was actually characterized by a relative decline in the association's more political activities, which was partly unexpected and partly natural. It was surprising because TÜSİAD had experienced in the late 1970s a heightened sense of its own growing political power, which manifested itself in the association's ability to precipitate the resignation of a civilian government over economic mismanagement, paving the way for the military to step in (see Chapter 4). However, during the period immediately following the coup, TÜSİAD reverted to its predominantly instrumentalist demands and did not formally expand on this newfound power. This was understandable to the extent that TÜSİAD was generally in favor of the types of economic reforms promoted by the IMF and adopted by the military, but also because the new constitution and political environment were generally unfavorable to the activities of civil society. Under the new rules set by the military, all institutions with the status of association, such as TÜSİAD, were explicitly barred from participating in political activity.⁴

Informally, however, the group witnessed the rise of two of its most vocal chairpersons Ali Koçman and Şahap Kocatopçu, who at many turns publicly criticized the government and its economic policy. Even though both TÜSİAD and the Özal government were proponents of liberalization, the conflict between the association's leadership and Özal was really, yet again, a good example of "the paradox of Turkish liberalism": even though the measures were ideologically intended to favor private entrepreneurship, their overall implementation crowded out investment by large capitalists. More specifically, government overspending through populist policies and presence of public enterprises caused a shortage of cheap credits, which industrialists needed in order to stay competitive.⁵ As such, some individuals close to the association have characterized this public spat as TÜSİAD's first significant break from the state in the 1980s during my interviews.⁶

The growing distance became more significant, however, when the new generation was elevated to positions of power from 1987 onward. With the business elite's heirs at its helm, TÜSİAD increasingly participated in more visible political activities and sustained efforts to develop the association's ideological power. The period thus started with the presidencies of Ömer Dinçkök and Cem Boyner, from two prominent families within the association. With this shift, Boyner's term as chairperson was accompanied by an increase in the association's publications and official activities. Even though they continued to mainly touch on Turkey's economic conditions, TÜSİAD materials that were published during this period started to advocate for more fundamental structural change, such as the policy reforms needed to achieve reindustrialization following the period of liberalization. In parallel, sociopolitical issues started to gain further visibility through such activities as the much-covered visit to the war-torn southeastern regions of Turkey, a significant gesture given how taboo the issue of minority rights and Kurdish identity was and continues to be.⁷

Strictly political topics came more formally to the forefront during the terms of the next two leaders, Bülent Eczacıbaşı and Halis Komili, from 1991 to 1996. During this period, TÜSİAD not only published reports on a range of issues spanning civic rights, privatization, local government, and the role of the state, but it also became in 1993 one of the only mainstream organizations to press for the liberalization of Kurdish as a language in Turkey, thus already touching on policies that challenged the ideology of the political elite three years before the publication of the *Democratization Report*.[8] The decision to commission the report on democracy taken under Komili's period in 1995 was therefore a natural evolution of the association's past activities rather than a radical shift or break.[9] Moreover, the series of panels organized by TÜSİAD on the topic of democratization following its publication attested to some degree the level to which the administration and some members had become committed to this goal.

Despite the fact that the report was foreshadowed by all of the above, its publication was greeted by much opposition and debate both by political actors and by some members of the association itself. Their objections rested either on the timing of the report or on specific topics it covered, ranging from the role of the military to religious education in schools to questioning the definition of Turkishness in the constitution. The first reaction came from members of the state, which went as far as summoning some of the association's members and leadership to appear in front of state prosecutors because the report directly tackled some of the ideologies traditionally imposed top-down by the state. The fact that some of my interviewees relished the opportunity to tell me that TÜSİAD leadership, like some romantic rebels, had to appear in court was particularly telling about the nature of state-business relations at the time.

However, reactions to the report from within TÜSİAD also demonstrated splits in the organization. Members from the two largest conglomerates clashed over it. Sakıp Sabancı hailed the report as something that TÜSİAD should be proud of and give its support to, while Rahmi Koç implied that he would not have allowed its publication had he been aware of its content. Despite these splits, TÜSİAD has made it its practice or informal policy to stand united on the issues it deals with and reports it publishes—a significant organizational element as will be discussed later in the chapter. As a result, TÜSİAD backed the report and continued scheduling activities revolving around its release.

As outlined in Chapter 1, the years surrounding the publication of the report also saw a rise in the individual participation of TÜSİAD members in activities outside of the organization. The change was significant because, as a few of my interviewees reminded me, it had never been historically customary for businesspeople to participate in civil society activities or to enter active politics, aside from a handful of parliamentarians who did not have very long political careers. This was explained by the precarious position that the bourgeoisie maintained throughout most of the country's history (see Chapter 3). Yet, the past twenty-five years saw them establish significant civil society organizations such as universities and museums, which, according to Şeni, was a new form of action for twentieth- and twenty-first-century Turkish businesspeople who pushed forth their own vision of the nation through these institutions. Museums and universities at once showcased the "Europeanness" of Turkey and in the process contributed to the development of previously underserved geographic areas through their locations in lower-income neighborhoods.[10]

In terms of more formal political action, as covered in Chapter 1, former chairperson Cem Boyner became the founding leader of the YDH political party, through which he made overtures to Kurdish citizens, intellectuals disillusioned with Kemalism, and individuals who wanted to find a more liberal solution to the secular-Muslim conflict. The YDH, which can be characterized as liberal (both politically and economically in the classic sense), also drew several of its members from TÜSİAD's ranks.[11] For some members, such as the famous banker and civil society actor Betil, it was therefore the political manifestation of the ideological shift that was impacting the association, even if no ties existed between the two. A similar and much-covered development in 1996 was the fact that a state prosecutor sought to indict Sakıp Sabancı, even though he ran the second largest Turkish conglomerate, with allegations of separatism because he published a report promoting increased government spending toward the southeast region's social and economic development. Instead of backing down, Sabancı responded by publishing a second edition of the report in book form. Two of my interviewees, who should be left anonymous, pointed to the existence of speculations about the state being behind the murder of Sakıp Sabancı's younger brother Özdemir Sabancı within that same year as a vendetta for the family's very visible political activities. Whether these suspicions are sound or not, the existence even of such theories points to the growingly precarious relationship between large business and the state—a monumental shift when compared to capital's shyer position in previous decades and also a significant difference from other country cases where capitalists are assumed to have some control over the state rather than be its subjects.

As significant as these changes are, it would be overly simplistic to imply that TÜSİAD's democratization efforts and ideological stance follow a linear path. Thus, projects like the current book that examine a wider timespan are able to offer a longer view of the extent to which the business elite's message has stayed consistent when compared to scholarship that focuses on specific temporal events. Informants from within and outside the organization have at multiple times described how the struggle between the "conservative" and "liberal" wings of the association play out on both a daily and long-term level. In the longer run, the conflict entails taking turns at the helm of the organization as chairperson to offer both sides some representation. On a day-to-day basis, it occasionally involves influential members reaching out to TÜSİAD administration to bring corrections to press releases or official statements if they stray too far away from its democratization agenda, a fact that amused a handful of the members I interviewed. A review of some of the association's positions does indeed reveal some difference in tone from period to period. For instance, during the Islamist AKP's years in power (2002 to present), chairperson Arzuhan Doğan Yalçındağ ran a much more conservative and staunchly secularist opposition, leading some scholars to conclude that the only motivation behind TÜSİAD's prodemocracy agenda was the EU.[12] However,

TÜSİAD leaders before and after her from the more liberal Sabancı and Boyner families were open to including more substantive dimensions of democracy, such as community rights, during the country's constitutional debates. Despite these conflicting messages, most of my interviewees underscored the fact that periods of oscillation were just blips in the broader steady trajectory the association followed in its democratization project. The next section will therefore explain further how organizational cohesion was maintained and how the association continued to pursue activities that increased its political and ideological power.

Institutionalizing the Business Elite's Ideological and Political Power

Examining changes to TÜSİAD's structure that took place over the same period as the adoption of its democratizing mission reveals an attempt to formalize the production of ideas rather than tackle them in an ad hoc fashion. It also uncovers a desire to keep the control of the organization within the hands of large capitalist families, while managing and taking advantage of a growingly diverse membership base. The fortuitous product of this balancing act has been, as will be shown in the following pages, the establishment of a structure better able to use the logics of "influence" and "leadership" in order to articulate large capital's ideology and interests as a unified front.

One of the hypotheses I had while conducting my interviews for TÜSİAD's prodemocracy turn was the impact of growing diversity within the association and the inclusion of members with needs that were different from those of its founders. Indeed, membership to TÜSİAD grew from 141, in 1975, to close to 500 in 2001 and over 600 during the following decades. As several interviewees reminded me, TÜSİAD is not a "monolith" and increase in the number of members has inevitably led to even further diversity on several separate levels. Younger, second- and third-generation businesspeople and industrialists had joined TÜSİAD during the 1980s. These were either the children of existing members from family-owned establishments or new entrepreneurs. Recent members with no organic ties to TÜSİAD have mostly joined from the rapidly growing, outward-oriented, dynamic industries such as textile.[13] Another change that is as, if not more, meaningful has been the inclusion of professional salaried managers and advisors as members. Although still limited, the inclusion of newer members and the entry of the next generation of holding owners has led to the greater inclusion of female entrepreneurs. Moreover, as hinted in the introduction to this chapter, there has been an ideological split between the "liberal" and "conservative" wings. Despite the fact that growing diversity on all of these fronts impacted the structure and effectiveness of the organization, my interviewees stressed that TÜSİAD still represents the interests of the business elite linked to the largest corporations.

It is therefore important to highlight the ways in which the founding members (or their families) have remained influential. The control that large capital established over the association operates on several crucial levels. First, the importance of large capital can be measured structurally. Interviews revealed that big business owners have been able to donate more money to the association than members from more modest backgrounds. The basic annual membership fee to be part of the association is around USD7,000 individually and finances TÜSİAD's operating budget. However, businesspeople from large holdings regularly make additional voluntary donations, which total up to millions of dollars, in order to help finance the bulk of the association's activities. Moreover, larger and more capital-intensive corporations still represented a sizeable portion of the Turkish economy and within TÜSİAD over the period leading up to the *Democracy Report*. The association had 215 members in 1985 and these were responsible for 80 percent of the production and employment generated by the top hundred Turkish firms.[14] In 1997, 223 companies and holdings linked to TÜSİAD members employed a little more than 370,000 workers and produced about 40.9 percent of the value-added in the Turkish manufacturing, construction and banking sectors.[15] Thus, the founding members and their holdings had some legitimate claim over the fact that they were important for the nation's economy.

Second, TÜSİAD founders also continued to exercise control through careful member selection. To remember, the association remains a voluntary organization and membership is based on the recommendation of two existing members and has to be approved by the board of directors.[16] Thus, often times, new members are drawn from the families of holding owners. Even in cases when prospective members have no organic ties to large corporations, they tend to be recruited from like-minded individuals with interests often linked to large capital.[17] Many professionals in large holdings have been introduced by their employers and in the case of smaller firms they are the ones who provide services—such as consulting, auditing, and capital goods—to larger holdings. For instance, two members, Oktay Varlıer and Tuğrul Erkin, gave me autobiographical accounts of how it was the owners of the holdings in which they had been executives in that had first tapped them for TÜSİAD membership.[18] Similarly, Cansen Başaran-Symes, who eventually became chairperson in 2018, emphasized that it was her position in PriceWaterhouse-Coopers' Turkey office and the services she had been offering to large holdings that compelled her to become a member.[19] Hence, although the growing introduction of professionals had brought a diversity of perspectives and expertise about more specific issues, the general direction of TÜSİAD did not change much.[20] Even though not from the same class background in the classical sense, the newer members nevertheless shared a similar ideology and value system as the owners of the business elite. However, their contributions should not be entirely dismissed, as the expertise they bring invariably enlarged the scope of issues the association was able to focus on (see Chapter 7).

Third, the political influence of larger members is further reinforced through the organizational structure the founders created and the election process in place. Coherence in goals is ensured through continuity in office holders. Two bodies have constituted the formal leadership function of TÜSİAD since its foundation in 1971. The first one, the Higher Advisory Council (Yüksek İstişare Konseyi), works more as an ideological body and determines the long-term goals of the organization, while the second, the Governing Board (Yönetim Kurulu), is an executive committee that ensures its day-to-day operations and whose president becomes the face of TÜSİAD in the media.[21] The former is made up of previous presidents of the Governing Board, while the latter is elected every two years by the members of TÜSİAD.[22] Moreover, the board and its president's election is not competitive and is reached through consensus. More specifically, it takes place during the General Council meeting through the approbation of a single list that has been predetermined through informal agreement between the owners of larger holdings, the core group of founders, and their heirs.[23] One essential feature of this model (as hinted to earlier in the chapter) has been to preserve peace between "liberal" and "conservative" families by alternating the ideological composition of TÜSİAD leadership and its connection to specific holdings. While this can lead to variations in message from year to year, the broader vision of the business elite for the association, however remains untouched and somewhat consistent.

TÜSİAD further manages some consistency of message through informal communication between its influential members and its administration. As mentioned above, some of my interviewees highlighted a few times when they reached out to the general secretary if they felt that a press release or official position went against their democratizing mission. Moreover, the Higher Advisory Council plays a crucial ideological role. It sets the broader objectives and is made up of former presidents. Because these were selected through consensus to begin with, there is an overrepresentation of members linked to large holdings in the ideological leadership of TÜSİAD. The system ensures that individuals who have served before or are connected to influential families really set the longer-term goals of the association in a formal capacity, not to mention their ability to do so through informal debates and discussions. Input by regular members, unless they serve in one of the commissions, is only given twice a year during the General Council meeting. During a conversation I had with Çağlar Keyder, one of the preeminent scholars on classes and politics in Turkey, he characterized this structure as allowing TÜSİAD to function as the nation's "bourgeois vanguard." In a society where no organic ties exist between members of the capitalist class and political parties, the association thus works as the political arm of large business.[24]

Finally, as iterated by multiple informants, TÜSİAD tries to establish some consistency and avoids public discord by choosing its publications (mainly reports) as a way to anchor its demands and has made it its policy to stand behind them without reservation. Hence, the report on democratization was eventually backed by TÜSİAD despite some disagreement about its content and timing.[25] For instance, a mildly more conservative member I spoke to dismissed opposition from within the association as a disagreement about the pace rather than the content of the demands that TÜSİAD formulates.[26]

Managing Diversity: The Logic of Influence and Leadership

The control established by large capital as described above has had its downsides. Four interviewees, who should be left anonymous, complained that TÜSİAD was not democratic enough internally. They wondered about the extent to which an organization, without a participatory culture itself, could embrace a democratizing role. Disillusionment about the shape and role of the organization have, however, not led to open disagreements. Part of the reason lies in the above-mentioned fact that new recruits tend to be business associates of existing members and, as someone I spoke to put it, there is a desire not to "hurt or ruffle any feathers by taking drastic measures such as leaving the organization in protest." Another reason is that, despite a tight ideological control of the organization by the founding members, the structure of the organization was changed over the years to accommodate diversity and to also make it more efficient in the pursuit of specific political goals. The need to manage diversity through greater institutionalization has allowed for the "logic of influence" and "leadership" to operate more effectively. This confirms the findings of studies conducted in comparative country cases, such as Argentina, which point to the fact that the role of business organizations was key to getting capitalists on board with political change through these dynamics that operate within them.[27] Therefore, the next few paragraphs will outline how institutional innovation positively impacted TÜSİAD's effectiveness as an additional source of evidence for the literature interested in business organizations and their impact on members. More importantly, it helps illustrate how associations can be used to increase the ideological power of the business elite.

One of the biggest organizational changes was the establishment of permanent commissions centered around predefined goals and issues. In 1996, these replaced ad hoc work groups to carry out research and manage TÜSİAD publications[28] and are now called "roundtables."[29] While previous work groups did include a few TÜSİAD members, they mostly drew from the knowledge of outside experts or professionals linked to large companies mainly based on their competencies on very specific topics. The new commissions or roundtables, on the other hand, are constituted of TÜSİAD members, and their chairs are drawn from members of the Governing Board. Moreover, because they have been modeled after the structure of the former Union of Industrial and Employers' Confederations of Europe (UNICE) and current BusinessEurope (of which TÜSİAD is a member since 1987), they also help coordinate with similar organizations at the level of the EU.[30] Accordingly, the following commissions have been created in 1996: Foreign Relations, Economic Research, Relations with Trade Organizations, Parliamentary Affairs, Industrial and Firm Affairs, Social Policy Research, Technology and Quality Management.[31] Newer roundtables have been added since to keep up with recent changes and include such areas as Digital Turkey and Energy and the Environment.

These groups had two significant impacts on the association's ability to press for its broader mission. First, they do not only do research, but also carry out more consistent activities linked to their topics, such as being responsible for liaising with the appropriate outside agencies on issues pertinent to their mandate.[32] This was important for state-business relations, as a few bureaucrats I spoke with from the state or the EU's Turkey Commission have commented that TÜSİAD is always very well represented in information sessions their institutions hold and that it is one of the civil society organizations that is diligent about maintaining this frequent contact. Having more permanent bodies as opposed to temporary groups seems to, at the very least, increase TÜSİAD's formal visibility in more administrative aspects of economic regulation and the EU membership process. Frequent contact also allows the association to inform and educate its members about changes to domestic and international regulations impacting the private sector. This has been reinforced by the fact the committees and their activities have been coordinated by what TÜSİAD calls the Council of Harmonization with the EU, which coordinates the commissions' activities to align their activities with the criteria needed for full membership into the union, affording some consistency of goals.

Second, and more crucially, the permanent presence of members within the commissions has allowed for increased input by TÜSİAD's more liberal and engaged wing, impacting the scope of the association's political activities. For instance, publications on subjects such as gender equality and income distribution in Turkey have been pushed for through the individual effort of one TÜSİAD member working in the Social Policy Research' Commission.[33] As significantly, the report on democracy, though written based on a decision taken by the board, was closely supervised by Can Paker and, to a certain extent, by İshak Alaton, who were active participants in the commissions and were closely associated with the prodemocratic wing of TÜSİAD. Several of my informants agreed that the more "radical" tone of the report and its willingness to tackle taboo issues was greatly driven by these two individuals' worldviews. To remember, Alaton had embraced a social-democratic ideology after having worked as a blue-collar worker in Sweden during his youth, while Paker studied in the 1960s when left-wing movements were at their height.

While large holding owners still maintained control of the broad ideological orientation of the organization, members' impact on the tone of reports can be explained by the publication process. The commissions decide to pen specific reports based on either the board's recommendation or the individual suggestion of their own participants. Furthermore, the commission chairs determine the publications' content and the experts they should seek to work on them. Hence, even if reports need the approval of the Governing Board to see daylight, committees and their individual members have some level of autonomy regarding the end product. This has impacted the issues TÜSİAD deals with both quantitatively and qualitatively. The presence of members who cared about gender equality increased the number of publications on the topic, while the choice of author and issues the *Democratization Report* should cover greatly impacted its final tone. Thus, the more formal participatory structure the association has established has put, for lack of a better word, the more enlightened members of the business community in leadership positions. The commissions also ensured some cohesion and allowed for the logic of influence to have an impact on the association.

When the *Democratization Report* was published in 1997, approximately a hundred members out of five hundred were active in commissions.[34] There is no doubt that one primary benefit of such a large participation rate has been to secure the sense of belonging that these individuals feel toward the association, further solidifying coalescence around the liberal democratic identity TÜSİAD pushes for.

One person I spoke to even lightheartedly emphasized that some members took so much pride in their roles in commissions that they went as far as printing them on their business cards. As such, this new organ not only enhanced the diffusion of ideology, but also afforded its members some sense of legitimacy as being part of a more enlightened and engaged business elite.

The organizational changes that made TÜSİAD more efficient politically have also been accompanied by the decision to expand its permanent staff, increasing the professionalization and international reach of the organization. This stands in sharp contrast to the TÜSİAD of the 1970s and early 1980s (highlighted in previous chapters), which was described to me by Feyyaz Berker, its first president, who worked out of a small office with one staff member and who organized meetings at other founders' homes. TÜSİAD today has a general secretary and two deputy secretaries, who coordinate a team of young experts. The latter offer administrative support and expertise to the commissions (or roundtables) in order to help coordinate TÜSİAD's activities.[35] I had the chance to meet and interview most of these experts, who were all energetic and had obtained graduate degrees in the social sciences or had worked in the private sector for a few years. They were all very knowledgeable about Turkey's political economy and really had a grasp of the issues that TÜSİAD deals with on both an academic and applied level. This change provided more consistency in ideology. According to Berker, it also positively impacted member participation as positions within TÜSİAD became less time consuming thanks to the support experts provided. As such, commission membership became more appealing to individuals from a wider range of professional backgrounds.[36]

Increased professionalization also allowed the business elite to expand its reach. TÜSİAD has opened an Ankara office to be close to administrative centers and in the 1990s established two international missions with permanent staff in Brussels and Washington DC. More missions followed around the world including France, England, Germany, China, the Gulf region, and Silicon Valley. Therefore, TÜSİAD's increased level of activity was not only directed toward the Turkish state, but was also geared toward EU membership and building more stable trade relations with other countries (see Chapter 7). The Brussels office was established in 1996 to "mediate the relationships between the Turkish private sector and the European Union and help incorporate considerations about a European dimension into TÜSİAD's agenda."[37] Within this framework, the Brussels mission has participated in UNICE (or BusinessEurope) activities and has coordinated meetings between the EU and TÜSİAD officials. These kinds of public diplomacy activities expanded both the association's and Turkey's reach around the world.[38] The offices have also increased the sense of legitimacy that capitalists have. The DC representative, for instance, mentioned that the US Chamber of Commerce had demonstrated great interest in TÜSİAD's activities and structure and that it had presented TÜSİAD as a model of success to other business associations in late-industrializing societies.[39]

While the above discussion highlighted organizational changes which made TÜSİAD more effective in the promotion of its demands, the following pages will underscore the next necessary condition behind TÜSİAD's push for democracy by tracing how the business elite perceived changes to their relation to the state. The overall theoretical argument is that large capital's growing economic, political, and ideological power did not translate to an immediate and parallel increase in influence over the state. Hence, the 1990s witnessed the emergence of a growing tension between capitalists who had newfound needs and powers and a political elite that still had great stakes in the informal state-society relations that the state had traditionally used to co-opt society. The rest of the chapter will therefore highlight the ways in which the business elite felt more legitimate. This will be followed by a discussion of how this shift, combined with the state's unwillingness to change, impacted TÜSİAD's demands.

State Autonomy and Democracy

The organizational structure built by TÜSİAD helps explain the formulation of a coherent capitalist ideology. As suggested by Poggi, however, ideas become salient when they mesh well with the changing position of a group.[40] Chapter 5 had demonstrated that economic liberalization and increased integration into world markets had transformed the needs of capital. But while the latter is important to understand why democracy became appealing and why TÜSİAD members felt that their economic power had changed, it is not sufficient to explain why they would go as far as break their ties with the state. Many other country cases with similar constraints did not witness the rise of a prodemocracy business class. Moreover, as demonstrated in Chapters 2 and 3, the Turkish state has traditionally been able to impose its ideology on a dependent capitalist class.

These points taken together make it crucial to explain the ways in which the position and psyche of capitalists have shifted, propelling them to focus on TÜSİAD in order to push for reform. The next few pages will highlight that this change operated on several parallel axes. First, economic liberalization and changes in economic policy have made capitalists reflect on the nature of a well-functioning liberal economic system and have given them a sense of greater autonomy from the state. Second, and linked to this point, the period (and TÜSİAD's activities) has increased the sense of legitimacy and ideological power capitalists enjoy. Finally, the new needs of capital created a tension between business and the Turkish state: the rising incompatibility between more formal private enterprise and a political elite that still relied on informal state-society relations to govern. All of these culminated in a greater willingness to accept and participate in TÜSİAD's prodemocracy agenda.

On the first point, the most obvious impact of economic liberalization has been on the discourse my informants have adopted and the link they built between capitalism and democracy. The ability to associate economic performance with different aspects of democracy, as opposed to just economic liberalization carried out with no concern for the institutional environment, can in part be explained by a process of intellectual maturation within TÜSİAD. Put differently, operating under market-oriented reforms for over a decade had propelled members of the private sector to reflect on the requirements of a well-functioning free trade economy. Indeed, when asked why they had not pressed for democracy sooner in the 1980s, several of my interviewees such as Eczacıbaşı or Varlıer, confirmed that whereas TÜSİAD gave its blanket support to economic liberalization in the early days, its members realized firsthand in the 1990s that a market economy really needed to be combined with changes in political and social institutions: "Of course, the radical decisions of 1980 comforted capital; it worked to its advantage. But [capitalists] then saw that this was not enough."[41]

Many of my interviewees admitted that the realization had been slow because the Turkish corporation owner was someone who still greatly benefited from state intervention. However, at the time of the interviews, they all nonetheless adopted arguments in favor of changes to the role of the state and for a greater role for the private sector as an engine of growth. All informants touched on various forms of state intervention that would be better suited for the current economic climate.

As was highlighted in the previous chapter, there were several immediate material needs that made the business elite reflect on the broader environment. Large corporation owners in particular had emphasized the need for a state more capable of managing a good education system and a large domestic market to make Turkey more competitive. Moreover, many interviewees had complained about higher energy prices in particular and higher input prices in general, but also inadequate infrastructure (mainly transportation and communication). While these issues are not directly related to demands for increased democracy (as they can be achieved under different conditions), they did lead the business elite to reevaluate the state on several levels.

The state's deficiencies highlighted by the business elite were as much about the types (or quality) of intervention as they were about its quantity, an idea also formulated by the academic literature on development strategies that emphasize the need for strong government institutions rather than a decrease in the level of the state's involvement.[42] TÜSİAD and its members have increasingly talked of the need for good governance in order to make the private sector more efficient. Furthermore, TÜSİAD, and some of my interviewees, emphasized liberalization of certain areas as a means to make the Turkish economy more productive by making more efficient use of resources. As such, the need to stay competitive and the broader international environment brought forth state reform as an important issue. Most importantly, by tackling these issues head on, TÜSİAD as an organization has given intellectual fodder to its members about the role of capitalists in society. They increasingly perceived private activity as legitimate and the state as failing on several levels. It was common for my interviewees to express this view:

> TÜSİAD started to see the changes in the social structure of the country and saw its dangers. Ankara has remained backwards on this issue; it continued to see issues through its statist mentality. They are afraid that their power is going to be taken from their hands. This is why the [state] is not open to reform. TÜSİAD wanted democracy even if it went against its own interests ... TÜSİAD members are refined individuals with good education. They can understand the issues and say, "the emperor has no clothes."[43]

> The Turkish government ... has pushed us to disaster because the form of governance was always wrong, especially in the last ten years.[44]

> Since [Özal's rule], Turkey has started to lose its position in the world in the 1990s. It had been one of the top sixteen nations in the world. It had achieved the rank of tenth nation in terms of gross national product; its level of education had increased. But politics became more corrupt. There was torture, conflicts, and killings within the sphere of politics. This is why we had come up with the report in 1996, to stop the corruption of politics in Turkey and describe how the Turkish people can live comfortably under the universal concept of democracy.[45]

In conjunction to outlining the shortcomings of the Turkish economy and state, economic liberalization had also given the private sector the opportunity to become more autonomous from the state when compared to the 1970s. The previous chapter had illustrated that the activities of holdings linked to TÜSİAD had expanded in scope and size since during the early 1980s. Moreover, it was shown that growing internationalization had given members the ability to form foreign partnerships domestically and to also acquire activities abroad, even if limited. The growing mobility and autonomy of Turkish capital has helped TÜSİAD members assess the shortcomings of the Turkish state on several additional levels.

First, they have been able to contrast the services and business environment offered by the Turkish state to other business opportunities. Growing internationalization and opportunities existing elsewhere is something that Turkish capital witnesses firsthand, raising issues of good governance. To remember, two interviewees gave specific examples of instances when they were offered very advantageous conditions for investment by foreign governments that reached out to them directly (Chapter 5). This, they pointed out, stood in sharp contrast to the lengthy bureaucratic process involved with investing in Turkey and higher input prices.[46] Second, partnerships with foreign companies and trade further reinforced this line of questioning and skepticism about the Turkish state's intervention by offering possibilities for growth that were previously not present under state-led models of development. One interviewee, who operates a medium-sized establishment, went into great detail to outline how he had formed a partnership with an American firm and how this eventually has changed all of his operation and perception of the Turkish state:

> The partnership in '98 started with thirty people. How large is it now? 380 people. And what is the difference between my receipt today and my receipt in '98? It is ten times more. How is this possible when everyone is going bankrupt in Turkey? It has to do with exportation. People who have decided that they have no other option than exporting are in [TÜSİAD] now. What has this brought us? A high value-added automotive sector and the exportation of textiles ... The businessman's mentality has changed ... Why does Turkey not go bankrupt with this political system? Because exports are still at 34 to 35 billions of dollars.[47]

As crucially, this intellectual reckoning about the inadequacies of state intervention was taking place in a context where my interviewees felt that they had more ideological power, to use Mann's theoretical framework. Indeed, some members stressed the fact that a growing sense of legitimacy among the private sector enabled TÜSİAD to tackle more sensitive issues previously under the ideological monopoly of the state. Many of the entrepreneurs I spoke to felt that their image after years of economic liberalism had improved greatly in public opinion. For instance, after referencing a 1950s' public perception survey in which Turkish people ranked entrepreneurs to be the least respectable from a list of institutions they were presented, because they were "perceived as thieves," Alaton went on with the interview:

> The same study was conducted in 1997. The most respectable [institution] was still the army, the second was businessmen and industrialists, third universities and the eleventh politicians ... This indicates an ideological revolution as a society. The somewhat shy attempts of the 1970s were the forebearers of this trend; the 1980–1990 period under Özal really underlined this.[48]

This increased sense of legitimacy translates into greater political power as outlined by several of my interviewees. Can Paker, who rued the fact that he had lacked ideological legitimacy in the past as a businessperson, emphasized the impact that the association was having:

> There is still in society a lack of confidence in businessmen, but it is now an admissible thing, what businessmen have to say is taken seriously. The things that TÜSİAD says do get echoed. When I was a member of the governing board, we even had done a study that revealed society was expecting TÜSİAD to find solutions to the country's problems. It has become that effective.[49]

A similar sentiment was echoed by an advisor to corporations when describing the ease with which they could now get meetings with the political elite:

> The biggest obstacle is for the mindset in Turkey to change. For example, we are going to meet [Prime Minister] Ecevit; we had lunch with Tayyip Erdoğan today. The point is that in the past it would have taken three months to get an appointment with Mr. Erdoğan; now he gives one within one day. In the past, the opposite side saw us as an adversary; now they have started to see us as a partner. When I say the opposite side, I mean politicians today.[50]

A conversation I had with another member helped illustrate how the association's spheres of activities and reports bolstered the business elite's confidence, despite a negative reception:

> Of course [the reports published by TÜSİAD] have gotten negative reactions from time to time. Because they do target the people who govern us and is

showing their shortcomings and what should be done. The people who were bothered by this have preferred to tell us to "mind our own business." But given what we have been talking about for the past half hour, given all the problems, the period where everyone "minded their own business" has passed. And it is a very healthy behavior; there isn't such a thing as not dealing with things that do not concern us. If I pay taxes and I am a citizen, what I say should be taken into account.[51]

The business elite thus felt that they had become significant political actors, thanks to both what society expects of entrepreneurs and their ability to reach the political class (gauged by their ability to secure meetings). As importantly, the notion that paying taxes and the business elite's unique vantage point provided them the legitimacy to be involved in civil society debates were themes that were often reiterated during interviews.

The increase in ideological power discussed above really crystalized to create a more reform-minded business elite when it is combined to the greater sense of economic power and autonomy from the state that capitalists were experiencing. Within this context, liberalization and a greater sense of autonomy from the state were paramount in increasing this sense of ideological power. For one thing, business does not rely on government contracts as much as it used to, as highlighted by the head of Eczacıbaşı Holding:

Incentives and contracts are not as they were before; the dependence of business to the state has decreased. I am not saying that it has completely disappeared. It is not at the level of Western countries; old habits still persist. But it is not exactly the same as before ...: today; entrepreneurs think "what can they do if they get angry? Would they make stones rain on our heads?"[52]

My informants also underscored the fact that economic liberalization had shifted the role of generating growth and wealth away from the state toward the private sector. Some like Erkut Yücaoğlu and Haluk Tükel even echoed ideas such as "no taxation without representation" when asked about the source of power behind TÜSİAD's demands.[53] Rona Yırcalı, of a major Turkish bank, has expressed this more specifically during our interview:

If I pay taxes, if I am also a citizen, what I want should be done and I should be heard. It is of course public government; political authority is free to do what it wants, but I will go and tell my side to the bureaucracy and ministers. And I will explain why my position is right and why things should be done this way by publishing reports as an association ... to become an autonomous source of pressure the way TÜSİAD is doing in a very healthy way.[54]

According to the interviewees that ventured an estimation, one-third of business taxes come from organizations that are linked to TÜSİAD members. This claim is partly supported by DIE (State Department of Statistics) data that reveal that manufacturing groups employing more than 1,000 employees, the pool from which the core and founding members of TÜSİAD are drawn, represented around only 1 percent of all manufacturing groups in Turkey, but employed 21.35 percent of the manufacturing labor force and created 31.58 percent of value-added in manufacturing. While not all these groups are linked to TÜSİAD members, and some are even state owned, this points to the structural importance of TÜSİAD members in generating employment, value-added, and taxes. Consequently, it can be observed that this economic structural power was something that my interviewees were translating into greater political and ideological confidence. Today, TÜSİAD estimates that its members and their firms contribute half of the entire economy's value-added. Thus, many saw the role of the private sector changing and the image of businesspeople improving:

> One may wonder why Turkey does no fail economically despite these policies and the economic environment. What holds Turkey on its feet is the fact that exports are still at 34 to 35 billion dollars and 10 to 12 billion comes from the trade balance. This is what solves all the problems. Lets return to the initial question: what happened to the businessman's mentality? People my age are slowly leaving. The young businessman is dynamic; he travels the world with his case and is willing to deal with the country's problems.[55]

Consequently, members of TÜSİAD have learned to live under a liberal economy and have witnessed the juxtaposition of increased economic autonomy with a growing sense of legitimacy. The contribution they feel they make toward the economy and the state gives them a legitimate political voice, which is quite different from the situation in the 1970s when large business was trying to carve a socially acceptable role for itself. This helps confirm findings of previous comparative studies which emphasize that living under a liberal economic regime has increased business's self-confidence in cases such as Chile, when compared to the more timid stance of Brazilian business that still heavily relied on the state.[56] Thus, a parallel rise in economic and ideological power worked together to increase the business elite's sense of its own transformative capacity. The next chapter will highlight that this greater sense of autonomy has also helped mitigate the association's relationship with the rising AKP Party's rule.

However, while the above discussion supports the claim that TÜSİAD and its members have gained enough power to press for meaningful change, they pose a new conundrum. Most of the literature has used the growing legitimacy of capitalist enterprise and structural power of capital to demonstrate that business in late-developing countries has enjoyed an increasing ability to isolate key aspects of economic polity from subordinate groups.[57] This has more often than not created elite resistance to the deepening of democracy. Furthermore, as noted in Chapter 2, many have underlined the existence of a wide range of regime and state-business arrangements able to promote the economic elite's interest.[58]

Turkish business was seen as historically being tied to an arbitrary state too, and this has been used by some of my interviewees to explain why some members have traditionally been reluctant to deal with political and social issues within TÜSİAD. Consequently, in addition to an intellectual process within TÜSİAD and the possibility of a more favorable intellectual climate for democratization, one must look into why and how the break from the state was seen as inevitable. Thus, the final section of the chapter will turn to the last parallel shift affecting the political power and autonomy of capital. More specifically, it will explore a growing tension between the needs of the private sector and the inadequacies of the state by looking at: (1) the relatively limited level of inclusion within the state that TÜSİAD members feel they experience and (2) a lag between the evolution of the private sector and the practices of the state.

Business Formalism and the Informal State

Chapters 3 and 4 had demonstrated the extent to which the political elite's reliance on informal state-society linkages had caused both the historical weakness of the bourgeoisie and had greatly shaped the way it was structured.[59] The practices of the Turkish private sector during the post-1980 period, were still shaped to certain degree by earlier traditions of state intervention and ongoing forms of state-business relations. One informant, with vast experience in corporate management thanks to her role as PriceWaterhouse's Turkey director, described how the structure and culture of private enterprise was greatly impacted:

> When you look at the management of the most powerful firms within TÜSİAD, you will still see individuals rooted in government and revenue; revenue is still a very important field of specialization in Turkey ... Despite recruiting people of different flavor to top management, the majority is still fiscal advisors and this indicates that they have a very Ankara and revenue style of management connected to Ankara. I think there are people with different vision, but I do not think that they have come to positions of power ... Change is not an easy thing. Turkey is very patriarchal; we have to look at the structure of society. I am not a sociologist, but when I look with an amateur eye I believe that many problems are rooted there. For example when you look at the second generation [of owners], a very important factor in Turkey, they have studied in very good schools. But you see that people who have studied in very important schools cannot do what they want in the firm's various positions because of family pressure. I think that social pressure, the family, respect for the family, and lack of opposition is still very important ... Professional managers are not able to be successful in this type of structure ... I have witnessed a lot of times that professionals adapt to the system rather than bring change.[60]

This quote largely echoes Ayşe Buğra's study of state-business relations in Turkey and indicates that state tradition is still important in determining the form of leadership and practices in business organizations.[61] However, one must distinguish between the microlevel practices of the business community and its broad political demands. Inclusion through individual particularistic ties may give economic benefits to business leaders, but it does not necessarily mean that they feel that large capital is able to influence the broad political direction of the country. Why particularistic ties and old practices lost their importance for the business elite, therefore, warrants some attention.

The negative reactions received by TÜSİAD from various segments of society, such as to the publication of the *Democratization Report*, and the seeming inability or reluctance of governments to act on issues that are important to large capital, such as EU membership, point to the fact that large capital does not have as much hold on the state as depicted by structuralist arguments. This was pointed out by one member of TÜSİAD, Kaslowski, during our interview as being one of the central paradoxes of my own research: why a group that is so privileged would feel the need to press for change.[62] Indeed, many informants have emphasized the extent to which the state was autonomous and not responsive to their more political demands, creating a tension with their growing economic and ideological power. One member noted the extent to which the political class was still reluctant to embrace the business elite's position:

> One of [the reactions from politicians] was: "I wish that this book [the *Democratization Report*] did not carry TÜSİAD's stamp and that we had passed these as laws ourselves. Because the fact that it comes from you forces us to take the opposite position." This was told to us by various heads of bureaucracies and parties during meetings we held in Ankara.[63]

After describing the ways in which paying taxes and their unique vantage point bestowed on capitalists enough legitimacy to press for change (see page 154 of this chapter), another prominent member involved in finance further described how the political elite continued to perceive them::

> What lies behind the resistance is the fact that politicians of the past fifty years have seen the businessman as someone [who] is self-interested, who steals and who does not care about the problems of the country. Even if this is not true they have always seen us this way, and they still do.[64]

Furthermore, several interviewees pointed to the historical weakness of civil society and the lack of formal class representation within the state, for instance through corporatist socioeconomic councils, as one of the more fundamental problems of Turkish democracy (see Chapters 3 and 4). Thus, capitalists felt that the state and its political elite did not incorporate (or listen to) their broader demands about the direction of the country.

It is important to underscore, however, that the above observations relate to the business elite's perceived lack of influence over broader policy debates and *not* their ability to use particularistic channels in order to gain favors. Thus, an important factor that has driven the business elite's political shift has been the juxtaposition of its growing need for broader change and declining use for informal access to the state. In other words, changes to the general environment and structure of private enterprise, as outlined in the previous Chapter 5. have created tensions between the business elite's broader demands and informal access that they enjoy from the state through particularistic, and not formal, channels. Several are worth noting.

To remember, it was already demonstrated that increased capital-intensive production created new needs for political certainty and social spending in sectors such as education. Moreover, since the 1980s, organizations linked to TÜSİAD have become more formal due to endogenous growth and also internationalization. The expansion of industry meant that the numbers of firms controlled by holdings and the size of the workforce they employ have grown. This means that the business elite now manage complex organizations that necessitate professional managers. Unlike owner families, the latter lack access to the state and therefore bring about the need an overall more efficient state bureaucracy. Hence, the previous chapter had illustrated several instances when interviewees, particularly consultants, had emphasized that the negative impact of widespread bad governance on the private sector should be distinguished from the privileged access to the state that the business elite enjoyed. For instance, they had discussed that it was "very easy to meet the minister at the top," but that the lack of good governance "in practice at the level of low-ranking officials" was not adequate for establishing the types of "everyday interaction" TÜSİAD member firms needed or for tackling problems such as the lack of cheap energy or infrastructure. [65]

Chapter 5 also demonstrated how growing internationalization constituted an additional source of tension for the business elite at the level of the enterprise. This was perhaps one of the more pervasive and long-term effect of growing trade and investment partnerships: they push international norms of corporate governance on the Turkish private sector. In more general terms, one of my interviewees close to TÜSİAD, who knows the needs of the private sector well, emphasized the fact that doing business internationally has forced the members of TÜSİAD to adopt "codes" that did not exist before. As Argüden, another consultant who helps the business elite navigate the international economy, reminded us in Chapter 5, the business elite's foreign partners and investors prefer places that have "transparency, ethics, and corporate governance." [66] Hence, according to him, firms tied to TÜSİAD were in a position where they had to "internalize these practices."

As such, growing internationalization has contributed to creating a tension between a segment of the private sector that has to adopt norms of accountability and performance on the one hand and a state that has shortcomings in the area of good governance on the other. One informant, Kaslowski, underscored the fact that he and other corporation owners had no choice but record every activity they did. He further provided a striking image of why the state did not heed their calls by stressing that the political elite was more interested in "hunting in the vast ocean that was the informal economy."[67]

Hence, the evolution of private enterprise made previous forms of access to the state the business elite enjoyed inadequate. As shown throughout the book, while the post-1980 period brought a radical transformation of the economy, state tradition has to some extent remained unchanged. Özal and his government continued to use state intervention to garner support (especially from the periphery), while unstable coalition governments in the 1990s also used these clientelistic networks for their advantage. Moreover, financial speculation engendered by the reforms created new sources of rent. Thus, the business elite felt that the informal practices of the state had become a burden, given their rising economic and ideological power. Before concluding the section, a word about the limits to TÜSİAD's newfound ambitions is warranted.

Limits to Power: TÜSİAD and the Periphery

During the period studied in the current chapter (1990s to early 2000s), TÜSİAD had managed to find a good balance between organizational effectiveness and the broader desire of the business elite to enhance its ideological-political power. However, some limits to its reach are also worth noting. Bureaucratization always carries risks for organizations. Industrialists from Brazil's São Paulo region were very similar to TÜSİAD founders to the extent that they controlled large corporations and did not feel represented by business associations imposed on them top-down by the Brazilian state. They had therefore established IEDI to act as a think tank that would become the business elite's voice in the country's democratization and development debates. Much like TÜSİAD, they would articulate the business elite's position through reports. Given that Brazilian business had also exhibited a tendency to be a democratizing force,[68] the hope was that IEDI would become an effective vehicle to enhance capitalists' ideological power. However, as soon as some of the position papers it published became too focused on technical minutia, members of the business elite stopped actively participating because they really were more interested in broad societal debates.[69] A similar shift has also occurred in TÜSİAD during AKP's rule from about 2010 onward. Its publications also became more microlevel and technical in nature during the period. The next chapter, which focuses on that period specifically, will therefore highlight the ways in which the association can use this to its advantage in coming years, instead of losing steam.

A more significant limit to TÜSİAD's power and ambitions has been the existence of new competing business associations. The 1990s and 2000s saw the rise of MÜSİAD and TUSKON, who were ideologically closer to the AKP and Gülenist movement respectively. Like TÜSİAD, these were voluntary associations that did not have any formal connections to the state and, as such, enjoyed the same level of autonomy and effectiveness in formulating the demands of parts of the business community.[70] While TUSKON witnessed the same demise as other Gülenist organizations following AKP's purge of the movement in 2016, scholarship on these two organizations have noted a few features that posed a challenge to TÜSİAD when they were both active:

(1) They share a cultural affinity with more religious entrepreneurs.
(2) As such, they have broad appeal to SME owners from regions outside of Turkey.

(3) They have helped build trade networks within Turkey and with regions like the Middle East and Africa. Although their members have increasingly experienced the benefit of trade with the EU, they may not be as staunch supporters of Turkey's candidacy process in the union as TÜSİAD members.
(4) All of these taken together, along with their proximity to AKP, has meant that they have successfully organized the bourgeoisie from the country's periphery, while TÜSİAD has remained a part of the center.

The political significance of these factors for TÜSİAD's approach to Erdoğan's presidency and the AKP government will be discussed in the next chapter. However, it is worth noting in the current discussion that the success of these two associations at the beginning of the century forced TÜSİAD to scale down its ambitions for even higher levels of ideological and political power. More specifically, following the *Democratization Report*, my conversations with TÜSİAD leadership had revealed that they were hoping to act as a broader umbrella organization for the private sector as a whole. Growing member diversity, the fact that bigger members were active in several sectors, and greater institutional effectiveness had given the Istanbul business elite a sense that it could represent the interests of the private sector as a whole, pretty much like semiformal organizations were mandated to do. Within this framework, TÜSİAD had in the first half of the decade started to organize and offer support to smaller regional "SİADs" (Industrialists' and Businesspeople's Associations) in the hopes of grouping them under a confederation that it would spearhead. While it was successful to some extent (see Chapter 7), MÜSİAD's and TUSKON's broader appeal led Istanbul capitalists to scale back their ambitious project. A MÜSİAD representative I interviewed for the book was flatly dismissive of TÜSİAD's power and democratizing role, stressing that his association's ability to mobilize thousands of entrepreneurs made it a more effective and democratic representative of the private sector by helping connect so many previously excluded regions to the government. TUSKON's president was more tactful. He devoted an entire afternoon to demonstrate his association's effectiveness and, to a lesser extent, the Gülen community's capacity for interfaith dialogue. He accomplished the latter by urging me to eat and drink the array of treats and beverages that I had been politely ignoring and that an aide had been steadily laying in front of me during the month of Ramadan (they had correctly surmised that I was someone who would not fast and wanted to demonstrate that they were accepting of my values). As far as TUSKON's effectiveness, the presentations were focused on showcasing the thousands of members that the network had and the ways in which it contributed to regional and international development by linking them to business opportunities abroad.

Given the large numbers of entrepreneurs these two organizations were able to mobilize, TÜSİAD's efforts were short lived. When I raised the issue again with TÜSİAD administration and members in the 2010s, they underscored that they were satisfied with primarily focusing on the interests of large industry. They still saw it as being a significant representative of the private sector as a whole by virtue of its members' diverse sectoral activities and due to the fact that they did also engage in business with more pious entrepreneurs in regions outside of Istanbul (as SMEs from the periphery worked as suppliers of intermediary goods or vendors of consumer goods produced by holdings).[71] Thus, today TÜSİAD continues to work pretty much as the representative of large capital, but it does so in a more coherent fashion and in a way that helps formulate the ideology of this group. Like the increased professionalization of the association, its attempt to forge a federation still impacts the tone of some of its activities, however. This, as will be seen in the next chapter, presents a series of opportunities and challenges for its broader political mission.

Conclusion

The above analysis has demonstrated that there is more to business's relation to the state than its instrumental needs by illustrating that the capital's growing ideological power was the product of deliberate thought process and institution building Consequently, looking at the structural power of the economic elite is not enough to understand its political position; the interplay between its economic and politico-ideological functions must also be taken into account. The discussion has also revealed that economic liberalization and the evolution of TÜSİAD members has done more than create new instrumentalist needs. By shifting the role of entrepreneurship away from the state to the private sector, changes in the economic and political environment have led members of TÜSİAD to go through a period of intellectual reflection and increased legitimacy that now permit them to think of the broader interests of capital and oppose the state.

However, because of the dual nature of the Turkish state, large capital still cannot use its structural power to affect a state whose tradition is to reproduce its rule based on informal relations. Thus, democracy has become particularly appealing as a way to both legitimize capital's power and gain access to the state more formally. The next chapter will discuss how TÜSİAD's new political role played out during the religious AKP's rule. More specifically, it will assess the extent to which the factors discussed in Chapter 5 and the current chapter impacted the business elite's ability to stay committed to democratization despite threats to its reign from new, more religious, political and economic classes. It will also assess the ways in which TÜSİAD can stay committed to its democratizing mission in the face of rising authoritarianism in Turkey and around the world.

Chapter 7

NEW AUTHORITARIANISM, CONFLICT, AND THE BUSINESS ELITE'S COMMITMENT TO DEMOCRACY

One primary concern with the business elite's regime preference has been that it is too often short-term and reactionary (see Chapter 2). The historical weakness of capitalist classes in late-industrializing societies like Turkey can accentuate the problem, as this group might feel powerless in the face of sociopolitical change. This final chapter examines the extent to which TÜSİAD and its members' prodemocracy stance has changed in light of a momentous shift in current Turkish politics: the religious AKP's growing hold on power in a country where the ruling elite had historically been secularist.

The process was of significance because it transferred control of the state away from the Kemalist center (mainly the military and bureaucracy) toward a new group of technocrats that came to prominence through the party's and other religious organizations' ranks from Turkey's periphery. Of specific concern for TÜSİAD is the fact that AKP's success partly lies on the support it garnered from a rising religious entrepreneurial class poised to challenge old Istanbul-based capital's privileged position.[1] While the previous chapter demonstrated that the business elite growingly felt confident enough in its economic and ideological power to formulate a coherent political position, the tradition in Turkey was for the political elite to rule top-down, focusing on the more authoritative functions of the state. All these factors taken together raise the question of how the secular business elite would react to a seeming threat to its status.

Recent scholarship has adopted a longer view (thanks to the passage of time) to trace more aptly the roots of President Erdoğan's autocratic impulses to a decade's long takeover of the country's institutions by a "political society" from the periphery.[2] This observation is lodged in the existence of a center-periphery tension and the fact that, given the lack of formal state-society relations, influence over the state must pass through capturing its institutions. Moreover, given the state tradition of top-down rule using authoritative power, it is expected or observed that the new political class is doing the same. While this longer view is important to remember to ultimately gauge the business elite's power vis-à-vis the state and government in coming years, the challenges and opportunities that AKP's reign presented for big business and other political actors have not been uniform over the course of its twenty years in power (see Chapter 2). As such, specific political cleavages during each period must be remembered more specifically to put TÜSİAD's stance over the years in context.

During the government's early years from around 2002 to 2007, the AKP championed the process of EU membership and the democratic reforms that this required. Moreover, the party was lauded by Western commentators, including the US presidency, for its ability to align Islam with liberal values and market principles.[3] This meshed well with TÜSİAD's prodemocracy agenda and its desire for Turkey to remain close to the West.[4] Between 2007 and 2013, however, political liberalization undertaken by a religious party created more noticeable splits among non-pious, secular actors. Civil society organizations representing diverse groups, such as Kurdish and feminist movements, were energized by the possibility to gain more rights. Military generals and more staunchly secularist parties like the CHP and some of its supporters were, however, highly suspicious of any reform achieved through the leadership of a government set on bringing Islam to prominence. The more secularist circles' passions were ignited in 2007 by the prospect of an AKP and, especially, an Erdoğan takeover of the presidency, which was perceived as a line of defense against the Islamization of the state. They organized street demonstrations (aka the "democracy protests") and the movement culminated in the drafting of a threatening memorandum by military top brass, which was interpreted by many as a "virtual (or unarmed) coup" attempt to remove the AKP from power. A protracted political battle against secularist segments of society and the state eventually led to a series of AKP-sponsored constitutional referenda (in 2007, 2010, 2017) that afforded the presidency greater powers, made it possible for Erdoğan to be elected through popular vote, and ultimately made the executive the most important branch of government.[5] Because the first two sets of reforms proposed in 2007 and 2010 tackled some of the deficiencies of Turkish democracy, they had garnered the votes of not only AKP loyalists, but also outside supporters who were moved by the prospect of increased democracy even if achieved under the umbrella of a religious conservative party. Ultimately, however, the prospect of increased democratization faded.[6]

The final period, from 2013 onward, has been marked by Erdoğan's firmer grip on power and his devotees' increased reliance on previous state traditions to crackdown on opposing voices. These included the Gezi Park protesters,[7] Kurdish populations in southeastern towns that had voted for the HDP in key mayoral and parliamentary races,[8] members of the Gülenist movement who were accused of undertaking the coup attempt of 2016,[9] and academics who had signed a petition for peace with Turkey's Kurdish militants.[10] Despite its privileged position, the business elite was not spared. Osman Kavala (a left-wing holding owner and civil society activist) was put under custody in 2017 and was sentenced to life in prison in 2022 for allegedly "attempting to overthrow the state" using his connection to Soros's Open Society. Many commentators believe that Kavala's sponsorship of several left-leaning prodemocracy organizations was seen as too threatening by the AKP regime who wanted to send a stern warning to the rest of civil society.[11] The episode also highlights the fact that the new state elite has used the same repertoire of undemocratic tools used throughout the republic's history, including ill-defined legal concepts such as protecting the nation.

The different stages of AKP's reign therefore present a unique opportunity to test the business elite's contribution and commitment to democracy. The first years allow for assessing the extent to which TÜSİAD managed to play a significant democratizing role during a period ripe for growing pluralism and political liberalization. The second phase of AKP's reign and growing conflicts with secular actors helps shed additional light on the topic. Given that both camps justified their position in terms of protecting democracy, TÜSİAD's stance as a prodemocracy secular actor therefore also warrants greater scrutiny. For one thing, the association itself exhibited some degree of hesitancy about the message it should adopt in the face of the ongoing political struggle. For another, the environment was ripe for the business elite to revert its prodemocracy position to support a military takedown of AKP, which would have confirmed predictions about the reactionary tendencies of the capitalist class. The third and final act of Erdoğan's growing grip on power helps reflect on how the business elite reacts to a threat emanating from a state apparatus that seemingly has been as, if not more, authoritarian as in previous decades. Even though the political and state actors have changed, the kinds of practices that TÜSİAD denounced under the Kemalist period have remained constant. However, this time around, as illustrated by the Kavala example above and the parallel ascent of a Muslim bourgeoisie, the business elite's and the association's positions in Turkish society were also under direct threat. This last period in one crucial way encapsulates the question dealt with throughout the current book: would the business elite be able to prove its democratic credentials and use all the sources of power it had accumulated in order to challenge a political class that was becoming more coercive? The question is of further comparative significance because it echoes the test the business elite in many de-democratizing societies are likely to have to pass over the next several years, given the rise of leaders with autocratic tendencies across the world.[12]

The findings in Chapters 5 and 6 suggest that understanding TÜSİAD and the business elite's position involves disentangling their trajectory along two axes: the impact that TÜSİAD's organizational efforts to increase ideological and political power had on its prodemocracy mission's long-term prospect, and the business elite's power in the face of a potential exogenous (AKP-led) challenge to their status. The role that these two axes played for the business elite's position during the AKP government will, thus, figure throughout the narrative. The first half of the chapter will focus on the periods of growing pluralism (2002–7) and constitutional debate (2007–10). Because this timespan was marked by the prospect of increased democratization and the types of reforms that TÜSİAD wanted, they will be examined more closely by focusing on: (1) potential shifts to the business elite's economic power during the period, (2) TÜSİAD's attempts at democratization through public diplomacy efforts during the EU membership process, and (3) the association's level of commitment to democratization during debates that pitted secularist actors against the AKP. While this exercise will help determine whether TÜSİAD actually managed to commit to democracy during a period ripe for change, the second half of the chapter will trace how the association was impacted by the rise of a seemingly more authoritarian state apparatus than even in previous, secularist decades. Even though the political and state actors have changed, the kinds of practices that TÜSİAD denounced under the Kemalist period seem to have remained constant. However, this time around, as illustrated by the Kavala example above and the establishment of a large Muslim corporate sector, the business elite's and the association's statures in Turkish society were also under direct threat, as was Turkey's rapprochement to the West. The last part of chapter will therefore examine TÜSİAD more closely during AKP's authoritarian turn by outlining the degree to which the business elite was politically impacted and the extent to which the association changed its strategies, including forging intra-class alliances and entering new fields of research. The overview will help conclude the chapter by commenting on the potential efficacy of new avenues TÜSİAD leadership has been exploring to counteract authoritarianism. In order to provide some context to the reader, however, the next few pages will offer a broader view of the challenges posed by AKP and the consistency of TÜSİAD's prodemocracy discourse over the years.

AKP's Initial Rise and the Business Elite

The book so far has demonstrated that the business elite and TÜSİAD were increasingly confident in their ideological and economic power. Moreover, the association had increased its organizational capacity to form a cohesive ideology centered on its democratization mission. This had allowed the business elite to challenge the secularist state and previous political classes during the period preceding the AKP government. Unlike the AKP, Turkey's political class had been throughout the post-1980 and post-coup era characterized by a series of coalition governments that were unwilling or unable to undertake significant political reform (see Chapters 1, 3, and 6). When combined with the state's tendency to rule top-down and insulate policy areas from societal pressure, the latter meant that the business elite had to publicly push for the kinds of reforms it felt were needed. To remember, TÜSİAD's director of the board at the time of the *Democratization Report*, Halis Komili, had even prefaced the document with a call to action: "If not us who? If not now when?"

The AKP's initial rise, therefore, posed a conundrum for large capitalists. Unlike its predecessors, the AKP government during its first years in power was seemingly open to deepening democratic reform and Turkey's ties with the EU.[13] Moreover, there is growing consensus in the political economy literature that Erdoğan resumed Özal's vision for Turkish economic liberalization, which had been interrupted by frequent crises of mismanagement in the 1990s.[14] More specifically, privatization efforts, greater openness of the economy to foreign capital, and regional development through aid to SMEs all gained speed under the AKP government. These were carried out in tandem with effort to expand the middle classes through housing projects and reforms to parts of the public sector such as healthcare.[15] It is also generally accepted that all of these reforms shaped the way through which political Islam's rise incorporated individuals from the periphery into rising middle classes and the capitalist market, rather than bringing about revolution from below. In many ways, the AKP government increasingly integrated Turkey into the global capitalist economy. Thanks to all of these measures, Western powers, the United States in particular, welcomed the transformation Turkey was undergoing and saw in it a model that could be applied to the rest of the Muslim world.[16] To remember, EU membership, the ability to attract foreign investment, and staying connected to the West were the kinds of changes TÜSİAD had been pushing for. As will be seen below, the association, therefore, continued to publicly endorse democratization despite its ideological differences with the AKP.[17]

However, Erdoğan's government also represented a threat to the business elite for four interrelated reasons hinted at in the first few pages. First, Erdoğan has adopted a confrontational tone against the business elite in populist discourse challenging their status. Among other things, he has accused them of being "thieves" and whenever they failed to publicly endorse his reforms, he had threatened to "cast them aside."[18] This type of discourse was worrying for the capitalist class, given the Turkish state tradition and the historical importance of keeping close ties to officials. Second, an additional threat to the business elite's prominent position came from the fact that the AKP's popularity and power rested in part on the emergence of a more religiously devout entrepreneurial class. The "Anatolian tigers" from the periphery were believed to be eroding the dominant role played in the Turkish economy by Istanbul-based holdings linked to TÜSİAD.[19] This group had come to prominence as early as the 1980s thanks to Özal and ANAP's liberal economic policies that made government credit available to the smaller export-oriented entrepreneurs from the periphery. While export promotion had also been beneficial to the protectionist era business elite (see Chapter 5), it also led to a boom in economic activity in provinces with a surge in the number of manufacturers that often served as subcontractors. Individuals at the helm of these companies were drawn from smaller commercial, agricultural, and working-class background and had common networks and values that contributed to their dynamism by facilitating economic cooperation. AKP's continuity with earlier 1980s-era policies helped fuel the further expansion of this group, elevating some of them to the status of large holding, which brings about the third source of threat for TÜSİAD members.

Third, this new rising elite had a more direct link to the AKP government with the help of their own association MÜSİAD, also a voluntary organization based on individual membership. Unlike TÜSİAD, the latter was organically aligned with the AKP's cadres and vision.[20] The symbolic and strategic placement of MÜSİAD offices close to AKP headquarters had, from the get-go, also raised questions about the kinds of clientelist networks that the new political and economic classes were building.[21] As such, the AKP did not change the fundamental nature of state-business relations. Economic policy geared at creating a new rising middle class still included big construction projects, changes to public procurement laws, and the privatization of the energy sector, all of which ultimately gave the executive great discretionary powers when selecting clients. Buğra and Savaşkan have traced the extent to which these practices have led to the emergence of new large holdings such as Cengiz Holing, IC Holding, and individual investors such as Ethem Sancak with direct AKP (and Erdoğan) ties.[22] They note that lucrative government contracts and timely investments in the energy sector propelled these families to the rank of richest Turkish citizens in the world as ranked by Forbes. Soon after the publication of this book, visitors to the United Nations headquarters in Manhattan will get to see a thirty-six-story tulip-shaped building erected by IC Holding after a successful bid for Erdoğan's vision for a new Turkish Cultural Center reminiscent of the Ottoman period's past glory. How these kinds of activities directly threatened the business elite was best summed up vividly during an interview I had with a now former TÜSİAD chairperson, Başaran-Symes:

> I like to look at the little packages of cheese and butter they serve on airplane meals when I travel. When you look at the Turkish Airlines' tray [Turkey's flagship state owned airline], it used to be brands that we all knew very well growing up, now all the little packages have labels of brands I do not recognize.[23]

Finally, and related to the above, as much as TÜSİAD in the 1990s and 2000s was willing to challenge the secularist state and its central Kemalist tenets, AKP's rise tested further the extent to which the business elite was willing to break its ties from it. After all, the corporations controlled by the latter historically owed their existence to the state and its attempt to build a national bourgeoisie (see Chapters 3 and 4). As much as they were less dependent on the state, as was seen in previous chapters, some members of the business elite still managed to secure lucrative contracts during the secularist period. Moreover, even if TÜSİAD was willing to take on the laic political elite, most of its members are secular and its politically more "conservative" (or reluctant) wing were still attached to some of the Kemalist values.[24] When combined with threats that Erdoğan directed toward the business elite and civil society organizations, all these points raise the question of how TÜSİAD and the business elite would react to democratization undertaken by the religious AKP.

To this day, TÜSİAD and its leadership (with varying levels of enthusiasm) have officially reiterated their commitment to their mission of promoting democratization, such as in 2018 when its chairperson, Erol Bilecik, emphasized the link the organization made between democratic institutions and economic development:

> When we did all this work, the message we gave to the public was the economy cannot be strengthened only through economic reforms, and to emphasize that strengthening the economy first and foremost needs to go through the creation of a transparent, consensus-building, fair and democratic society. The best and tried formula for Turkey is: democracy, the rule of law, a free and creative society, quality education, technology-based production and speeding up the EU candidacy process.[25]

TÜSİAD has even dedicated part of its Higher Advisory Council meeting in 2014 to the memory of the *Democratization Report*'s author Bülent Tanör by holding a panel on the history of democracy in Turkey. This kind of demonstrative public commitment to a project undertaken two decades ago speaks to the role the democratizing mission played in increasing the business elite's ideological power (see Chapter 6). It proves further the validity of what Schmitter and Streeck call the "logic of influence" when discussing associations' role in shaping capitalists' political positions. TÜSİAD's ability to stay on message as such serves to reinforce the prediction made by scholars who have studied business organizations' role in the stability of democracy in other comparative cases such as Latin American countries: associations smooth out the reactionary tendencies of their members by formulating a coherent mission.[26] In the case of Turkey too, acting through TÜSİAD has allowed the business elite to stay focused on its democratization mission despite changes to the wider political environment.[27]

TÜSİAD's consistent message, however, does not mean that the association's structure and spheres of activity have remained stagnant over the past two decades. TÜSİAD has continued to undertake organizational changes in line with its previous attempts to build an efficient vehicle for private-sector representation (see Chapter 6). These have included the establishing five think tanks in academic settings; helping establish the Women Entrepreneurs Association of Turkey (Türkiye Kadın Girişimciler Derneği, KADIGER), and forging alliances with some of the regional business associations in the hopes of acting as an umbrella association through the Turkish Enterprise and Business Confederation (Türk Girişim ve İş Dünyası Konfederasyonu, TÜRKONFED). Parts of these measures can be explained by an endogenous drive that all movements undergo with the aim of enhancing what their leadership perceive to be organizational effectiveness. However, as will be seen below, some of these changes were also driven by a reaction to the changing external environment. For instance, TÜSİAD heightened its foreign presence by continuing to open missions abroad in response to EU governments' seeming opposition to Turkey's membership to the union. In addition, it has expanded its focus on newer topics, such as gender equality, in what seems to be an attempt to avoid criticizing the AKP government head-on, while still touching on issues that deal with democratization. The extent to which TÜSİAD stayed on message and the exact impact of the above organizational changes will be examined more closely, whenever appropriate, in sections dealing with AKP's first years in power and its turn to authoritarian practices. The next section, however, will highlight the degree to which the economic power of the association's core (the business elite) changed during the AKP's first decade in power.

Economic Power under the New Order

The business elite's growing economic power (see Chapter 5) has made the AKP government and rising Muslim bourgeoisie more tolerable. In terms of sheer size,

TÜSİAD members and the business elite continued to play a prominent role in the Turkish economy. In 2010, nearly a decade into AKP's rule, the association estimated that its members still held a significant place in industry by producing 65 percent of total manufacturing output. Moreover, their establishments generated 50 percent of private sector value-added and were responsible for roughly half of declared employment during the past decade (from 2010 until 2020).[28]

As for the new Muslim entrepreneurial class, several dynamics made its expansion potentially beneficial for the business elite. First, their ascent has not posed as significant a challenge to the status of large conglomerates from within TÜSİAD as one might assume. At the onset of AKP's electoral victory in 2001, there were forty TÜSİAD-member owned businesses among the largest hundred Turkish industrial establishments (ranked by the Istanbul Chamber of Industry, or İSO, based on the amount of revenue from production they generate). In 2006 and 2011, during AKP's first decade in power, forty-six and forty TÜSİAD-controlled firms, respectively, sat among the largest hundred (see Table 7.1). While TÜSİAD members generated a little less than a third of the revenue on the list in 2001, they managed to grow their shares to around 50 percent in 2006 and 2011. This is considerable given that more than a quarter of the establishments on the list were either owned by foreign corporations, the state, the military, or the army's pension plan. As such, TÜSİAD represented more than half of the largest domestically and privately owned establishments over the entire period. At least during the AKP's initial years, TÜSİAD member firms' prominent economic position in industry was not directly jeopardized by pro-AKP manufacturing firms.

Second, given the ability of TÜSİAD-controlled establishments to preserve their competitiveness, there emerged a synergic relationship between the business elite and entrepreneurs from the regions. To remember, policies that were started in the 1980s under Özal's ANAP and picked up later by the AKP had led to a surge in

Table 7.1 Share of TÜSİAD Member Businesses in Turkey's Largest 100 Industrial Establishments According to Revenue from Production

	2001	2006	2011	2016	2020
TÜSİAD establishments in top 10	4	6	5	5	4
TÜSİAD establishments in top 100	40	46	39	36	32
Foreign establishments	12	14	16	13	11
State or military owned	19	12	13	14	15
Total revenue of all top 100 firms in billions USD	72.4	118.6	123.5	125.8	175.5
Share of TÜSİAD %	32.23	53.01	46.48	47.45	41.7
100th establishment's revenue in billions USD	0.24	0.34	0.40	0.40	0.57
TÜSİAD's revenue in Billions USD	23.3	56.1	57.4	59.7	73.

Note: İSO provides revenue data in nominal Turkish lira. The data has been adjusted for comparison using the IMF's Consumer Price Index (based on 2010 values) and the Turkish Central Bank's historical exchange rate for December 31, 2010.

Source: İstanbul Sanayi Odası, "Türkiye'nin 500 Büyük Sanayi Kuruluşu," http://www.iso500.org.tr/#. Accessed August 5, 2022; "World Development Indicators," https://databank.worldbank.org/source/world-development-indicators. Accessed August 5, 2022.

the number of private-sector establishments in the periphery.[29] By contributing to employment and prosperity in traditionally underdeveloped regions, the Muslim entrepreneurial class directly benefitted TÜSİAD members by helping expand the domestic market. This is further accentuated, according to one of my informants, by the fact that small-town capitalists own a series of official dealerships or franchises in which products manufactured by large holdings are prominently featured. A stroll through any Turkish town, reveals Beko, Arçelik, and Fiat dealerships or Migros and Carrefour supermarkets (all produced and supplied by top holdings within TÜSİAD) Chapter 6 had demonstrated that TÜSİAD had already emphasized the need for regional development and that owners of large holdings tended to favor the social dimensions of democracy in order to benefit from economies of scale. Smaller entrepreneurs and their dynamism, thus, directly contributed to the performance of businesses linked to TÜSİAD.

Finally, many Muslim entrepreneurs and their association MÜSİAD had tended to favor trade with Middle Eastern and Central Asian nations to which they felt closer. I was reminded of this fact when discussing the topic of Turkish business with a representative from MÜSİAD and the president of TUSKON when they outlined the extent to which they helped their members network in these regions. However, with the greater integration of Turkey in world markets, entrepreneurs in the periphery and MÜSİAD have also increasingly started to favor proximity to the EU as a means to expand and gain expertise.[30] Over the period, the business community from a large range of the ideological spectrum has, therefore, undertaken public diplomacy efforts to compel the Turkish government to align with the EU. Thus, there are times when both TÜSİAD's and MÜSİAD's lobbying efforts have tended to mesh. All in all, the rise of an entrepreneurial class from outside the traditional business elite has not presented an imminent existential danger and has not engendered intra-class conflict.

Despite the above dynamics, it would be hasty to dismiss the threat that new political leadership has posed for TÜSİAD members, given the historical importance of state actors for the national bourgeoisie. Indeed, at the end of AKP's second decade in power the number of TÜSİAD establishments among the largest hundred industrial firms fell to thirty-two, according to the same İSO data collected over the period. This is partly due to the natural growth of industry and cannot be attributed to direct action by the political class. More specifically, while the relative share of total revenue TÜSİAD members generated decreased over the period, the absolute revenue they managed to bring in increased. This is evidenced by the fact that the total revenue generated by all one-hundred establishments grew from USD120 billion to USD175 billion in 2020, while the bottom establishment generated USD575 million in revenue in 2020, up from around USD400 million during the previous decade. Put differently, TÜSİAD members were sharing a smaller slice of a growing pie during the more authoritarian Erdoğan years.

However, part of this loss in status is also due to direct political action, and its impact should not be overlooked. As traced by Buğra and Savaşkan, changes to the fortunes of Turkey's billionaires cannot be explained by economic factors alone and should be understood in light of the state's ability to punish opponents and reward allies through sources of rent developed, even under economic liberalization.[31] Erdoğan has ramped up his criticism of some members of the business elite (see next section), and his ire has often engendered tax audits of firms linked to TÜSİAD. The most visible early victim of this threat has been Aydın Doğan, a media mogul, who had come under constant scrutiny of an AKP-led bureaucracy for his secularist news outlets' critical coverage of the government.[32] In 2009, Doğan Holding was fined USD3.8 billion for unpaid taxes and had to eventually sell several major newspapers to the AKP-linked Demirören Holding. This not only raised questions about freedom of the press in Erdoğan's Turkey, but also caused Doğan Holding–owned businesses to slip from the ranks of largest establishments.[33] While tax audits were used as a powerful tool to silence some members of the business elite, tax breaks, state-commissioned construction projects, and the privatization of energy have all been used to reward allies and elevate a business class close to the government (as had been the case throughout much of Turkish history). Thus, in recent years, companies with close ties to the Erdoğan presidency have moved up the ranks, thanks to timely acquisitions of state-owned energy plants and defense companies.[34] Given that these are presumably moves that TÜSİAD-linked holdings would have made successfully in previous decades (see Chapters 3 and 4), the impact that AKP's rule has had in changing the landscape of dominant businesses has been profound.

The implications of this shift on TÜSİAD's political position will be discussed in greater detail in the second half of the chapter when the impact of Erdoğan's presidency is more directly discussed. For the more immediate discussion, however, a few factors that helped buffer the above shift and made it more tolerable for the traditional business elite should be underlined. The amount of revenue, employment, and production that the latter has continued to generate still points to the significant levels of economic power and autonomy from state action that TÜSİAD members had accrued over previous decades (see Chapters 5 and 6). Moreover, during follow-up interviews I conducted around the early 2010s, a handful of TÜSİAD members acknowledged that, despite its attempts to build and use new clientelistic networks, the AKP government and its cadres seemed surprisingly attuned with the business elite's needs. They further noted that the government and civil service, at least during the first decade in power, were more open to talking about policy with them when compared to the pre-2000 coalitions. This is confirmed by the fact that, during its initial phases, the AKP had proposed the establishment of a Social-Economic Council in the new constitution to represent the interests of labor and business. Given that the lack of such formal representation within the state was something that my interviewees had complained about, AKP's openness to the idea was undeniably a factor that smoothed out tensions between the political and economic elite. It should be reemphasized that the past two decades have not been uniform. The above discussion about the rise of new businesspeople, and the increasingly discretionary powers that the AKP government has had when rewarding them, raises grave concerns about the extent to which this relationship has been tenable in recent years. As far as the first decade of the government's rule is concerned, however, the combination of the business elite's economic power and hints of changing state-business relations have made reform more acceptable. As such, TÜSİAD used its organizational capacity to try and become an ally for change. However, it is vital not to overstate TÜSİAD's influence on the process. As one informant from TÜSİAD put it:

> It would not be shrewd of politicians to admit that they passed reforms because capitalists wanted it. I have talked to many of them, and they all told me that [the *Democratization Report*] was a wonderful document but that they wished it had come from someone else and not TÜSİAD.[35]

Therefore, rather than attempt to build a direct link between the association's demands and reform it is worth examining what Turam has termed "politics of engagement" between governing classes and TÜSİAD during the first decade.[36] How the association used its institutional capacity during the period to situate itself in the country's debates is worth looking at through this prism.

TÜSİAD's Political Structure and Public Diplomacy

As seen in chapter 6, TÜSİAD has become a more formal organization over the years by creating committees on a range of topics and opening administrative offices in various locations staffed by administrators. This expansion continued during AKP's first years in power. Internationally, TÜSİAD proceeded to open missions in order to create a political presence in Paris, Berlin, London, Washington DC, and the EU (through its Brussels office). It also established business networks in Shanghai, the Silicon Valley, and Dubai with more instrumentalist goals in mind.

During the same period, TÜSİAD sought to build a think-tank style sphere of influence, similar to business representation in the United States. Although some individual members of the business elite and their foundations already had centers focused on timely research, the most notable of which was TESEV, TÜSİAD became more formally involved by setting up institutions of its own. Domestically, it established and funded five research centers in university settings within Turkey.[37] Internationally, TÜSİAD promoted discussion with foreign politicians and scholars by establishing institutes in Paris and Berlin: the Institut du Bosphore (Bosphorus Institute) and Bosphorus Initiative, respectively. The association also deepened its intellectual ties with actors outside of Turkey by establishing partnerships with the Brookings Institution and the German Marshall Fund.

TÜSİAD's expansion has impacted the business elite's participation in Turkey's democratization process on several levels. For starters, the inclusion of think tanks more formally within TÜSİAD made the organization more prolific. In addition to organizing frequent panels, this initiative has allowed TÜSİAD to triple the number of reports it published from 47 in the 1990s to 141 from 2010 onward, as some of its publications came directly from panels or projects undertaken by its research centers (see next section). Hence, TÜSİAD shifted its attention to a greater range of topics through a more formal organization, as opposed to focusing on a few timely publications (such as the *Democratization Report*) that were directly commissioned from its leadership. It also tried to increase its sphere of influence through a wider network, which entailed reliance on permanent staff and greater participation of members or professional managers with technical experience. The efficacy of these choices for the business elite's political agenda and their rationale will be discussed in greater detail in the next section on AKP's more authoritarian period, while its implications for the broader comparative literature will be discussed in the concluding chapter.

However, as far as the particular period under review is concerned (AKP's democratizing years), TÜSİAD used its new offices in two specific ways to advance the democratization process. The first step it took was to use its organizational presence abroad to directly lobby European governments and attempt to sway public opinion using their organizational capacity. This was done in the hopes of promoting Turkey's membership to the EU and led the association to focus on think tanks as a tool to achieve its goals. As highlighted in a release by Arzuhan Doğan Yalçındağ, president of TÜSİAD in 2009, during the Institut du Bosphore's inauguration, think tanks were deliberately chosen to shape international opinion about Turkey:

> Within the scope of TÜSİAD's five-year International Communication Programme that covers the period between 2008–2012, France will be in the spotlight for 2009. Therefore, TÜSİAD has opted to establishing a think tank in order to create direct communication with the French public opinion … Successful communication requires identifying the specific model of communication that is used to address each countries' own public opinion. Interaction with the French public opinion is generally achieved through think tanks.[38]

Moreover, TÜSİAD continued to use its formal membership in European organizations, such as UNICE (now BusinessEurope) to create a presence within the union and establish itself as a prodemocracy voice for Turkey.[39] More specifically, TÜSİAD leadership used its formal connections to BusinessEurope and its organic connections to other business associations to undertake public diplomacy efforts by organizing panels and visits. For instance, TÜSİAD met with Movement of the Enterprises of France (Mouvement des entreprises de France, MEDEF) nine times between 2004 and 2009, both in France and in Turkey. During those meetings, eleven French ministers and parliamentarians, in addition to two French prime ministers, were present. Erdoğan was also in attendance during two of those events, as the prime minister of Turkey, while Abdullah Gül attended twice (as foreign minister and president of Turkey). Most of TÜSİAD's meetings with foreign politicians were similarly attended by ministers from the AKP. All in all, twenty-seven high-ranking officials from the party, including Gül and Erdoğan, were in attendance at TÜSİAD's international visits during the period. It should be emphasized that a source close to the organization who witnessed some of these events characterized AKP's presence as brief and symbolic. However, given the lack of TÜSİAD's formal status and Erdoğan's attacks on the association, the fact that there would be frequent ceremonial interactions is still noteworthy.

In addition to bilateral meetings, over the same period, TÜSİAD used its European presence to undertake lobbying efforts within the EU by meeting with representatives of BusinessEurope five times (in addition to the organization's annual summit) as well as the EU minister responsible for expansion a total of four times in less than four years. It also used its connections with foreign business organizations to leverage for Turkey's ascension to the EU by coming out with joint statements. For instance, the French and Turkish business elite, in a joint statement, recognized the work that needed to be done for the candidacy process to be successful:

> TÜSİAD and MEDEF believe that Turkey's EU membership requires, in addition to global reforms, a deep transformation. Throughout this process, there will be opportunities for significant cooperation between France and Turkey on issues as diverse as the environment, education, finance, tourism, local government, transportation, infrastructure, security, telecommunication, and information technology. TÜSİAD and MEDEF are aware of negative social and cultural perceptions about Turkey in European public opinion. For this reason, the two organizations believe that aligning Turkish and French public opinion will require using every opportunity to develop mutual understanding and friendly relations.[40]

In using its political capital and cosmopolitanism in these public diplomacy efforts, the business elite thus compelled and facilitated AKP's relationship with European leaders and tried to ensure that the democratization process was on track to meet EU membership criteria. However, some commentators have been wary about the possibility that the association's only end goal was joining the EU and that it acted cautiously in national politics to avoid alienating the secularist establishment in the process of AKP-led reform.[41] Its domestic role during the period should, therefore, be examined more closely, as TÜSİAD was compelled to weigh in during political conflicts that pitted the AKP to secular actors.

TÜSİAD and Domestic Political Conflict

Domestically, two key years, 2007 and 2010, are worth looking into during the AKP's first decade in power because the party was pushing for constitutional reform despite opposition from secularist circles (see Chapter 1). The position that TÜSİAD would take in the country's constitutional debates came under scrutiny not only because of its links to the previous state elite and the threat of a rising Muslim bourgeoisie, but also in light of Erdoğan's repeated populist attacks on the association. A very ostensible example came during his criticism of the association's stance on the 2007 referendum when he declared that "Bitaraf olmayan ber taraf olur." This statement was confounding because Erdoğan's use of old Turkish led to two different interpretations of the warning he directed toward TÜSİAD and its members: "Those who remain neutral will be eliminated" or "those who remain neutral will be cast aside," the former, like many commentators saw it, implying a more direct existentialist threat. Hence, the association found itself in the same predicament as many other prodemocracy actors. The reforms were tackling many of the country's earlier political problems but were carried out by a political group whose commitment to pluralism was being increasingly questioned.[42] In the case of the business elite, there was the real prospect of losing economic power.

As far as Erdoğan's direct attacks are concerned, my conversation with someone close to TÜSİAD revealed that the association understood the statement to mean the latter rather than the more menacing threat of annihilation. This was confirmed by the fact that rather than side with the Kemalist establishment, TÜSİAD tried to adopt a moderating role around democratization debates. During the first significant conflict between secular circles and the AKP, in 2007, TÜSİAD's policy of sticking to its goals and previous publications allowed it to stay on the prodemocracy side of the debate by continuously standing behind its call for reforms. In 2007, it published a summary of all of its previous reports and opinions called *Güçlü Demokrasi, Güçlü Sosyal Yapı, Güçlü Ekonomi* (Strong Democracy, Strong Social Structure and Strong Economy), and emphasized that the country's political debates should revolve around these three major issues.[43] In so doing it took a position that moved away from the conflict by restating the type of political reforms it had been pressing for since the 1990s. Moreover, TÜSİAD signaled that it favored replacing the military constitution of 1982 and situated itself as a secular actor in the debate by stating that it should be done on the condition civil society actors participate.[44]

As importantly, in addition to publicly reiterating its support for the democratization process and for constitutional change, TÜSİAD signaled that it would not act as a reactionary force in Turkish politics the way it had before the coup of 1980. When other secularist political actors called on the Constitutional Court to close-down the AKP, TÜSİAD welcomed the court's decision not to ban the party by reiterating its commitment to pluralism in a press release:

> TÜSİAD has consistently emphasized that the closure of a political party will not resolve a country's political problems … there is still much that must be done to make Turkish democracy stronger and more pluralistic. Firstly, political parties must develop their political agendas, programs, and activities based on the fact that Turkey is a secular, democratic, social and constitutional state. All constitutional and legal barriers that prevent Turkey from strengthening its democracy must be changed. In light of this experience, … and to commence this process of change, we reiterate our call for the establishment of a Constitutional Convention which will include all groups of society as well as civil society organizations. We believe this decision will be regarded as a milestone in the history of Turkish democracy.[45]

Through this statement the association also urged the AKP to respect the democratization process and the rule of law, situating itself as a moderating voice within the political conflict.

As for the referendum of 2010, which made it possible to try military personnel involved in the 1980 coup, lifted restrictions on civil servants' unionization, changed the makeup of the supreme court, and established the Economic and Social Council, TÜSİAD came out in support of constitutional change. This was underscored often in Chairperson Ümit Boyner's speeches and press releases, such as when she commented on the constitutional debates by stating that "the aim should be a 21st century Constitution that is a true social contract and the expression of our will to live together and freely," or again, when she linked the debate to development and called for a more participatory constitutional process: "[the] lack of democracy prevents Turkey from ascending to higher leagues in terms of economy and development. [TÜSİAD's] goal is to work toward increased participation from diverse groups in society."[46]

Hence, TÜSİAD continued to emphasize the importance of political change, but also reiterated its desire for the AKP to stay committed to pluralism. A point that was further emphasized by the association's commission that deals with political reform when it highlighted its meetings' agenda during the period: identity issues, freedoms of conscience and religion, separations of power.[47] In sum, TÜSİAD's confidence as a secular actor during a period when the reforms were being carried out by a religious party helps confirm the findings of previous chapters. A combination of its economic power with the political organization it built through TÜSİAD ensured that the business elite stayed ideologically consistent with its message during the AKP's first decade in power.

However, a cautionary note is warranted. While the above mediating role and commitment to democracy were of significance, they came nowhere close to the radical tone of TÜSİAD's first *Democratization Report* in 1996. The types of statements delivered over the period betray a desire to appease both the AKP and secularist center. Moreover, my conversation with the association's administration at the time revealed a desire to advocate for individual rights rather than communal or group rights as advocated by the more religious government. In other words, TÜSİAD's preferred mechanism to accommodate religion in public life was more compatible with secular values rather than a wholesale acceptance of the Islamic character of Turkey and its periphery. Several factors help explain this lukewarm attitude to reform. First, given the historical weakness of the Turkish bourgeoisie, it was trying to achieve a balancing act. Second, personal conversations I have had with two of my informants revealed that some members of the business elite had been irked by Erdoğan's personality and authoritarian tendencies during in-person meetings, foreshadowing events to come. In that sense, they faced the same kinds of dilemmas that secular members of Turkish society grappled with during his ascent.[48] Finally, the leadership under Chairperson Doğan Yalçındağ from 2006 to 2009 (before Boyner quoted above stepped in) was from the more politically conservative wing of TÜSİAD. As emphasized in the previous chapter, swings in leadership were common, and the association's tone about specific issues (not the broader mission) has tended to vary. Thus, there have been fluctuations over the period depending on who was at TÜSİAD's helm. However, despite these factors and rumblings from secularist circles (including from among its ranks), TÜSİAD was still able to adopt a moderating tone during the constitutional debates. To a large extent this attests to the strength of the organization that the more reform-minded founders of TÜSİAD had been able to build. A conversation I have had with someone who has been privy to internal conversations within TÜSİAD has acknowledged that, while the broader membership base is politically shyer, the association's leadership has continued to use the megaphone that TÜSİAD provides to push forth a prodemocracy agenda. Whether this can survive and continue to be effective during Erdoğan's growing grip on power will be examined in the next section.

Rising Authoritarianism and the Business Elite

As outlined in the introduction to this chapter, the final phase of AKP's and Erdoğan's rule has seen them rely increasingly on undemocratic practices. Several factors beyond the scope of this book explain their political turn. However, the current government displays a striking continuity with previous Turkish state traditions (discussed in Chapters 3 through 6). More specifically, the AKP has not transformed, but rather has taken over the practice of ruling top-down by manning the bureaucracy and by focusing on a dominant ideology (Sunni Islam in this case), which the party views as a rallying point for Turkey's population. Thus, even though some gains have been significant, such as changing the role of the military or bringing voices from the periphery of Turkish society to politics (see Chapter 1), the democratization process seems to have been stalled.[49] This has been further heightened by the increased role the presidency has played under Erdoğan, through the centralization of power. Because the historical weakness of civil society lies in arbitrary state action, centralizing rather than building more formal state-society relations can most likely accentuate the problem. Thus, political actors who had found a democratic opening up until 2013 have come increasingly under threat.

In this environment, the role that the Divan Hotel played during the Gezi Park protests in 2013 epitomizes the threat that the AKP posed specifically for the business elite. The luxury Divan Hotel is an Istanbul institution owned by TÜSİAD's Koç family (whose holding company also happens to control five of the ten largest Turkish industrial establishments). The hotel grabbed public attention when it was a literal stone's throw away from the Gezi protests, during which an "Occupy"-inspired alliance of movements took over a park of the same name to block an urban development project the government had undertaken. The park was initially used to advocate a diverse range of social movement causes. But the protests grew the moment security forces decided to breakdown the encampment with tear gas, compelling allies of the movement from across Istanbul to join in solidarity.

For days, the park's vicinity, including the Divan, were engulfed in smoke and surrounded by clashes. Soon into the events, hotel management (allegedly with the blessing of the Koç family itself) decided to open their doors in order to provide protesters a safe haven, where they could get medical attention, water, and reprieve from police violence. The hotel also blocked security forces from entering the premises and ultimately won the PKF hotel experts' "Innovation in Hospitality Award" for displaying "civil solidarity, courage and hospitality in crisis situations."[50] More importantly, the Koç family was perceived as supporting a prodemocracy movement in line with the business elite's political stance.

In response, Erdoğan and the AKP started what many interpreted to be a series of politically motivated punitive measures against the holding, including tax audits of its companies, the withdrawal of a defense contract, and calls to investigate any possible linkages between capitalist moguls and the military memorandum of February 28, 1997, which had put an end to the AKP's predecessor, the Refah Party.[51] Thus, TÜSİAD and the business elite found themselves in a situation where acting against the government attracted arbitrary state action. This incident, along others mentioned in the previous section, raises the question of how TÜSİAD would (or could) operate during the AKP's second term, without losing economic privileges. As importantly, the shift in the government's tone raises the question of how effective the business elite can be in impacting political change when the ruling elite continues the same state tradition of insulating itself from private-sector pressure in order to rule top-down.

TÜSİAD's position was further complicated by Turkey's gradual move away from EU membership. Ascension talks have stalled in part because of Erdoğan's desire to break with previous Turkish foreign policy in order to become a regional (and even global) power; a problem that was exacerbated by France's and Germany's opposition to Turkey's membership. Overall, the initial political model proposed by Erdoğan's AKP and lauded by the West, therefore, veered off course during the period.[52] While Chapter 5 had revealed that EU membership and the global environment were not the sole factors driving the business elite's demands for democracy, the shift away from the union and international community caused TÜSİAD to lose an additional source of legitimacy and ideological anchor for its democratization mission. Thus, the association and large capitalists' prodemocracy stance has become more fragile. Given the historical political weakness of the Turkish business elite in the face of authoritarian state tradition, all of these changes raise the question of the direction the association would take.

Shifting Strategies under Authoritarianism

The book so far has demonstrated that rather than rely solely on its economic power, that TÜSİAD has made strategic choices throughout its history to effect change by transforming its structure in order to enhance its ideological power. The 1970s had been a period where the business elite were in search of new strategies to amplify their political voice (see Chapter 4), while the early 1990s saw large corporation owners make a conscious decision to hand over TÜSİAD's reins to its second-generation members in an attempt to become more effective. According to three individuals who were privy to internal discussions, thanks to their outsider/insider status, the period from 2010 to 2020 was marked by a similar attempt to switch gears. They observed in various meetings, especially within the think tanks that TÜSİAD had established, that there was increased discussion to move the association's fields of activity toward more meso-level issues that were more institutional and technical in nature. The following paragraphs will outline how four factors were instrumental to this change. First, TÜSİAD's organizational restructuring continued to increase the participation of individuals with technical expertise and expanded its fields of activity. Moreover, the association's permanent staff increased from forty-four to sixty-two between 2001 and 2022.[53] Second, despite limited success, the association continued to engage other entrepreneurs from Turkey's private sector. Third, TÜSİAD devoted its energy to commenting on subject areas that can potentially strengthen civil society and bring change to lower levels of government rather than tackle broader questions that the state and political elite have been unresponsive to. Finally, as will be shown in the last section, these three factors taken together have potentially presented TÜSİAD with a fortuitous road map through which it can try to promote democratization while avoiding authoritarian backlash from Erdoğan's government. An analysis of TÜSİAD's fields of activity over the period helps reveal how the first two factors came into play in the face of growing authoritarianism.

To remember, TÜSİAD publications and the policy to stand behind their content is one main tool the association uses to formulate its stance on a number of issues of importance for the business elite. Their breakdown by subject and how they changed over the last few years are, therefore, good indicators of how TÜSİAD has adapted to mounting political pressure on civil society organizations. As importantly, changes to the number of reports and the topics they cover serve as a gauge of how the association's organizational structure has evolved over the course of the past few decades, as they reveal the areas TÜSİAD feels proficient in.

Unsurprisingly during the 1990s and 2000s, when the business elite decided to push for increased democratization, TÜSİAD had published more extensively on political issues, ten and seventeen publications respectively, when compared to one report on good governance it had published in the 1980s. As discussed in the previous section on AKP's first years in power, TÜSİAD's willingness to participate in the democratization process, unlike other mainstream secularist actors, helps explain this increased focus. In addition to the *Democratization Report*, which continued to serve as an ideological anchor, the association published several reports on constitutional reform and the political standards needed for EU membership between 2000 and 2010 (Table 7.2).

However, the place strictly political issues (such as democratization) held among the areas that TÜSİAD devoted its energy to decreased in relation to that of others during the AKP government. Indeed, there was an increase in the sheer number of publications up from 47 in the 1990s to 112 in 2000s and 141 in 2010s. Thus, publications on strictly economic topics outpaced others over the same period and more than doubled when compared to the 1990s (56 and 81 during the 2000s and 2010s respectively). More importantly, of the reports on strictly economic issues, 42 out of 81 were on firm and sector-level analyses or handbooks intended to inform the business community rather than sway the general public and political elite.

Table 7.2 TÜSİAD Reports by Topic and Decade

Decade		1970s	1980s	1990s	2000s	2010s
Political	Democracy	0	0	5	8	5
	Good governance	1	1	4	4	6
	Total political	3	1	10	17	11
Social Issues	Education	1	0	1	9	9
	Income distribution	3	3	3	4	2
	Gender	0	0	0	3	7
	Total social	12	16	11	33	46
Economic	Macro	19	30	18	22	27
	Micro	4	3	3	20	42
	Foreign trade	9	10	5	14	12
	Total economic	32	43	27	56	81
Topics under multiple fields	Environment	0	0	3	10	17
	Judiciary and governance	5	8	9	13	21
Total		47	60	47	112	141

Source: Author classification based on https://tusiad.org/45-yil/.

This did not, however, mean that the business elite shifted its attention completely to instrumentalist concerns. Over the same period, TÜSİAD also devoted energy to topics that were more socioeconomic in nature. Two areas in particular—gender equality and education—came to the fore. Between 2000 and 2020, TÜSİAD published eighteen reports and documents on the topic of education, which ranged from model textbooks for a more global education to the importance of trades to have a more efficient labor market. Moreover, the association reflected on the need for STEM education and the importance of early childhood education for Turkey to become truly integrated into the rest of the world. As for gender, the association published ten studies ranging from broader surveys of gender inequality in society to more particular questions, such as women's media representation.

TÜSİAD also became increasingly engaged on the topics of the environment and of governance, which were both covered in a range of publications that fell under the broader spectrums of all three fields the association works on (political, socioeconomic, and strictly economic). Efforts on the environment intensified between 2010 and 2020, especially after the Paris accord, with seventeen publications that TÜSİAD put out. These were very diverse and included children's books that sensitized younger generations to the perils of global warming, as well as guides for the private sector on how to integrate increasingly greener global supply chains. As for governance, the reports (all twenty-nine of them since 2000) were even more wide-ranging and included analyses of local government as well as compliance advice for corporations.

In sum, the relative proportion of reports on democracy and broader political issues declined over the period as TÜSİAD expanded its sphere of interest to incorporate a greater range of fields to include the environment, governance, gender, and education. The next section will address the extent to which this was due to AKP's years in power, TÜSİAD's own organizational structure, or the business elite's ideology and political strategy. The previous sections had highlighted that some members of the business elite, Doğan and Koç Holdings, had been punished for their political stances by an AKP-led government and bureaucracy. When combined with the cynical observation that large establishments from TÜSİAD continued to do relatively well despite Erdoğan's presidency, a source close to the association I spoke to speculated that the change might partially be motivated by the desire to accommodate members who were shyer politically. The state has historically played a central role for the private sector. As such, it is very likely that the increased focus on instrumentalist issues was partly driven by Turkey's political climate, which made dabbling in current affairs more perilous.

However, endogenous factors inherent to the association, which operated on several interrelated levels, also made TÜSİAD more prolific on a wider range of topics. First, the sheer increase in the number of publications, regardless of subject, confirms the efficiency of the "roundtables" formed by the association and of its strategy to call on members to provide input on specific issues of import by participating in them (see Chapter 6). In 2021, there were ten such roundtables working on thirty-five subfields.[54] In addition, the think tanks formed by TÜSİAD also organized activities around specific issues. The work of roundtables and think tanks often culminated in the publication of reports on more technical topics. Many professionals from large holdings within the association participated in specific commissions (or committees) within roundtables that focused on topics of practical interest to private enterprise, including Digital Turkey, which according to the association works "to support the transformation to the information society and enhance the innovation capacity in order to raise the added value and competitiveness" or the Energy and Environment roundtable which was tasked with "embedding sustainable development principles and to the environmental protection and spreading out the principles of low carbon economy into the business practices."[55] While the former published reports ranging from e-commerce to IT and growth in Turkey, the latter has worked on the sustainability of various sectors in Turkey, including energy and tourism. While TÜSİAD's organizational structure can help explain the shift in focus, its work with members of the capitalist class from outside the business elite can also help explain part of the change.

Intraclass Alliances

The focus on more microlevel instrumental concerns further signals TÜSİAD's desire to become a peak association able to organize the rest of the private sector as a civil society actor. It does so more specifically by serving the needs of the wider capitalist class. More specifically, since AKP's reign, TÜSİAD has founded two side organizations: KADİGER and TÜRKONFED in 2002 and 2004, respectively. KADİGER was founded through the initiative of TÜSİAD members such as Meltem Kurtsan who had been active in the association's Social Policy Commission (roundtable) in the 2000s. During our interview, Kurtsan (the CEO of a natural pharmaceuticals company) had sarcastically pointed out the "Businessman of the

7. New Authoritarianism

Year" award she had received and had displayed prominently in her office. Around the same time, she spearheaded the establishment of KADIGER in order to mentor and promote female entrepreneurs for successful careers in the private sector.

According to its own mission statement, TÜRKONFED was established to contribute to the development of regional, sectoral, and national economic policies. My interviews with TÜSİAD's deputy general secretary at the time of the confederation's establishment revealed that it was done to try and form an umbrella peak organization that could bring the interests of the entire capitalist class to the fore with the help of the business elite. Thus, it was really the product of TÜSİAD's attempt to act as a nationwide organization. This was significant given AKP's rule, as MÜSİAD and TUSKON were two competing organizations that more successfully rallied SMEs from the regions thanks to their religious identities.[56] TÜRKONFED, which started with 6 federations and 69 associations, however, had managed by 2021 to expand its reach and represented 20 federations and 141 subassociations. It currently has over 11,000 members, roughly the same figure as its pro-AKP counterpart MÜSİAD, which also has 11,000 members and eighty-nine regional offices.

Of significance is the fact that TÜSİAD is present at many levels of the confederation through its membership in all twenty of its federations and through the organization of common events and summits. Because TÜRKONFED "focuses on enhancing the structures and competitiveness of Small and Medium Size Enterprises (SMEs) throughout Turkey,"[57] TÜSİAD's heightened interest on more technical or practical issues can in part be explained by its attempt to rally smaller capitalists. Moreover, its focus on gender, especially in the workplace, meshes well with KADIGER's mission. In sum, TÜSİAD's increasing interest in issues that move beyond broader political questions can be explained by a combination of the more authoritarian environment, its own endogenous growth, and its desire to play an organizing role for the rest of the private sector. However, TÜSİAD's growing professionalization, its focus on more meso- or microlevel issues, and the external political environment raise questions about its ability to focus on the issue of democratization beyond more than ceremonial or symbolic adherence to the mission.

However, there is also another narrative arc. During an interview, General Secretary Ebru Dicle outlined that the Turkish private sector's challenges with global integration, through compliance issues in such fields as intellectual property, or dealing with institutional change, inevitably require focus on finer grain issues that demand more technical expertise. Thus, according to her, topics that fall under the broad umbrella of Turkey's economic and political change became inevitably linked to more micro- or meso-level analyses, which TÜSİAD feels knowledgeable about. As the last section of this chapter will highlight, this focus on narrower issues with greater expertise has allowed the association to stay committed to the democratization mission.[58] Interestingly, during the current period, TÜSİAD's vanguard—or more prodemocracy leadership—has managed to connect these activities back to the broader concern of democratization.

New Democratization Strategies?

TÜSİAD's Higher Advisory Council is the association's body that defines its mission and shapes its longer-term vision (see Chapter 6). The council is still made up of individuals with family ties or, in the least, close connections to the business elite. Its yearly meetings are paramount for setting goals and serve as markers for the business elite's political mood. As someone I spoke to between 2021 and 2022 emphasized, even if the political environment has become more repressive, the association's leadership always finds a way to address democratization, whether it is in a section of a report or part of a speech. Three interviewees, who enjoy an outsider-insider perspective, felt that the council's June 17, 2021 gathering had been the most significant in recent years because TÜSİAD's chairperson, Simone Kaslowski, provided its members with a consequential road map. Specifically, he laid out a vision on how to combine TÜSİAD's recent foci and professionalization with the question of democracy.

As he was delivering his speech, three seemingly unrelated events were taking place in Turkey: Erdoğan announced that the country would be leaving the Istanbul Convention (a human rights treaty that seeks to protect women from violence); students from the prestigious Bosphorus University had been protesting the appointment of an AKP loyalist as their institution's rector by Erdoğan; and a mysterious foam had oozed to the shores of the Marmara Sea, presumably because of environmental degradation. Kaslowski's presentation was deliberate to the extent that he tied all these issues back to democratization and showcased how TÜSİAD's evolution over the past ten years, as discussed above, made the association a key actor for change.[59]

More specifically, Kaslowski focused on the problem of deinstitutionalization at all levels of government, which had been occurring because of the takeover of an already insular state by AKP cadres and the centralization of power in the hands of the presidency.[60] Deinstitutionalization was presented as the root cause of Turkey's ills and was juxtaposed to the private sector's and TÜSİAD's formalism as a potential source of change. On the problem of deinstitutionalization and the economy, Kaslowski opined thus:

> The cost of deinstitutionalization constantly increases. Every passing day, we see the extent to which the erosion of institutions damage our system of government, the welfare and happiness of our society, and our nation's perception, prestige and trustworthiness in international markets. Questions about the reliability of official statistics, the fact that institutions do not have the authority to fulfill their duties, that performance standards are ill-defined, all make it harder to enter a strong economic period and to establish healthy communication and relationships with the outside world.

He further added how deinstitutionalization hurt democracy:

> Institutions are also important for the functioning of democracy. It is the primary condition for the political system to be effective and transparent.

Political parties are the most important element of democracy. Doing politics without closing parties and banning them, but by keeping democratic channels open, developing accountability, funding politics through ethical standards, and establishing a legal basis that adheres to universal laws and EU standards will undoubtably make our democracy stronger.

Rather than limit himself to the broader questions of economic performance and democratization, however, Kaslowski went on to address how deinstitutionalization hurt the meso-level issues TÜSİAD had been working on and how they were essential to democracy and economic development. On gender equality, after reminding listeners of the association's stance, his speech emphasized the role of institutions for this issue as well:

In almost all of our meetings we emphasize women's rights. We want and expect our country to rejoin the Istanbul agreement. We expect nothing less from our security forces and judiciary but to adopt the strongest stance possible in preventing violence against women. Enabling women's participation in education, employment and government should be seen as an integral part of our goal to become a developed nation.

In evoking an international treaty, TÜSİAD's leadership sought to bind the Turkish state to international standards, but also put the onus of protecting women's rights on effective state institutions (namely, the judiciary and law enforcement). As importantly, the remarks built a tacit link between TÜSİAD's and KADIGER's activities on gender equality and female empowerment that operate at several societal levels. Kaslowski's speech further highlighted how TÜSİAD's work on education was driven by international standards and was equally needed for the protection of individual rights:

It is impossible for generations that have not had access to quality education to look at the future with confidence. The possibility for our children to compete with their peers during adulthood will be unattainable if we do not provide them with the ability to ask questions, critical thinking, communication, and science and math skills. The Turkish education system should at all levels focus on critical thought, without hindering creativity, to educate free individuals.

Finally, by using the issue of the environment, Kaslowski demonstrated how TÜSİAD's general direction was equally timely in order to impact political change. First, he emphasized why nations and the private sector could not ignore the issue of decay and—once again—international norms:

The West is combining its plans to combat climate change with multiple other objectives. As measures to combat climate change are undertaken, they will also bring about a large wave of economic development. Large investments and financing will flow to nations that have adopted a circular economic system, that have a plan to become carbon neutral and that use their natural resources in a sustainable way ... It is clear that over the next 15–20 years that countries that contribute to environmental deterioration in their forests, seas and environment will be pushed out of global economic chains.

Thus, TÜSİAD leadership drew a link between international norms and the issues of gender equality, education, and the environment through Kaslowski's emphasis on the Istanbul accord, the need for Turkish students to compete with other nations, and greener global supply chains. The issues presented as such not only put forward the interest of the business elite that does not want to be isolated from the rest of the world (see Chapters 5 and 6), but it also reminded that Erdoğan's AKP government is not insular and would likely have to adjust should they want Turkey to do well internationally. A commentator I spoke to felt that TÜSİAD was attempting to find meso-level topics that were binding to both economic and political actors because of international standards.

Moreover, through Kaslowski's speech the business elite sought to carve a role for civil society actors and TÜSİAD more specifically. On the environment and how the latter could be helpful, Kaslowski affirmed thus:

We experienced the latest environmental catastrophe in the Marmara Sea. For the Marmara Sea Action Plan Coordination Council (Marmara Denizi Eylem Planı Koordinasyon Kurulu), which was formed by a Presidential directive, to be successful, it is of outmost important that academics, the private sector, and civil society organizations are included in it. Within this perspective, TÜSİAD will continue to be part of the solution on issues that deal with the environment.

Framing the issue in this way helped underscore the expertise that TÜSİAD built over the years through its roundtables, think tanks, and publications. As importantly, Kaslowski concluded his remarks by emphasizing that all the issues they had been working on increased civil society's strength and its ability to bring about democratization.

While children and youth were going through the hardest period of their education during the pandemic; while women relied on the Istanbul agreement to protect them against the vicious cycle of violence; while academics were fighting for their freedom; while farmers were protecting their ecosystems; while businesspeople and shopkeepers were making efforts to keep their businesses and employment afloat; while workers were trying to adapt to new conditions under the pandemic; they all voiced their demands by reiterating their desire to live in a wealthier and freer country ... [TÜSİAD] will continue to devotedly share our ideas, studies and activities, supported through scientific knowledge, with the government and public to contribute to our country's progress and development.

Through Kaslowski's speech, the business elite has identified several ways in which they can use TÜSİAD's recent path to push for democratization despite growing limits imposed by the AKP government. More importantly, the speech was very well received by the association's members who felt that it was consequential both in terms of its content and timing. Ebru Dicle, the general secretary, further underscored that the administration had gotten a wave of positive feedback from members who were very supportive of this new direction.[61] As such, the council meeting was soon followed by the publication of a new report *Building the Future with a New Mindset*, which built on this new vision. Through it, the business elite focused on an institutional-level analysis (like Kaslowski had done) of human and social development in Turkey, addressing democratic deficiencies throughout the system of government.[62] As importantly, according to Dicle, the new report offered an agenda for the types of issues the association plans to tackle over the next few years.

Both Kaslowski's speech and the new agenda must be remembered in the context of TÜSİAD's growing professionalization, expanding spheres of activity, and attempts to build links with the rest of civil society through its think tanks. First, the speech and report have linked all of TÜSİAD's recent spheres of activity (gender equality, education, the efficiency of institutions, and the environment) back to issues of democracy. The report also highlighted many of the areas my informants had previously complained about, including regional inequality, government inefficiency, and the lack of scientific research and innovation (see Chapters 5 and 6). Second, by focusing on deinstitutionalization as the main deficiency of Turkey's current government and as the root cause of problems in the above areas, TÜSİAD not only is able to indirectly criticize the government, but it can also situate the role of the private sector as an agent of change. Chapter 6 had outlined that one source of tension between the business elite and the state was the fact that private sector was becoming more formal, while the political elite still relied on informal state-society relations. Moreover, the current chapter has traced how TÜSİAD too is becoming more professional or formal as an organization, through greater involvement of its members and other professionals in roundtables in order to expand the scope of its reports. Thus, Kaslowski and the business elite feel that the association has found a source of legitimacy in its more institutionalized nature. Finally, the chairperson's speech situates the private sector and TÜSİAD as potential resources for grassroots change rather than top-down reform, through their formalism and the work that the association had been doing with think tanks and other business organizations (TÜRKONFED and KADIGER). To this end, Dicle has also emphasized that they had visited other business associations with the report in order to get their support. The observers I spoke to, with varying levels of enthusiasm about its prospect for success, felt that Kaslowski defined the next few years of the organization.

Conclusion

The rise of a more religious government that drew strength from the traditionally more peripheral actors in Turkish society and politics posed a challenge for the business elite's prodemocracy stance. During its first decade in power, the AKP's push for reforms provided TÜSİAD a choice between a more democratizing role and a more reactionary stance, in the face of threats to the secularist establishment and the industrial elite's privileged position. The chapter demonstrated that TÜSİAD member firms' economic power made the prospect of reform achieved by outsiders more tolerable. In addition, the organizational capacity the association has built allowed the business elite to stay committed to its democratizing mission and to contribute to the process of change. As such, the period has helped confirm the findings of the previous chapter: a prodemocracy stance developed through the business elite's institutions provide capitalists with a sense of legitimacy and some confidence in its ability to affect change.

The second phase of AKP's rule, however, presented a bigger problem through the new state elite's attack on democratic institutions and civil society actors. TÜSİAD and the business elite found themselves in a situation where a prodemocracy stance became less sustainable. Moreover, TÜSİAD's own evolution has led it to focus on more instrumentalist, less controversial issues. The two taken together raised the question of whether a prodemocracy stance is bound to become strictly symbolic and legitimizing or whether the business elite can effect change. Recent developments suggest that TÜSİAD has combined its political views, the private sector's growing formalism, and the kinds of meso-level institutional issues they have tackled in the past to formulate a new strategy. The latter can potentially help the business elite carve itself a democratizing role in a growingly autocratic country. My conversations with the general secretary and other insiders have also revealed that there is member enthusiasm and support for such a strategy. The viability of such a position and its implications for the broader comparative literature will be discussed in the next and final chapter.

CONCLUSION

The main thrust of the book was to help understand why the business elite would push for increased democracy at the risk of severing its ties from the state in late-industrializing societies. Large Turkish capitalists had historically benefited from some of the illiberal strategies of the political elite, which had used incentives to co-opt various segments of society to garner support in its attempt to impose a dominant ideology top-down (see Chapters 1 and 3). Yet, by acting through their main association—TÜSİAD—the country's wealthiest corporation owners had pushed for democratization and had tackled highly contentious issues, challenging the state.

Through the examination of AKP's reign over the past two decades, the book also demonstrated that, unlike what is typically predicted by the comparative literature,[1] the business elite's prodemocracy stance appears to have become long term, despite threats to its interest emanating from a new political elite and a new class of entrepreneurs. In so doing, large Turkish capitalists not only challenged assumptions about business conservatism in Turkey, but also elsewhere in late-developing nations. A note of caution on this point was made in Chapter 7, however. President Erdoğan's firmer grip on power and tighter control of clientelistic networks have also exposed to a certain extent the limits of the traditional business elite's sway, even posing an existentialist threat. With this observation in mind, a few lessons for the social sciences can still be drawn from the business elite's political activities.

Understanding the factors that shaped their stance can help assess the prospect of full democracy in countries where it is lacking or under threat or, at the very least, can help determine whether the business elite will move away from acting as a pro-authoritarian conservative force (as it had done during the military coup of 1980 in Turkey and during the rise of bureaucratic authoritarian regimes in Latin America). A close examination of cases like TÜSİAD where capitalists have acted in unique and unpredicted fashion can, therefore, inform broader debates about capitalist development and democracy. Moreover, the AKP's more autocratic tendencies and the business elite's response can offer a potential roadmap for how the capitalist class can not only stay committed to the democratization project, but also contribute to it in more meaningful ways.

Through in-depth qualitative interviews with members of TÜSİAD, the business elite, and individuals close to them, I had found three theoretical tools to be of particular use in understanding the business elite's prodemocracy turn: (1) the importance of not just structural power, but also other sources of power that shape state-business relations (political, ideological, economic, and military) as defined by Mann,[2] (2) the fact that states can at times be autonomous from societal pressure and the business elite,[3] (3) and that in the case of late-industrializing nations, such as Turkey, the types of representation capitalists have within the state can be informal rather than formal. With this in mind, the conclusion will highlight some of the main findings.

Economic Power

Within the above framework, the economic power and material needs of the business elite were, as predicted by the more Marxian literature, influential in predicting their political stance. Chapter 4 demonstrated that large Turkish industrialists' initial impulse to organize politically happened within the context of the 1960s and 1970s, when years of growth and transition to more sophisticated sectors had given them a sense that their interests were distinct from the rest of the private sector. The 1970s became a decade when the business elite founded TÜSİAD to experiment with new forms of interest representation that moved away from the informal access they enjoyed to the state and from other semiformal business associations that the state had imposed top-down.

While the 1970s were a period when Turkish corporations found their political voice, the 1980s and 1990s became a period when they started to perceive the need for increased democratization. An analysis of economic power and changing material conditions during this period demonstrated that the business elite saw a clear link between the various dimensions of democracy and the need to operate in an increasingly global, complex, and liberal economy (see Chapter 5). The 1980s were a period of economic liberalization in Turkey and around the world. Thus, the business elite needed to adjust to an environment where it was confronted to increased competition. Economic liberalization was all the more important because the private sector became a more significant engine of economic development. But the business elite was also experiencing a series of endogenous changes, in particular the growth of industry and its continued move to more sophisticated forms of production. The period can be characterized as affording the capitalist class new opportunities, but also constraints through its greater integration in world markets. This made them realize the importance of such institutions as political certainty and the rule of law to make long-term investment decisions needed for innovation. In addition, similar concerns made some members of the business elite appreciate the social dimensions of democracy (such as education, income distribution, and regional development) as being pivotal in creating large markets and a skilled labor force. The business elite was economically more confident, but it also realized what needed to change politically.

As important as these economic factors were, they also brought to the fore the need to bring in additional analytical tools to understand the full transformation TÜSİAD and its members underwent politically. One of the biggest puzzles I confronted when I conducted research on the Turkish business elite was the apparent disconnect between their economic power (TÜSİAD member firms generate 50 percent of Turkey's official private-sector employment) and the fact that the political class was not responsive to their needs large capitalists had to organize politically and had to publicly criticize the lack of democracy in the country in order to advance their material needs.

State Autonomy

State autonomy and the informal nature of interest representation in Turkey were, therefore, particularly useful in understanding the business elite's prodemocratic turn and willingness to take on the state. The Turkish state and political elite had historically prioritized insulating the state from societal pressures to create a dominant national ideology over granting various groups formal access to the state (see Chapter 3). During the period of state-led development up until the 1980s, economic policy had primarily been used to make sure that the business elite, which needed state resources, would also embrace the goals of the political elite.[4] The state's autonomy as such created a particular tension for the private sector from the 1980s onwards. Even under economic liberalization, governments stayed in power through clientelist networks that they built, and the state elite characterized by the military and bureaucrats still insulated certain policy areas, such as those touching national identity, from public debate (see Chapters 1, 3, and 6). Hence, the state was not responsive to the new needs of capitalists. As importantly, private-sector establishments controlled by the business elite were becoming more formal because of international integration and their own endogenous growth, while the state still relied on informal channels of incorporation. While privileged access to the state had helped the business elite build their industrial empires between the 1940s and 1980s, this type of relationship became too uncertain for more capital-intensive production and world integration, which required greater stability. This tension brought about the need to look at power as more multifaceted than just structural power.

Ideological and Political Power

Chapter 4 demonstrated that as early as the 1970s the business elite had entered a phase of political experimentation to increase its voice and sense of legitimacy through accumulating political and ideological power. From forming TÜSİAD as an association autonomous from other semiformal business organizations, to begin with, to publishing full-page newspaper ads condemning the government's inability to adopt policy reforms, the period was characterized by the business elite trying to find its place in politics. Chapter 6 showed how ideological and political powers became even more central for understanding the business elite's regime preferences throughout the post-1980 period. For starters, capitalists had become less dependent on the state, and there was less fear of reprisal for criticizing it (political power).

More importantly, TÜSİAD continued to build on the experience it had amassed throughout the 1970s to make the association more effective. Though its overall size grew, TÜSİAD made sure that the association's control remained in the hands of its influential leaders, at the same time as it increased participation and drew on the expertise of a greater range of members by creating workgroups (later renamed commissions and roundtables). It also developed a culture of standing behind every report it published (an important vehicle for expressing the association's views). In so doing, the business elite formulated a more coherent prodemocracy position that stayed consistent throughout the post-1980 period. Because in the case of industrialized Western nations, entrepreneurial activity has been socially sanctioned and capitalist interest has traditionally been incorporated within the state, these kinds of activities are generally not examined as closely by the literature on capitalism and democracy. But, for the case of Turkey and other comparable cases, the work that goes into building interest representation is more essential.[5] In sum, by forging and constantly reshaping TÜSİAD, the business elite has been able to more openly challenge the state.

Acting through an association was of further importance because, through some of its influential leaders and through its commitment to democratization, TÜSİAD was able to instill in its members an appreciation for the importance of the mission. Members I interviewed over the past two decades as well as official statements made by the association suggest that (in a country where the business elite has lacked legitimacy) embracing a democratizing role has provided them with an enhanced sense of ideological legitimacy.

AKP's Rise and Its Implications

Erdoğan and the AKP's reign confirms some of these findings, but also opens up new topics for further discussion. During its first years in power, the AKP pursued a democratizing agenda and seemed committed to joining the EU. Rather than feel threatened, like other secular actors, by the fact that some of these goals were achieved under the umbrella of a more religious government, the business elite adopted a more moderating tone during the country's political debates (see Chapter 7). TÜSİAD, at least in its official statements, also stayed committed to its democratization mission. This stance, adopted from 2002 to at least 2013, and again in 2021, confirms the findings that a combination of its economic power, acting through an association, and the importance of a democratizing discourse for its ideological power allowed the business elite to stay on message. During the first act of AKP's rule, TÜSİAD and the business elite, thus, avoided a reactionary authoritarian turn by participating in rather than opposing Turkey's period of reform.

The second phase of AKP's rule under Erdoğan's more centralized presidency, however, posed a much greater challenge and existential threat for TÜSİAD, the business elite, and other prodemocracy civil society actors (see Chapter 7). Rather than staying the course on Turkey's democratization process, the AKP's style of rule became more autocratic. As importantly for business representation, its use of clientelistic networks and arbitrary state action through staffing the bureaucracy demonstrated continuity with previous Turkish political tradition. This raises several interrelated questions that warrant further comparative research and that are beyond the scope of the current book.

First, even though TÜSİAD stayed committed to its mission by emphasizing the need for democracy and through such actions as meeting with Kurdish party leaders (see Chapters 1 and 7), the fact that the business elite was unable to prevent the rise of a more authoritarian regime in the first place confirms that dealing conceptually with the state and political classes as autonomous actors is warranted in cases such as Turkey. This approach will prove particularly useful in cases where the state has tended to manage the business elite rather than be subjugated to its will. On a grimmer note, AKP's autocratic style of rule also suggests that capitalist support for the democratization process is not a sufficient condition in itself to promote political change. Rueschemeyer, Huber, and Stephens' vast comparative study has already revealed that historically democratization under capitalism was achieved through interclass alliances.[6] Thus, while TÜSİAD's demands have meshed well during the period with such groups as Kurds, feminists, and more progressive unions such as DİSK, Erdoğan's rise begs the question of whether the association could have done even more to build more formal coalitions for change. Future comparative research can help determine whether nations in which "third wave" democracy has proven more stable enjoyed greater cooperation between the business elite and popular classes.

Second, the current book has avoided the overly linear explanations of the international diffusion literature in order to highlight the significance of endogenous factors and of the deliberate labor that TÜSİAD put into formulating its political goals. However, in the case of Turkey, the EU had played a significant role in legitimizing the demands of prodemocracy actors—including TÜSİAD—during the AKP's first years in power and during the 1990s (see Chapters 5 and 7).[7] While not the only determining factor, if the EU had been more open to Turkey's candidacy, TÜSİAD's public diplomacy efforts would have been more successful in binding the AKP and Turkey's political classes to an agenda for change. Hence, transnational actors who want to promote change can and should work with local associations such as TÜSİAD that represent the interests of the elite in order to press for significant change in country cases such as Turkey.

Third, the book demonstrated that it was in part the state's poor economic performance (during the 1970s and then 1990s) combined with the lack of formal business representation that compelled larger capitalists to press for change during the pre-AKP era. As much as Chapter 7 has demonstrated TÜSİAD has stayed committed to its democratization mission under Erdoğan, one significant factor raises questions about its future continuity. As noted by commentators, the AKP government has done relatively well in terms of economic performance up until recently.[8] Chapter 7 further highlighted that the business elite tied to TÜSİAD has accumulated enough experience and capital to maintain its economic power during the period. However, some of them suffered losses due to arbitrary state action and were even jailed. Given that it was the state's poor economic performance and the lack of business representation that had partially compelled the business elite to press for change during earlier governments, one can legitimately wonder whether Erdoğan's better performance and ability to punish opponents will tame the capitalist class. If in coming years TÜSİAD reverts to an apolitical stance, it would confirm the importance of material interests and the historical importance of keeping close ties to the state. If, however, the business elite continues to push for change, it would confirm Weberian notions that a democratization discourse has become too important for the elite to abandon.

Finally, and related to the above, Chapter 7 has illustrated that TÜSİAD is establishing a new strategy to push for democratization in an environment that is not conducive to dissent. The business elite is drawing on its growing formalism and on its years of expertise in areas such as gender equality, the environment, regional development, and good government through the work of TÜSİAD and its think tanks in order to push for change at the level of society. These include its work with TÜRKONFED in heavily Kurdish regions or its attempt to achieve women's empowerment in the workforce through KADIGER. TÜSİAD's leadership seems to think that by promoting formalism throughout civil society and by holding all sectors of society, including the state, accountable to international norms within these spheres of life, that it can achieve grassroots change. My conversations with some insiders have also revealed that there is a great level of enthusiasm from the members. While beyond the scope of this book, future research can try and determine from a comparative perspective whether a growingly formal private sector is able to affect change in other civil society organizations and the state in an environment that has relied on more informal state-society relations historically. Within this context, the model built by TÜSİAD can serve as an example. The association's top leadership, according to my interviews, seem to relish their democratizing mission and the ability to speak about democracy when they can, it has given them a great source of ideological legitimacy. At the same time, General Secretary Ebru Dicle has described the organizational structure that TÜSİAD has built as a "kitchen where there are always cooks working on a number of timely issues."[9] The two combined can offer a road map for future research and future directions the business elite can take to protect democracy.

NOTES

Preface

1 James Duesenberry, "Comment on 'An Economic Analysis of Fertility,'" *Demographic and Economic Change in Developed Countries*, no. 3 (1960): 7. Quoted in Mark Granovetter, "Economic Institutions as Social Constructions: A Framework for Analysis," *Acta Sociologica* 35, no. 1 (1992): 3–11, 6.

Introduction

1 Published and commissioned by TÜSİAD in 1997, the *Perspectives on Democratization in Turkey Report* (*Türkiye'de Demokratikleşme Perspektifleri*) was written by a well-known, left-leaning constitutional law scholar Bülent Tanör in consultation with several TÜSİAD members. The report was really an analysis of the laws at the time, and its aim was to determine how they could be made more democratic. The document was organized under three broad headings: "the Political Dimension [of Democracy]," "Human Rights," and "the Rule of Law." The section on the political dimension spanned laws that regulated political parties, the parliament, and the role of the military; the one on human rights touched on individual rights and immunity, freedoms of conscience, collective rights, and the lack of minority rights for Turkey's Kurdish population; and the section on the rule of law mainly emphasized the need to have an impartial judiciary. Moreover, the report's foreword—drafted by TÜSİAD's chairperson at the time, Halis Komili—called on the association and its members to adopt a more democratizing role in part by asking "if not us who, if not now when?"
2 Metin Heper, *The State Tradition in Turkey* (Beverley, North Humberside: Eothen Press, 1985); Ahmet İnsel, *La Turquie Entre l'Ordre et le Développement: Éléments d'Analyse sur Le Rôle de l'État dans le Processus de Développement* (Paris: L'Harmattan, 1984).
3 Roger Kaplan and Freedom House, eds., *Freedom in the World: The Annual Survey of Political Rights and Civil Liberties, 1997–1998* (New Brunswick, NJ: Transaction Publishers, 1998).
4 For a broad overview see Feroz Ahmad, *The Making of Modern Turkey*, The Making of the Middle East Series (London: Routledge, 1993); Çağlar Keyder, *State and Class in Turkey: A Study in Capitalist Development* (London: Verso, 1987); Irvin Cemil Schick and Ertuğrul Ahmet Tonak, *Turkey in Transition: New Perspectives* (Oxford: Oxford University Press, 1987); İnsel, *La Turquie Entre l'ordre et Le Développement*.
5 Dietrich Rueschemeyer, Evelyne Huber, and John D. Stephens, *Capitalist Development and Democracy* (Chicago: University of Chicago Press, 1992).
6 For the case of Turkey see Ayşe Buğra, *State and Business in Modern Turkey: A Comparative Study*. SUNY Series in the Social and Economic History of the Middle East (Albany: State University of New York Press, 1994) and Keyder, *State and*

Class in Turkey. For comparative cases see, for instance, Peter B. Evans, *Dependent Development: The Alliance of Multinational, State, and Local Capital in Brazil* (Princeton, NJ: Princeton University Press, 1979) and Guillermo A. O'Donnell *Modernization and Bureaucratic-Authoritarianism: Studies in South American Politics* (Berkeley: Institute of International Studies, University of California Press, 1979).

7 For a review of the rise and subsequent turn to authoritarianism of the AKP, see Cihan Tuğal, *The Fall of the Turkish Model: How the Arab Uprisings Brought down Islamic Liberalism* (London: Verso, 2016); Yeşim Arat and Şevket Pamuk, *Turkey between Democracy and Authoritarianism* (Cambridge: Cambridge University Press, 2019). For a review of its relationship to Muslim entrepreneurs, see Ayşe Buğra and Osman Savaşkan, *New Capitalism in Turkey: The Relationship between Politics, Religion and Business* (Cheltenham, UK: Edward Elgar Publishing, 2014).

8 Rueschemeyer, Huber, and Stephens, *Capitalist Development and Democracy*.

9 Ibid.; E. Huber and J. D. Stephens, "The Bourgeoisie and Democracy: Historical and Contemporary Perspectives," *Social Research* 66, no. 3 (Fall 1999): 759–88.

10 Ernest J. Bartell and Leigh A. Payne, *Business and Democracy in Latin America*, Pitt Latin American Series (Pittsburgh: University of Pittsburgh Press, 1995); Fernando Henrique Cardoso, "Entrepreneurs and the Transition to Democracy in Brazil," in *Transitions from Authoritarian Rule: Comparative Perspectives*, ed. Guillermo O'Donnell, Philippe Schmitter, and Laurence Whitehead (Baltimore: John Hopkins University Press, 1986), 137–53.

11 Guillermo A. O'Donnell, Philippe C. Schmitter, Laurence Whitehead, and Woodrow Wilson International Center for Scholars, *Transitions from Authoritarian Rule* (Baltimore: Johns Hopkins University Press, 1986); Eduardo Silva, "From Dictatorship to Democracy—The Business-State Nexus in Chile's Economic Transformation, 1975–1994," *Comparative Politics* 28, no. 3 (April 1996): 299–320.

12 Samuel P. Huntington, *The Third Wave: Democratization in the Late Twentieth Century*, vol. 4 (Oklahoma: University of Oklahoma Press, 1993), 63.

13 David Collier and Steven Levitsky, "Democracy with Adjectives: Conceptual Innovation in Comparative Research," *World Politics* 49, no. 3 (April 1, 1997): 430–51; Steven Levitsky and Lucan A. Way, *Competitive Authoritarianism: Hybrid Regimes after the Cold War* (Cambridge: Cambridge University Press, 2010); Guillermo A. O'Donnell, "Illusions about Consolidation," *Journal of Democracy* 7, no. 2 (1996): 34–51.

14 İshak Alaton, personal interview with author (TÜSİAD member, then member of the Parliamentary Affairs Commission, president and cofounder of Alarko Holding), July 31, 2001.

15 Karl Marx and Friedrich Engels, "Manifesto of the Communist Party," in *The Marx-Engels Reader*, ed. Robert C. Tucker (New York: Norton, 1978), 475; hereafter referred as *Communist Manifesto*.

16 Ibid., 474.

17 Ibid., 475.

18 Thomas H. Marshall, *Citizenship and Social Class* (Cambridge: Cambridge University Press, 1950).

19 Barrington Moore, *Social Origins of Dictatorship and Democracy: Lord and Peasant in the Making of the Modern World* (Boston: Beacon Press, 1967).

20 Can Paker (TÜSİAD member, Türk Henkel AS), personal interview by author, August 7, 2001.

21 Max Weber, *The Protestant Ethic and the Spirit of Capitalism And Other Writings* (London: Penguin, 2002), 14.
22 Max Weber, *Max Weber: Selections in Translation* (Cambridge: Cambridge University Press, 1978), 339.
23 Moore, *Social Origins of Dictatorship and Democracy*.
24 Charles Tilly, *Coercion, Capital, and European States, AD 990-1992* (Hoboken, NJ: Wiley-Blackwell, 1992).
25 Michael Mann, *The Sources of Social Power. Vol. 2: The Rise of Classes and Nation-States, 1760-1914* (Cambridge: Cambridge University Press, 1993), 9.
26 Tim Jacoby, *Social Power and the Turkish State* (Routledge, 2004).
27 Francis Fukuyama, *The End of History and the Last Man* (New York: Simon and Schuster, 2006); Beth A. Simmons, Frank Dobbin, and Geoffrey Garrett, eds., *The Global Diffusion of Markets and Democracy* (Cambridge: Cambridge University Press, 2008).
28 Michael Hardt and Antonio Negri, *Empire* (Cambridge, MA: Harvard University Press, 2001).
29 David Harvey, "Between Space and Time: Reflections on the Geographical Imagination1," *Annals of the Association of American Geographers* 80, no. 3 (1990): 418-34; Saskia Sassen, *Cities in a World Economy* (London: Sage, 2018).
30 Leslie Sklair, "The Transnational Capitalist Class and Global Politics: Deconstructing the Corporate-State Connection," *International Political Science Review* 23, no. 2 (April 2002): 159-74.
31 Scott Greenwood, "Bad for Business? Entrepreneurs and Democracy in the Arab World," *Comparative Political Studies* 41, no. 6 (2008): 837-60, http://cps.sagepub.com/content/early/2007/09/17/0010414007300123.short.
32 An Chen, "Capitalist Development, Entrepreneurial Class, and Democratization in China," *Political Science Quarterly* 117, no. 3 (Fall 2002): 401-22.
33 Ziya Öniş and Umut Türem, "Entrepreneurs, Democracy, and Citizenship in Turkey," *Comparative Politics* 34, no. 4 (July 2002): 439-56.
34 Simmons, Dobbin, and Garrett, *Global Diffusion of Markets and Democracy*.
35 For a critique of cultural explanations and argument for a structuralist or state-centric explanation in a different context, see J. Samuel Valenzuela and Arturo Valenzuela, *Modernization and Dependency: Alternative Perspectives in the Study of Latin American Underdevelopment Comparative Politics* (New York: City University of New York Press, 1978).
36 Bartell and Payne, *Business and Democracy in Latin America*.
37 Kevin J. Middlebrook, *The Paradox of Revolution: Labor, the State, and Authoritarianism in Mexico* (Baltimore: Johns Hopkins University Press, 1995).
38 O'Donnell, *Modernization and Bureaucratic-Authoritarianism*.
39 Ibid.; Nicos P. Mouzelis, *Politics in the Semi-Periphery: Early Parliamentarism and Late Industrialization in the Balkans and Latin America* (London: Macmillan, 1986).
40 John A. Hall, *Powers and Liberties: The Causes and Consequences of the Rise of the West* (Oxford: Blackwell, 1985); Michael Mann, "Ruling-Class Strategies and Citizenship," *Sociology—The Journal of the British Sociological Association* 21, no. 3 (August 1987): 339-54.
41 Peter B. Evans, *Embedded Autonomy: States and Industrial Transformation* (Princeton, NJ: Princeton University Press, 1995).
42 Theda Skocpol and Edwin Amenta, "States and Social Policies," *Annual Review of Sociology* (1986): 131-57.

43 Buğra, *State and Business in Modern Turkey*.
44 Yemile Mizrahi, "Rebels without a Cause? The Politics of Entrepreneurs in Chihuahua," *Journal of Latin American Studies* 26 (1994): 137–58.
45 For business interests as "capital flows" or investment, see Albert O. Hirschman, *Exit, Voice, and Loyalty: Responses to Decline in Firms, Organizations, and States* (Cambridge, MA: Harvard University Press, 1970), who famously outlined how investors, unlike workers, can use the threat of disinvestment—or the "exit" option—to push the hand of government officials. This line of investigation has been useful for gauging the structural power of capitalists and understanding cases (like Mexico in 1994) where the state had to adopt reforms following its financial crisis, as outlined by Sylvia Maxfield, *Governing Capital: International Finance and Mexican Politics* (Ithaca, NY: Cornell University Press, 1990). As for business as sector, Evans, *Embedded Autonomy*, has convincingly used the IT sector to hone his highly influential concept of "embedded autonomy," which helps illustrate that the right mix of distance and cooperation between state officials and private-sector actors was paramount to implementing coherent development policy for emerging industries. Conversely, the lack of such linkages leads to corruption and poor policymaking, thus hurting good governance. Some scholars have looked at the existence (or absence) of entrepreneurial behavior among the national bourgeoisie and private-sector establishments, see Seymour Martin Lipset and Aldo E. Solari, *Elites in Latin America* (New York: Oxford University Press, 1967). However, Buğra, in *State and Business in Modern Turkey*, notes that most research on the decision-making process of businesspeople and specific firms are based on Chandler's classic account of the growth of the modern US corporation, which has tended to expand and adopt a more formal structure to absorb transaction costs associated with doing business with other private-sector organizations. Firms will choose to do many activities in-house if it will help save such things as legal and transportation costs involved with production, leading to the bureaucratization of the corporation. According to Buğra, however, what can be classified as the lack of entrepreneurship in Turkey can be tied to the nature of state-business relations, which have tended to reward the capacity to maintain informal ties to the government. As such, the behavior of capitalists through more structural and state-centric factors is an important building block for understanding why capitalists might be traditionally shyer politically than what is customarily assumed.
46 Buğra, *State and Business in Modern Turkey*.
47 Ibid.
48 For a discussion of family control in non-Turkish settings, see Ben Ross Schneider, *Hierarchical Capitalism in Latin America* (Cambridge: Cambridge University Press, 2013).
49 Sylvia Maxfield and Ben Ross Schneider, *Business and the State in Developing Countries* (Ithaca, NY: Cornell University Press, 1997); Ben Ross Schneider, *Business Politics and the State in Twentieth-Century Latin America* (Cambridge: Cambridge University Press, 2004).
50 Philippe C. Schmitter and Wolfgang Streeck, *The Organization of Business Interests: A Research Design to Study the Associative Action of Business in the Advanced Industrial Societies of Western Europe*. Discussion papers, International Institute of Management: Labour Market Policy (Berlin: Wissenschaftszentrum Berlin, 1981).

51 Francisco Durand and Eduardo Silva, *Organized Business, Economic Change, and Democracy in Latin America* (Coral Gables, FL: North-South Center Press at the University of Miami, 1998).
52 Melani Claire Cammett, *Globalization and Business Politics in Arab North Africa: A Comparative Perspective* (Cambridge: Cambridge University Press, 2007); Pete W. Moore, *Doing Business in the Middle East: Politics and Economic Crisis in Jordan and Kuwait* (Cambridge: Cambridge University Press, 2004).
53 Michael Useem, "The Social Organization of the American Business Elite and Participation of Corporation Directors in the Governance of American Institutions," *American Sociological Review* 44, no. 4 (August 1, 1979): 553–72.
54 Nicos P. Mouzelis, *Sociological Theory: What Went Wrong?: Diagnosis and Remedies* (London: Routledge, 1995).
55 These included several TÜSİAD permanent staff members, including the general secretary and their deputies. As for members of the business elite, a combination of purposive and snowball sampling was used to interview forty TÜSİAD members, which included three large corporation owners, professional managers from corporations, and several SME owners. In addition, some care was given to interview members who had been active within the association, members who were identified as being more conservative, and, conversely, members who are more liberal politically, female and male entrepreneurs, as well as members from the younger and older generation. Given the difficulty to reach elite informants and the importance of networks in Turkey, in addition to reaching out to specific individuals, I used every opportunity to talk to interviewees through references. A handful of outside observers, such as the editor of an economic news magazine and members of the state bureaucracy, were also included for their outsider perspective.
56 For a review of Muslim entrepreneurs, see Buğra and Savaşkan, *New Capitalism in Turkey*. TUSKON was a confederation representing 40,000 entrepreneurs who identified with the religious Gülenist movement, while MÜSİAD represented the interests of SMEs from regions outside of the traditional industrial hubs and was ideologically close to the AKP. Their rise because of their differing political values and economic dynamism was thought to pose a challenge for the established business elite.

Chapter 1

1 Roger Owen, *State, Power and Politics in the Making of the Modern Middle East* (New York: Routledge, 2013).
2 See https://books.google.com/ngrams/graph?content=deep+state&year_start=1800&year_end=2019&corpus=28&smoothing=3#, accessed July 17, 2021.
3 "Lies, Damn Lies and the Deep State: Plenty of Americans See Them All," ABC News/Washington Post Poll: Deep State and Fake News, April 27. 2017, https://www.langerresearch.com/wp-content/uploads/1186a4DeepStateFakeNews.pdf, accessed July 17, 2021.
4 "In Turkey, New Accusations of Links Between Police, Politicians and Criminals," *New York Times*, December 31, 1996, https://www.nytimes.com/1996/12/31/world/in-turkey-new-accusations-of-links-between-police-politicians-and-criminals.html?searchResultPosition=2, accessed July 17, 2021.

5. Metin Heper, *The State Tradition in Turkey* (Beverley, North Humberside: Eothen Press, 1985); Merve Kavakcı, "Turkey's Test with Its Deep State," *Mediterranean Quarterly* 20, no. 4 (2009): 83–97.
6. Ahmet Insel, *La Turquie Entre l'ordre et Le Développement: Éléments d'analyse Sur Le Rôle de l'État Dans Le Processus de Développement* (Paris: L'Harmattan, 1984).
7. Ibid.; Robert Bianchi, *Interest Groups and Political Development in Turkey* (Princeton, NJ: Princeton University Press, 1984); Çağlar Keyder, *State and Class in Turkey: A Study in Capitalist Development* (London: Verso, 1987); Şerif Mardin, "Center-Periphery Relations: A Key to Turkish Politics?," *Daedalus* (1973): 169–90; Ellen Kay Trimberger, *Revolution from above: Military Bureaucrats and Development in Japan, Turkey, Egypt, and Peru* (New Brunswick, NJ: Transaction Publishers, 1978).
8. Yeşim Arat and Şevket Pamuk, *Turkey between Democracy and Authoritarianism* (Cambridge: Cambridge University Press, 2019); Cihan Tuğal, *The Fall of the Turkish Model: How the Arab Uprisings Brought down Islamic Liberalism* (London: Verso, 2016); Berna Turam, ed., *Secular State and Religious Society: Two Forces in Play in Turkey* (New York: Springer, 2011); M. Hakan Yavuz, *Secularism and Muslim Democracy in Turkey* (Cambridge: Cambridge University Press, 2009).
9. Guillermo A. O'Donnell, "Illusions about Consolidation," *Journal of Democracy* 7, no. 2 (1996): 34–51.
10. Luiz Carlos Bresser Pereira, Adam Przeworski, and José María Maravall, *Economic Reforms in New Democracies: A Social-Democratic Approach* (Cambridge: Cambridge University Press, 1993).
11. Evelyne Huber, Dietrich Rueschemeyer, and John D. Stephens, "The Paradoxes of Contemporary Democracy: Formal, Participatory, and Social Dimensions," *Comparative Politics* 29, no. 3 (1997): 323–42; Ronald A. Dahl, *Polyarchy: Participation and Opposition* (New Haven, CT: Yale University Press, 1971).
12. David Collier and Steven Levitsky, "Democracy with Adjectives: Conceptual Innovation in Comparative Research," *World Politics* 49, no. 3 (April 1, 1997): 430–51; Francis Fukuyama, "Why Is Democracy Performing So Poorly?," *Journal of Democracy* 26, no. 1 (2015): 11–20; O'Donnell, "Illusions about Consolidation."
13. Steven Levitsky and Lucan A. Way, *Competitive Authoritarianism: Hybrid Regimes after the Cold War* (Cambridge: Cambridge University Press, 2010).
14. Ibid.; Thomas Carothers, "The End of the Transition Paradigm," *Journal of Democracy* 13, no. 1 (2002): 5–21.
15. Dietrich Rueschemeyer, Evelyne Huber, and John D. Stephens, *Capitalist Development and Democracy* (Chicago: University of Chicago Press, 1992), 10.
16. Daron Acemoglu and James A. Robinson, *Economic Origins of Dictatorship and Democracy* (Cambridge: Cambridge University Press, 2006).
17. Carothers, "The End of the Transition Paradigm."
18. Collier and Levitsky, "Democracy with Adjectives"; David Collier and Steven Levitsky, "Conceptual Hierarchies in Comparative Research: The Case of Democracy," in *Concepts and Method in the Social Science: The Tradition of Giovanni Sartori*, ed. David Collier and John Gerring (London: Routledge, 2009).
19. Huber, Rueschemeyer, and Stephens, "The Paradoxes of Contemporary Democracy."
20. Arat and Pamuk, *Turkey between Democracy and Authoritarianism*.
21. Cengiz Gunes, *The Kurdish National Movement in Turkey: From Protest to Resistance* (London: Routledge, 2013); Durukan Kuzu, *Multiculturalism in Turkey: The Kurds and the State* (Cambridge: Cambridge University Press, 2018).

22 Yeşim Bayar, *Formation of the Turkish Nation-State, 1920–1938* (New York: Springer, 2016).
23 Feroz Ahmad, *The Young Turks and the Ottoman Nationalities: Armenians, Greeks, Albanians, Jews, and Arabs, 1908–1918* (Salt Lake City: University of Utah Press, 2014).
24 Robert Olson, *The Emergence of Kurdish Nationalism and the Sheikh Said Rebellion, 1880–1925* (Austin: University of Texas Press, 2013).
25 Bayar, *Formation of the Turkish Nation-State*; Keyder, *State and Class in Turkey*.
26 Kuzu, *Multiculturalism in Turkey*.
27 Ibid.
28 Scholars of Kurdish political demands see these kinds of materialist or structuralist explanations as too simplistic because of their inability to discern the importance that more cultural and historical factors, like a shared Kurdish national identity, have played for demands for autonomy. Moreover, the extent to which the conflict has impacted human rights is beyond the scope of the current book. For a detailed account, see David Romano, *The Kurdish Nationalist Movement: Opportunity, Mobilization and Identity* (Cambridge: Cambridge University Press, 2006); Gunes, *The Kurdish National Movement in Turkey*.
29 For a review of all the actors involved, see Turam, *Secular State and Religious Society*.
30 Berna Turam, *Between Islam and the State: The Politics of Engagement* (Stanford, CA: Stanford University Press, 2007).
31 Mardin, "Center-Periphery Relations"; Yavuz, *Secularism and Muslim Democracy in Turkey*.
32 Ramazan Kılınç, *Alien Citizens: The State and Religious Minorities in Turkey and France* (Cambridge: Cambridge University Press, 2019).
33 Keyder, *State and Class in Turkey*; Mardin, "Center-Periphery Relations"; Trimberger, *Revolution from Above*.
34 Mardin, "Center-Periphery Relations."
35 Huri Islamoğlu and Çağlar Keyder, "Agenda for Ottoman History," *Review (Fernand Braudel Center)* (1977): 31–55; Keyder, *State and Class in Turkey*; Sevket Pamuk, *The Ottoman Economy and Its Institutions* (Farnham, UK: Ashgate Publishing, 2009).
36 Bayar, *Formation of the Turkish Nation-State*; Mardin, "Center-Periphery Relations"; Yavuz, *Secularism and Muslim Democracy in Turkey*.
37 For a comprehensive analyses of how all these factors came into play during the period, see Bayar, *Formation of the Turkish Nation-State*.
38 Mardin, "Center-Periphery Relations."
39 Ayhan Aktar, *Varlık Vergisi ve" Türkleştirme" Politikaları*, vol. 4 (Istanbul: İletişim Yayınları, 2000).
40 Dilek Güven, "Riots against the Non-Muslims of Turkey: 6/7 September 1955 in the Context of Demographic Engineering," *European Journal of Turkish Studies. Social Sciences on Contemporary Turkey* 12, no. 12 (2011).
41 Elçin Aktoprak, *Bir" Kurucu Öteki" Olarak: Türkiye'de Gayrimüslimler* (Ankara: Ankara Üniversitesi, Siyasal Bilgiler Fakültesi, İnsan Hakları Merkezi, 2010).
42 Quoted in Asharq Al-awsat, "Turkish Exceptionalism: Interview with Serif Mardi," https://eng-archive.aawsat.com/theaawsat/features/turkish-exceptionalism-interview-with-serif-mardin, accessed April 26, 2021.
43 Doğan Gürpınar and Ceren Kenar, "The Nation and Its Sermons: Islam, Kemalism and the Presidency of Religious Affairs in Turkey," *Middle Eastern Studies* 52, no. 1 (2016): 60–78.

44 Emir Kaya, *Secularism and State Religion in Modern Turkey: Law, Policy-Making and the Diyanet* (London: Bloomsbury, 2017); Kılınç, *Alien Citizens*.
45 Yeşim Arat, "The Project of Modernity and Women in Turkey"; Yeşim Arat, "From Emancipation to Liberation: The Changing Role of Women in Turkey's Public Realm," *Journal of International Affairs* 54, no. 1 (2000): 107–23.
46 Mardin, "Center-Periphery Relations," 179.
47 Arat, "From Emancipation to Liberation."
48 Berna Turam, "Gender and Sexuality of the State," *Turkish Review* 4, no. 3 (2014): 346–8; Berna Turam, "Turkish Women Divided by Politics," *International Feminist Journal of Politics* 10, no. 4 (December 2008): 475–94; Arat, "From Emancipation to Liberation"; Arat, "The Project of Modernity and Women in Turkey."
49 Nicos P. Mouzelis, *Politics in the Semi-Periphery: Early Parliamentarism and Late Industrialization in the Balkans and Latin America* (London: Macmillan, 1986); Guillermo A. O'Donnell, *Bureaucratic Authoritarianism: Argentina, 1966–1973, in Comparative Perspective* (Berkeley: University of California Press, 1988); and Peter B. Evans, *Dependent Development: The Alliance of Multinational, State, and Local Capital in Brazil* (Princeton, NJ: Princeton University Press, 1979) have offered a more Marxist interpretation for the rise of authoritarianism, noting that an alliance of technocrats, capitalists, and multinational corporations came together to promote the next stage of capitalist development and crush popular mobilization engendered by increased wealth at higher stages of development (see Chapter 2). While, Samuel P. Huntington, *Political Order in Changing Societies* (New Haven, CT: Yale University Press, 2006), has offered a more functionalist perspective.
50 Insel, *La Turquie Entre l'ordre et Le Développement*; Keyder, *State and Class in Turkey*.
51 Arat and Pamuk, *Turkey between Democracy and Authoritarianism*.
52 Şahan Savaş Karataşlı, "The Origins of Turkey's 'Heterodox' Transition to Neoliberalism: The Özal Decade and Beyond," *Journal of World-Systems Research* 21, no. 2 (2015): 387–416.
53 Metin Heper and Ahmet Evin, *State, Democracy, and the Military: Turkey in the 1980s* (Berlin: Walter de Gruyter, 1988); Metin Heper and Barry M. Rubin, *Political Parties in Turkey* (London: Routledge, 2002).
54 Yeşim Arat, "Social Change and the 1983 Governing Elite in Turkey," in *Structural Change in Turkish Society*, ed. Mübeccel Belik Kıray (Bloomington: Indiana University Turkish Studies Department, Indiana University Press, 1991), 163–78; Arat and Pamuk, *Turkey between Democracy and Authoritarianism*, 61–3.
55 Ibid.
56 Korkut Boratav, "Inter-Class and Intra-Class Relations of Distribution under 'Structural Adjustment': Turkey during the 1980s," in *The Political Economy of Turkey: Debt, Adjustment and Sustainability*, ed. Tosun Arıcanlı and Dani Rodrik (New York: St Martin's Press, 1990); Metin Heper, "The State, Political Party and Society in Post-1983 Turkey," *Government and Opposition* 25, no. 3 (1990): 321–33; Karataşlı, "The Origins of Turkey's 'Heterodox' Transition to Neoliberalism."
57 For a comprehensive account of how the RP and AKP used grassroots organizing successfully, see Jenny White, *Islamist Mobilization in Turkey: A Study in Vernacular Politics* (Seattle: University of Washington Press, 2011).
58 William M. Hale, *Islamism, Democracy, and Liberalism in Turkey the Case of the AKP*, Routledge Studies in Middle Eastern Politics 11 (Abingdon, Oxon: Routledge, 2009); Ahmet Kuru, *Democracy, Islam, and Secularism in Turkey*, Religion, Culture and Public Life (New York: Columbia University Press, 2012).

59 Turam, *Between Islam and the State*.
60 White, *Islamist Mobilization in Turkey*.
61 Ayşe Buğra and Osman Savaşkan, *New Capitalism in Turkey: The Relationship between Politics, Religion and Business* (Cheltenham, UK: Edward Elgar Publishing, 2014); Karataşlı, "The Origins of Turkey's 'Heterodox' Transition to Neoliberalism."
62 Tuğal, *The Fall of the Turkish Model*.
63 Ibid.; Arat and Pamuk, *Turkey between Democracy and Authoritarianism*; Yavuz, *Secularism and Muslim Democracy in Turkey*.
64 Berk Esen and Sebnem Gumuscu, "The Perils of 'Turkish Presidentialism,'" *Review of Middle East Studies* 52, no. 1 (2018): 43–53.
65 Kuru, *Democracy, Islam, and Secularism in Turkey*; Turam, *Between Islam and the State*; Turam, *Secular State and Religious Society*.
66 Buğra and Savaşkan, *New Capitalism in Turkey*; Ziya Öniş and Umut Türem, "Business, Globalization and Democracy: A Comparative Analysis of Turkish Business Associations," *Turkish Studies* 2, no. 2 (Autumn 2001): 94–120; Işik D. Özel, "Market Integration and Transformation of Business Politics: Diverging Trajectories of Corporatisms in Mexico and Turkey," *Socio-Economic Review*, 2018.
67 Tuğal, *The Fall of the Turkish Model*.
68 Turam, *Secular State and Religious Society*; Yavuz, *Secularism and Muslim Democracy in Turkey*.
69 Arat and Pamuk, *Turkey between Democracy and Authoritarianism*; Tuğal, *The Fall of the Turkish Model*.
70 While beyond the scope of this book, religious organizations in the periphery, such as the Gülenist movement, previously engaged the state through forming educational institutions to provide avenues of upward social mobility and jobs for its youth membership in various agencies (such as the judiciary, law enforcement, healthcare, and education). While the movement's relationship with the AKP soured after the attempted coup of 2016 against Erdoğan, for which it was held responsible, many secular Turks feared that this new network of career bureaucrats would be used to forge a religious order. For an ethnography of the movement, see Turam, *Between Islam and the State*.
71 Kuzu, *Multiculturalism in Turkey*.
72 Tuğal, *The Fall of the Turkish Model*; Ergun Özbudun, "Turkey's Judiciary and the Drift toward Competitive Authoritarianism," *International Spectator* 50, no. 2 (2015): 42–55.
73 Yeşim Arat, "Violence, Resistance, and Gezi Park," *International Journal of Middle East Studies* 45, no. 4 (2013): 807–9; Donatella della Porta and Kivanc Atak, "The Spirit of Gezi: A Relational Approach to Eventful Protest and Its Challenges," in *Global Diffusion of Protest*, ed. Donatella della Porta, Riding the Protest Wave in the Neoliberal Crisis (Amsterdam: Amsterdam University Press, 2017), 31–58.
74 Ömer Turan and Burak Özçetin, "Football Fans and Contentious Politics: The Role of Çarşı in the Gezi Park Protests," *International Review for the Sociology of Sport* 54, no. 2 (2019): 199–217.
75 "I am neither leftist nor rightist, I am an avid footballer" ("ne sağcıyım ne solcu futbolcuyum futbolcu").
76 Ödül Celep, "The Moderation of Turkey's Kurdish Left: The Peoples' Democratic Party (HDP)," *Turkish Studies* 19, no. 5 (2018): 723–47; Ioannis N. Grigoriadis, "The Peoples' Democratic Party (HDP) and the 2015 Elections," *Turkish Studies* 17, no. 1 (2016): 39–46; Francis O'Connor and Bahar Baser, "Communal Violence and Ethnic

Polarization before and after the 2015 Elections in Turkey: Attacks against the HDP and the Kurdish Population," *Journal of Southeast European and Black Sea Studies* 18, no. 1 (2018): 53–72.

77 Mehmet Arısan, "From 'Clients' to 'Magnates': The (Not So) Curious Case of Islamic Authoritarianism in Turkey," *Southeast European and Black Sea Studies* 19, no. 1 (2019): 11–30; Berk Esen and Sebnem Gumuscu, "Building a Competitive Authoritarian Regime: State–Business Relations in the AKP's Turkey," *Journal of Balkan and Near Eastern Studies* 20, no. 4 (2018): 349–72; Ziya Öniş, "Turgut Özal and His Economic Legacy: Turkish Neo-Liberalism in Critical Perspective," *Middle Eastern Studies* 40, no. 4 (2004): 113–34; Buğra and Savaşkan, *New Capitalism in Turkey*.

78 Michael M. Gunter, "Erdogan's Future: The Failed Coup, The Kurds & The Gulenists," *Journal of South Asian and Middle Eastern Studies* 41, no. 2 (2018): 1–15; Gunes, *The Kurdish National Movement in Turkey*; Tuğal, *The Fall of the Turkish Model*.

79 Buğra and Savaşkan, *New Capitalism in Turkey*.

80 "Sabancı, 'Kürt raporu' nedeniyle öldürüldü," Radikal.com.tr, August 3, 2012, http://www.radikal.com.tr/turkiye/sabanci-kurt-raporu-nedeniyle-olduruldu-1096138/, accessed July 22, 2021.

81 Ibid.

82 "Cem Boyner: Zeytini yorduk," Milliyet, August 14, 2005,https://www.milliyet.com.tr/yazarlar/serpil-yilmaz/cem-boyner-zeytini-yorduk-244134, accessed July 22, 2021.

83 "Doğu ve Güneydoğu Anadolu'da Sosyal ve Ekonomik Öncelikler," September 1, 2006, Tesev, https://www.tesev.org.tr/tr/research/dogu-ve-guneydogu-anadoluda-sosyal-ve-ekonomik-oncelikler/, accessed July 22, 2021.

84 TÜSİAD, "TÜSİAD Başkanı Dinçer Ankara Temaslarına Ilişkin Basın Toplantısı Düzenledi," Press Release, 2014, https://tusiad.org/tr/tum/item/7899-tusiad-baskani-dincer-ankara-temaslarina-iliskin-basin-toplantisi-duzenledi, accessed July 15, 2022.

85 TÜSİAD, "TÜSİAD Statement on the General Elections in Turkey," Press Release, June 24, 2015, https://tusiad.org/en/press-releases/item/8463-tusiad-statement-on-the-general-elections-in-turkey, accessed July 15, 2022.

Chapter 2

1 Karl Marx and Friedrich Engels, "Manifesto of the Communist Party," in *The Marx-Engels Reader*, ed. Robert C. Tucker (New York: Norton, 1978), 475.

2 T. H. Marshall, *Citizenship and Social Class* (Cambridge: Cambridge University Press, 1950).

3 Barrington Moore, *Social Origins of Dictatorship and Democracy: Lord and Peasant in the Making of the Modern World* (Boston: Beacon Press, 1967).

4 Adam Przeworski, *The State and the Economy under Capitalism* (Chur, Switzerland: Harwood Academic Publishers, 1990); Joseph A. Schumpeter, *Capitalism, Socialism and Democracy* (London: Routledge, 2003).

5 Schumpeter, *Capitalism, Socialism and Democracy*.

6 For example, see Dietrich Rueschemeyer, Evelyne Huber, and John D. Stephens, *Capitalist Development and Democracy* (Chicago: University of Chicago Press, 1992).

7 Seymour Martin Lipset and Aldo E. Solari, *Elites in Latin America* (New York: Oxford University Press, 1967).

8 Jagdish N. Bhagwati, "Democracy and Development," *Journal of Democracy* 3, no. 3 (1992): 37–44; Atul Kohli, "Democracy and Development," in *Development Strategies Reconsidered*, ed. John P. Lewis and Valeriana Kallab (Washington, DC: Overseas Development Council, 1986); Atul Kohli, "Democracy amid Economic Orthodoxy: Trends in Developing Countries," *Third World Quarterly* 14, no. 4 (1993): 671–89; Adam Przeworski and Fernando Limongi, "Political Regimes and Economic Growth," *Journal of Economic Perspectives* 7, no. 3 (1993): 51–69.
9 Jose Maria Maravall, "The Myth of the Authoritarian Advantage," *Journal of Democracy* 5, no. 4 (1994): 17–31.
10 Guillermo A. O'Donnell, *Bureaucratic Authoritarianism: Argentina, 1966-1973, in Comparative Perspective* (Berkeley: University of California Press, 1988).
11 Terry L. Karl, "Dilemmas of Democratization in Latin-America," *Comparative Politics* 23, no. 1 (October 1990): 1–21.
12 Francisco Durand and Eduardo Silva, *Organized Business, Economic Change, and Democracy in Latin America* (Coral Gables, FL: North-South Center Press at the University of Miami, 1998); Ernest J. Bartell and Leigh A. Payne, *Business and Democracy in Latin America*, Pitt Latin American Series (Pittsburgh: University of Pittsburgh Press, 1995).
13 A. Chen, "Capitalist Development, Entrepreneurial Class, and Democratization in China," *Political Science Quarterly* 117, no. 3 (Fall 2002): 401–22; Scott Greenwood, "Bad for Business? Entrepreneurs and Democracy in the Arab World," *Comparative Political Studies* 41, no. 6 (2007): 837–60.
14 Stephan Haggard and Robert R. Kaufman, *Dictators and Democrats* (Princeton, NJ: Princeton University Press, 2016).
15 Francis Fukuyama, "Why Is Democracy Performing So Poorly?," *Journal of Democracy* 26, no. 1 (2015): 11–20, https://doi.org/10.1353/jod.2015.0017; Guillermo A. O'Donnell, "Illusions about Consolidation," *Journal of Democracy* 7, no. 2 (1996): 34–51.
16 For example, Moore, *Social Origins of Dictatorship and Democracy*.
17 For example, Peter B. Evans, *Embedded Autonomy: States and Industrial Transformation* (Princeton, NJ: Princeton University Press, 1995).
18 Nicos Poulantzas, *Pouvoir Politique et Classes Sociales* (Paris: F. Maspero, 1971).
19 Linda Weiss, "Infrastructural Power, Economic Transformation, and Globalization," in *An Anatomy of Power: The Social Theory of Michael Mann*, ed. J. Hall and R. Schroeder (Cambridge: Cambridge University Press, 2006), 167–86.
20 Michael Mann, "The First Failed Empire of the 21st Century," *Review of International Studies* 30, no. 4 (2004): 631–53.
21 Linda Weiss, *The Myth of the Powerless State* (Ithaca, NY: Cornell University Press, 1998).
22 Bartell and Payne, *Business and Democracy in Latin America*, xi.
23 Schumpeter, *Capitalism, Socialism and Democracy*, 56.
24 Nicos Poulantzas, " Capitalist State," *New Left Review* 1, no. 58 (December 1969): 67–78.
25 Peter B. Evans, Dietrich Rueschemeyer, and Theda Skocpol, *Bringing the State Back in* (Cambridge: Cambridge University Press, 1985).
26 Evans, *Embedded Autonomy*.
27 Weiss, *The Myth of the Powerless State*.
28 G. William Domhoff, *The Power Elite and the State: How Policy Is Made in America* (New Brunswick, NJ: Transaction Publishers, 1990).

29. Roger Owen, *State, Power and Politics in the Making of the Modern Middle East* (New York: Routledge, 2013).
30. Lisa Anderson, "The State in the Middle East and North Africa," *Comparative Politics* 20, no. 1 (1987): 1–18.
31. Michael Mann, *The Sources of Social Power. Vol. 2: The Rise of Classes and Nation-States, 1760–1914* (Cambridge: Cambridge University Press, 1993), 59.
32. John A. Hall, *Powers and Liberties: The Causes and Consequences of the Rise of the West* (Oxford: Blackwell, 1985).
33. Ibid.
34. Anderson, "The State in the Middle East and North Africa"; Owen, *State, Power and Politics in the Making of the Modern Middle East*.
35. Michael Mann, *The Sources of Social Power* (Cambridge: Cambridge University Press, 1986).
36. Ibid.
37. Talcott Parsons, "The Distribution of Power in American Society," *World Politics* 10, no. 1 (1957): 123–43.
38. Karl Marx, "The German Ideology," in *The Marx-Engels Reader*, ed. Robert C. Tucker (New York: Norton, 1978), 172.
39. Domhoff, *The Power Elite and the State*.
40. Philippe C. Schmitter and Wolfgang Streeck, *The Organization of Business Interests: A Research Design to Study the Associative Action of Business in the Advanced Industrial Societies of Western Europe.* Discussion papers, International Institute of Management: Labour Market Policy (Berlin: Wissenschaftszentrum Berlin, 1981).
41. Schumpeter, *Capitalism, Socialism and Democracy*.
42. Gianfranco Poggi, *Calvinism and the Capitalist Spirit* (Amherst: University of Massachusetts Press, 1984).
43. Mann, *The Sources of Social Power. Vol. 2*.
44. S. Mainwaring, "The State and the Industrial Bourgeoisie in Peron Argentina, 1945–1955," *Studies in Comparative International Development* 21, no. 3 (Fall 1986): 3–31.
45. Kevin J. Middlebrook, *The Paradox of Revolution: Labor, the State, and Authoritarianism in Mexico* (Baltimore: Johns Hopkins University Press, 1995).
46. Kevin J. Middlebrook, "Caciquismo and Democracy: Mexico and Beyond," *Bulletin of Latin American Research* 28, no. 3 (2009): 411–27; O'Donnell, *Bureaucratic Authoritarianism*.
47. Joab B. Eilon and Yoav Alon, *The Making of Jordan: Tribes, Colonialism and the Modern State*, vol. 61 (London: I.B. Tauris, 2007); Owen, *State, Power and Politics in the Making of the Modern Middle East*.
48. Bartell and Payne, *Business and Democracy in Latin America*.
49. Adam Smith, *An Inquiry into the Nature and Causes of the Wealth of Nations*, vol. 2 (Edinburgh: Printed for Mundell, Doig, and Stevenson, 1809), 186.
50. Albert O. Hirschman, *The Passions and the Interests: Political Arguments for Capitalism before Its Triumph* (Princeton, NJ: Princeton University Press, 1977).
51. Marx and Engels, "Manifesto of the Communist Party."
52. R. Collins, "Weber Last Theory of Capitalism—A Systematization," *American Sociological Review* 45, no. 6 (1980): 925–42; Schumpeter, *Capitalism, Socialism and Democracy*; Max Weber, *General Economic History* (New Brunswick, NJ: Transaction Publishers, 1981).
53. Max Weber, *The Protestant Ethic and the Spirit of Capitalism* (New York: Scribner, 1976).

54 Marx and Engels, "Manifesto of the Communist Party."
55 Polanyi, albeit from a different perspective, traces the political struggle between capitalist and feudal interests over the legal institutional changes that brought about the commodification of land, labor, and capital: Karl Polanyi, *The Great Transformation* (Boston: Beacon Press, 1957).
56 Schumpeter, *Capitalism, Socialism and Democracy*.
57 Moore, *Social Origins of Dictatorship and Democracy*.
58 Marshall, *Citizenship and Social Class*.
59 Weber, *The Protestant Ethic and the Spirit of Capitalism*.
60 Schumpeter, *Capitalism, Socialism and Democracy*.
61 Rueschemeyer, Huber, and Stephens, *Capitalist Development and Democracy*.
62 Marshall, *Citizenship and Social Class*; Schumpeter, *Capitalism, Socialism and Democracy*.
63 While beyond the scope of this review, another tradition has linked debates about Western European democracy and its stability to industrial relations. Some have focused on the role that class compromises and a tripartite accord between the state, labor, and business to explain the lack of class struggle and opposition to democracy. See, for example, P. C. Schmitter, "Democratic-Theory and Neocorporatist Practice," *Social Research* 50, no. 4 (1983): 885–928; Theda Skocpol and Edwin Amenta, "States and Social Policies," *Annual Review of Sociology* 12 (1986): 131–57; E. O. Wright, "Working-Class Power, Capitalist-Class Interests, and Class Compromise," *American Journal of Sociology* 105, no. 4 (January 2000): 957–1002. Others, however, have focused on the ability of businesses to create a dependent working class through the labor process and control over production to explain workers' inability to become a significant political force. See, for example, Harry Braverman, *Labor and Monopoly Capital: The Degradation of Work in the Twentieth Century* (New York: Monthly Review Press, 1974); Stephen Marglin, "What Do Bosses Do?," in *The Division of Labour: The Labour Process and Class-Struggle in Modern Capitalism*, ed. André Gorz (Sussex: Harvester Press, 1976), 13–54. They assert that technological changes under capitalism have been implemented to deskill workers and give capitalists control over production. Some, like Mann, further demonstrate that although conditions for radical labor movements exist, that industrialism has created a system of dependency that has made it difficult to raise class consciousness: Michael Mann, *Consciousness and Action among the Western Working Class* (London: Macmillan, 1973). Some studies, however, have refuted these claims by demonstrating that changes under capitalism are not due to the deliberate attempt of the capitalist class to control workers, but more so the natural extension of industrialism. See Paul Attewell, "The Deskilling Controversy," *Work and Occupation* 14, no. 3 (August 1987): 323–46; David S. Landes, "What Do Bosses Really Do?," *Journal of Economic History* 46, no. 3 (September 1986): 585–623, for critiques of Braverman and Marglin, respectively. Some authors have further opposed the negative view presented by these studies to emphasize that neither control over production nor the lack of a militant working class can be explained through class struggle entirely. Goldthorpe has demonstrated that workers in advanced industrial countries are more concerned with material well-being than they are with control over production: John H. Goldthorpe, *The Affluent Worker: Political Attitudes and Behaviour* (Cambridge: Cambridge University Press, 1968). Blackburn and Mann have adopted an approach in between the two by demonstrating that capitalist production does indeed restrict the life chances of workers, but that these are still satisfied because they derive an actual level of satisfaction from the perceived diversity jobs offered by capitalism: R. M. Blackburn

and Michael Mann, *The Working Class in the Labour Market* (London: Macmillan, 1979). Furthermore, Przeworski has demonstrated that where democracy emerged, the working class preferred to join electoral politics through more centrist social-democratic parties to guarantee redistributive policies rather than press for radical change through socialist movements. This has had the benefit of pushing labor-friendly policies while curbing the potential for labour militancy: Adam Przeworski, *Capitalism and Social Democracy* (Cambridge: Cambridge University Press; Editions de la Maison des Sciences de l'Homme, 1985).

64 Przeworski, *Capitalism and Social Democracy*.
65 Michael Mann, "Ruling-Class Strategies and Citizenship," *Sociology—The Journal of the British Sociological Association* 21, no. 3 (1987): 339–54.
66 Mann, *The Sources of Social Power. Vol. 2*.
67 Moore, *Social Origins of Dictatorship and Democracy*.
68 For example, Collins, "Weber Last Theory of Capitalism."
69 Ibid.
70 Weber, *General Economic History*.
71 Mann, "Ruling-Class Strategies and Citizenship."
72 Mann, *The Sources of Social Power. Vol. 2*.
73 Mann, "Ruling-Class Strategies and Citizenship."
74 Mann, *The Sources of Social Power. Vol. 2*.
75 Schumpeter, *Capitalism, Socialism and Democracy*.
76 Albert O. Hirschman, "The Turn to Authoritarianism in Latin America and the Search for Its Economic Determinants," in *The New Authoritarianism in Latin America*, ed. D. Collier (Princeton, NJ: Princeton University Press, 1979).
77 Ibid., 63–6.
78 Alexander Gerschenkron, *Economic Backwardness in Historical Perspective: A Book of Essays* (Cambridge: Belknap Press of Harvard University Press, 1962).
79 Fernando Henrique Cardoso and Enzo Faletto, *Dependency and Development in Latin America* (Berkeley: University of California Press, 1979); Immanuel Wallerstein, "A World-System Perspective on the Social Sciences," *British Journal of Sociology* 61 (2010): 167–76.
80 Theda Skocpol and Ellen Kay Trimberger, "Revolutions and the World-Historical Development of Capitalism," *Berkeley Journal of Sociology* 22 (1977): 101–13; Ellen Kay Trimberger, *Revolution from Above: Military Bureaucrats and Development in Japan, Turkey, Egypt, and Peru* (New Brunswick, NJ: Transaction Publishers, 1978).
81 Ayşe Buğra, *State and Business in Modern Turkey: A Comparative Study*, SUNY Series in the Social and Economic History of the Middle East (Albany: State University of New York Press, 1994); Çağlar Keyder, *State and Class in Turkey: A Study in Capitalist Development* (London: Verso, 1987); Trimberger, *Revolution from Above*.
82 O'Donnell, *Bureaucratic Authoritarianism*.
83 Ibid.; Cardoso and Faletto, *Dependency and Development in Latin America*; Peter B. Evans, *Dependent Development: The Alliance of Multinational, State, and Local Capital in Brazil* (Princeton, NJ: Princeton University Press, 1979).
84 Nicos P. Mouzelis, *Politics in the Semi-Periphery: Early Parliamentarism and Late Industrialization in the Balkans and Latin America* (London: Macmillan, 1986).
85 Lipset and Solari, *Elites in Latin America*.
86 J. Samuel Valenzuela and Arturo Valenzuela, *Modernization and Dependency: Alternative Perspectives in the Study of Latin American Underdevelopment Comparative Politics* (New York: City University of New York Press, 1978).

87 Skocpol and Trimberger, "Revolutions and the World-Historical Development of Capitalism."
88 Buğra, *State and Business in Modern Turkey*.
89 Ben Ross Schneider, "Organized Business Politics in Democratic Brazil," *Journal of Interamerican Studies and World Affairs* 39, no. 4 (Winter 1997): 95–127.
90 Robert Bianchi, "Interest Group Politics in the Third-World," *Third World Quarterly* 8, no. 2 (April 1986): 507–39; Durand and Silva, *Organized Business*; Ben Ross Schneider, *Business Politics and the State in Twentieth-Century Latin America* (Cambridge: Cambridge University Press, 2004).
91 Samuel P. Huntington, *The Third Wave: Democratization in the Late Twentieth Century*, vol. 4 (Oklahoma: University of Oklahoma Press, 1993).
92 Guillermo O'Donnell, Philippe Schmitter, and Laurence Whitehead, eds., *Transitions from Authoritarian Rule: Comparative Perspectives* (Baltimore: Johns Hopkins University Press, 1986).
93 Eduardo Silva, "From Dictatorship to Democracy—The Business-State Nexus in Chile's Economic Transformation, 1975–1994," *Comparative Politics* 28, no. 3 (April 1996): 299–320.
94 Fernando Henrique Cardoso, "Entrepreneurs and the Transition to Democracy in Brazil," in *Transitions from Authoritarian Rule: Comparative Perspectives*, ed. Guillermo O'Donnell, Philippe Schmitter, and Laurence Whitehead (Baltimore: John Hopkins University Press, 1986), 137–53.
95 Karl, "Dilemmas of Democratization."
96 Patrick S. Barrett, "The Limits of Democracy: Socio-Political Compromise and Regime Change in Post-Pinochet Chile," *Studies in Comparative International Development* 34, no. 3 (Fall 1999): 3–36; Patrick S. Barrett, "Labour Policy, Labour-Business Relations and the Transition to Democracy in Chile," *Journal of Latin American Studies* 33 (August 2001): 561–97; Silva, "From Dictatorship to Democracy."
97 Jeffrey M. Paige, "Coffee and Power in El Salvador," *Latin American Research Review* 28, no. 3 (1993): 7–40.
98 Stephan Haggard and Robert R. Kaufman, *The Political Economy of Democratic Transitions* (Princeton, NJ: Princeton University Press, 1995).
99 Schneider, *Business Politics and the State*.
100 Cardoso, "Entrepreneurs and the Transition to Democracy in Brazil."
101 The term Washington Consensus (or neoliberalism in many academic circles), coined by John Williamson, refers to the set of economic reforms the IMF, World Bank, and US Treasury Department generally agreed were good for developing nations. Part of the hope was that they would also curb arbitrary state policy and help put an end to practices such as clientelism and populism that hurt democracy. See, for instance, Moises Naim, "Washington Consensus or Washington Confusion?," *Foreign Policy* (2000): 87–103; John Williamson, "Democracy and the 'Washington Consensus,'" *World Development* 21, no. 8 (1993): 1329–36.
102 Evans, *Embedded Autonomy*.
103 Blanca Heredia, "Making Economic Reform Politically Viable," in *Democracy, Markets, and Structural Reform in Latin America: Argentina, Bolivia, Brazil, Chile, and Mexico*, ed. William C. Smith, Carlos H. Acuna, and Eduardo A. Gamarra (Miami: University of Miami North-South Center, 1994), 265–96; Philip Oxhorn and Graciela Ducatenzeiler, *What Kind of Democracy? What Kind of Market?: Latin America in the Age of Neoliberalism* (University Park, PA: Pennsylvania State University Press, 1998); Luiz Carlos Bresser Pereira, José María Maravall, and Adam Przeworski, *Economic*

Reforms in New Democracies: A Social-Democratic Approach (Cambridge: Cambridge University Press, 1993); Carlos H. Waisman, "Capitalism, the Market, and Democracy," *American Behavioral Scientist* 35, nos. 4–5 (March 1992): 500–16.

104 Melanie Claire Cammett, *Globalization and Business Politics in Arab North Africa: A Comparative Perspective* (Cambridge: Cambridge University Press, 2007).

105 Bartell and Payne, *Business and Democracy in Latin America*.

106 Korkut Boratav, "Inter-Class and Intra-Class Relations of Distribution under 'Structural Adjustment': Turkey during the 1980s," in *The Political Economy of Turkey: Debt, Adjustment and Sustainability*, ed. Tosun Arıcanlı and Dani Rodrik (New York: St Martin's Press, 1990); Şahan Savaş Karataşlı, "The Origins of Turkey's 'Heterodox' Transition to Neoliberalism: The Özal Decade and Beyond," *Journal of World-Systems Research* 21, no. 2 (2015): 387–416; Ziya Öniş, "Turgut Özal and His Economic Legacy: Turkish Neo-Liberalism in Critical Perspective," *Middle Eastern Studies* 40, no. 4 (2004): 113–34.

107 Pereira, Maravall, and Przeworski, *Economic Reforms in New Democracies*.

108 Mouzelis, *Politics in the Semi-Periphery*.

109 For discussions, see Edward L. Gibson, *Class and Conservative Parties: Argentina in Comparative Perspective* (Baltimore: Johns Hopkins University Press, 1996); James W. McGuire, *Peronism without Peron: Unions, Parties, and Democracy in Argentina* (Stanford, CA: Stanford University Press, 1997); Pereira, Maravall, and Przeworski, *Economic Reforms in New Democracies*; William C. Smith, "State, Market and Neoliberalism in Posttransition Argentina—The Menem Experiment," *Journal of Interamerican Studies and World Affairs* 33, no. 4 (Winter 1991): 45–82; Kurt Weyland, "Neopopulism and Neoliberalism in Latin America: Unexpected Affinities," *Studies in Comparative International Development* 31, no. 3 (Fall 1996): 3–31.

110 Frances Hagopian, "Democracy by Undemocratic Means—Elites, Political Pacts, and Regime Transition in Brazil," *Comparative Political Studies* 23, no. 2 (July 1990): 147–70.

Chapter 3

1 Six if one considers the forced ousting of the Islamist RP coalition in 1997 by the military, the memorandum written by the military in 2009 to try and oust the AKP government, and the coup attempt of 2016, which has caused the AKP to restrict freedoms in order to prosecute individuals with alleged ties to the coup.

2 For a more recent and broad overview, see, for example, Yeşim Arat and Şevket Pamuk, *Turkey between Democracy and Authoritarianism* (Cambridge: Cambridge University Press, 2019).

3 Metin Heper, *The State Tradition in Turkey* (Beverley, North Humberside: Eothen Press, 1985); Ahmet Insel, *La Turquie Entre l'ordre et le Développement: Éléments d'analyse Sur Le Rôle de l'État Dans Le Processus de Développement* (Paris: L'Harmattan, 1984); Çağlar Keyder, *State and Class in Turkey: A Study in Capitalist Development* (London: Verso, 1987).

4 Lisa Anderson, "The State in the Middle East and North Africa," *Comparative Politics* 20, no. 1 (1987): 1–18; Roger Owen, *State, Power and Politics in the Making of the Modern Middle East* (New York: Routledge, 2013).

5   David Collier and Steven Levitsky, "Conceptual Hierarchies in Comparative Research: The Case of Democracy," in *Concepts and Method in the Social Science: The Tradition of Giovanni Sartori*, ed. David Collier and John Gerring (London: Routledge, 2009).
6   Heper, *The State Tradition in Turkey*; Keyder, *State and Class in Turkey*; Levent Köker, *Modernleşme, Kemalizm ve Demokrasi* (Istanbul: Iletişim Yayınları, 1999). For a discussion of how the IEMP model explains this see Tim Jacoby, *Social Power and the Turkish State* (Routledge, 2004).
7   Yeşim Bayar, *Formation of the Turkish Nation-State, 1920–1938* (New York: Springer, 2016).
8   Şerif Mardin, "Center-Periphery Relations: A Key to Turkish Politics?," *Daedalus* (1973): 169–90.
9   Metin Heper, *Strong State and Economic Interest Groups: The Post-1980 Turkish Experience* (Berlin: Walter de Gruyter, 1991); Çağlar Keyder, "Bureaucracy and Bourgeoisie: Reform and Revolution in the Age of Imperialism," *Review (Fernand Braudel Center)* 11, no. 2 (1988): 151–65; Ellen Kay Trimberger, *Revolution from Above: Military Bureaucrats and Development in Japan, Turkey, Egypt, and Peru* (New Brunswick, NJ: Transaction Publishers, 1978).
10 Yeşim Arat, "Politics and Big Business: Janus-Faced Link to the State," in *Strong State and Economic Interest Groups: The Post-1989 Experience*, ed. Metin Heper (Berlin: Walter de Gruyter, 1991), 135–48; Ayşe Buğra, *State and Business in Modern Turkey: A Comparative Study*, SUNY Series in the Social and Economic History of the Middle East (Albany: State University of New York Press, 1994); Keyder, *State and Class in Turkey*.
11 Mardin, "Center-Periphery Relations."
12 John A. Hall, *Powers and Liberties: The Causes and Consequences of the Rise of the West* (Oxford: Blackwell, 1985).
13 Karen Barkey, *Empire of Difference: The Ottomans in Comparative Perspective* (Cambridge: Cambridge University Press, 2008); Şevket Pamuk, "Institutional Change and the Longevity of the Ottoman Empire, 1500–1800," *Journal of Interdisciplinary History* 35, no. 2 (2004): 225–47.
14 Fernand Braudel, *The Mediterranean and the Mediterranean World in the Age of Philip II*, vol. 2 (Berkeley: University of California Press, 1995); Halil Inalcik, "Impact of the Annales School on Ottoman Studies and New Findings [with Discussion]," *Review (Fernand Braudel Center)* (1978): 69–99.
15 Barkey, *Empire of Difference*.
16 Pamuk, "Institutional Change and the Longevity."
17 There has been a Marxian debate among economic historians as to whether Turkey's relative lack of development compared to Western Europe should be attributed to the Ottoman Empire's land-holding system or whether it was its increased dependence during the latter phases of the empire that stunted its growth. See, for instance, Halil Berktay and Suraiya Faroqhi, *New Approaches to State and Peasant in Ottoman History* (London: Routledge, 1992); Huri Islamoğlu and Çağlar Keyder, "Agenda for Ottoman History," *Review (Fernand Braudel Center)* (1977): 31–55. Proponents of land-based explanations, which have adopted a more class-centric approach, maintain that the lack of feudalism and presence of the Asiatic mode of production inhibited the type of dynamism that had set Europe's transition to capitalism in motion, while the second camp maintains that dominance of the world system by Western imperial powers greatly impacted Turkish class structure and the state under the Ottoman Empire. This debate

is similar to the one that seeks to understand the relative importance of exogenous and endogenous factors in understanding late-development in the rest of the world. Given that the nature of state-business relations is the primary focus and explanatory variable of this chapter, both approaches offer some information as to how they were shaped. Thus I will not attempt to weigh in on the debate and will rather outline what each has to say about the nature of states in general and the Turkish state in particular.

18 Gianfranco Poggi, *The State: Its Nature, Development, and Prospects* (Stanford, CA: Stanford University Press, 1990).
19 Michael Mann, *The Sources of Social Power* (Cambridge: Cambridge University Press, 1986); Barrington Moore, *Social Origins of Dictatorship and Democracy: Lord and Peasant in the Making of the Modern World* (Boston: Beacon Press, 1967).
20 Karl Marx and Friedrich Engels, "Manifesto of the Communist Party," in *The Marx-Engels Reader*, ed. Robert C. Tucker (New York: Norton, 1978).
21 Hall, *Powers and Liberties*; Mann, *The Sources of Social Power*; Charles Tilly, *Coercion, Capital, and European States, AD 990–1992* (Hoboken, NJ: Wiley-Blackwell, 1992).
22 Mann, *The Sources of Social Power*.
23 Max Weber, *General Economic History* (New Brunswick, NJ: Transaction Publishers, 1981).
24 T. H. Marshall, *Citizenship and Social Class* (Cambridge: Cambridge University Press, 1950).
25 Mann, *The Sources of Social Power*.
26 Michael Mann, *The Sources of Social Power. Vol. 2: The Rise of Classes and Nation-States, 1760–1914* (Cambridge: Cambridge University Press, 1993).
27 John Haldon, *A Social History of Byzantium* (Chichester: Wiley-Blackwell, 2009).
28 Keyder, *State and Class in Turkey*.
29 Ibid.
30 Barkey, *Empire of Difference*.
31 Keyder, *State and Class in Turkey*.
32 Buğra, *State and Business in Modern Turkey*, notes the existence of several large landholding families. As such, one should not overemphasize their absence. However, these were not as numerous and powerful as was the case under Western European feudalism. Furthermore, they were not the ones who formed the basis of the subsequent political and economic elite in Turkey. For further reading on the landholding system and the economic structure of the empire, see Halil Inalcik and Donald Quataert, *An Economic and Social History of the Ottoman Empire, 1300–1914* (Cambridge: Cambridge University Press, 1994); Huri Islamoğlu and Çağlar Keyder, "Agenda for Ottoman History," *Review (Fernand Braudel Center)* (1977): 31–55; and Çağlar Keyder and Faruk Tabak, *Landholding and Commercial Agriculture in the Middle East* (Albany: State University of New York Press, 1991),
33 Keyder, "Bureaucracy and Bourgeoisie"; Trimberger, *Revolution from Above*.
34 Barkey, *Empire of Difference*.
35 Ibid.; Keyder, *State and Class in Turkey*; Roger Owen, and Şevket Pamuk, *A History of Middle East Economies in the Twentieth Century* (Cambridge, MA: Harvard University Press, 1998).
36 For further readings on the manufacturing sector during the Ottoman period, see Keyder, *State and Class in Turkey*; Buğra, *State and Business in Modern Turkey*; Donald Quataert, *Ottoman Manufacturing in the Age of the Industrial Revolution*, vol. 30 (Cambridge: Cambridge University Press, 2002); Donald Quataert, *Manufacturing in the Ottoman Empire and Turkey, 1500–1950* (Albany: State University of New York

Press, 1994); Fatma Müge Göçek, *Rise of the Bourgeoisie, Demise of Empire: Ottoman Westernization and Social Change* (Oxford: Oxford University Press on Demand, 1996).

37 Göçek, *Rise of the Bourgeoisie*.
38 Most serious studies on entrepreneurship in the Ottoman period have refuted cultural differences and have focused on structural factors. See, for example, Keyder, *State and Class in Turkey*; Buğra, *State and Business in Modern Turkey*; and Göçek, *Rise of the Bourgeoisie*.
39 Göçek, *Rise of the Bourgeoisie*.
40 Keyder, "Bureaucracy and Bourgeoisie"; Trimberger, *Revolution from Above*.
41 Feroz Ahmad, "The Late Ottoman Empire," in *The Great Powers and the End of the Ottoman Empire*, ed. Marian Kent (London: Routledge, 2005), 15–40.
42 Ibid.; Carter V. Findley, *Bureaucratic Reform in the Ottoman Empire: The Sublime Porte, 1789–1922*, Princeton Studies on the Near East (Princeton, NJ: Princeton University Press, 2012); Göçek, *Rise of the Bourgeoisie*; Keyder, "Bureaucracy and Bourgeoisie"; Elisabeth Özdalga, *Late Ottoman Society the Intellectual Legacy*, SOAS/Routledge Curzon Studies on the Middle East 3 (London: Routledge Curzon, 2005); Trimberger, *Revolution from Above*.
43 Keyder, "Bureaucracy and Bourgeoisie"; Erik J. Zürcher, *The Young Turk Legacy and Nation Building: From the Ottoman Empire to Atatürk's Turkey* (London: Bloomsbury, 2014).
44 Zürcher, *The Young Turk Legacy and Nation Building*.
45 Buğra, *State and Business in Modern Turkey*.
46 One reason why these joint ventures have been preferred as opposed to more direct state involvement is the presence of some liberal tendency within the CUP that made these more desirable than directly interventionist policies. For further details, see Buğra, *State and Business in Modern Turkey*.
47 Buğra, *State and Business in Modern Turkey*.
48 Michael Mann, *The Dark Side of Democracy: Explaining Ethnic Cleansing* (Cambridge: Cambridge University Press, 2005).
49 Feroz Ahmad, *The Young Turks and the Ottoman Nationalities: Armenians, Greeks, Albanians, Jews, and Arabs, 1908–1918* (Salt Lake City: University of Utah Press, 2014); Zürcher, *The Young Turk Legacy and Nation Building*.
50 Ahmet İçduygu, Şule Toktas, and B. Ali Soner, "The Politics of Population in a Nation-Building Process: Emigration of Non-Muslims from Turkey," *Ethnic and Racial Studies* 31, no. 2 (2008): 358–89.
51 Şahan Savaş Karataşlı and Sefika Kumral, "Capitalist Development in Hostile Conjunctures: War, Dispossession, and Class Formation in Turkey," *Journal of Agrarian Change* 19, no. 3 (2019): 528–49; Erik J. Zürcher, *Turkey: A Modern History* (London: Bloomsbury, 2017).
52 Taner Akçam, *The Young Turks' Crime against Humanity: The Armenian Genocide and Ethnic Cleansing in the Ottoman Empire*, ACLS Humanities E-Book (Princeton, NJ: Princeton University Press, 2012); Fatma Muge Göçek, *Denial of Violence: Ottoman Past, Turkish Present, and Collective Violence against the Armenians, 1789–2009* (Oxford: Oxford University Press, 2014); Nesim Şeker, "Demographic Engineering in the Late Ottoman Empire and the Armenians," *Middle Eastern Studies* 43, no. 3 (2007): 461–74.
53 Akçam, *The Young Turks' Crime against Humanity*; Karataşlı and Kumral, "Capitalist Development in Hostile Conjunctures"; Şeker, "Demographic Engineering in the Late Ottoman Empire and the Armenians."

54 Akçam, *The Young Turks' Crime against Humanity*; Göçek, *Denial of Violence*.
55 Ibid.
56 It should be noted that, given its large size, the Armenian population was diverse and included both urban and rural, both lower- and upper-class individuals. Thus, the transfer not only involved capitalist enterprises, but also afforded the opportunity for dispossessing smaller farmers of their dwellings and their lands, leading to a land grab in Anatolia. The review of similar cables sent by CUP officials reveal that the desired policy was to use these to harbor new Muslim immigrants. Akçam, *The Young Turks' Crime against Humanity*; Karataşlı and Kumral, "Capitalist Development in Hostile Conjunctures."
57 Quoted in Akçam, *The Young Turks' Crime against Humanity*, 363.
58 Karataşlı and Kumral, "Capitalist Development in Hostile Conjunctures"; Keyder, *State and Class in Turkey*.
59 Göçek, *Denial of Violence*.
60 Buğra, *State and Business in Modern Turkey*.
61 Zürcher, *Turkey*.
62 Zürcher, *The Young Turk Legacy and Nation Building*.
63 Keyder, *State and Class in Turkey*; Mardin, "Center-Periphery Relations."
64 Zürcher, *The Young Turk Legacy and Nation Building*.
65 Trimberger, *Revolution from Above*.
66 Erdal Yavuz, "The State of the Industrial Workforce, 1923–1940," in *Workers and the Working Class in the Ottoman Empire and the Turkish Republic 1839–1950*, ed. Donald Quataert and Eric Zürcher (London: Tauris Academic Studies, 1994), 95–125; Keyder, *State and Class in Turkey*, 1987.
67 Nicos P. Mouzelis, *Politics in the Semi-Periphery: Early Parliamentarism and Late Industrialization in the Balkans and Latin America* (London: Macmillan, 1986).
68 Zürcher, *The Young Turk Legacy and Nation Building*.
69 Bayar, *Formation of the Turkish Nation-State, 1920–1938*.
70 Feroz Ahmad, *The Making of Modern Turkey*, The Making of the Middle East Series (New York: Routledge, 1993).
71 For an extensive review of economic policies covering the period from 1918 to 1960, see Yahya Sezai Tezel, *Cumhuriyet Döneminin Iktisadi Tarihi* (Ankara: Yurt Yayınevi, 1982).
72 Karataşlı and Kumral, "Capitalist Development in Hostile Conjunctures."
73 Tezel, *Cumhuriyet Döneminin Iktisadi Tarihi*; Köker, *Modernleşme, Kemalizm ve Demokrasi*.
74 Selim İlkin and İlhan Tekeli, *Uygulamaya Geçerken Türkiye'de Devletçiligin Olusumu* (Ankara: Orta Dogu Teknik Üniversitesi, 1982); Korkut Boratav, *Türkiye'de Devletçilik*, vol. 3 (Ankara: Savaş Yayınevi, 1982); Keyder, *State and Class in Turkey*; Buğra, *State and Business in Modern Turkey*.
75 Buğra, *State and Business in Modern Turkey*.
76 İlkin and Tekeli, *Uygulamaya Geçerken Türkiye'de Devletçiligin Olusumu*; Köker, *Modernleşme, Kemalizm ve Demokrasi*.
77 Ibid.; Keyder, *State and Class in Turkey*.
78 Keyder, *State and Class in Turkey*; Ahmad, *The Making of Modern Turkey*.
79 Buğra, *State and Business in Modern Turkey*.
80 Ibid.
81 Seven Ağır and Cihan Artunç, "The Wealth Tax of 1942 and the Disappearance of Non-Muslim Enterprises in Turkey," *Journal of Economic History* 79, no. 1

(2019): 201–43; Ayhan Aktar, *Varlık Vergisi ve" Türkleştirme" Politikaları*, vol. 4 (Istanbul: İletişim Yayınları, 2000).
82 Keyder, *State and Class in Turkey*; Buğra, *State and Business in Modern Turkey*.
83 For an exhaustive review of economic policy in the post-World War II period, see Korkut Boratav, *Türkiye İktisat Tarihi 1908-2002*. 9th edition (Ankara: İmge Kitabevi, 2005). For how this impacted the powers of Western states see Michael Mann, *The Sources of Social Power. Vol. 4: Globalizations, 1945-2011* (Cambridge: Cambridge University Press, 2012).
84 Şahan Savaş Karataşlı, "The Origins of Turkey's 'Heterodox' Transition to Neoliberalism: The Özal Decade and Beyond," *Journal of World-Systems Research* 21, no. 2 (2015): 387–416.
85 Feroz Ahmad, *The Turkish Experiment in Democracy, 1950–1975* (London: Royal Institute of International Affairs, 1977); Myron Weiner and Ergun Özbudun, *Competitive Elections in Developing Countries* (Durham, NC: Duke University Press, 1987); Kemal H. Karpat, "Turkey's Politics," in *Turkey's Politics: The Transition to a Multi-Party System* (Princeton, NJ: Princeton University Press, 2015).
86 Karataşlı, "The Origins of Turkey's 'Heterodox' Transition to Neoliberalism."
87 Robert Bianchi, *Interest Groups and Political Development in Turkey* (Princeton, NJ: Princeton University Press, 1984); Heper, *Strong State and Economic Interest Groups*, 15.
88 Buğra, *State and Business in Modern Turkey*.
89 Mardin, "Center-Periphery Relations."
90 Çağlar Keyder, *The Definition of a Peripheral Economy* (Cambridge: Cambridge University Press; Editions de la Maison des sciences de l'homme, 1981).
91 Keyder, *State and Class in Turkey*.
92 Ahmad, *The Turkish Experiment in Democracy, 1950-1975*; Weiner and Özbudun, *Competitive Elections in Developing Countries*.
93 Keyder, *State and Class in Turkey*.
94 Buğra, *State and Business in Modern Turkey*.
95 Ibid.
96 Ibid.
97 Karataşlı and Kumral, "Capitalist Development in Hostile Conjunctures"; Dilek Güven, "Riots against the Non-Muslims of Turkey: 6/7 September 1955 in the Context of Demographic Engineering," *European Journal of Turkish Studies. Social Sciences on Contemporary Turkey*, no. 12 (2011); Buğra, *State and Business in Modern Turkey*.
98 Ahmad, *The Turkish Experiment in Democracy, 1950-1975*; Kemal H. Karpat, "The Military and Politics in Turkey, 1960-64: A Socio-Cultural Analysis of a Revolution," *American Historical Review* 75, no. 6 (1970): 1654–83; Kemal H. Karpat, "Military Interventions: Army-Civilian Relations in Turkey before and after 1980," in *Studies on Turkish Politics and Society* (Leiden: Brill, 2004), 353–77.
99 Fikret Şenses, *Recent Industrialization Experience of Turkey in a Global Context*, Contributions in Economics and Economic History, No. 155 (Westport, CT: Greenwood Press, 1994); Keyder, *State and Class in Turkey*; Buğra, *State and Business in Modern Turkey*.
100 Heper, *Strong State and Economic Interest Groups*; Bianchi, *Interest Groups and Political Development in Turkey*.
101 Keyder, *State and Class in Turkey*.
102 Buğra, *State and Business in Modern Turkey*.

103 Ibid.; Keyder, *State and Class in Turkey*.
104 Keyder, *State and Class in Turkey*.

Chapter 4

1 Yeşim Arat, "Politics and Big Business: Janus-Faced Link to the State," in *Strong State and Economic Interest Groups: The Post-1989 Experience*, ed. Metin Heper (Berlin: Walter de Gruyter, 1991), 135–48; Ayşe Buğra, *State and Business in Modern Turkey: A Comparative Study*, SUNY Series in the Social and Economic History of the Middle East (Albany: State University of New York Press, 1994); Robert Bianchi, *Interest Groups and Political Development in Turkey* (Princeton, NJ: Princeton University Press, 1984).
2 TÜSİAD, *TÜSİAD 1975 Yılı Çalışmaları* (Istanbul: TÜSİAD, 1975).
3 Bülent Eczacıbaşı (TÜSİAD member, TÜSİAD chairman [1991–2] and president and copresident of the Higher Advisory Council [1992–9], president of Eczacıbaşı Holding AS), personal interview by author, August 6, 2001.
4 Buğra, *State and Business in Modern Turkey*.
5 Ibid.; Çağlar Keyder, *State and Class in Turkey: A Study in Capitalist Development* (London: Verso, 1987).
6 Bianchi, *Interest Groups and Political Development in Turkey*; Buğra, *State and Business in Modern Turkey*; Arat, "Politics and Big Business."
7 Buğra, *State and Business in Modern Turkey*; Keyder, *State and Class in Turkey*.
8 Buğra, *State and Business in Modern Turkey*.
9 "İshak Alaton's Biography—Alarko Holding," https://www.alarko.com.tr/en/about-us/founders/ishak-alaton/biography, accessed April 26, 2022.
10 Buğra, *State and Business in Modern Turkey*.
11 Being active in several sectors give holding owners and members of TÜSİAD a vantage point very similar to the "inner circle" of American capitalists: those individuals who sit on the board of several corporations and who are, therefore, able to see the broader needs of capital. These tend to be more progressive when compared to single-sector or local capital on issues such as labor relations, as they are able to discern the broader needs of capitalism as a system. Jill S. Quadagno, "Welfare Capitalism and the Social Security Act of 1935," *American Sociological Review* 49, no. 5 (October 1, 1984): 632–47, https://doi.org/10.2307/2095421; Michael Useem, "The Inner Group of the American Capitalist Class," *Social Problems* 25, no. 3 (February 1, 1978): 225–40, https://doi.org/10.2307/800061. However, in Turkey, they are not necessarily able to turn this into political action, since holding owners have been successful at obtaining individual favors from the state and historically did not want to jeopardize their links to government officials. As was seen in the previous chapter, classes were not represented effectively by formal channels, thus compounding the problem.
12 Eczacıbaşı, personal interview by author, August 6, 2001.
13 Korkut Boratav, *Türkiye İktisat Tarihi 1908–2002, 9th edition* (Ankara: İmge Kitabevi, 2005); Korkut Boratav, *Türkiye'de Devletçilik*, vol. 3 (Ankara: Savaş Yayınevi, 1982); Keyder, *State and Class in Turkey*; Feroz Ahmad, *The Making of Modern Turkey*, The Making of the Middle East Series (London: Routledge, 1993).

14 Keyder, *State and Class in Turkey*; Boratav, *Türkiye İktisat Tarihi*; Ahmad, *The Making of Modern Turkey*.
15 For shifts in industrialization policy, see Fikret Şenses, "Stabilization and Structural Adjustment Program and the Process of Turkish Industrialization: Main Policies and Their Impact," in *Recent Industrialization Experience of Turkey in a Global Context*, ed. Fikret Şenses (Wesport, CT: Greenwood Press, 1994). For a review of how SEEs impacted industrialization, see Boratav, *Türkiye'de Devletçilik*; Korkut Boratav and Ergun Türkcan, *Türkiye'de Sanayileşmenin Yeni Boyutları ve KİT'ler* (Ankara: Tarih Vakfı Yurt Yayınları, 1993).
16 Bianchi, *Interest Groups and Political Development in Turkey*.
17 Şenses, "Stabilization and Structural Adjustment," 52–3.
18 Bianchi, *Interest Groups and Political Development in Turkey*.
19 Ibid.
20 Ibid.; Arat, "Politics and Big Business."
21 Melani Claire Cammett, *Globalization and Business Politics in Arab North Africa: A Comparative Perspective* (Cambridge: Cambridge University Press, 2007); Pete W. Moore, *Doing Business in the Middle East: Politics and Economic Crisis in Jordan and Kuwait* (Cambridge: Cambridge University Press, 2004).
22 Vedat Milor and Jesse Biddle, "Economic Governance in Turkey: Bureaucratic Capacity, Policy Networks, and Business Associations," in *Business and the State in Developing Countries*, ed. Sylvia Maxfield and Ben Ross Schneider (Ithaca, NY: Cornell University Press, 1997), 277–309.
23 Arat, "Politics and Big Business," 137.
24 Bianchi, *Interest Groups and Political Development in Turkey*.
25 Ibid.; Keyder, *State and Class in Turkey*.
26 Metin Heper, "Interest Group Politics in Post-1980 Turkey: Lingering Monism," in *Strong State and Economic Interest Groups: The Post-1980 Turkish Experience*, ed. Metin Heper (Berlin: Walter de Gruyter, 1991); Ergun Özbudun, "The Post-1980 Legal Framework for Interest Group Associations," in *Strong State and Economic Interest Groups: The Post-1989 Experience*, ed. Metin Heper (Berlin: Walter de Gruyter, 1991), 41–54.
27 Bianchi, *Interest Groups and Political Development in Turkey*.
28 Ibid.
29 Ben Ross Schneider, "Organized Business Politics in Democratic Brazil," *Journal of Interamerican Studies and World Affairs* 39, no. 4 (Winter 1997): 95–127; Ben Ross Schneider, *Business Politics and the State in Twentieth-Century Latin America* (Cambridge: Cambridge University Press, 2004).
30 Oktay Varlıer (TÜSİAD member, Alarko Holding), personal interview by author, June 17, 2002.
31 Arat, "Politics and Big Business"; Bianchi, *Interest Groups and Political Development in Turkey*; Keyder, *State and Class in Turkey*.
32 Buğra, *State and Business in Modern Turkey*; Fatma Muge Göçek, *Denial of Violence: Ottoman Past, Turkish Present, and Collective Violence against the Armenians, 1789–2009* (Oxford: Oxford University Press, 2014).
33 Varlıer, personal interview by author, 2002.
34 İshak Alaton (TÜSİAD member, then member of the Parliamentary Affairs Commission, president and cofounder of Alarko Holding), personal interview by author, July 31, 2001.

35 Gianfranco Poggi, *Calvinism and the Capitalist Spirit* (Amherst: University of Massachusetts Press, 1984); Max Weber, *The Protestant Ethic and the Spirit of Capitalism* (New York: Scribner, 1976).
36 Poggi, *Calvinism and the Capitalist Spirit*.
37 Keyder, *State and Class in Turkey*; Buğra, *State and Business in Modern Turkey*.
38 Alaton, personal interview by author, 2001.
39 Varlıer, personal interview by author, 2002.
40 TÜSİAD, *TÜSİAD 1975 Yılı Çalışmaları*.
41 Rona Yırcalı (TÜSİAD member, chairman of Yapı Kredi Bank), personal interview by author, July 23, 2002.
42 Buğra, *State and Business in Modern Turkey*.
43 Ibid.
44 TÜSİAD, *TÜSİAD 1977 Yılı Çalışmaları* (Istanbul: TÜSİAD, 1977); TÜSİAD, *TÜSİAD 1978 Yılı Çalışmaları* (Istanbul: TÜSİAD, 1978); TÜSİAD, *TÜSİAD 1979 Yılı Çalışmaları* (Istanbul: TÜSİAD, 1979).
45 TÜSİAD, *TÜSİAD 1979 Yılı Çalışmaları*.
46 Keyder, *State and Class in Turkey*; Ahmad, *The Making of Modern Turkey*.
47 Mustafa Sönmez, *Türkiye'de Holdingler Kırk Haramiler* (Istanbul: Arkadaş Yayınevi, 1988).
48 Arat, "Politics and Big Business"; Buğra, *State and Business in Modern Turkey*.
49 Ziya Öniş, "The Political Economy of Turkey in the 1980s: The Anatomy of Unorthodox Liberalism," *Interest Group Politics in Turkey* (Berlin: Walter de Gruyter, 1991); Şahan Savaş Karataşlı, "The Origins of Turkey's 'Heterodox' Transition to Neoliberalism: The Özal Decade and Beyond," *Journal of World-Systems Research* 21, no. 2 (2015): 387–416.
50 Karataşlı, "The Origins of Turkey's 'Heterodox' Transition."

Chapter 5

1 Feyyaz Berker, speech delivered on January 23, 1997, www.tusiad.org.tr.
2 For a complete overview of the reforms, see Tosun Arıcanlı and Dani Rodrik, eds., *The Political Economy of Turkey: Debt, Adjustment and Sustainability* (New York: Springer, 1990).
3 Ziya Öniş, "Turgut Özal and His Economic Legacy: Turkish Neo-Liberalism in Critical Perspective," *Middle Eastern Studies* 40, no. 4 (2004): 113–34; Fikret Şenses, "Stabilization and Structural Adjustment Program and the Process of Turkish Industrialization: Main Policies and Their Impact," in *Recent Industrialization Experience of Turkey in a Global Context*, ed. Fikret Şenses (Westport, CT: Greenwood Press, 1994); Ümit Sönmez, "The Political Economy of Market and Regulatory Reforms in Turkey: The Logic and Unintended Consequences of Ad-Hoc Strategies," *New Political Economy* 16, no. 1 (2011): 101–30.
4 Feyyaz Berker (TÜSİAD member, TÜSİAD chairman [1971–9] and High Advisory Board member and president [1985–6], cofounder and copresident of Tekfen Holding AS), personal interview by author, August 19, 2002.
5 Paul Kubicek, *The European Union and Democratization* (London: Routledge, 2003).
6 Peter B. Evans, *Embedded Autonomy: States and Industrial Transformation* (Princeton, NJ: Princeton University Press, 1995); Luiz Carlos Bresser Pereira, Adam Przeworski,

and Jose Maria Maravall, *Economic Reforms in New Democracies: A Social-Democratic Approach* (Cambridge: Cambridge University Press, 1993).
7   Michael Mann, "Has Globalization Ended the Rise and Rise of the Nation-State?," *Review of International Political Economy* 4, no. 3 (1997): 472–96; Linda Weiss, *The Myth of the Powerless State* (Ithaca, NY: Cornell University Press, 1998).
8   Şahan Savaş Karataşlı, "The Origins of Turkey's 'Heterodox' Transition to Neoliberalism: The Özal Decade and Beyond," *Journal of World-Systems Research* 21, no. 2 (2015): 387–416; Öniş, "Turgut Özal and His Economic Legacy"; Sönmez, "The Political Economy of Market and Regulatory Reforms in Turkey."
9   Karataşlı, "The Origins of Turkey's 'Heterodox' Transition to Neoliberalism."
10 Yılmaz Akyüz and Korkut Boratav, "The Making of the Turkish Financial Crisis," *World Development*, 31, no. 9 (2003): 1549–66.
11 Ayşe Buğra and Osman Savaşkan, *New Capitalism in Turkey: The Relationship between Politics, Religion and Business* (Cheltenham, UK: Edward Elgar Publishing, 2014); Ziya Öniş and Umut Türem, "Business, Globalization and Democracy: A Comparative Analysis of Turkish Business Associations," *Turkish Studies* 2, no. 2 (Autumn 2001): 94–120.
12 Guillermo A. O'Donnell, "Illusions and Conceptual Flaws," *Journal of Democracy* 7, no. 4 (1996): 160–8.
13 Karataşlı, "The Origins of Turkey's 'Heterodox' Transition to Neoliberalism"; Öniş, "Turgut Özal and His Economic Legacy."
14 Arıcanlı and Rodrik, *The Political Economy of Turkey*.
15 Korkut Boratav, "Inter-Class and Intra-Class Relations of Distribution under 'Structural Adjustment': Turkey during the 1980s," in *The Political Economy of Turkey: Debt, Adjustment and Sustainability*, ed. Tosun Arıcanlı and Dani Rodrik (New York: St Martin's Press, 1990); Karataşlı, "The Origins of Turkey's 'Heterodox' Transition to Neoliberalism"; Öniş, "Turgut Özal and His Economic Legacy."
16 Şenses, "Stabilization and Structural Adjustment."
17 Karataşlı, "The Origins of Turkey's 'Heterodox' Transition to Neoliberalism."
18 Ibid.; Buğra and Savaşkan, *New Capitalism in Turkey*; Ömer Demir, Mustafa Acar, and Metin Toprak, "Anatolian Tigers or Islamic Capital: Prospects and Challenges," *Middle Eastern Studies* 40, no. 6 (2004): 166–88, https://doi.org/10.1080/0026320042000282937; Evren Hosgör, "Islamic Capital/Anatolian Tigers: Past and Present," *Middle Eastern Studies* 47, no. 2 (2011): 343–60.
19 TÜSİAD, *Brochure* (Istanbul: TÜSİAD, 1997).
20 Linda Weiss, *States in the Global Economy: Bringing Domestic Institutions Back in*, vol. 86 (Cambridge: Cambridge University Press, 2003).
21 Ayşe Buğra, *State and Business in Modern Turkey: A Comparative Study*, SUNY Series in the Social and Economic History of the Middle East (Albany: State University of New York Press, 1994); Öniş, "Turgut Özal and His Economic Legacy."
22 Buğra, *State and Business in Modern Turkey*.
23 Ziya Öniş, "Liberalization, Transnational Corporations, and Foreign Direct Investment in Turkey: The Experience of the 1980s," in *Recent Industrialization Experience of Turkey in a Global Context*, ed. Fikret Şenses (Westport, CT: Greenwood Press, 1994).
24 TÜSİAD, *Brochure*.
25 Ziya Öniş, "Organization of Export-Oriented Industrialization: The Turkish Foreign Trade Companies in Comparative Perspective," in *Economics and Politics of Turkish*

Liberalization, ed. Tevfik F. Nas and Mehmet Odekon (London: Lehigh University Press, 1992), 76.
26 Ibid., 76–7.
27 Bülent Eczacıbaşı (TÜSİAD member, TÜSİAD chairman [1991–2] and president and copresident of the Higher Advisory Council [1992–9], president of Eczacıbaşı Holding AS, personal interview by author, August 6, 2001.
28 Reşat Bayer and Ziya Öniş, "Turkish Big Business in the Age of Democratic Consolidation: The Nature and Limits of Its Influence," *South European Society and Politics* 15, no. 2 (June 2010): 181–201, https://doi.org/10.1080/13608746.2010.503043.
29 Eczacıbaşı, personal interview by author, August 6, 2001.
30 Ibid.
31 For a more detailed analysis of business's position toward EU integration please see Öniş and Türem, "Business, Globalization and Democracy and Işık Özel, "Market Integration and Transformation of Business Politics: Diverging Trajectories of Corporatisms in Mexico and Turkey," *Socio-Economic Review* 19, no. 1 (2018): 219–45.
32 Şerif Kaynar (TÜSİAD member, K-Partners, Turkey), personal interview by author, July 8, 2002.
33 Buğra and Savaşkan, *New Capitalism in Turkey*.
34 Yılmaz Argüden (TÜSİAD member, then member of the ARGE danismanlik AS), personal interview by author, August 2001.
35 Ibid.
36 Bayer and Öniş, "Turkish Big Business in the Age of Democratic Consolidation."
37 Tuğrul Kudatgobilik (Koç Holding AS), personal interview by author, July 24, 2002.
38 Ebru Dicle (TÜSİAD deputy general secretary), personal interview by author, July 24, 2001.
39 Kudatgobilik, personal interview by author, July 24, 2002.
40 Akyüz and Boratav, "The Making of the Turkish Financial Crisis."
41 Cem Duna, TÜSİAD's European Union Affairs Commission, Founder of AB Consultancy & Investment Services. July 13, 2001, personal interview by author.
42 Eczacıbaşı, personal interview by author, August 6, 2001.
43 Aldo Kaslowski (TÜSİAD member and chairman of Organik Holding), personal interview by author, July 30, 2002.
44 Bülent Eczacıbaşı, speech delivered on April 8, 1997, www.tusiad.org.tr.
45 Meltem Kurtsan (Kurtsan Ilaclari AS), personal interview by author, July 10, 2002; Erkut Yücaoğlu (TÜSİAD member, TÜSİAD chairman [1999–2001]), personal interview by author, July 24, 2001.
46 Mehmet Şuhubi (TÜSİAD member, Teslo Tekstil Urunleri Sanayi ve Ticaret AS), personal interview by author, July 10, 2002.
47 Argüden, personal interview by author, August 2001.
48 Varlıer, personal interview by author, June 17, 2002.
49 Buğra, *State and Business in Modern Turkey*.
50 John Waterbury, "Export-Led Growth and the Centre Right Coalition in Turkey," *Comparative Politics* 24, no. 2 (1992): 45–62.
51 Şuhubi, personal interview by author, July 10, 2002.
52 World Bank Group, "World Development Indicators" (Washington, DC: World Bank Group, 2005)
53 Tuğrul Kudatgobilik (Koç Holding AS), personal interview by author, July 24, 2002.
54 World Bank Group, "World Development Indicators."

Notes 221

55 TÜSİAD, *Brochure*.
56 Devlet-Istatistik-Enstitüsü, "İşyeri Büyüklük Grubuna Göre Katma Deyer," *DIE Newsletter*, 1999.
57 Akyüz and Boratav, "The Making of the Turkish Financial Crisis."
58 Eczacıbaşı, speech delivered on April 8, 1997.
59 Halis Komili, speech delivered on December 9, 1994, www.tusiad.org.tr.
60 World-Bank-Group, "World Development Indicators."
61 Haluk Tükel (TÜSİAD member, TÜSİAD secretary general), personal interview by author, 2002.
62 Kaslowski, personal interview by author, 2002; Şuhubi, personal interview by author, July 10, 2022.
63 Muharrem Kayhan, speech delivered as chairman of TÜSİAD on January 22, 1998, www.tusiad.org.tr.
64 Halis Komili, speech delivered on December 8, 1995, www.tusiad.org.tr.
65 TÜSİAD (1990) "Türkiye'de Eğitim" (Education in Turkey) and TÜSİAD (2000) *Türkiye'de Bireysel Gelir Dağılımı ve Yoksulluk* (Individual Income Distribution and Poverty in Turkey).
66 For a detailed analysis of income distribution during the post-1980 period, please see Korkut Boratav, "Inter-Class and Intra-Class Relations of Distribution under 'Structural Adjustment': Turkey during the 1980's," in *The Political Economy of Turkey: Debt, Adjustment and Sustainability*, ed. Tosun Arıcanlı and Dani Rodrik (New York: St Martin's Press, 1990), 199–29.
67 Berker, personal interview by author, August 19, 2002; Eczacıbaşı, personal interview by author, 2001.
68 Eczacıbaşı, personal interview by author, August 6, 2001.
69 Varlıer, personal interview by author, June 17, 2002.
70 Ibid.
71 Vedat Milor and Jesse Biddle, "Economic Governance in Turkey: Bureaucratic Capacity, Policy Networks, and Business Associations," in *Business and the State in Developing Countries*, ed. Sylvia Maxfield and Ben Ross Schneider (Ithaca, NY: Cornell University Press, 1997), 277–309.
72 Cansen Başaran-Symes (TÜSİAD member and founder of PriceWaterhouse, Turkey), personal interview by author, 2002, 2008; Kaynar, personal interview by author, July 8, 2002.
73 Kaynar, personal interview by author, July 8, 2002.
74 Berker, personal interview by author, June 17, 2002.
75 Eroğlu Galip, TÜSİAD member, Hidrotek Arıtma İnşaat Sanayi ve Ticaret Ltd, personal interview by author, July 2002.
76 Argüden, personal interview by author, 2002.

Chapter 6

1 Erkut Yücaoğlu (TÜSİAD member, TÜSİAD chairman [1999–2001]), personal interview by author, 2001.
2 Philippe C. Schmitter and Wolfgang Streeck, *The Organization of Business Interests: A Research Design to Study the Associative Action of Business in the Advanced Industrial Societies of Western Europe*. Discussion papers, International Institute of Management: Labour Market Policy (Berlin: Wissenschaftszentrum Berlin, 1981).

3 Bülent Eczacıbaşı (TÜSİAD member, TÜSİAD chairman [1991–2] and president and copresident of the Higher Advisory Council [1992–9], president of Eczacıbaşı Holding AS), personal interview by author, August 21, 2002; Alp Orçun (Eczacıbaşı Holding), personal interview by author, 2001.
4 Ergun Özbudun, "The Post-1980 Legal Framework for Interest Group Associations," in *Strong State and Economic Interest Groups: The Post-1989 Experience*, ed. Metin Heper (Berlin: Walter de Gruyter, 1991), 41–54.
5 Yeşim Arat, "Politics and Big Business: Janus-Faced Link to the State," in *Strong State and Economic Interest Groups: The Post-1989 Experience*, ed. Metin Heper (Berlin: Walter de Gruyter, 1991), 135–48; Tosun Arıcanlı and Dani Rodrik, *The Political Economy of Turkey: Debt, Adjustment and Sustainability* (Basingstoke: Macmillan, 1990); Ziya Öniş, "The Political Economy of Turkey in the 1980s: The Anatomy of Unorthodox Liberalism," in *Interest Group Politics in Turkey* (Berlin: Walter de Gruyter, 1991).
6 Işık Özel, "Beyond the Orthodox Paradox: The Breakup of State-Business Coalitions in 1980s Turkey," *Journal of International Affairs* 57, no. 1 (2003): 97–112.
7 TÜSİAD, *TÜSİAD 1989 Yili Çalismalari* (Istanbul: TÜSİAD, 1989).
8 TÜSİAD activity reports from 1990 to 1996, available at https://tusiad.org/45-yil/.
9 Ebru Dicle (TÜSİAD deputy general secretary), personal interview by author, July 24, 2001; Alp Orçun, personal interview by author, 2001 to 2002.
10 Nora Şeni, "Le Mécène, Un Acteur Méconnu de La Ville. Istanbul à l'heure Des Musées Privés," *Transcontinentales. Sociétés, Idéologies, Système Mondial*, no. 7 (2009): 105–28.
11 John Doxey, "Turkey's New Reformer," *New Leader (New York)* 78, no. 6 (1995): 8; Ibrahim Betil (former TÜSİAD member, then chairman of Turkey's Educational Volunteers), personal interview by author, 2002.
12 Reşat Bayer and Ziya Öniş, "Turkish Big Business in the Age of Democratic Consolidation: The Nature and Limits of Its Influence," *South European Society and Politics* 15, no. 2 (2010): 181–201.
13 Arat, "Politics and Big Business"; Anonymous (entrepreneur in the textile sector and TÜSİAD member), personal interview by author, 2001.
14 Arat, "Politics and Big Business" 137.
15 TÜSİAD, *Brochure* (Istanbul: TÜSİAD, 1997).
16 Cansen Başaran-Symes (TÜSİAD member and founder of PriceWaterhouse, Turkey), personal interview by author, 2002.
17 Ibid.; Betil, personal interview by author, 2001; Çağlar Keyder (Bosphorus University), personal interview by author, 2001; Orçun, personal interview by author, 2001.
18 Oktay Varlıer (TÜSİAD member, Alarko Holding), personal interview by author, June 17, 2002; Tuğrul Erkin (TÜSİAD member), personal interview by author, July 9, 2002.
19 Başaran-Symes, personal interview by author, 2002.
20 During interviews, Ebru Dicle and Tuğrul Kudatgobilik confirmed that the contribution of professionals has been mostly felt through their expertise about specific technical issues (Dicle, personal interview by author, 2001, 2002; Tuğrul Kudatgobilik [Koç Holding AS], personal interview by author, July 24, 2002).
21 TÜSİAD, "TÜSİAD Charter," https://tusiad.org/en/tusiad/charter, accessed July 25, 2022.
22 Dicle, personal interview by author, July 24, 2001.
23 Ibid.; Arat, "Politics and Big Business."

24 Keyder, personal interview by author, 2001.
25 Haluk Tükel (TÜSİAD member, TÜSİAD secretary general), personal interview by author, 2002; Orçun, personal interview by author, 2001; Eczacıbaşı, personal interview by author, August 21, 2002.
26 Mehmet Şuhubi (TÜSİAD member, Teslo Tekstil Urunleri Sanayi ve Ticaret AS), personal interview by author, July 10, 2002.
27 Carlos H. Acuna, "Political Struggle and Business Peak Associations: Theoretical Reflections on the Argentine Case," in *Organized Business, Economic Change, and Democracy in Latin America*, ed. Francisco Durand and Eduardo Silva (Coral Gables, FL: North-South Center Press at the University of Miami, 1998).
28 Dicle, personal interview by author, 2001.
29 TÜSİAD, "TÜSİAD Faaliyet Raporu 2019," https://tusiad.org/tr/faaliyet-raporlari/item/10523-tusi-ad-faaliyet-raporu-2019, accessed July 25, 2022; Dicle, personal interview by author, 2001, 2022.
30 Dicle, personal interview by author, 2001 to 2002; Bahadır Kaleağası (TÜSİAD Brussel representative), personal interview by author, 2001;.
31 The "Perspectives on Democracy in Turkey Report" as well as other work relating to political reform has been for the most part carried under the auspices of the Parliamentary Affairs Commission.
32 Dicle, personal interview by author, 2002; Ümit Izmen (TÜSİAD deputy general secretary), personal interview by author, 2002.
33 Dicle, personal interview by author, 2001.
34 TÜSİAD, *TÜSİAD 1997 Yılı Çalışmaları* (Istanbul: TÜSİAD, 1997).
35 TÜSİAD, "TÜSİAD Faaliyet Raporu 2019," https://tusiad.org/tr/faaliyet-raporlari/item/10523-tusi-ad-faaliyet-raporu-2019, accessed July 25, 2022.
36 Feyyaz Berker (TÜSİAD member, TÜSİAD chairman [1971-9] and High Advisory Board member and president [1985-6], cofounder and copresident of Tekfen Holding AS), personal interview by author, August 19, 2002.
37 TÜSİAD, *TÜSİAD 1997 Yılı Çalışmaları* (Istanbul: TÜSİAD, 1997).
38 Kaleağası, personal interview by author, 2001.
39 Abdullah Akyüz (TÜSİAD Washington DC representative), personal interview by author, 2011.
40 Gianfranco Poggi, *Calvinism and the Capitalist Spirit* (Amherst: University of Massachusetts Press, 1984).
41 Varlıer, personal interview by author, June 17, 2001.
42 Peter B. Evans, *Embedded Autonomy: States and Industrial Transformation* (Princeton, NJ: Princeton University Press, 1995); Linda Weiss, *The Myth of the Powerless State* (Ithaca, NY: Cornell University Press, 2018).
43 Varlıer, personal interview by author, June 17, 2002.
44 İshak Alaton (TÜSİAD member, then member of the Parliamentary Affairs Commission, president and cofounder of Alarko Holding), personal interview by author, 2001.
45 Şuhubi, personal interview by author, July 10, 2002.
46 Meltem Kurtsan (Kurtsan Ilaclari AS), personal interview by author, July 10, 2002; Erkut Yücaoğlu (TÜSİAD member, TÜSİAD chairman [1999-2001]), personal interview by author, 2001.
47 Şuhubi, personal interview by author, July 10, 2002.
48 Alaton, personal interview by author, July 31, 2001.
49 Can Paker (TÜSİAD member, Türk Henkel AS), personal interview by author, 2001.

50 Yılmaz Argüden (TÜSİAD member, then member of the ARGE danismanlik AS), personal interview by author, 2002.
51 Rona Yırcalı (TÜSİAD member, chairman of Yapı Kredi Bank), personal interview by author, July 23, 2002.
52 Eczacıbaşı, personal interview by author, 2001.
53 Tükel, personal interview by author, 2002; Yücaoğlu, personal interview by author, 2001.
54 Yırcalı, personal interview by author, July 23, 2002.
55 Şuhubi, personal interview by author, 2001.
56 Ernest J. Bartell, "Perceptions by Business Leaders and the Transition to Democracy in Chile," in *Business and Democracy in Latin America*, ed. Leigh A. Payne and Ernest J. Bartell (Pittsburgh: University of Pittsburgh Press, 1995).
57 Eduardo Silva, "From Dictatorship to Democracy—The Business-State Nexus in Chile's Economic Transformation, 1975-1994," *Comparative Politics* 28, no. 3 (April 1996): 299–320; E. Huber and J. D. Stephens, "The Bourgeoisie and Democracy: Historical and Contemporary Perspectives," *Social Research* 66, no. 3 (Fall 1999): 759–88.
58 Michael Mann, "Ruling-Class Strategies and Citizenship," *Sociology—The Journal of the British Sociological Association* 21, no. 3 (1987): 339–54; Charles Edward Lindblom, *Politics and Markets: The World's Political Economic Systems* (New York: Basic Books, 1977); Dietrich Rueschemeyer, Evelyne Huber, and John D. Stephens. *Capitalist Development and Democracy* (Chicago: University of Chicago Press, 1992).
59 Ayşe Buğra, *State and Business in Modern Turkey: A Comparative Study*, SUNY Series in the Social and Economic History of the Middle East (Albany: State University of New York Press, 1994).
60 Başaran-Symes, personal interview by author, July 2002.
61 Buğra, *State and Business in Modern Turkey*.
62 Aldo Kaslowski (TÜSİAD member, chairman of Organik Holding), personal interview by author, 2002.
63 Şuhubi, personal interview by author, 2001.
64 Yırcalı, personal interview by author, July 23, 2002.
65 Argüden, personal interview by author, 2002.
66 Ibid.
67 Kaslowski, personal interview by author, 2002.
68 Fernando Henrique Cardoso, "Entrepreneurs and the Transition to Democracy in Brazil," in *Transitions from Authoritarian Rule: Comparative Perspectives*, ed. Guillermo O'Donnell, Philippe Schmitter, and Laurence Whitehead (Baltimore: John Hopkins University Press, 1986), 137–53.
69 Peter R. Kingstone, "Corporatism, Neoliberalism, and the Failed Revolt of Big Business: Lessons from the Case of IEDI," *Journal of Interamerican Studies and World Affairs* 40, no. 4 (Winter 1998): 73–95.
70 Ayşe Buğra and Osman Savaşkan, *New Capitalism in Turkey: The Relationship between Politics, Religion and Business* (Cheltenham, UK: Edward Elgar Publishing, 2014).
71 Devrim Yavuz, "Conflict, Democratic Reform, and Big Business: Factors Shaping the Economic Elite's Position for Change," in *Secular State and Religious Society: Two Forces in Play in Turkey*, ed. Berna Turam (New York: Springer, 2011), 143–66.

Chapter 7

1 Ayşe Buğra and Osman Savaşkan, *New Capitalism in Turkey: The Relationship between Politics, Religion and Business* (Cheltenham, UK: Edward Elgar Publishing, 2014); Işik Özel, "Political Islam and Islamic Capital: The Case of Turkey," in *Religion and Politics in Europe, the Middle East and North Africa*, ed. Jeffrey Haynes (New York: Routledge, 2009), 155–77.
2 Cihan Tuğal, *The Fall of the Turkish Model: How the Arab Uprisings Brought down Islamic Liberalism* (London: Verso, 2016).
3 Ibid.
4 Reşat Bayer and Ziya Öniş, "Turkish Big Business in the Age of Democratic Consolidation: The Nature and Limits of Its Influence," *South European Society and Politics* 15, no. 2 (June 2010): 181–201, https://doi.org/10.1080/13608746.2010.503043.
5 For a review of the period and these cleavages, see Yeşim Arat and Şevket Pamuk, *Turkey between Democracy and Authoritarianism* (Cambridge: Cambridge University Press, 2019).
6 Tuğal, *The Fall of the Turkish Model*.
7 Yeşim Arat, "Violence, Resistance, and Gezi Park," *International Journal of Middle East Studies* 45, no. 4 (2013): 807–9.
8 Elçin Aktoprak, "Between Authoritarianism and Peace: The Kurdish Opening in Turkey (2013–2015)," in *Democratic Representation in Plurinational States* (Cham: Springer, 2018), 137–58; Ödül Celep, "The Moderation of Turkey's Kurdish Left: The Peoples' Democratic Party (HDP)," *Turkish Studies* 19, no. 5 (2018): 723–47.
9 Michael M. Gunter, "Erdoğan's Future: The Failed Coup, the Kurds & the Gulenists," *Journal of South Asian and Middle Eastern Studies* 41, no. 2 (2018): 1–15.
10 Cem Özatalay, "Purge, Exile, and Resistance: Rethinking the Conflict of the Faculties through the Case of Academics for Peace in Turkey," *European Journal of Turkish Studies* 30, no. 30 (2020), https://doi.org/10.4000/ejts.6746; Omer Tekdemir, Mari Toivanen, and Bahar Baser, "Peace Profile: Academics for Peace in Turkey," *Peace Review* 30, no. 1 (2018): 103–11, https://doi.org/10.1080/10402659.2017.1419968.
11 "From Prominent Turkish Philanthropist to Political Prisoner," *New York Times*, April 9, 2020, https://www.nytimes.com/2020/04/09/world/middleeast/osman-kavala-turkey.html?smid=url-share, accessed June 19, 2022.
12 Stephan Haggard and Robert R. Kaufman, "Dictators and Democrats," in *Dictators and Democrats* (Princeton, NJ: Princeton University Press, 2016).
13 Sevgi Akarçeşme, "The EU Anchor, Turkish Democracy and the Future of the AK Party," *Insight Turkey* 10, no. 2 (2008): 125–33.; Hakan M. Yavuz, *Secularism and Muslim Democracy in Turkey*, vol. 28 (Cambridge: Cambridge University Press, 2009).
14 Buğra and Savaşkan, *New Capitalism in Turkey*; Şahan Savas Karataşlı, "The Origins of Turkey's 'Heterodox' Transition to Neoliberalism: The Özal Decade and Beyond," *Journal of World-Systems Research* 21, no. 2 (2015): 387–416; Tuğal, *The Fall of the Turkish Model*.
15 Ayşe Buğra and Çağlar Keyder, "The Turkish Welfare Regime in Transformation," *Journal of European Social Policy* 16, no. 3 (2006): 211–28; Ayşe Buğra and Çağlar Keyder, *New Poverty and the Changing Welfare Regime of Turkey* (Ankara: UNDP, 2003); Ziya Öniş, "The Triumph of Conservative Globalism: The Political Economy of the AKP Era," *Turkish Studies* 13, no. 2 (2012): 135–52; Volkan Yılmaz, *The Politics of Healthcare Reform in Turkey* (New York: Springer, 2017).

16 Tuğal, *The Fall of the Turkish Model.*
17 Bayer and Öniş, "Turkish Big Business in the Age of Democratic Consolidation."
18 "Erdogan: Those Who Are Neutral Will Be Eliminated," Milliyet, August 18, 2010, https://www.milliyet.com.tr/siyaset/erdogan-bitaraf-olan-bertaraf-olur-1277904, accessed June 19, 2022.
19 Emin Baki Adas, "The Making of Entrepreneurial Islam and the Islamic Spirit of Capitalism," *Journal for Cultural Research* 10, no. 2 (2006): 113–37; Buğra and Savaşkan, *New Capitalism in Turkey*; Ömer Demir, Mustafa Acar, and Metin Toprak, "Anatolian Tigers or Islamic Capital: Prospects and Challenges," *Middle Eastern Studies* 40, no. 6 (2004): 166–88; Evren Hosgör, "Islamic Capital/Anatolian Tigers: Past and Present," *Middle Eastern Studies* 47, no. 2 (2011): 343–60, https://doi.org/10.1080/00263206.2011.534336; Özel, "Political Islam and Islamic Capital."
20 Buğra and Savaşkan, *New Capitalism in Turkey*; Ziya Öniş and Umut Türem, "Business, Globalization and Democracy: A Comparative Analysis of Turkish Business Associations," *Turkish Studies* 2, no. 2 (Autumn 2001): 94–120; Özel, "Political Islam and Islamic Capital."
21 Berk Esen and Sebnem Gumuscu, "Building a Competitive Authoritarian Regime: State–Business Relations in the AKP's Turkey," *Journal of Balkan and Near Eastern Studies* 20, no. 4 (2018): 349–72; Esra Çeviker Gürakar, *Politics of Favoritism in Public Procurement in Turkey: Reconfigurations of Dependency Networks in the AKP Era* (New York: Springer, 2016).
22 Buğra and Savaşkan, *New Capitalism in Turkey*, 88–9.
23 Cansen Başaran-Symes (TÜSİAD member and founder of PriceWaterhouse, Turkey), personal interview by author, 2008.
24 This had been made apparent during debates surrounding the publication of the *Democratization Report* (see Chapter 6) and throughout AKP's reign when a prominent member İnan Kıraç left the organization in protest because it "did not work for the welfare and integrity of the nation." Hürriyet, "İnan Kıraç'tan TÜSİAD'dan istifa açıklaması," bigpara.hurriyet.com.tr, https://bigpara.hurriyet.com.tr/haberler/ekonomi-haberleri/inan-kiractan-tusiaddan-istifa-aciklamasi_ID450131/, accessed July 25, 2022.
25 Erol Bilecik quoted in the TÜSİAD, "TÜSİAD Faaliyet Raporu 2018," https://tusiad.org/tr/faaliyet-raporlari/item/10233-tusiad-faaliyet-raporu-2018, 3, accessed July 25, 2022 (Author's translation),.
26 Ernest J. Bartell and Leigh A. Payne, *Business and Democracy in Latin America*, Pitt Latin American Series (Pittsburgh: University of Pittsburgh Press, 1995); Francisco Durand and Eduardo Silva, *Organized Business, Economic Change, and Democracy in Latin America* (Coral Gables, FL: North-South Center Press at the University of Miami, 1998).
27 Devrim Yavuz, "Conflict, Democratic Reform, and Big Business: Factors Shaping the Economic Elite's Position for Change," in *Secular State and Religious Society: Two Forces in Play in Turkey*, ed. Berna Turam (New York: Springer, 2011), 143–66.
28 See http://www.TÜSİAD.org.tr/Content.aspx?mi=1_43, accessed October 8, 2010 and July 6, 2021.
29 Karataşlı, "The Origins of Turkey's 'Heterodox' Transition to Neoliberalism"; Buğra and Savaşkan, *New Capitalism in Turkey*.
30 Derya Büyüktanır, "Public Diplomacy Activities of TÜSİAD and MÜSİAD during the AK Party Era," *Gazi Akademik Bakış* 11, no. 23 (2018): 73–98; Öniş, "The Triumph

of Conservative Globalism"; Işık Özel, *State–Business Alliances and Economic Development: Turkey, Mexico and North Africa* (New York: Routledge, 2014).
31 Buğra and Savaşkan, *New Capitalism in Turkey*, 88–101.
32 Ibid.
33 Daren Butler, "Sale of Dogan Set to Tighten Erdogan's Grip over Turkish Media," Reuters, https://www.reuters.com/article/us-dogan-holding-m-a-demiroren/sale-of-dogan-set-to-tighten-erdogans-grip-over-turkish-media-idUSKBN1GY0EL, March 22, 2018, accessed July 7, 2021.
34 Buğra and Savaşkan, *New Capitalism in Turkey*.
35 Mehmet Şuhubi (TÜSİAD member, Teslo Tekstil Urunleri Sanayi ve Ticaret AS), personal interview by author, July 10, 2002.
36 Berna Turam, *Between Islam and the State: The Politics of Engagement* (Stanford, CA: University Press, 2007); Berna Turam, ed., *Secular State and Religious Society: Two Forces in Play in Turkey* (New York: Springer, 2011).
37 The Information Society Forum (Bilgi Toplumu Forumu, BTF) at Bilkent University; The Foreign Policy Forum (Dış Politika Forumu, DPF) at the Boğaziçi University; Koç University's Economic Research Forum (Ekonomik Araştırma Forumu, EAF); a center on Sustainable Development (Sürdürülebilir Kalkınma Forumu, SKF) at Özyeğin University; and a Sabancı University forum on competition (Rekabet Forumu, REF).
38 "Paris Boğaziçi Enstitüsü çalışmalarına başlıyor," TÜSİAD.org, https://tusiad.org/tr/basin-bultenleri/item/1657-paris-bogazici-enstitusu-calismalarina-basliyor, accessed April 30, 2022.
39 BusinessEurope was founded with the goal of acting as a trans-European umbrella organization for national business federations and associations in the hopes of enhancing cooperation and impacting the direction of the EU (https://www.businesseurope.eu/history-organisation, accessed July 7, 2021).
40 "MEDEF-TÜSİAD Ortak Açıklaması: MEDEF ve TÜSİAD, Avrupa'nın Siyasi ve Ekonomik Alanda Küresel Bir Güç Olarak Hareket Etmesinin Önemine Dikkat Çekti," TÜSİAD.org, 2007, https://tusiad.org/tr/basin-bultenleri/item/1380-medef-tusiad-ortak-aciklamasi--medef-ve-tusiad--avrupanin-siyasi-ve-ekonomik-alanda-kuresel-bir-guc-olarak-hareket-etmesinin-onemine-dikkat-cekti.
41 Bayer and Öniş, "Turkish Big Business in the Age of Democratic Consolidation."
42 Tuğal, *The Fall of the Turkish Model*.
43 TÜSİAD, *1 Ocak 2014 Tarihinde Avrupa Birliği'ne Tam Üyelik Hedefine Doğru: Güçlü Demokrasi, Güçlü Sosyal Yapı, Güçlü Ekonomi* (Istanbul: TÜSİAD, 2007).
44 TÜSİAD, "Anayasa Konvansiyonu Nedir, Neden Gereklidir?," press release, June 18, 2008.
45 TÜSİAD, "Turkey's Democracy Proves to Be Strong," press release, July 31, 2008.
46 TÜSİAD, *TÜSİAD 2010 Yılı Çalışmaları* (Istanbul: TÜSİAD, 2010); TÜSİAD, *TÜSİAD 2011 Yılı Çalışmaları* (Istanbul: TÜSİAD, 2011).
47 TÜSİAD, *TÜSİAD 2010 Yılı Çalışmaları*, 29.
48 Tuğal, *The Fall of the Turkish Model*.
49 Arat and Pamuk, *Turkey between Democracy and Authoritarianism*; Tuğal, *The Fall of the Turkish Model*.
50 Svante E. Cornell, "Erdogan versus Koç Holding: Turkey's New Witch Hunt," *Turkey Analyst* 6, no. 18 (2013), https://www.turkeyanalyst.org/publications/turkey-analyst-articles/item/64-erdogan-vs-ko%C3%A7-holding-turkeys-new-witch-hunt.html.

51 Ibid.; Semih Idiz, "The AKP Shoots its Goose," *Hurriyet Daily News*, July 30, 2013, sec. Opinion, https://www.hurriyetdailynews.com/opinion/semih-idiz/the-akp-shoots-its-goose--51639.
52 Tuğal, *The Fall of the Turkish Model*.
53 Ebru Dicle (TÜSİAD general secretary), personal interview by author, April 22, 2022.
54 TÜSİAD, "Focus Areas," 2021, https://tusiad.org/en/focus-areas.
55 Ibid.
56 TUSKON was linked to the Gülenist movement. When I had interviewed its president in 2010, the association had managed to establish an impressive national network and successfully organized missions in regions such as Sub-Saharan Africa to create trade and investment opportunities. At the time of my interview, during the month of Ramadan, its president showcased the Gülenist tendency to engage in interfaith dialogue by pointing to a plate of treats and cup of coffee that had been brought out for me, urging me to eat (my first name, research subject, and nervous demeanor had probably been hints that I was most likely not fasting). The association became ineffective following the coup of 2016, when the Gülenist movement and its organizations were purged.
57 TÜRKONFED, "About Us," TÜRKONFED, https://turkonfed.org/en/page/about-us, accessed July 25, 2022.
58 Ebru Dicle (TÜSİAD general secretary), personal interview by author, April 22, 2022.
59 See https://TÜSİAD.org/tr/konusma-metinleri/item/10745-simone-kaslowski-genel-kurul-toplantisi-acilis-konusmasi, accessed July 10, 2021.
60 The full transcript of his speech can be found here: "Simone Kaslowski Yüksek İstişare Konseyi Toplantısı Açılış Konuşması," TÜSİAD.org, https://tusiad.org/tr/konusma-metinleri/item/10857-simone-kaslowski-yuksek-i-stisare-konseyi-toplantisi-acilis-konusmasi, accessed April 30, 2022. All quoted text from Kaslowski are taken from this speech.
61 Dicle, personal interview by author, April 22, 2022.
62 "Yeni Bir Anlayışla Geleceği İnşa: İnsan, Bilim, Kurumlar," TÜSİAD.org, https://tusiad.org/tr/yayinlar/raporlar/item/10855-yeni-bir-anlayisla-gelecegi-i-nsa-i-nsan-bilim-kurumlar, accessed April 30, 2022.

Conclusion

1 Dietrich Rueschemeyer, Evelyne Huber, and John D. Stephens, *Capitalist Development and Democracy* (Chicago: University of Chicago Press, 1992).
2 Michael Mann, *The Sources of Social Power. Vol. 2: The Rise of Classes and Nation-States, 1760–1914* (Cambridge: Cambridge University Press, 1993).
3 Peter B. Evans, Dietrich Rueschemeyer, and Theda Skocpol, *Bringing the State Back in* (Cambridge: Cambridge University Press, 1985).
4 Ayşe Buğra, *State and Business in Modern Turkey: A Comparative Study*, SUNY Series in the Social and Economic History of the Middle East (Albany: State University of New York Press, 1994).
5 Ernest J. Bartell and Leigh A. Payne, *Business and Democracy in Latin America*, Pitt Latin American Series (Pittsburgh: University of Pittsburgh Press, 1995); Melani Claire Cammett, *Globalization and Business Politics in Arab North Africa: A Comparative Perspective* (Cambridge: Cambridge University Press, 2007); Francisco

Durand and Eduardo Silva, *Organized Business, Economic Change, and Democracy in Latin America* (Coral Gables, FL: North-South Center Press at the University of Miami, 1998).
6 Rueschemeyer, Huber, and Stephens, *Capitalist Development and Democracy*.
7 Cihan Tuğal, *The Fall of the Turkish Model: How the Arab Uprisings Brought down Islamic Liberalism* (London: Verso, 2016).
8 Ayşe Buğra and Osman Savaşkan, *New Capitalism in Turkey: The Relationship between Politics, Religion and Business* (Cheltenham, UK: Edward Elgar Publishing, 2014).
9 Ebru Dicle (TÜSİAD general secretary), personal interview by author, 2022.

BIBLIOGRAPHY

Acemoglu, Daron, and James A. Robinson. *Economic Origins of Dictatorship and Democracy.* Cambridge: Cambridge University Press, 2006.

Adas, Emin Baki. "The Making of Entrepreneurial Islam and the Islamic Spirit of Capitalism." *Journal for Cultural Research* 10 (2) (2006): 113–37.

Ağır, Seven, and Cihan Artunç. "The Wealth Tax of 1942 and the Disappearance of Non-Muslim Enterprises in Turkey." *Journal of Economic History* 79 (1) (2019): 201–43.

Ahmad, Feroz. "The Late Ottoman Empire." In *The Great Powers and the End of the Ottoman Empire*, edited by Marian Kent, 15–40. London: Routledge, 2005.

Ahmad, Feroz. *The Making of Modern Turkey.* The Making of the Middle East Series. London: Routledge, 1993.

Ahmad, Feroz. *The Turkish Experiment in Democracy, 1950–1975.* London: Royal Institute of International Affairs, 1977.

Ahmad, Feroz. *The Young Turks and the Ottoman Nationalities: Armenians, Greeks, Albanians, Jews, and Arabs, 1908–1918.* Salt Lake City: University of Utah Press, 2014.

Akarçeşme, Sevgi. "The EU Anchor, Turkish Democracy and the Future of the AK Party." *Insight Turkey* 10 (2) (2008): 125–33.

Akçam, Taner. *The Young Turks' Crime against Humanity: The Armenian Genocide and Ethnic Cleansing in the Ottoman Empire.* ACLS Humanities E-Book. Princeton, NJ: Princeton University Press, 2012.

Aktar, Ayhan. *Varlık Vergisi ve" Türkleştirme" Politikaları.* Vol. 4 Istanbul: İletişim Yayınları, 2000.

Aktoprak, Elçin. "Between Authoritarianism and Peace: The Kurdish Opening in Turkey (2013–2015)." In *Democratic Representation in Plurinational States*, edited by Nimni, Ephraim and Elcin Aktoprak, 137–58. Cham: Springer, 2018.

Aktoprak, Elçin. *Bir "Kurucu Öteki" Olarak: Türkiye'de Gayrimüslimler.* Ankara: Ankara Üniversitesi, Siyasal Bilgiler Fakültesi, İnsan Hakları Merkezi, 2010.

Akyüz, Yılmaz, and Korkut Boratav. "The Making of the Turkish Financial Crisis." *World Development* 31 (9) (2003): 1549–66.

Al-awsat, Asharq. "Turkish Exceptionalism: Interview with Serif Mardin," December 12, 2007, https://eng-archive.aawsat.com/theaawsat/features/turkish-exceptionalism-interview-with-serif-mardin. Accessed April 26, 2021.

Anderson, Lisa. "The State in the Middle East and North Africa." *Comparative Politics* 20 (1) (1987): 1–18.

Arat, Yeşim. "From Emancipation to Liberation: The Changing Role of Women in Turkey's Public Realm." *Journal of International Affairs* 54 (1) (2000): 107–23.

Arat, Yeşim. "Politics and Big Business: Janus-Faced Link to the State." In *Strong State and Economic Interest Groups: The Post-1980 Experience*, edited by Metin Heper, 135–48. Berlin: Walter de Gruyter, 1991.

Arat, Yeşim. "The Project of Modernity and Women in Turkey." In *Rethinking Modernity and National Identity in Turkey*, edited by Sibel Bozdogan and Reşat Kasaba, 95–112. Seattle: University of Washington Press, 1997.

Arat, Yeşim. "Social Change and the 1983 Governing Elite in Turkey." In *Structural Change in Turkish Society*, edited by Mübeccel Belik Kıray, 163-78. Bloomington: Indiana University Turkish Studies Department, Indiana University Press, 1991.

Arat, Yeşim. "Violence, Resistance, and Gezi Park." *International Journal of Middle East Studies* 45 (4) (2013): 807-9.

Arat, Yeşim, and Şevket Pamuk. *Turkey between Democracy and Authoritarianism*. Cambridge: Cambridge University Press, 2019.

Arıcanlı, Tosun, and Dani Rodrik, eds. *The Political Economy of Turkey: Debt, Adjustment and Sustainability*. Basingstoke: Macmillan, 1990.

Arısan, Mehmet. "From 'Clients' to 'Magnates': The (Not So) Curious Case of Islamic Authoritarianism in Turkey." *Southeast European and Black Sea Studies* 19 (1) (2019): 11-30.

Attewell, Paul. "The Deskilling Controversy." *Work and Occupation* 14 (3) (1987): 323-46.

Barkey, Karen. *Empire of Difference: The Ottomans in Comparative Perspective*. Cambridge: Cambridge University Press, 2008.

Barrett, P. S. "Labour Policy, Labour-Business Relations and the Transition to Democracy in Chile." *Journal of Latin American Studies* 33 (August 2001): 561-97.

Barrett, P. S. "The Limits of Democracy: Socio-Political Compromise and Regime Change in Post-Pinochet Chile." *Studies in Comparative International Development* 34 (3) (Fall 1999): 3-36.

Bartell, Ernest J., and Leigh A. Payne. *Business and Democracy in Latin America*. Pitt Latin American Series. Pittsburgh: University of Pittsburgh Press, 1995.

Bayar, Yeşim. *Formation of the Turkish Nation-State, 1920-1938*. New York: Springer, 2016.

Bayer, Reşat, and Ziya Öniş. "Turkish Big Business in the Age of Democratic Consolidation: The Nature and Limits of Its Influence." *South European Society and Politics* 15 (2) (2010): 181-201.

Berktay, Halil, and Suraiya Faroqhi. *New Approaches to State and Peasant in Ottoman History*. London: Routledge, 1992.

Bhagwati, Jagdish N. "Democracy and Development." *Journal of Democracy* 3 (3) (1992): 37-44.

Bianchi, R. "Interest Group Politics in the Third-World." *Third World Quarterly* 8 (2) (1986): 507-39.

Bianchi, Robert. *Interest Groups and Political Development in Turkey*. Princeton, NJ: Princeton University Press, 1984.

Blackburn, R. M., and Michael Mann. *The Working Class in the Labour Market*. London: Macmillan, 1979.

Boratav, Korkut. "Inter-Class and Intra-Class Relations of Distribution under 'Structural Adjustment': Turkey during the 1980s." In *The Political Economy of Turkey: Debt, Adjustment and Sustainability*, edited by Tosun Arıcanlı and Dani Rodrik, 199-229. New York: St. Martin's Press, 1990.

Boratav, Korkut. *Türkiye'de Devletçilik*. Vol. 3. Ankara: Savaş Yayınevi, 1982.

Boratav, Korkut. *Türkiye İktisat Tarihi 1908-2002*. 9th edition. Ankara: İmge Kitabevi, 2005.

Boratav, Korkut, and Ergun Türkcan. *Türkiye'de Sanayileşmenin Yeni Boyutları ve KİT'ler*. Ankara: Tarih Vakfı Yurt Yayınları, 1993.

Braudel, Fernand. *The Mediterranean and the Mediterranean World in the Age of Philip II*. Vol. 2. Berkeley: University of California Press, 1995.

Braverman, Harry. *Labor and Monopoly Capital: The Degradation of Work in the Twentieth Century*. New York: Monthly Review Press, 1974.

Buğra, Ayşe. *State and Business in Modern Turkey: A Comparative Study*. SUNY Series in the Social and Economic History of the Middle East. Albany: State University of New York Press, 1994.

Buğra, Ayşe, and Çağlar Keyder. *New Poverty and the Changing Welfare Regime of Turkey*. Ankara: UNDP, 2003.

Buğra, Ayşe, and Çağlar Keyder. "The Turkish Welfare Regime in Transformation." *Journal of European Social Policy* 16 (3) (2006): 211–28.

Buğra, Ayşe, and Osman Savaşkan. *New Capitalism in Turkey: The Relationship between Politics, Religion and Business*. Cheltenham, UK: Edward Elgar Publishing, 2014.

Büyüktanır, Derya. "Public Diplomacy Activities of TÜSİAD and MÜSİAD during the AK Party Era." *Gazi Akademik Bakış* 11 (23) (2018): 73–98.

Cammett, Melani Claire. *Globalization and Business Politics in Arab North Africa: A Comparative Perspective*. Cambridge: Cambridge University Press, 2007.

Cardoso, Fernando Henrique. "Entrepreneurs and the Transition to Democracy in Brazil." In *Transitions from Authoritarian Rule: Comparative Perspectives*, edited by Guillermo O'Donnell, Philippe Schmitter, and Laurence Whitehead, 137–53. Baltimore: John Hopkins University Press, 1985.

Cardoso, Fernando Henrique, and Enzo Faletto. *Dependency and Development in Latin America*. Berkeley: University of California Press, 1979.

Carothers, Thomas. "The End of the Transition Paradigm." *Journal of Democracy* 13 (1) (2002): 5–21.

Celep, Ödül. "The Moderation of Turkey's Kurdish Left: The Peoples' Democratic Party (HDP)." *Turkish Studies* 19 (5) (2018): 723–47.

Chen, A. "Capitalist Development, Entrepreneurial Class, and Democratization in China." *Political Science Quarterly* 117 (3) (Fall 2002): 401–22.

Collier, David, and Steven Levitsky. "Conceptual Hierarchies in Comparative Research: The Case of Democracy." *Concepts and Method in the Social Science: The Tradition of Giovanni Sartori*, edited by David Collier and John Gerring, 269–88. London: Routledge, 2009.

Collier, David, and Steven Levitsky. "Democracy with Adjectives: Conceptual Innovation in Comparative Research." *World Politics* 49 (3) (1997): 430–51.

Collins, R. "Weber Last Theory of Capitalism—A Systematization." *American Sociological Review* 45 (6) (1980): 925–42.

Cornell, Svante E. "Erdogan versus Koç Holding: Turkey's New Witch Hunt." *Turkey Analyst* 6 (18) (2013), https://www.turkeyanalyst.org/publications/turkey-analyst-articles/item/64-erdogan-vs-ko%C3%A7-holding-turkeys-new-witch-hunt.html.

Dahl, Robert A. *Polyarchy: Participation and Opposition*. New Haven, CT: Yale University Press, 1971.

della Porta, Donatella, and Kivanc Atak. "The Spirit of Gezi: A Relational Approach to Eventful Protest and Its Challenges." In *Global Diffusion of Protest: Riding the Protest Wave in the Neoliberal Crisis*, edited by Donatella della Porta, 31–58. Amsterdam: Amsterdam University Press, 2017.

Demir, Ömer, Mustafa Acar, and Metin Toprak. "Anatolian Tigers or Islamic Capital: Prospects and Challenges." *Middle Eastern Studies* 40 (6) (2004): 166–88.

Domhoff, G. William. *The Power Elite and the State: How Policy Is Made in America*. New Brunswick, NJ: Transaction Publishers, 1990.

Doxey, John. "Turkey's New Reformer." *New Leader* 78 (6) (1995): 8.

Duesenberry, James. "Comment on 'An Economic Analysis of Fertility.'" *Demographic and Economic Change in Developed Countries*, 3 (1960): 17.

Durand, Francisco, and Eduardo Silva. *Organized Business, Economic Change, and Democracy in Latin America*. Coral Gables, FL: North-South Center Press at the University of Miami, 1998.

Eilon, Joab B., and Yoav Alon. *The Making of Jordan: Tribes, Colonialism and the Modern State*. Vol. 61. London: I.B. Tauris, 2007.

Esen, Berk, and Sebnem Gumuscu. "Building a Competitive Authoritarian Regime: State-Business Relations in the AKP's Turkey." *Journal of Balkan and Near Eastern Studies* 20 (4) (2018): 349–72.

Esen, Berk, and Sebnem Gumuscu. "The Perils of 'Turkish Presidentialism.'" *Review of Middle East Studies* 52 (1) (2018): 43–53.

Evans, Peter B. *Dependent Development: The Alliance of Multinational, State, and Local Capital in Brazil*. Princeton, NJ: Princeton University Press, 1979.

Evans, Peter B. *Embedded Autonomy: States and Industrial Transformation*. Princeton, NJ: Princeton University Press, 1995.

Evans, Peter B., Dietrich Rueschemeyer, and Theda Skocpol. *Bringing the State Back in*. Cambridge: Cambridge University Press, 1985.

Findley, Carter V. *Bureaucratic Reform in the Ottoman Empire: The Sublime Porte, 1789–1922*. Princeton Studies on the Near East. Princeton, NJ: Princeton University Press, 2012.

Fukuyama, Francis. *The End of History and the Last Man*. New York: Simon and Schuster, 2006.

Fukuyama, Francis. "Why Is Democracy Performing So Poorly?" *Journal of Democracy* 26 (1) (2015): 11–20.

Gerber, Haim. *Economy and Society in an Ottoman City: Bursa, 1600–1700*. Jerusalem: Hebrew University Press, 1988.

Gerschenkron, Alexander. *Economic Backwardness in Historical Perspective: A Book of Essays*. Cambridge: Belknap Press of Harvard University Press, 1962.

Gibson, Edward L. *Class and Conservative Parties: Argentina in Comparative Perspective*. Baltimore: Johns Hopkins University Press, 1996.

Göçek, Fatma Müge. *Denial of Violence: Ottoman Past, Turkish Present, and Collective Violence against the Armenians, 1789–2009*. Oxford: Oxford University Press, 2014.

Göçek, Fatma Müge. *Rise of the Bourgeoisie, Demise of Empire: Ottoman Westernization and Social Change*. Oxford: Oxford University Press on Demand, 1996.

Goldthorpe, John H. *The Affluent Worker: Political Attitudes and Behaviour*. Cambridge: Cambridge University Press, 1968.

Granovetter, M. "Economic Institutions as Social Constructions: A Framework for Analysis." *Acta Sociologica* 35 (1) (1992): 3–11.

Greenwood, Scott. "Bad for Business? Entrepreneurs and Democracy in the Arab World." *Comparative Political Studies* 41 (6) (2008): 837–60, http://cps.sagepub.com/content/early/2007/09/17/0010414007300123.short.

Grigoriadis, Ioannis N. "The Peoples' Democratic Party (HDP) and the 2015 Elections." *Turkish Studies* 17 (1) (2016): 39–46.

Gunes, Cengiz. *The Kurdish National Movement in Turkey: From Protest to Resistance*. London: Routledge, 2013.

Gunter, Michael M. "Erdogan's Future: The Failed Coup, the Kurds & the Gulenists." *Journal of South Asian and Middle Eastern Studies* 41 (2) (2018): 1–15.

Gürakar, Esra Çeviker. *Politics of Favoritism in Public Procurement in Turkey: Reconfigurations of Dependency Networks in the AKP Era*. New York: Springer, 2016.

Gürpinar, Doğan, and Ceren Kenar. "The Nation and Its Sermons: Islam, Kemalism and the Presidency of Religious Affairs in Turkey." *Middle Eastern Studies* 52 (1) (2016): 60–78.

Güven, Dilek. "Riots against the Non-Muslims of Turkey: 6/7 September 1955 in the Context of Demographic Engineering." *European Journal of Turkish Studies. Social Sciences on Contemporary Turkey* 12 (12) (2011).

Haggard, Stephan, and Robert R. Kaufman. "Dictators and Democrats." In *Dictators and Democrats*. Princeton, NJ: Princeton University Press, 2016.

Haggard, Stephan, and Robert R. Kaufman. *The Political Economy of Democratic Transitions*. Princeton, NJ: Princeton University Press, 1995.

Hagopian, F. "Democracy by Undemocratic Means—Elites, Political Pacts, and Regime Transition in Brazil." *Comparative Political Studies* 23 (2) (1990): 147–70.

Haldon, John. *A Social History of Byzantium*. Chichester: Wiley-Blackwell, 2009.

Hale, William M. *Islamism, Democracy, and Liberalism in Turkey the Case of the AKP*. Routledge Studies in Middle Eastern Politics 11. Abingdon, Oxon: Routledge, 2009.

Hall, John. A. *Powers and Liberties: The Causes and Consequences of the Rise of the West*. Oxford: Blackwell, 1985.

Hardt, Michael, and Antonio Negri. *Empire*. Cambridge, MA: Harvard University Press, 2001.

Harvey, David. "Between Space and Time: Reflections on the Geographical Imagination." *Annals of the Association of American Geographers* 80 (3) (1990): 418–34.

Heper, Metin. "Interest Group Politics in Post-1980 Turkey: Lingering Monism." In *Strong State and Economic Interest Groups: The Post-1980 Turkish Experience*, edited by Metin Heper, 163–76. Berlin: Walter de Gruyter, 1991.

Heper, Metin. "The State, Political Party and Society in Post-1983 Turkey." *Government and Opposition* 25 (3) (1990): 321–33.

Heper, Metin. *The State Tradition in Turkey*. Beverley, North Humberside: Eothen Press, 1985.

Heper, Metin. *Strong State and Economic Interest Groups: The Post-1980 Turkish Experience*. Berlin: Walter de Gruyter, 1991.

Heper, Metin, Ahmet Evin, and Deutsches Orient Institut. *State, Democracy, and the Military: Turkey in the 1980s* Berlin: Walter de Gruyter, 1988.

Heper, Metin, and Barry M. Rubin. *Political Parties in Turkey*. London: Routledge, 2002.

Heredia, Blanca. "Making Economic Reform Politically Viable." In *Democracy, Markets, and Structural Reform in Latin America: Argentina, Bolivia, Brazil, Chile, and Mexico*, edited by William C. Smith, Carlos H. Acuna, and Eduardo A. Gamarra, 265–96. Miami: University of Miami North-South Center Press, 1994.

Hirschman, Albert O. *Exit, Voice, and Loyalty: Responses to Decline in Firms, Organizations, and States*. Cambridge, MA: Harvard University Press, 1970.

Hirschman, Albert O. *The Passions and the Interests: Political Arguments for Capitalism Before Its Triumph*. Princeton, NJ: Princeton University Press, 1977.

Hirschman, Albert O. "The Turn to Authoritarianism in Latin America and the Search for Its Economic Determinants." In *The New Authoritarianism in Latin America*, edited by D. Collier, 61–98. Princeton, NJ: Princeton University Press, 1979.

Hosgör, Evren. "Islamic Capital/Anatolian Tigers: Past and Present." *Middle Eastern Studies* 47 (2) (2011): 343–60.

Huber, E., and J. D. Stephens. "The Bourgeoisie and Democracy: Historical and Contemporary Perspectives." *Social Research* 66 (3) (Fall 1999): 759–88.

Huber, Evelyne, Dietrich Rueschemeyer, and John D. Stephens. "The Paradoxes of Contemporary Democracy: Formal, Participatory, and Social Dimensions." *Comparative Politics* 29 (3) (1997): 323–42.

Huntington, Samuel P. *Political Order in Changing Societies*. New Haven, CT: Yale University Press, 2006.

Huntington, Samuel P. *The Third Wave: Democratization in the Late Twentieth Century*. Vol. 4. Oklahoma: University of Oklahoma Press, 1993.

İçduygu, Ahmet, Şule Toktas, and B. Ali Soner. "The Politics of Population in a Nation-Building Process: Emigration of Non-Muslims from Turkey." *Ethnic and Racial Studies* 31 (2) (2008): 358–89.

Ilkin, Selim, and Ilhan Tekeli. *Uygulamaya Geçerken Türkiye'de Devletçiligin Olusumu*. Ankara: Orta Dogu Teknik Üniversitesi, 1982.

Inalcik, Halil. "Impact of the Annales School on Ottoman Studies and New Findings [with Discussion]." *Review (Fernand Braudel Center)* 1 (3/4) (1978): 69–99.

Inalcik, Halil, and Donald Quataert. *An Economic and Social History of the Ottoman Empire, 1300–1914*. Cambridge: Cambridge University Press, 1994.

Insel, Ahmet. *La Turquie Entre l'ordre et Le Développement: Éléments d'analyse Sur Le Rôle de l'État Dans Le Processus de Développement*. Paris: L'Harmattan, 1984.

Islamoğlu, Huri, and Çağlar Keyder. "Agenda for Ottoman History." *Review (Fernand Braudel Center)* 1 (1) (1977): 31–55.

Jacoby, Tim. *Social Power and the Turkish State*. Routledge, 2004.

Kaplan, Roger, and Freedom House, eds. *Freedom in the World: The Annual Survey of Political Rights and Civil Liberties, 1997–1998*. New Brunswick, NJ: Transaction Publishers, 1998.

Karataşlı, Şahan Savaş. "The Origins of Turkey's 'Heterodox' Transition to Neoliberalism: The Özal Decade and Beyond." *Journal of World-Systems Research* 21 (2) (2015): 387–416.

Karataşlı, Şahan Savaş, and Sefika Kumral. "Capitalist Development in Hostile Conjunctures: War, Dispossession, and Class Formation in Turkey." *Journal of Agrarian Change* 19 (3) (2019): 528–49.

Karl, T. L. "Dilemmas of Democratization in Latin-America." *Comparative Politics* 23 (1) (1990): 1–21.

Karpat, Kemal H. "Military Interventions: Army-Civilian Relations in Turkey before and after 1980." In *Studies on Turkish Politics and Society*, 353–77. Leiden: Brill, 2004.

Karpat, Kemal H. "Turkey's Politics." In *Turkey's Politic: The Transition to a Multi-Party Systems*. Princeton, NJ: Princeton University Press, 2015.

Kavakci, Merve. "Turkey's Test with Its Deep State." *Mediterranean Quarterly* 20 (4) (2009): 83–97.

Kaya, Emir. *Secularism and State Religion in Modern Turkey: Law, Policy-Making and the Diyanet*. London: Bloomsbury, 2017.

Keyder, Çağlar. "Bureaucracy and Bourgeoisie: Reform and Revolution in the Age of Imperialism." *Review (Fernand Braudel Center)* 11 (2) (1988): 151–65.

Keyder, Çağlar. *The Definition of a Peripheral Economy: Turkey, 1923–1929*. Cambridge: Cambridge University Press; Editions de la Maison des sciences de l'homme, 1981.

Keyder, Çağlar. *State and Class in Turkey: A Study in Capitalist Development*. London: Verso, 1987.

Keyder, Çağlar and Faruk Tabak. *Landholding and Commercial Agriculture in the Middle East*. Albany: State University of New York Press, 1991.

Kılınç, Ramazan. *Alien Citizens: The State and Religious Minorities in Turkey and France*. Cambridge: Cambridge University Press, 2019.

Kingstone, Peter R. "Corporatism, Neoliberalism, and the Failed Revolt of Big Business: Lessons from the Case of IEDI." *Journal of Interamerican Studies and World Affairs* 40 (4) (1998): 73–95.

Kohli, Atul. "Democracy amid Economic Orthodoxy: Trends in Developing Countries." *Third World Quarterly* 14 (4) (1993): 671–89.

Kohli, Atul. "Democracy and Development." In *Development Strategies Reconsidered*, edited by John P. Lewis and Valeriana Kallab, 153–76. Washington, DC: Overseas Development Council, 1986.

Köker, Levent. *Modernleşme, Kemalizm ve Demokrasi*. Istanbul: Iletisim, 1999.

Kubicek, Paul. *The European Union and Democratization*. London: Routledge, 2003.

Kuru, Ahmet. *Democracy, Islam, and Secularism in Turkey*. Religion, Culture and Public Life Book 11. New York: Columbia University Press, 2012.

Kuzu, Durukan. *Multiculturalism in Turkey: The Kurds and the State*. Cambridge: Cambridge University Press, 2018.

Landes, David S. "What Do Bosses Really Do?" *Journal of Economic History* 46 (3) (1986): 585–623.

Levitsky, Steven, and Lucan A. Way. *Competitive Authoritarianism: Hybrid Regimes after the Cold War*. Cambridge: Cambridge University Press, 2010

Lindblom, Charles Edward. *Politics and Markets : The World's Political Economic Systems*. New York: Basic Books, 1977.

Lipset, Seymour Martin, and Aldo E. Solari. *Elites in Latin America*. New York: Oxford University Press, 1967.

Mainwaring, S. "The State and the Industrial Bourgeoisie in Peron Argentina, 1945–1955." *Studies in Comparative International Development* 21 (3) (1986): 3–31.

Mann, Michael. *Consciousness and Action among the Western Working Class*. London: Macmillan, 1973.

Mann, Michael. *The Dark Side of Democracy: Explaining Ethnic Cleansing*. Cambridge: Cambridge University Press, 2005.

Mann, Michael. "The First Failed Empire of the 21st Century." *Review of International Studies* 30 (4) (2004): 631–53.

Mann, Michael. "Has Globalization Ended the Rise and Rise of the Nation-State?" *Review of International Political Economy* 4 (3) (1997): 472–96.

Mann, Michael. "Ruling-Class Strategies and Citizenship." *Sociology—The Journal of the British Sociological Association* 21 (3) (1987): 339–54.

Mann, Michael. *The Sources of Social Power*. Cambridge: Cambridge University Press, 1986.

Mann, Michael. *The Sources of Social Power. Vol. 2: The Rise of Classes and Nation-States, 1760–1914*. Cambridge: Cambridge University Press, 1993.

Mann, Michael. *The Sources of Social Power. Vol. 4: Globalizations, 1945–2011*. Cambridge: Cambridge University Press, 2012.

Maravall, Jose Maria. "The Myth of the Authoritarian Advantage." *Journal of Democracy* 5 (4) (1994): 17–31.

Mardin, Şerif. "Center-Periphery Relations: A Key to Turkish Politics?" *Daedalus* 102 (1) (1973): 169–90.

Marglin, Stephen. "What Do Bosses Do?" In *The Division of Labour: The Labour Process and Class-Struggle in Modern Capitalism*, edited by André Gorz, 13–54. Sussex: Harvester Press, 1976.

Marshall, Thomas H. *Citizenship and Social Class*. Cambridge: Cambridge University Press, 1950.

Marx, Karl, and Friedrich Engels. "Manifesto of the Communist Party." In *The Marx-Engels Reader*, edited by Robert C. Tucker, 469–500. New York: Norton, 1978.

Maxfield, Sylvia. *Governing Capital: International Finance and Mexican Politics*. Ithaca, NY: Cornell University Press, 1990.

Maxfield, Sylvia, and Ben Ross Schneider. *Business and the State in Developing Countries*. Ithaca, NY: Cornell University Press, 1997.

McGuire, James W. *Peronism without Peron: Unions, Parties, and Democracy in Argentina*. Stanford, CA: Stanford University Press, 1997.

Middlebrook, Kevin J. "Caciquismo and Democracy: Mexico and Beyond." *Bulletin of Latin American Research* 28 (3) (2009): 411–27.

Middlebrook, Kevin J. *The Paradox of Revolution: Labor, the State, and Authoritarianism in Mexico*. Baltimore: Johns Hopkins University Press, 1995.

Milor, Vedat, and Jesse Biddle. "Economic Governance in Turkey: Bureaucratic Capacity, Policy Networks, and Business Associations." In *Business and the State in Developing Countries*, edited by Sylvia Maxfield and Ben Ross Schneider, 277–309. Ithaca, NY: Cornell University Press, 1997.

Mizrahi, Yemile. "Rebels without a Cause? The Politics of Entrepreneurs in Chihuahua." *Journal of Latin American Studies* 26 (1994): 137–58.

Moore, Barrington. *Social Origins of Dictatorship and Democracy: Lord and Peasant in the Making of the Modern World*. Boston: Beacon Press, 1967.

Moore, Pete Watson. *Doing Business in the Middle East: Politics and Economic Crisis in Jordan and Kuwait*. Cambridge: Cambridge University Press, 2004.

Moore, Pete Watson. "Doing Business with the State: Explaining Business Lobbying in the Arab World." PhD Thesis, McGill University, Montreal, Canada,1998.

Mouzelis, Nicos P. *Politics in the Semi-Periphery: Early Parliamentarism and Late Industrialization in the Balkans and Latin America*. London: Macmillan, 1986.

Mouzelis, Nicos P. *Sociological Theory: What Went Wrong?: Diagnosis and Remedies*. London: Routledge, 1995.

O'Connor, Francis, and Bahar Baser. "Communal Violence and Ethnic Polarization before and after the 2015 Elections in Turkey: Attacks against the HDP and the Kurdish Population." *Journal of Southeast European and Black Sea Studies* 18 (1) (2018): 53–72.

O'Donnell, Guillermo A. *Bureaucratic Authoritarianism: Argentina, 1966–1973, in Comparative Perspective*. Berkeley: University of California Press, 1988.

O'Donnell, Guillermo A. "Illusions about Consolidation." *Journal of Democracy* 7 (2) (1996): 34–51.

O'Donnell, Guillermo A. "Illusions and Conceptual Flaws." *Journal of Democracy* 7 (4) (1996): 160–8.

O'Donnell, Guillermo A. *Modernization and Bureaucratic-Authoritarianism: Studies in South American Politics*. Berkeley: Institute of International Studies, University of California Press, 1979.

O'Donnell, Guillermo A., Philippe C. Schmitter, Laurence Whitehead, and Woodrow Wilson International Center for Scholars, Latin American Program, 1986. *Transitions from Authoritarian Rule*. Baltimore: Johns Hopkins University Press.

Olson, Robert. *The Emergence of Kurdish Nationalism and the Sheikh Said Rebellion, 1880–1925*. Austin: University of Texas Press, 2013.

Öniş, Ziya. "Liberalization, Transnational Corporations, and Foreign Direct Investment in Turkey: The Experience of the 1980s." In *Recent Industrialization Experience of Turkey in a Global Context*, edited by Fikret Şenses (Westport, CT: Greenwood Press, 1994).

Öniş, Ziya. "Organization of Export-Oriented Industrialization: The Turkish Foreign Trade Companies in Comparative Perspective." In *Economics and Politics of Turkish Liberalization*, edited by Tevfik F. Nas and Mehmet Odekon, 73–100. London: Lehigh University Press, 1992.

Öniş, Ziya. "The Political Economy of Turkey in the 1980s: The Anatomy of Unorthodox Liberalism." In *Strong State and Economic Interest Groups: The Post-1989 Experience*, edited by Metin Heper, 27–40. Berlin: Walter de Gruyter, 1991.

Öniş, Ziya. "The Triumph of Conservative Globalism: The Political Economy of the AKP Era." *Turkish Studies* 13 (2) (2012): 135–52.

Öniş, Ziya. "Turgut Özal and His Economic Legacy: Turkish Neo-Liberalism in Critical Perspective." *Middle Eastern Studies* 40 (4) (2004): 113–34.

Öniş, Ziya and Umut Türem. "Business, Globalization and Democracy: A Comparative Analysis of Turkish Business Associations." *Turkish Studies* 2 (2) (2001): 94–120.

Öniş, Ziya, and Umut Türem. "Entrepreneurs, Democracy, and Citizenship in Turkey." *Comparative Politics* 34 (4) (2002): 439–56.

Owen, Roger. *State, Power and Politics in the Making of the Modern Middle East*. New York: Routledge, 2013.

Oxhorn, Philip, and Graciela Ducatenzeiler. *What Kind of Democracy? What Kind of Market?: Latin America in the Age of Neoliberalism*. University Park, PA: Pennsylvania State University Press, 1998.

Özatalay, Cem. "Purge, Exile, and Resistance: Rethinking the Conflict of the Faculties through the Case of Academics for Peace in Turkey." *European Journal of Turkish Studies* 30 (30) (2020), https://doi.org/10.4000/ejts.6746.

Özbudun, Ergun. "The Post-1980 Legal Framework for Interest Group Associations." In *Strong State and Economic Interest Groups: The Post-1989 Turkish Experience*, edited by Metin Heper, 41–54. Berlin: Walter de Gruyter, 1991.

Özbudun, Ergun. "Turkey's Judiciary and the Drift toward Competitive Authoritarianism." *International Spectator* 50 (2): 42–55, 2015.

Özdalga, Elisabeth. *Late Ottoman Society the Intellectual Legacy*. SOAS/Routledge Curzon Studies on the Middle East 3. London: Routledge Curzon, 2005.

Özel, Işık. "Market Integration and Transformation of Business Politics: Diverging Trajectories of Corporatisms in Mexico and Turkey." *Socio-Economic Review* 19 (1) (2021): 219–45.

Özel, Işık. "Political Islam and Islamic Capital: The Case of Turkey." In *Religion and Politics in Europe, the Middle East and North Africa*, edited by Jeffrey Haynes, 155–77. New York: Routledge, 2009.

Özel, Işık. *State-Business Alliances and Economic Development: Turkey, Mexico and North Africa*. New York: Routledge, 2014.

Paige, J. M. "Coffee and Power in El Salvador." *Latin American Research Review* 28 (3) (1993): 7–40.

Pamuk, Şevket. "Institutional Change and the Longevity of the Ottoman Empire, 1500–1800." *Journal of Interdisciplinary History* 35 (2) (2004): 225–47.

Pamuk, Şevket. *The Ottoman Economy and Its Institutions*. Farnham, UK: Ashgate Publishing, 2009.

Parsons, Talcott. "The Distribution of Power in American Society." *World Politics* 10 (1) (1957): 123-43.
Pereira, Luiz Carlos Bresser, Adam Przeworski, and José María Maravall. *Economic Reforms in New Democracies: A Social-Democratic Approach*. Cambridge: Cambridge University Press, 1993.
Poggi, Gianfranco. *Calvinism and the Capitalist Spirit*. Amherst: University of Massachusetts Press, 1984.
Poggi, Gianfranco. *The State: Its Nature, Development, and Prospects*. Stanford, CA: Stanford University Press, 1990.
Polanyi, Karl. *The Great Transformation*. Boston: Beacon Press, 1957.
Poulantzas, Nicos. "The Problem of the Capitalist State." *New Left Review* 1 (58) (December 1969): 67-78.
Poulantzas, Nicos. *Pouvoir Politique et Classes Sociales*. Paris: F. Maspero, 1971.
Przeworski, Adam. *Capitalism and Social Democracy*. Cambridge: Cambridge University Press; Editions de la Maison des Sciences de l'Homme, 1985.
Przeworski, Adam. *The State and the Economy under Capitalism*. Chur, Switzerland: Harwood Academic Publishers, 1990.
Przeworski, Adam, and Fernando Limongi. "Political Regimes and Economic Growth." *Journal of Economic Perspectives* 7 (3) (1993): 51-69.
Quadagno, Jill S. "Welfare Capitalism and the Social Security Act of 1935." *American Sociological Review* 49 (5) (1984): 632-47.
Quataert, Donald. *Manufacturing in the Ottoman Empire and Turkey, 1500-1950*. Albany: State University of New York Press, 1994.
Quataert, Donald. *Ottoman Manufacturing in the Age of the Industrial Revolution*. Vol. 30. Cambridge: Cambridge University Press, 2002.
Quataert, Donald. *Workers, Peasants and Economic Change in the Ottoman Empire, 1730-1914*. Istanbul: Isis Press, 1993.
Romano, David. *The Kurdish Nationalist Movement: Opportunity, Mobilization and Identity*. Vol. 22. Cambridge: Cambridge University Press, 2006.
Rueschemeyer, Dietrich, Evelyne Huber, and John D. Stephens. *Capitalist Development and Democracy*. Chicago: University of Chicago Press, 1992.
Sassen, Saskia. *Cities in a World Economy*. London: Sage, 2018.
Schick, İrvin Cemil, and Ertuğrul Ahmet Tonak. *Turkey in Transition: New Perspectives*. Oxford: Oxford University Press, 1987.
Schmitter, Philippe. C. "Democratic Theory and Neocorporatist Practice." *Social Research* 50 (4) (1983): 885-928.
Schmitter, Philippe C., and Wolfgang Streeck. *The Organization of Business Interests: A Research Design to Study the Associative Action of Business in the Advanced Industrial Societies of Western Europe*. Discussion papers, International Institute of Management: Labour Market Policy. Berlin: Wissenschaftszentrum Berlin, 1981.
Schneider, Ben Ross. "Organized Business Politics in Democratic Brazil." *Journal of Interamerican Studies and World Affairs* 39 (4) (Winter 1997): 95-127.
Schneider, Ben Ross. *Business Politics and the State in Twentieth-Century Latin America*. Cambridge: Cambridge University Press, 2004.
Schneider, Ben Ross. *Hierarchical Capitalism in Latin America*. Cambridge: Cambridge University Press, 2013.
Schumpeter, Joseph A. *Capitalism, Socialism and Democracy*. London: Routledge, 2003.
Şeker, Nesim. "Demographic Engineering in the Late Ottoman Empire and the Armenians." *Middle Eastern Studies* 43 (3) (2007): 461-74.

Seni, Nora. "Le Mécène, Un Acteur Méconnu de La Ville. Istanbul à l'heure Des Musées Privés." *Transcontinentales. Sociétés, Idéologies, Système Mondial*, no. 7 (2009): 105–28.

Şenses, Fikret. *Recent Industrialization Experience of Turkey in a Global Context*. Contributions in Economics and Economic History, No. 155. Westport, CT: Greenwood Press, 1994.

Şenses, Fikret. "Stabilization and Structural Adjustment Program and the Process of Turkish Industrialization: Main Policies and Their Impact." In *Recent Industrialization Experience of Turkey in a Global Context*, edited by Fikret Şenses, 51–74. Westport, CT: Greenwood Press, 1994.

Silva, E. "From Dictatorship to Democracy—The Business-State Nexus in Chile's Economic Transformation, 1975–1994." *Comparative Politics* 28 (3) (1996): 299–320.

Simmons, Beth A., Frank Dobbin, and Geoffrey Garrett, eds. *The Global Diffusion of Markets and Democracy*. Cambridge: Cambridge University Press, 2008.

Sklair, L. "The Transnational Capitalist Class and Global Politics: Deconstructing the Corporate-State Connection." *International Political Science Review* 23 (2) (2002): 159–74.

Skocpol, Theda, and Edwin Amenta. "States and Social Policies." *Annual Review of Sociology* 12 (1986): 131–57.

Skocpol, Theda, and Ellen Kay Trimberger. "Revolutions and the World-Historical Development of Capitalism." *Berkeley Journal of Sociology* 22 (1977): 101–13.

Smith, Adam. *An Inquiry into the Nature and Causes of the Wealth of Nations*. Vol. 2. Edinburgh: Printed for Mundell, Doig, and Stevenson, 1809, https://link-gale-com.lehman.ezproxy.cuny.edu/apps/doc/U0107045052/MOME?u=lehman_main&sid=bookmark-MOME&xid=0174f62d&pg=192.

Smith, William C. "State, Market and Neoliberalism in Posttransition Argentina—The Menem Experiment." *Journal of Interamerican Studies and World Affairs* 33 (4) (Winter 1991): 45–82.

Sönmez, Mustafa. *Türkiye'de Holdingler Kırk Haramiler*. Istanbul: Arkadaş Yayınevi, 1988.

Sönmez, Ümit. "The Political Economy of Market and Regulatory Reforms in Turkey: The Logic and Unintended Consequences of Ad-Hoc Strategies." *New Political Economy* 16 (1) (2011): 101–30.

Tekdemir, Omer, Mari Toivanen, and Bahar Baser. "Peace Profile: Academics for Peace in Turkey." *Peace Review* 30 (1) (2018): 103–11, https://doi.org/10.1080/10402659.2017.1419968.

Tezel, Yahya Sezai. *Cumhuriyet Döneminin İktisadi Tarihi*. Ankara: Yurt Yayınevi, 1982.

Tilly, Charles. *Coercion, Capital, and European States, AD 990–1992*. Hoboken, NJ: Wiley-Blackwell, 1992.

Trimberger, Ellen Kay. *Revolution from Above: Military Bureaucrats and Development in Japan, Turkey, Egypt, and Peru*. New Brunswick, NJ: Transaction Publishers, 1978.

Tuğal, Cihan. *The Fall of the Turkish Model: How the Arab Uprisings Brought down Islamic Liberalism*. London: Verso, 2016.

Turam, Berna. *Between Islam and the State: The Politics of Engagement*. Stanford, CA: Stanford University Press, 2007.

Turam, Berna. "Gender and Sexuality of the State." *Turkish Review* 4 (3) (2014): 346–8.

Turam, Berna, ed. *Secular State and Religious Society: Two Forces in Play in Turkey*. New York: Springer, 2011.

Turam, Berna. "Turkish Women Divided by Politics." *International Feminist Journal of Politics* 10 (4) (2008): 475–94, https://doi.org/10.1080/14616740802393882.

Turan, Ömer, and Burak Özçetin. "Football Fans and Contentious Politics: The Role of Çarşı in the Gezi Park Protests." *International Review for the Sociology of Sport* 54 (2) (2019): 199–217.

TÜSİAD. *Brochure*. Istanbul: TÜSİAD, 1997.

TÜSİAD. *Türkiye'de Bireysel Gelir Dağılımı ve Yoksulluk: Avrupa Birliği Ile Karşılaştırma*. Istanbul: TÜSIAD, 2000.

TÜSİAD. *Türkiye'de Demokratikleşme Perspektifleri (Perspectives on Democratization in Turkey)* Istanbul: TÜSİAD, 1997.

TÜSİAD. *Türkiye'de Eğitim*. Istanbul: TÜSİAD, 1990.

TÜSİAD. "TÜSİAD Başkanı Dinçer Ankara Temaslarına İlişkin Basın Toplantısı Düzenledi," Press Release, 2014, https://tusiad.org/tr/tum/item/7899-tusiad-baskani-dincer-ankara-temaslarina-iliskin-basin-toplantisi-duzenledi. Accessed July 15, 2022

TÜSİAD. "TÜSİAD Charter," https://tusiad.org/en/tusiad/charter. Accessed July 25, 2022.

TÜSİAD, "TÜSİAD Faaliyet Raporu 2018," https://tusiad.org/tr/faaliyet-raporlari/item/10233-tusiad-faaliyet-raporu-2018. Accessed July 25, 2022.

TÜSİAD. "TÜSİAD Faaliyet Raporu 2019," https://tusiad.org/tr/faaliyet-raporlari/item/10523-tusi-ad-faaliyet-raporu-2019. Accessed July 25, 2022.

TÜSİAD. "TÜSİAD Statement on the General Elections in Turkey," Press Release, June 24, 2015, https://tusiad.org/en/press-releases/item/8463-tusiad-statement-on-the-general-elections-in-turkey. Accessed July 15, 2022.

TÜSİAD. *TÜSİAD 1975 Yılı Çalışmaları*. Istanbul: TÜSİAD, 1975.

TÜSİAD. *TÜSİAD 1977 Yılı Çalışmaları*. Istanbul: TÜSİAD, 1977.

TÜSİAD. *TÜSİAD 1978 Yılı Çalışmaları*. Istanbul: TÜSİAD, 1978.

TÜSİAD. *TÜSİAD 1979 Yılı Çalışmaları*. Istanbul: TÜSİAD, 1979.

TÜSİAD. *TÜSİAD 1997 Yılı Çalışmaları*. Istanbul: TÜSİAD, 1997.

TÜSİAD, *TÜSİAD 2010 Yılı Çalışmaları*. Istanbul: TÜSİAD, 2010.

Useem, Michael. "The Inner Group of the American Capitalist Class." *Social Problems* 25 (3) (1978): 225–40.

Useem, Michael. "The Social Organization of the American Business Elite and Participation of Corporation Directors in the Governance of American Institutions." *American Sociological Review* 44 (4) (1979): 553–72.

Valenzuela, J. Samuel, and Arturo Valenzuela. *Modernization and Dependency: Alternative Perspectives in the Study of Latin American Underdevelopment Comparative Politics*. New York: City University of New York Press, 1978.

Waisman, C. H. "Capitalism, the Market, and Democracy." *American Behavioral Scientist* 35 (4–5) (1992): 500–16.

Wallerstein, Immanuel. "A World-System Perspective on the Social Sciences." *British Journal of Sociology* 61 (2010): 167–76.

Waterbury, John. "Export-Led Growth and the Centre Right Coalition in Turkey." *Comparative Politics* 24 (2) (1992): 127–45.

Weber, Max. *General Economic History*. New Brunswick, NJ: Transaction Publishers, 1981.

Weber, Max. *Max Weber: Selections in Translation*. Cambridge: Cambridge University Press, 1978.

Weber, Max. *The Protestant Ethic and the Spirit of Capitalism: And Other Writings*. London: Penguin, 2002.

Weiner, Myron, and Ergun Özbudun. *Competitive Elections in Developing Countries*. Durham, NC: Duke University Press, 1987.

Weiss, Linda. "Infrastructural Power, Economic Transformation, and Globalization." In *An Anatomy of Power: The Social Theory of Michael Mann*, edited by J. Hall and R. Schroeder, 167–86. Cambridge: Cambridge University Press, 2006.

Weiss, Linda. *The Myth of the Powerless State*. Ithaca, NY: Cornell University Press, 1998.

Weiss, Linda. *States in the Global Economy: Bringing Domestic Institutions Back in*. Vol. 86. Cambridge: Cambridge University Press, 2003.

Weyland, K. "Neopopulism and Neoliberalism in Latin America: Unexpected Affinities." *Studies in Comparative International Development* 31 (3) (1996): 3–31.

White, Jenny. *Islamist Mobilization in Turkey: A Study in Vernacular Politics*. Seattle, WA: University of Washington Press, 2011.

World Bank Group. "World Development Indicators." Washington, DC: World Bank Group, 2005.

Wright, E. O. "Working-Class Power, Capitalist-Class Interests, and Class Compromise." *American Journal of Sociology* 105 (4) (2000): 957–1002.

Yavuz, Devrim. "Conflict, Democratic Reform, and Big Business: Factors Shaping the Economic Elite's Position for Change." In *Secular State and Religious Society: Two Forces at Play in Turkey*, edited by Berna Turam, 143–66. New York: Springer, 2012.

Yavuz, Erdal. "The State of the Industrial Workforce, 1923–1940." In *Workers and the Working Class in the Ottoman Empire and the Turkish Republic 1839–1950*, edited by Donald Quataert and Eric Zürcher, 95–125. London: Tauris Academic Studies, 1994.

Yavuz, Hakan M. *Secularism and Muslim Democracy in Turkey*. Vol. 28. Cambridge: Cambridge University Press, 2009.

Yılmaz, Volkan. *The Politics of Healthcare Reform in Turkey*. New York: Springer, 2017.

Zürcher, Erik J. *Turkey: A Modern History*. London: Bloomsbury, 2017.

Zürcher, Erik J. *The Young Turk Legacy and Nation Building: From the Ottoman Empire to Atatürk's Turkey*. London: Bloomsbury, 2014.

INDEX

Note: Page numbers in *italics* denote figures and tables.

Abdul Hamid II, Sultan 77
Africa 44, 160
agriculture and agricultural lands 55, 58, 72, 84–6, 130, *131*, 167
Akçam, Taner 79
Alarko Holding 4, 95, *131*, 137
Alaton, İshak
  background 43–4
  business background 4
  and diversity issues in TÜSİAD 148
  and origins of Alarko Holding 95
  on paths to European democracy 54
  on public perception of entrepreneurs 153
  and structure of study 18
Amazon (company) ix
Amnesty International 2
Anatolia 73, 78–9, 214 n.56. *See also* center-periphery dialectic; Islam and Muslims, Muslim entrepreneurs
Anatolian tigers 113, 167
ancien régime 6, 55
Ankara University 118
Arat, Yeşim 31–2, 106
arbitrary state power
  and AKP's rise to power 178–9, 193–4
  and the Kurdish minority 25–6
  and multiparty democracy period 84–5
  and path to democracy in Europe 58
  and top-down rule in Turkey 80–1
  and TÜSİAD critiques of government 106
  and TÜSİAD's leadership 41
  and the Washington Consensus 209 n.101
  Washington Consensus view on 66
  See also despotic power

Arçelik 171
Argentina 53, 65, 147
Argüden, Yılmaz 158
aristocracy
  and bureaucratic authoritarianism 61
  influence in late-developing societies 62
  and late-developing societies 62
  and paths to European democracy 54–5, 57–8
  and path to democracy in Europe 57
  and theoretical approach to state-business relations 43–4
  and typology of state-business relations 52–3
  and Western European feudal dynamics 72–3
  See also landed classes
Armenians/Armenian genocide 2, 29, 36, 79–80, 214 n.56
Asia 44
assassinations 39, 104, 143
assimilation 26. *See also* Kurds and Kurdish issue
associational life. *See* civil society
Atatürk, Mustafa Kemal 28, 76, 81, 83, 88
Atatürkism. *See* Kemalism
authoritarianism
  and AKP's rise to power 169, 171–2, 178–9, 192–3
  and alliances of capitalist development 202 n.49
  authoritarian revolutions 8
  bureaucratic authoritarianism 60–2
  and challenges to Turkish democratization 69
  and factors shaping the business elite 189
  and imposition of martial law x, 26, 33
  and intraclass alliances 183

and late-developing societies 60–2
and origins of the *Democratization Report* 2
and path to democracy in Europe 57
and public diplomacy of TÜSİAD 174
and state power in late-industrializing societies 11
and state tradition of top-down political rule 163
and theoretical approach to state-business relations 45
and threats to TÜSİAD's status 171
and TÜSİAD strategies under AKP rule 165–6, 179–80
automation 56
automotive sector 130, 132, 152
autonomy. *See also* state autonomy
ayan system 74

Balkans 62, 120
Bartell, Ernest J. 46, 54
Başaran-Symes, Cansen 136, 145, 168
Baudouy, Joseph 91
Bayar, Celal 84–5, 121
Beko 171
Berker, Feyyaz 91, 105, 137, 149
Bezos, Jeff ix
Bianchi, Robert 101
bilateral trade agreements 75, 78, 97
Bilecik, Erol 168
Blackburn, R. M. 207 n.63
black market 83
Borusan Holding *131*, 137
Bosphorus Initiative 173
Bosphorus University 184
bourgeoisie
and AKP's rise to power 168–70
bourgeois democracy 23, 44
and bureaucratic authoritarianism 60–1
and business elite's ideological power 102, 104
and center-periphery tensions 160
democratizing role of 5–8
and domestic political conflict 175, 177
and dual nature of Turkish state 71
and Early Ottoman period 72–3, 75–6
and "embedded autonomy" 198 n.44
and EU integration efforts 120

and evolution of TÜSİAD's prodemocracy position 110, 142
forces leading to creation of 18
and impact of capital-intensive production 99
and informal state-society linkages 156
and interview sources 16
and origins of Turkish capitalist class 2–3, 94
and paths to European democracy 54–5, 56–9
and state autonomy concept 47
and theoretical approach to state-business relations 43–5
and threats to TÜSİAD's status 165, 171
and top-down Ottoman reforms 77–9
and the Turkish Republic 80–4, 87
and typologies of power 52
and the Young Turk movement 79–80
Boyner, Cem 39, 141, 143, 177
Boyner, Ümit 177
Boyner family 144
Braverman, Harry 207 n.63
Brazil 3, 49, 65, 97, 155, 159
Britain (and Great Britain) 18, 57–9, 76. *See also* England
Brookings Institute 173
Buğra, Ayşe
on cause of military coup 106–7
on decision-making research 198 n.44
on informal state-business relations 136
on landholding families in Turkey 212 n.32
on new rising Muslim elite and Muslim holdings in Turkey 167–8
on "paradox of Turkish liberalism" 86, 89
on problems created by informal state links 156
research on Turkish capitalists 79
on state-business relations 11
on Turkish holding companies 93–4
Building the Future with a New Mindset (report) 187
bureaucracy and bureaucratization
bureaucratic authoritarianism 60–2, 189
and center-periphery tensions 27, 28
and competition for state subsidies 94–5
and EU integration efforts 118

and state autonomy concept 48, 49
as threat to business associations 159
and top-down rule 22
and typologies of power 50
Burundi 125
business associations 14–15, 65, 99–100
business elite
   and AKP's rise to power 166–9, 169–73, 192–4
   and autonomy from the state 155
   and capital-intensive production 96–9
   and capital's political power 106–7
   and case-study approach 16–17
   and democratization strategies 184–7, 188
   and domestic political conflict 175–8
   economic and ideological power 5–8, 190–1
   and the globalization debate 9–11
   and holding companies 93–6
   and ideological power 102–6, 191–2
   and intraclass alliances 182–3
   in newly industrialized countries 13–16
   paradigm shift 113–17
   and political power 99–102
   reactionary tendencies 163
   and responses to AKP rule 164–6
   responses to rising authoritarianism 178–9, 179–82
   and scope/methods of study 1–4, 190
   and social dimensions of democracy 134–5
   and state autonomy 191
   and state-business relations under late-industrialization 11–13
   and state repression 164
   and TÜSİAD's origins 91–3
   and TÜSİAD's political structure 173–5
BusinessEurope 174–5, 227 n.39
Byzantine Empire 72–3

caliphate 28, 73
Calvinism 52
capital accumulation 131–3
capital flows 198 n.44
capital goods 82, 86, 97, 100–1, 114, 115, 145

capital-intensive production
   and evolution of Turkish business elite 96–9
   and heavy industrialization 129–30, 131–5
   and market expansion 128–9
   and need for business formalism 158
capital investment 98, 132
capitalist ideology
   and accommodation of ideological diversity 144, 146–50
   and business elite's ideological and political power 144–6
   and business formalism 156–9
   and capital's political power 106–7
   and challenges to Turkish democratization 69–70
   and dual nature of Turkish state 70–1
   of early Ottoman period 71–6
   of late Ottoman period 76–80
   and limits of TÜSİAD's power 159–61
   and path to democracy in Europe 56–9
   and schisms within TÜSİAD 139–40
   and state autonomy 150–6
   and theoretical approach to state-business relations 45
   and TÜSİAD's political activities 140–4
   See also business elite
capitulation treaties 75, 78
Cardoso, Fernando Henrique 66
Carrefour supermarkets 171
Carrier Corporation 95
case-study approach 16–17
Cengiz Holding 168
center-periphery dialectic
   and AKP governance 37–8
   and dual nature of Turkish state 70
   and limits to TÜSİAD's power 159–61
   and secular-Muslim conflict 26–8
   and secular-religious conflict 29
   and state tradition of top-down political rule 163
   and top-down rule in Turkey 30–1
   and the Turkish Republic 85
Central Asia 135, 171
central bank 116
centralization of power 23, 45, 67, 71–2, 74–5
chaebols 94, 116

charismatic leadership 15, 34, 53, 62, 65
Chile 3, 65, 155
China 10, 45, 50, 97
Christians. *See* Armenians/Armenian genocide; Greek minority
citizenship
  citizenship rights 39
  civic citizenship 26
  ethnic citizenship 26, 28, 81
  and the Kurdish minority 25–6
  and path to democracy in Europe 58–9
  and Turkish identity 78
  universal citizenship 39, 58
civil rights 41
civil service 49, 67, 75, 104
civil society
  and AKP governance 32, 35, 164, 168, 193
  business associations as 15
  and business elite's political power 99–101
  and business formalism 194
  and capital-intensive production 134
  and "deep state" networks 22
  and development of Turkish democracy 23–4
  distrust of 89
  and diversity issues in TÜSİAD 147–8
  and divided opinions on democratization 41–2
  and domestic political conflict 176, 178
  and dual nature of Turkish state 70
  and evolution of Turkish democracy 1–2
  and evolution of TÜSİAD's prodemocracy position 110, 141–3
  and Gezi protests 36–7, 40, 178
  and growing legitimacy of business sector 154
  and impact of 1980 coup 30–1
  and interview sources 16
  and intraclass alliances 182
  and late-developing societies 64
  and problems created by informal state links 157
  and secular-religious conflicts 29
  and the Turkish Republic 81, 83, 87–8
  and TÜSİAD strategies under AKP rule 180, 186–8
  and typologies of power 50, 53
  and weak coalition governments 33
class identity and consciousness 18, 71–6, 98, 207 n.63
clientelism
  and ANAP's majority rule 32
  and AKP governance 37, 193
  and AKP's rise to power 167
  and bureaucratic authoritarianism 62
  coalition governments' use of 159
  and Erdoğan's grip on power 189
  and multiparty democracy 89
  and state autonomy 191
  and state-business relations under late-industrialization 11–12
  and third wave of democratization 66
  and the Turkish Republic 81, 88
  and TÜSİAD strategies under AKP rule 172
  and typologies of power 53
  and the Washington Consensus 209 n.101
  and weak coalition governments 33
climate control industry 95
clothing industry *115*
coalition governments 32–4
collective power 52, 63
Collier, David 70
Committee for National Union (Milli Birlik Komitesi) 87
Committee for Union and Progress (İttihat ve Terakki Cemiyeti, CUP) 77–82, 213 n.46, 214 n.56. *See also* Young Turk movement
communication technology 79, 137
Communist Manifesto (Marx and Engels) 5–6, 43
comparative approach to study 4, 17, 24
comprador bourgeoisie 6, 43
Confederation of Businessmen and Industrialists (Türkiye İşadamları ve Sanayicileri Konfederasyonu, TUSKON) 16, 120, 159–60, 171, 183, 199 n.55, 228 n.56
Confederation of Revolutionary Workers' Unions (Türkiye Devrimci İşçi Sendikaları Konfederasyonu, DİSK) 66
Constantinople 73
Constitutional Court 176

Constitutional Reform and the Democratization of the State (report) 10
constitutions
  and challenges to democracy 23
  constitutional reforms 3, 35
  and coup of 1980 31
  and domestic political conflict 177
  and Ottoman era 77
  and path to democracy in Europe 58
  and schisms within TÜSİAD 139
  and TÜSİAD strategies under AKP rule 165
consumer goods 97, 115, 130, 161
corporativismo (corporatism) 83
corporate governance 137, 158
corporatism 52, 83, 87, 97, 100, 157
corruption 9, 23, 152, 198 n.44
cosmopolitanism of business class 74, 117, 119, 125–8, 138, 175
coups
  and AKP governance 37–8
  and capital's political power 106
  and challenges to Turkish democratization 69
  and domestic political conflict 177
  and evolution of Turkish democracy 1
  and factors shaping the business elite 189
  goals of 97
  and the Gülenist movement 203 n.70
  impact on Turkish industry 18
  and multiparty democracy 85
  origins and impact of 1980 coup 30–1
  and ousting of RP coalition 33–4, 210 n.1
  and Paker's background 43
  and popular perception of Turkish capitalists 38
  in Southern Cone nations 12
"cruel choice" thesis 45
cultural diversity 75, 77–9, 144

Dahl, Robert A. 23
Dark Side of Democracy (Mann) 79
debt crises 30, 63–4, 76, 106, 107
"deep state" networks 21–3, 33, 36, 38–9
deinstitutionalization 184–5, 187
Demirel, Süleyman 32–3, 101, 106–7

Demirören Holding 172
democracy and democratization
  and AKP governance 34–8, 166–9, 171, 173–5, 176–8, 178–81
  and ANAP's majority rule 31–2
  and business interests 38–41
  and center-periphery dichotomy 26–8
  and coup of 1980 30–1
  and "deep state" networks 21–3, 36, 38
  and EU integration efforts 117–22
  and individual attitudes 41–2
  and the Kurdish minority 25–6
  and microorganizational change in TÜSİAD firms 136–8
  notions of democracy 23–4
  protests supporting 36
  and role of bourgeoisie 5–6
  and secular-religious conflicts 29–30
  since 1980 24–34
  and state autonomy 150–6
  third-wave 3–4, 9, 23, 46, 63–4, 64–7, 109, 193
  and TÜSİAD reports 181
  and weak coalitions 32–4
Democratic Left Party (Demokratik Sol Parti, DSP) 34, 36
Democratization Report
  and capital's political power 106
  and center-periphery tensions 38–9
  and diversity issues in TÜSİAD 148
  and evolution of Turkish democracy 2–3
  and evolution of TÜSİAD's prodemocracy position 110, 142
  influence of liberal TÜSİAD members 15
  internal divisions on 41
  key figures behind 43
  and Komili's influence 166
  negative reactions to 157
  organization and content of 196 n.1
  and Paker's influence 6
  radical tone of 177
  and schisms within TÜSİAD 139–40, 226 n.24
  and Tanör's influence 169
  and TÜSİAD strategies under AKP rule 173, 180

Democrat Party (Demokrat Parti, DP) 13, 85–8, 101
dependency theory 61–2, 211 n.17
dependent business 59–64
deregulation 23, 110, 112, 123
despotic power 50, 70, 73–5
Development Bank 95
devşirme system 75
Dicle, Ebru 16–17, 183, 187, 194
dictatorships 59–61. *See also* coups
Dinçkök, Ömer 141
Directorate of Religious Affairs (Diyanet İşleri Başkanlığı) 29
distributive power 52
Divan Hotel 178
diversity
  and capitalist ideology 144, 146–50
  cultural 75, 77–9
  religious 75, 203 n.70
Doğan, Aydın 172
Doğan Holding 172, 182
Domhoff, G. William 49
drug trafficking 21
dual nature of Turkish state 70–1, 161
Duesenberry, James xi
Duna, Cem 118, 123

Ecevit, Bülent 34, 104, 106, 153
Economic and Social Council 177
economic power
  and business cosmopolitanism 125–8
  and capital-intensive production 128–9, 134–5
  and capitalists' role in democratization 4–8
  and CHP's rule 81
  and dual nature of Turkish state 70
  and economic liberalization x, 9–11, 25, 33, 85, 105–6, 138, 150, 154
  and EU integration efforts 117–22
  and foreign investment in Turkish business 122–5
  and heavy industrialization 129–34
  and the Kurdish issue 40
  and microorganizational change 136–8
  and paradigm shift of the business elite 113–17
  and political environment 111–13
  and theoretical approach to state-business relations 43–4, 190–1
Eczacıbaşı, Bülent 117–19, 142, 151
Eczacıbaşı family 40
Eczacıbaşı Holding *131*, 137, 154
education
  and capital-intensive production 134
  and center-periphery tensions 27
  and divided opinions on democratization 41
  and evolution of TÜSİAD's prodemocracy position 142
  and the Gülenist movement 203 n.70
  and impact of 1980 coup 31
  and need for business formalism 158
  and social dimensions of democracy 135
  and state autonomy 151–2
  and structural limits to Turkish democracy 26
  and TÜSİAD reports 181, *181*
elections and electoral politics
  and AKP governance 36–7
  and centrism of working class 208 n.63
  and challenges to Turkish democratization 23, 69
  and coalition governments 32–4
  and formal democracy 25
  and paths to European democracy 56
  and secular-religious conflict 30
  and stability fostering economic growth 132–3
  transition to the multiparty period 85
electronics industry *115*
El Salvador 65
embedded autonomy 198 n.44
Embedded Autonomy (Evans) 198 n.44
"end of history" thesis 9. *See also* globalization
energy costs 126, 151
Engels, Friedrich 5–6, 44, 48, 72
England 8, 55, 57, *120*, 121, 136, 149. *See also* Britain (and Great Britain)
Enka Holding *131*, 137
Enlightenment 58, 59
entrepreneurship
  and business elite's ideological power 102–3
  and business elite's political power 102

and democratizing role of TÜSİAD 92
and embedded autonomy 198 n.44
and the Gülenist movement 199 n.55
and late-development 62
and origins of Turkish capitalist class 94
and state-business relations 6–7, 11
and top-down Ottoman reforms 78–9
and Turkish holding companies 96
and TÜSİAD strategies under AKP rule 180
environmental issues 181, 181–4, 185–7, 190, 194
Erbakan, Necmettin 33–4, 101, 177
Erdoğan, Recep Tayyip
  and AKP governance 34, 35–6
  and AKP's rise to power 166–8, 192–4
  autocratic tendencies 17
  and domestic political conflict 175–8
  and evolution of TÜSİAD's prodemocracy position 3
  and factors shaping the business elite 189
  and growing legitimacy of business sector 153
  and the Gülenist movement 203 n.70
  and Islamization of the state 164–5
  and the Kurdish issue 40
  and public diplomacy of TÜSİAD 174–5
  and rising authoritarianism 178–9
  and state tradition of top-down political rule 163
  and structural limits to Turkish democracy 25
  and threats to TÜSİAD's status 171–2
  and TÜSİAD strategies under AKP rule 180, 182, 184, 186
  and weak coalition governments 34
Erkin, Tuğrul 145
Eroğlu, Galip 137
Étatism (statism) 83
ethnicity
  and AKP governance 37
  ethnic citizenship 26, 28, 81
  ethnic cleansing 77
  ethnic identity in Turkish culture 22, 41
  ethnic pluralism 79
  ethnic policies 79, 84, 86, 96
  and ethnonationalism 29, 40, 78
  ethno-religious minorities during Ottoman era 94, 102
  See also Armenians/Armenian genocide; diversity; Kurds and Kurdish issue
European Union (EU) membership
  and AKAP's majority rule 32
  and AKP governance 35, 164
  and AKP's rise to power 167
  and BusinessEurope 227 n.39
  and center-periphery tensions 160
  and diversity issues in TÜSİAD 147–9
  and domestic political conflict 175
  and EU integration and democratization 117–22
  and fostering economies of scale 135
  and problems created by informal state links 157
  and rising Turkish authoritarianism 179
  and the Turkey Commission 147
  and TÜSİAD strategies under AKP rule 165–6, 180
  and weak coalition governments 34
Evans, Peter B. 48
Evren, Kenan 30, 31
executive power 67, 69, 114, 167
export-led growth (ELG) 66–7, 116
Export Promotion Fund 116
exports
  and AKP's rise to power 167
  and business cosmopolitanism 126–7
  and capital-intensive production 128
  destinations of Turkish exports *120, 121*
  and economic liberalization of the 80s and 90s 112–16, *113*
  export-led growth model of development 66–7, 109, 116
  and foreign investment in Turkish business 123
  and fostering economies of scale 135
  and heavy industrialization 129–31
  and state autonomy 152
  and structural adjustment programs 112
  and tax revenues from TÜSİAD members 155
extrajudicial murders 21

family ownership 14, 63, 93–6, 136, 144, 146, 156. *See also specific family names*
fascist Italy 83
feudalism
  and democratizing role of the bourgeoisie 5–6
  and Marxian debate on Turkish development 211 n.17
  and Ottoman period 71–4, 211 n.17
  and path to democracy in Europe 55–6, 58
  and theoretical approach to state-business relations 44
  and Turkish landholding families 212 n.32
  and typologies of power 50–1
Fiat 171
financial crises 34, 132
financial deregulation 123
five-year plans 83, 97
Fırt 38
football hooligans 36
foreign direct investment 123, *124*, 128, 132
foreign exchange 85, 116
foreign investment 122–5
foreign partnerships 114, 122–4, 152, 158. *See also* joint ventures and partnerships
foreign policy 179
foreign trade *181*
foreign trade companies (FTCs) 115
formalism 11, 53, 138, 156–9, 187–8, 194
France
  French Revolution 55, 57, 77
  and Industrial Revolution 76
  and paths to European democracy 55
  and path to democracy in Europe 56–7
  and rising Turkish authoritarianism 179
  and state autonomy concept 48
  taxation systems 74
  and Turkish exports *120*, 121
free speech ix, 25
free-trade ideology 52, 81, 83, 92–3
French Revolution 55, 57, 77

Garih, Üzeyir 95
GDP of Turkey 69, 97, 112, *113*, 123, *124*, 132–3

gender equality 29, 41, 169, 181, *181*, 194
generational shift in Turkish business class
  and business elite's ideological and political power 144
  and democratizing role of TÜSİAD 92
  and environmental issues 181
  and evolution of TÜSİAD's prodemocracy position 140–1
  and interview sample selection 199 n.54
  and Paker's background 43
  and problems created by informal state links 156
  and rising Turkish authoritarianism 179
  and TÜSİAD strategies under AKP rule 185
Germany
  and Industrial Revolution 76
  and path to democracy in Europe 57, 60
  and rising Turkish authoritarianism 179
  and Turkish exports *120*, 121
  and typology of state-business relations 52
Gezi protests 36–7, 40, 178
Giddens, Anthony 5
Gırgır 38
globalization 9–11, 16, 46, 52, 92, 118, 183
Global South 44, 61, *120*
Göçek, Fatma Müge 80
Goldthorpe, John H. 207 n.63
good governance 41, 69, 139, 152, 158, *181*, 198 n.44
Governing Board (Yönetim Kurulu) 145–7, 148
grassroots change 187
Great Depression 82
Greece 62, 77, 86
Greek minority 79, 102
Gül, Abdullah 36, 174
Gülenist movement 37, 120, 159–60, 199 n.55, 203 n.70, 228 n.56

heavy industrialization 129–34
Higher Advisory Council (Yüksek İstişare Konseyi) 145–6, 169, 184
Hirschman, Albert O. 54, 59
holding companies 93–6, 97–9, 99–102, 107, 114, 116, 216 n.11. *See also specific company names*
Holland *120*

Huber, Evelyne 24–5, 56, 193
human rights 61, 119, 184, 196 n.1
Huntington, Samuel 3–4, 63

IC Holding 168
ideological, economic, military, and political (IEMP) power model
  and comparative approach to study 17
  described 8
  and path to democracy in Europe 58
  and state autonomy concept 49
  and theoretical approach to state-business relations 46, 190
  and "third wave" of democratization 66–7
  and typology of state-business relations 51, 53
ideological power
  and capitalists' role in democratization 4–8
  and divided opinions on democratization 42
  and dual nature of Turkish state 70
  and late-developing societies 62–3
  and Ottoman despotic power 76
  and theoretical approach to state-business relations 191–2
  of Turkish business elite 102–5, 144–6
importation of goods 84
import-export companies 115
import substitution industrialization (ISI)
  and business elite's ideological power 103
  and business elite's political power 100
  and capital-intensive production 97
  and challenges of late-development 60
  and CHP's rule 83
  and Özal's background 114
  and state-led development policies 87–8
  and "third wave" of democratization 66–7
income inequality 9, 41, 134, 181
independence movements 81
independent cities 72–3
Independent Industrialists and Businessmen Association (Müstakil Sanayici ve İşadamları Derneği, MÜSİAD) 10, 35, 159–60, 167, 183
India 49, 97

industrial capitalism 57
Industrial Development Bank 98
industrialization
  and business elite's political power 101
  and capital-intensive production 96–7
  and CHP's rule 82
  and heavy industrialization 129–33
  and militarization of European states 76
  state-led 87–8
  and theoretical approach to state-business relations 43–4
  and TÜSİAD's ideological transformation 8
  and typologies of power 53
Industrial Revolution 76
inflation 33, 86, 132, 135
informal economy 158, 191
informal state-society relations 22, 53, 114, 136, 150, 156–9, 187
infrastructural power 50–1, 151
infrastructure spending 86
inheritance 75, 102, 136
"Innovation in Hospitality Award," 179
İnönü, Erdal 33
input prices 126, 151–2
Institut du Bosphore (Bosphorus Institute) 173–4
Institute for the Study of Industrial Development (Instituto de Estudos para o Desenvolvimento Industrial, IEDI) 65, 159
institutionalization 144–6
institutional power 52
Institutional Revolutionary Party (Partido Revolucionario Institucional, PRI) 13, 53
intellectual property 183
interfaith dialogue 160, 228 n.56
intermediate goods 97, *115*
International Monetary Fund (IMF) 30, 106, 209 n.101
international trade 75, 115
interview subjects 16–17, 199 n.54
interwar period 18
intraclass alliances 182–3
intraclass conflict 14–15
"invisible hand of the market," 54. *See also* free-trade ideology
Iran 25

Iraq 25
Islam and Muslims
    and AKP governance 34, 164
    and CHP's rule 84
    Islamic character of Turkey 177
    Islamic fundamentalism 35
    Muslim bourgeoisie of Turkey 113, 165, 167, 169–71
    Muslim capitalists 77, 82
    Muslim entrepreneurs 84, 159, 170–1
    and Ottoman despotic power 75
    and ousting of RP coalition 33–4, 210 n.1
    political Islam 166–7
    and secular-religious conflict 30, 163–6, 168, 175–7, 188
    and structural limits to Turkish democracy 25
    Sunni Islam 27–9, 37, 73, 178
    and weak coalition governments 33
    See also center-periphery dialectic; Kurds and Kurdish issue
Israel 120
Istanbul, Turkey 88
Istanbul Chamber of Industry (Istanbul Sanayi Odası, ISO) 99, 104, 170
Istanbul Convention 184
Istanbul Technical University 95
Italy 120, 121
IT sector 48, 198 n.44

Japan 49
Jews and Judaism 75, 84
joint ventures and partnerships
    and capital-intensive production 114
    and foreign partnerships 126
    government-private joint ventures 78, 82, 213 n.46
    private joint ventures 94
    and state reforms 123
Justice and Development Party (Adalet ve Kalkınma Partisi, AKP)
    authoritarian tendencies 69
    and center-periphery tensions 27, 159–60
    and domestic political conflict 175–8
    and economic power 169–73
    and Erdoğan's centralization of power 193

    and evolution of TÜSİAD's prodemocracy position 3, 143
    and factors shaping the business elite 189
    and growing legitimacy of business sector 155
    impact on Turkish industry 18
    and intraclass rivalries 182–3
    and the Kurdish issue 40
    and local government 33, 34, 175, 181
    and new democratization strategies 184–7
    and ousting of RP coalition 33–4, 210 n.1
    phases of rule 34–8
    rise to power 166–9, 171–2, 192–4
    rising authoritarianism of 178–9, 192–4
    and secular-religious conflict 30
    and shift to authoritarian rule 163–5
    and structural limits to Turkish democracy 25
    and TÜSİAD's political structure 173–5
    and TÜSİAD strategies under AKP rule 19, 179–82
Justice Party (Adalet Partisi, AP) 101

Karataşlı, Şahan Savaş 107
Kaslowski, Aldo 125, 133, 157–8
Kaslowski, Simone 184–7
Kavala, Osman 164
Kayhan, Muharrem 119
Kaynar, Şerif 136
Kemalism (Atatürkism)
    and AKP governance 36, 37
    and AKP's rise to power 168
    and CHP's rule 82–3
    and democratizing role of TÜSİAD 92–3
    described 1
    and domestic political conflict 176
    and dual nature of Turkish state 70
    and evolution of Turkish democracy x
    and evolution of TÜSİAD's prodemocracy position 143
    and impact of 1980 coup 30–1
    and the Kurdish issue 39
    and schisms within TÜSİAD 139
    and shifting centers of power 163
    and state-led development policies 88
    and structural limits to Turkish democracy 26

and TÜSİAD strategies under AKP
    rule 165
and typology of state-business relations 51
See also Republican People's Party
    (Cumhuriyet Halk Partisi, CHP)
Keyder, Çağlar 146
Kıraç, İnan 226 n.24
Koç, Rahmi 142
Koç, Vehbi 86
Kocatopçu, Şahap 141
Koç family 14, 178–9
Koç Holding
    and business elite in NICs 13–14
    diversity of activities 94, *131*
    and EU integration efforts 121
    and foreign investment 123
    government contracts and subsidies 95
    and joint ventures 114
    subsidiaries and employees of 136–7
    and TÜSİAD strategies under AKP
        rule 182
Koç University 134
Koçman, Ali 141
Kohli, Atul 45
Komili, Halis 133, 139, 142, 166, 195 n.1
Korea 49, 94
Kurdistan's Workers' Party (Partiya
    Karkerên Kurdistan, PKK) 25, 33
Kurds and Kurdish issue
    and AKP governance 36–7, 164
    and AKP's rise to power 193–4
    and autonomy pressures 201 n.28
    and business elite's break with the
        state 39–41
    and business elite's ideological
        power 104
    and center-periphery tensions 28
    and economic inequality studies 134
    and evolution of Turkish democracy x
    and secular-religious conflict 30
    and structural limits to Turkish
        democracy 25–6
    and threats to Turkish pluralism 21
    and weak coalition governments 33
Kurtsan, Meltem 126, 182

labor
    and evolution of TÜSİAD's
        prodemocracy position 2
    and growth of Turkish
        manufacturing 155
    labor costs and markets 117, 181
    labor organizations 4–5, 65–6, 102
    and path to democracy in Europe 55
    and reformism of working class
        208 n.63
    and state autonomy 48
    and typology of states 53
laicism 27–9, 163. *See also* Kemalism
    (Atatürkism)
laissez-fairism 82
landed classes
    and bureaucratic authoritarianism 61
    and Early Ottoman period 74–6
    landholding families 212 n.32
    minority capitalists under Young
        Turks 79
    and path to democracy in Europe 57
    and third-wave of democratization 65
    and top-down Ottoman reforms 77
    and typology of state-business
        relations 53
    and Western European feudal
        dynamics 72
late-industrialization
    and elite resistance to the deepening of
        democracy 155
    and evolution of TÜSİAD's
        prodemocracy position 2
    and factors shaping the business
        elite 189
    and role of the state 59–64
    and state autonomy 48
    and state-business relations 11–13,
        17–18
    and theoretical approach to state-
        business relations 46, 190
    and third wave of democratization 66–7
    and Turkish holding companies 94
Latin America
    and bureaucratic authoritarianism
        60–1, 189
    business associations in 15
    and business organizations' role in
        democratization 169
    dictatorships 12
    and factors shaping the business
        elite 189

landed aristocracy in 53
and late-developing societies 59–60, 62
and national development strategies 81–2
Southern Cone nations 12, 62
and theoretical approach to state-business relations 44
Lausanne treaty 82
laws and legal systems 7, 100, 133, *181*
legitimacy 154–5. *See also* ideological power
Lenin, Vladimir 48
Levitsky, Steven 70
LGBTQ community 37
liberalism 6, 111–17, 164, 199 n.54
lobbying 114
logic of influence 140, 146–50, 169

machinery 5, 98, 114, *115*, 129–30, 132. *See also* capital-intensive production; heavy industrialization
majority rule 31–2
managerial class 63
mandatory religion classes 31
Mann, Michael
  on CUP ethnic cleansing policies 79
  on forms of power 8–9, 13, 50
  IEMP model of 8–9, 46, 49–51, 53, 153, 190
  on paths to European democracy 57, 58
  and state-business relations under late-industrialization 13
  and structure of study 17
  on working-class dependency fostered by industrialization 207 n.63
manufacturing 86, 97–8, 130
Mardin, Şerif 27–9, 40, 70, 107
Marglin, Stephen 207 n.63
Marmara region 98
Marmara Sea Action Plan Coordination Council (Marmara Denizi Eylem Planı Koordinasyon Kurulu) 186
Marshall, Thomas H. 56
Marshall Fund 173
Marshall plan 84–5, 96–7
martial law x, 26, 33
Marx, Karl (and Marxian philosophy)
  and bureaucratic authoritarianism 61–2
  and capital's influence on the state 93
  and causes of military coup 106
  and evolution of Turkish democracy 23
  and evolution of TÜSİAD's prodemocracy position 18–19
  on impact of capital-intensive production 98
  Marxian debate on Turkish development 211 n.17
  and paths to European democracy 55, 56
  on rise of authoritarianism 202 n.49
  and schisms within TÜSİAD 139–40
  and state autonomy concept 47–8
  and theoretical approach to state-business relations 43–4, 190–1
  and TÜSİAD's ideological transformation 5–9
  and typologies of power 50
  and typology of state-business relations 52
  on Western European feudal dynamics 72
Menderes, Adnan 84–5
merchant cities 72–3
merchants 101
Metropolitan Museum ix
Mexico 3, 13, 53, 97
microorganizational change 136–8
Middle Ages 50, 71, *120*
middle class 34, 56, 107
Middle East
  and business associations 15
  and business authoritarianism 10
  and globalization forces 10
  military dictatorships in 44–5
  and MÜSİAD trade preferences 171
  and periphery networks 160
  and state autonomy 49
  and typologies of power 50, 53
Migros supermarkets 171
military power
  and bureaucratic authoritarianism 61–2
  and business elite's political power 102
  and challenges to Ottoman rule 76
  and European feudalism 72
  and evolution of TÜSİAD's prodemocracy position 142
  and late-developing societies 62–3
  military governments 25, 88–9, 100, 106

and third-wave of democratization 65
and Turkish dictatorships 44–5
and TÜSİAD's ideological transformation 8
See also coups
minority capitalists 79–80
minority populations 25–6. *See also* diversity; ethnicity
minority rights 41. *See also* Armenians/Armenian genocide; Greek minority; Kurds and Kurdish issue
Mobutu Sese Seko 48
"model textbooks," 134
modernization
  and center-periphery tensions 26–7
  and CHP's rule 82
  and evolution of Turkish democracy 22
  and late-developing societies 60–2
  and Ottoman reforms 76
  and paths to European democracy 57
  and reforms from above 77
  and theoretical approach to state-business relations 44
Moore, Barrington 5–6, 8, 44, 57, 76
Motherland Party (Anavatan Partisi, ANAP) 31–4, 36–7, 167, 170
Mouzelis, Nicos 30, 81
Movement of the Enterprises of France (Mouvement des entreprises de France, MEDEF) 174–5
multiculturalism 25–6, 78
multinational corporations 202 n.49
multiparty democracy in Turkey: transition to 21, 32–4, 84–7
Musk, Elon ix
Muslims. *See* Islam and Muslims
Mussolini, Benito 83

National Action Party (Partido Acción Nacional, PAN) 13
National Assembly 28, 31, 35, 85, 107
nationalism
  and challenges of late-development 60
  and challenges to Ottoman rule 76
  and CHP's rule 82
  and divided opinions on democratization 41
  and forms of citizenship 26, 28

and Kurdish identity 201 n.28
and late-developing societies 62–3
and reforms from above 77
and state autonomy 191
and state-led development policies 88
Turkish national identity 22
and typology of state-business relations 50, 51
and weak coalition governments 33
and the Young Turk movement 80
Nationalist Democratic Party (Milliyetçi Demokrasi Partisi, MDP) 31–2
Nationalist Movement Party (Milliyetçi Hareket Partisi, MHP) 34, 36
National Salvation Party (Milli Selamet Partisi, MSP) 101, 107
National Security Council (Milli Güvenlik Kurulu, MGK) 31
nation-building 13, 18
neoliberalism 107, 209 n.101. *See also* export-led growth (ELG); structural adjustment
neo-Ottomanism 27
New Democracy Movement (Yeni Demokrasi Hareketi, YDH) 39–40, 143. *See also* Boyner, Cem
newly industrialized countries (NICs)
  business elite in 13–16
  and challenges of international competition 117
  and evolution of TÜSİAD's prodemocracy position 4
  and globalization forces 10–11
  See also late-industrialization
noblesse de robe (nobility of the robe) 74
North Africa 15

Occupy Gezi protests 36–7, 40, 178
O'Donnell, Guillermo A. 60
Öniş, Ziya 121
Organisation for Economic Co-operation and Development (OECD) 123
Orthodox Church 29
Ottoman Empire
  and center-periphery tensions 27–8
  composition of business elite 94, 102
  defeat in World War I 80–1
  and despotic power 73–5
  and Early Ottoman period 75–6

ethno-religious minority business class 94, 102
and ideological power of business elite 102
land-holding system 211 n.17
and late-industrialization forces 18
and legacy of despotic power 73-6
and origins of Turkish capitalist class 94
and Turkish nationalism 26
and TÜSİAD's headquarters 91
and typologies of power 50-1
and Western European feudal dynamics 72-3
Özal, Turgut
and AKAP's majority rule 32
and AKP governance 34, 37
and AKP's rise to power 166-7
background of 107
conflict with TÜSİAD 141, 152
and the DP 85
and informal state power 158-9
and lobbying pressures for liberalization 114
and periphery networks 170-1

Paker, Can 6, 43, 148, 153
Pamuk, Orhan 1-2, 31-2
paradigm shift of the business elite 113-17
Paris accord 181
parliamentary democracy 1, 33, 35, 37, 44, 58, 77, 164
partenariats (joint public-private ventures) 78
participatory democracy 23
The Passions and the Interests (Hirschman) 59
patronage 45, 101
Payne, Leigh A. 46, 54
peace process 36
peasantry 61, 72-3, 78
Peoples' Democratic Party (Halkların Demokratik Partisi, HDP) 37, 40, 164, 302 n.76
periphery. See center-periphery dialectic
Peronist Party 53
Perspectives on Democratization in Turkey Report. See Democratization Report
pharmaceutical industry 126
Pinochet, Augusto 3

pluralism 9, 15, 79, 165, 177. See also democracy and democratization; diversity
Poggi, Gianfranco 52, 103, 150
political stability
and business organizations' role in democratization 169
and foreign investment in Turkish business 125, 128
and heavy industrialization 131-3
and state autonomy 191
theoretical explanations for 207 n.63
and TÜSİAD's prodemocracy position 16
polyarchy 23
populism
and bureaucratic authoritarianism 62
and CHP's rule 83
and domestic political conflict 175
and evolution of TÜSİAD's prodemocracy position 3, 4
and state-business relations under late-industrialization 11-12
and state economic enterprises 97
and third-wave of democratization 65
and typologies of power 53
Poulantzas, Nicos 48
poverty 44, 95, 102, 106, 134
price controls 83-4
PriceWaterhouse-Coopers 145, 156
privatization
and AKP governance 172
and AKP's rise to power 166, 167
and economic liberalization of the 80s and 90s 112
and evolution of TÜSİAD's prodemocracy position 142
and heavy industrialization 133
ideological transformation towards democratization 109-10
and transitions to democracy 64
and TÜSİAD criticisms of civilian government 2
procedural democracy 24, 31
professionalization of business class
and diversity issues in TÜSİAD 149
and intraclass alliances 183
and microorganizational change in TÜSİAD firms 136-7

and scope of TÜSİAD's efforts 161
and TÜSİAD strategies under AKP rule 184, 187
protectionism
 and AKP's rise to power 167
 and business elite's ideological power 103
 and challenges of late-development 60
 and CHP's rule 83
 and foreign investment in Turkish business 123
 and globalization forces 9
 in late-industrializing societies 11
 and post–World War II period 84
 See also import substitution industrialization (ISI)
Protestant Ethic and the Spirit of Capitalism (Weber) 7, 12, 52, 103
Protestantism 7, 12, 52, 103
Przeworski, Adam 207 n.63
public diplomacy 174, 193
public opinion 39, 153, 174–5

quotas 82

radical youth movements 39–40
Ramadan 160
raw materials 55, 97, 115, *115*, 130
redistribution 134–5
Refah Party 179
reforms and reformism
 constitutional reforms 3, 35
 and domestic political conflict 176
 and foreign investment in Turkish business 122–5
 ideological transformation towards democratization 188
 and path to democracy in Europe 56
 reform from above 81
 top-down Ottoman reforms 77–9, 96, 187
regional inequalities and development
 and AKP's rise to power 166, 194
 and center-periphery dialectic 27, 170–1
 and economic liberalization of the 80s and 90s 112–13
 and economic power of business elite 190

and evolution of TÜSİAD's prodemocracy position 3, 143
and the Gülenist movement 160, 199 n.55, 228 n.56
and Kurdish regions 26, 39, 40–1
and Latin American dictatorships 12
and TÜSİAD's agenda 183, 187
and TÜSİAD's founding 14
religion and religiosity
 and center-periphery dichotomy 26–8, 187–8
 religious diversity 75, 203 n.70
 religious entrepreneurs 159
 religious freedoms 27
 and secular-religious conflict 29–30
 See also Islam and Muslims
Republican Party (U.S.) 34
Republican People's Party (Cumhuriyet Halk Partisi, CHP)
 and AKP governance 36
 and business elite in NICs 13
 and business elite's ideological power 102, 104
 and business elite's political power 100
 and capital's political power 106
 and center-periphery tensions 28
 and CHP's rule 81–4
 and dual nature of Turkish state 71
 and multiparty democracy 84–6
 and secular-Muslim conflict 164
 and weak coalition governments 34
 See also Kemalism (Atatürkism)
research and development (R&D) 122–5, *124*
Roman Empire 71–3, 75
Romania *120*
Rueschemeyer, Dietrich 24–5, 48, 56, 193
rule of law 10, 41, 125, 196 n.1
Russia ix, *120*

Sabancı, Özdemir 143
Sabancı, Sakıp 39, 95, 134, 142–3
Sabancı family 144
Sabancı Foundation 134
Sabancı Holding 94, 107, 114, 116, *131*, 136–7
Sabancı University 134
Sackler family ix
Sancak, Ethem 168

sanitation sector 96
São Paulo, Brazil 159
Savaşkan, Osman 167–8, 171
Schmitter, Philippe 140, 169
Schumpeter, Joseph 44, 47–8, 52, 55–6, 96
Second Empire (France) 56
Second Republic (Turkey) 87
secular bureaucracy 29, 188
secularism
 and AKP governance 35
 and center-periphery tensions 26–8
 and evolution of TÜSİAD's prodemocracy position 143
 and the Kurdish issue 39
 secular-religious conflicts 29–30, 143
 and structural limits to Turkish democracy 25
 and TÜSİAD strategies under AKP rule 163–6
 See also Kemalism; laicism
secular-Muslim conflict 143
Serbia 77
Sezer, Necdet 36
"SIADs" (Industrialists' and Businesspeople's Associations) 160
single-party rule 1, 28
skilled labor 135
Skocpol, Theda 48
small and medium-sized enterprises (SMEs)
 and AKP governance 34–5, 183
 and AKP's rise to power 166
 and business elite in NICs 15
 and corruption problems 110
 economic power of 113
 and shifting centers of power 159, 161
 and TÜSİAD's permanent staff 199 n.54
 and TÜSİAD strategies under AKP rule 183
 and TUSKON 120
 See also Independent Industrialists and Businessmen Association (MÜSİAD); Islam and Muslims, Muslim entrepreneurs
Smith, Adam 54
social-democratic ideology 6, 33–4, 95, 148

Social-Democratic Populist Party (Sosyaldemokrat Halkçı Parti, SHP) 33
Social-Economic Council 172
social media ix
social mobility 107
social policy 82
Social Policy Commission (of TÜSİAD) 182
Social Policy Research' Commission (of TÜSİAD) 148
social rights 56, 65
South America 62
South Korea 44–5, 97, 116
Soviet Union 9, 84. *See also* Russia
Spain *120*
stabilization measures 106
State and Business in Modern Turkey (Buğra) 11, 198 n.44
state autonomy 46–54, 150–6, 191
state-centric approaches 13. *See also* state autonomy
state-driven industrialization 84
state economic enterprises (SEEs) 83, 85, 87–8, 97
state-led development/industrialization
 and business cosmopolitanism 126
 and business elite's ideological power 104
 and capital's political power 106
 and the globalization debate 9
 and late-industrialization forces 18
 replacement by export-driven policies 109
 and state autonomy 152
 and state-society relations 87–8
 and theoretical approach to state-business relations 191
stateless groups 25. *See also* Kurds and Kurdish issue
State Planning Agency (Devlet Planlama Teşkilatı, DPT) 32, 87, 107
state prosecutors 26, 30–1, 42, 142–3
State Security Courts (Devlet Güvenlik Mahkemeleri, DGM) 31
state spending 133
State Statistics Institute (Devlet İstatistik Enstitüsü, DİE) 104
statism 80–4

STEM education 181
Stephens, John D. 24–5, 56, 193
stock markets 14, 94
Streeck, Wolfgang 140, 169
Strong Democracy, Strong Social
  Structure and Strong Economy
  *(Güçlü Demokrasi, Güçlü Sosyal Yapı,
  Güçlü Ekonomi)* 176
structural adjustment 30, 66–7. *See also*
  neoliberalism
structural comparative approach 24
structural limits to democracy 25
subsidiaries 129, 136–7
subsidies 11, 60, 67, 86, 94–5, 103
suffrage 25, 56
Şuhubi, Mehmet 133
sultanic rule 73–4, 76, 81
sunk costs 132
Sunni Islam 27–9, 37, 73, 178
Sweden 4, 43, 95, 148
Syria 25

Tanör, Bülent 39, 169, 196 n.1
tariffs 82, 97
taxation
  and AKP governance 172
  and bureaucratic authoritarianism 62
  and business cosmopolitanism 126
  and capital-intensive production 97
  and center-periphery tensions 27
  and conflict with Kurdish militia 134
  and development of the bourgeoisie 5
  and Early Ottoman period 73–6
  and growing legitimacy of business
    sector 154–5
  and the Kurdish issue 40
  and multiparty democracy 85
  and problems created by informal state
    links 157
  and reform proposals 133
  and rising Turkish authoritarianism 179
  and secular-religious conflicts 29
  and Turkish holding companies 95
  and typologies of power 50, 52
  wealth taxes 84, 102
  and Western European feudal
    dynamics 72
technocrats
  and AKAP's majority rule 32
  and AKP governance 36–7
  and alliances of capitalist development
    202 n.49
  and bureaucratic authoritarianism 60–1
  and capitalist commitment to
    democratization 64
  and capital's political power 107
  and economic liberalization of the 80s
    and 90s 112
  and evolution of TÜSİAD's
    prodemocracy position 110
  and late-developing societies 62–3
  and Özal's background 114
  and shifting centers of power 163
  and weak coalition governments 33
technology imports 98, 114, 122–5,
  207 n.63
Tekfen Holding 91, *131*, 137
terrorists 26, 104
textiles *115*, 123, 127, 130, 144, 152
think tanks
  and AKP's rise to power 194
  and Brazilian business associations 159
  and business elite's ideological
    power 104
  and the Kurdish issue 40
  and public diplomacy of
    TÜSİAD 173–4
  and third-wave of democratization 65
  and TÜSİAD strategies under AKP rule
    169, 179–80, 187
  as unifying force in TÜSİAD 15
third-wave of democratization
  and AKP's rise to power 193
  and capitalist commitment to
    democratization 63–7
  and challenges to Turkish
    democratization 23
  and evolution of TÜSİAD's
    prodemocracy position 3–4
  and the globalization debate 9
  linkage with democratization 109
  and theoretical approach to state-
    business relations 46
Tilly, Charles 8
tımar system 73–5
Tocqueville, Alexis de 59
top-down reforms 22, 76–9, 96, 187
transnational capital 61

transnational organizations 107
transparency ethic 158
transportation industry 114, *115*, 126, 129–30, 151
transportation infrastructure 61, 86, 151, 175, 198 n.44
tribal affiliations 53
True Path Party (Doğru Yol Partisi, DYP) 32–3
Tükel, Haluk 133, 154
Turam, Berna 27, 173
Turgut Özal 31–2
Turkish Airlines 168
Turkish Confederation of Employer Associations (Türkiye İşveren Sendikaları Konfederasyonu, TISK) 98–100, 102
Turkish Cultural Center 168
Turkish Economic and Social Studies Foundation (Türkiye Ekonomik ve Sosyal Etüdler Vakfı, TESEV) 40, 173
Turkish Enterprise and Business Confederation (Türk Girişim ve İş Dünyası Konfederasyonu, TÜRKONFED) 169, 182–3, 187, 194
Turkish Industry and Business Association (TÜSİAD)
  adoption of prodemocracy position 2–4
  and AKP governance 38–9, 163–6, 166–9, 192–4
  and authoritarianism 178–9
  and business cosmopolitanism 125–8
  and business elite in NICs 14–16
  and business formalism 156–9
  and capital-intensive production 128–9, 134–5
  and capitalist commitment to democratization 65–6
  and challenges to Turkish democratization 69
  councils and governing boards of 145–6, 148
  and coup of 1980 106–7
  and democratization efforts 184–7
  and diversity challenges 146–50
  and divided opinions on democratization 41–2
  and domestic political conflict 175–8
  and dual nature of Turkish state 71
  and economic liberalization of the 80s and 90s 112–17
  and economic power 170–3
  and EU integration pressures 117–22
  evolution of political activities 140–50
  fees and budget of 145
  and foreign direct investment 123–5
  founding of 2, 14–15, 89, 100
  and globalization forces 10–11
  and heavy industrialization 129–33
  and Higher Advisory Council (Yüksek İstişare Konseyi) 145–6, 169, 184
  and ideological power of business elite 103–6
  ideological transformation towards democratization 4–8, 18–19, 91–3, 109–11, 139–40, 188
  and IEMP model 8
  and influence of holding owners 216 n.11
  influential progressive figures 43
  international missions 149–50
  and intraclass alliances 182–3
  and the Kurdish issue 39–41
  limits of power 159–61
  member selection 145
  and microorganizational changes 136–8
  and military coup of 1980 12
  mission statement 105
  and political power of business elite 99–102, 191–2
  political structure and public diplomacy 173–5
  representation in industrial economy *170*
  research sponsored by 105, 166, 173–4
  roundtables and commissions 91, 146–9, 177, 182, 186–7, 192
  schisms within 139, 144, 226 n.24
  shifting of strategy under authoritarian rule 179–82
  shift to democratization 1
  and social dimensions of democracy 134–5
  staff and structure of 149, 180, 199 n.54
  and state autonomy 47, 150–6
  and theoretical approach to state-business relations 190–1

Index

as tool for studying capitalist
  development 189–90
and Turkish holding companies 95–8
and typologies of power 52
See also Democratization Report
"Turkish model," 35, 167, 179
Turkish Union of Chambers and
  Commodity Exchanges (Türkiye
  Odalar ve Borsalar Birliği, TOBB) 85,
  87, 99, 100–2
"The Turn to Authoritarianism in
  Latin America and the Search
  for its Economic Determinants"
  (Hirschman) 59
Twitter ix
typologies of states 50–4

Ukraine ix
unelected officials 31. *See also* bureaucracy
  and bureaucratization; civil service
unionization ix, 177. *See also* labor
Union of Industrial and Employers'
  Confederations of Europe (UNICE)
  147, 149, 174
United Nations 85, 168
United States
  and capital-intensive production
    98
  and democracy and human rights
    agenda 119
  and Mann's IEMP model 46, 53
  and Özal's background 107
  and secularism 27
  and Turkish exports *120*
United States Chamber of Commerce
  66
universal citizenship 39, 58. *See also*
  Weber, Max-Weberian theory
universal suffrage 25, 56
universities 91, 95, 118, 134, 184
US Chamber of Commerce 149
US Treasury Department 209 n.101

value-added production 84, 152, 155
Varlıer, Oktay 135, 137, 145, 151
vassalage 72
vendettas 143
vertical integration 78. *See also* holding
  companies

Washington Consensus 66, 209 n.101
wealth taxes 29, 84, 102
Weber, Max-Weberian theory
  and AKP's rise to power 194
  and bourgeois class in Ottoman
    system 75–6
  and bureaucratic authoritarianism 61–2
  on "capitalist spirit," 23, 55, 103
  influence of ideology on
    organizations 150
  and paths to European democracy 57–8
  and role of the bourgeoisie in
    democratization 43
  and state autonomy concept 48–9
  and state-business relations under late-
    industrialization 12–13
  and third-wave of democratization 66
  and TÜSİAD's ideological
    transformation 7
  and typologies of power 52
Weiss, Linda 49
Welfare Party (Refah Partisi, RP) 33–4
Western Europe
  and capitalism/democracy
    relationship 56–9
  and centrism of working class 207 n.63
  early liberal democracy in 54–6
  and feudalism 72–3
  and feudal landholding 211 n.17,
    212 n.32
  and theoretical approach to state-
    business relations 43–4
  and typologies of power 53
  See also specific countries
Westernization 22, 27, 29
Williamson, John 209 n.101
Women Entrepreneurs Association of
  Turkey (Türkiye Kadın Girişimciler
  Derneği, KADIGER) 169, 182–3,
  185, 194
working class 56
World Bank 32, 107, *115*, 209 n.101
world-systems theory 61. *See also*
  dependency theory
World War I 28, 79–81
World War II 18, 29, 83, 95, 102

Yalçındağ, Arzuhan Doğan 143, 174, 177
Yeşilçam (Green Pine Street) 38

Yırcalı, Rona 154
Young Turk movement
  and business elite's ideological power 102
  and center-periphery tensions 28
  and CHP's rule 81–2, 84
  and economic policy 77–9, 80–2, 84, 86–8
  and minority capitalists 79–80
  and reforms from above 76–8
  and state-led development policies 88
Yücaoğlu, Erkut 126, 139–40, 154

Zaire 48

www.ingramcontent.com/pod-product-compliance
Lightning Source LLC
Chambersburg PA
CBHW052219300426
44115CB00011B/1750